COVID TRAVEL UPDATE

The Covid-19 pandemic has made travel to Japan difficult or impossible in recent years. As a consequence, it has been a tumultuous time for Japanese businesses that rely on tourism.

The author and contributors to *Tokyo Stroll* have been busy keeping the guide up to date on closures, relocations, and changes to hours of operation during this period. For general advice on travel to Japan during the pandemic, see the "Pandemic planning" heading on page 21.

TOKYO STROLL

A Guide to City Sidetracks and Easy Explorations

Gilles Poitras

Foreword by Jake Adelstein

Stone Bridge Press • *Berkeley, California*

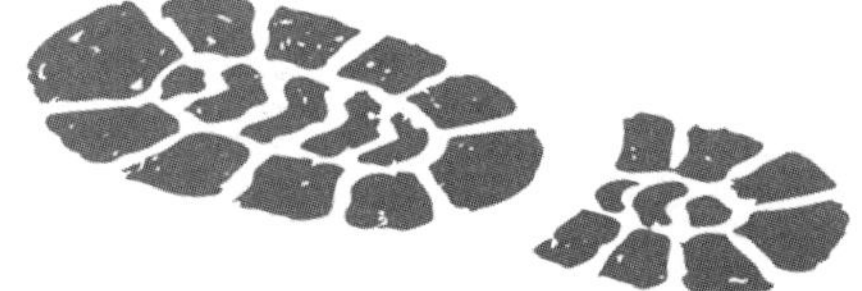

Published by
Stone Bridge Press
P. O. Box 8208, Berkeley, CA 94707
TEL 510-524-8732 • sbp@stonebridge.com • www.stonebridge.com

Maps by Cynthia Olen based on open-source OpenStreetMap data maps.

Book design and layout by John Sockolov.

Printed in the United States of America.

First printing, 2022.

p-ISBN 978-1-61172-058-7
e-ISBN 978-1-61172-942-9

Contents

Tokyo Stroll Guide

Foreword

Tokyo is a wonderful maze: multileveled, new and old, mysterious and boring, sacred and profane, sexy and prudish at the same time. For the glitz and glamour—to explore Roppongi Hills or Omotesandō Hills or whatever needless chrome and electronic modern day shopping mallstrosity that you might want to explore—there are guidebooks galore already available. If you want to know how it feels to live in an old neighborhood, dine on delights not yet splattered all over Instagram, see wonders hidden in narrow alleys, and know the meaning of the mystical monuments and statues in back alley shrines and temples, then this is the book for you.

It's so much more than a guidebook; it's a Japanese history lesson, a conversation, an invitation to explore areas of the city you had no idea existed and rediscover parts of city you thought you knew. There are things explained succinctly in this book that I have seen for years but never really understood or appreciated, like the Myth of Tomorrow mural in Shibuya station. For a jaded Tokyoite like myself, it gave me a fresh perspective on the familiar.

In some ways this is a demanding book: there is an assumption that you understand something about Japan and that you are curious about the history of Tokyo, the religions of the nation, and the superstitions and myths that still are subtly intertwined with modern Japanese life.

The description of Kōfukuji 弘福寺 found on page 293 is priceless:

> An Ōbaku Zen temple founded in 1673, with the main hall and two-story sanmon gate done in a Chinese style. Both were constructed in 1933 after the temple was destroyed in the Great Kantō Earthquake. This temple also has a small attractive garden on one

side—you pass under a short bridge to reach it. The grounds contain a shrine to Hotei and this temple is on the Shichifukujin tour. There is another shrine with statues of an elderly couple, the Jiji Baba. Praying here is said to be effective for treating coughing and asthma. These two statues were carved by a recluse priest named Fugai in the form of his parents. No one knows when the curative powers came to be ascribed to the statues.

I think the number of people who know what "Ōbaku Zen" is in modern Japan are far and few between. I am a Zen Buddhist priest and I barely know myself. I also wonder if prayers offered at the statues will work against coronavirus, but perhaps that is simply because I am a morbid person. There are some references difficult to decipher.

But that's OK, because even if you don't know the terms off the bat, Gilles usually does a wonderful job of explaining and exploring them eloquently. The level of detail is immense. The transient nature of Tokyo makes many guidebooks almost obsolete as soon as they are printed. However, by concentrating on businesses and establishments that have been around for over 50 years, there's a good chance that when you take this book in hand and explore and walk and stroll through both the famous and lesser-known districts of the city, you will find everything in its place, even when you want to come back.

Japan has a folk belief in the power of words, 言霊 (Kotodama) or literally "the spirit of words". It is an animist society at heart and so everything is imbued with a living presence. In this book that you have in your hands, or on your smartphone, or on your tablet, there's a little bit of the soul of the author and his love for Tokyo and Japanese culture. Pick a neighborhood from the book and take an afternoon wander through it, knowing that the author is there with you as a kind of guardian angel. You'll find that what seems to be ordinary becomes rather extraordinary, and you'll be glad you took the stroll.

Jake Adelstein

Why Another Tokyo Guidebook?

My goal was to produce the type of book I wish I'd had when I first visited Tokyo. Rather than being a typical guide to hot tourism sites and nightclub districts, this book is intended for those who wish to just walk about and observe interesting neighborhoods. It's a book designed to have in hand, rather than for armchair reading or to glance at on the flight. As I was doing research, I kept discovering places I did not know about, which necessitated a trip to look at them (an author's life can be so hard). Quite often I would see places and things in Tokyo and not know what they were, then discover information about them after I returned home. Part of the goal of this book is to reduce that problem for you on your trip.

While there have been guidebooks to walking interesting parts of Tokyo in the past, these have tended to use specific routes with directions. The problem with that model is that things change, making it hard to follow directions. For example, "Cross the bridge to the first intersection with a stop light and turn left at the gas station" sounds fine. But if a street in between has had a stop light added and the gas station has been replaced by a 7-11, then the directions are no longer useful.

Instead, this book provides location information for interesting sights in various neighborhoods and you can choose which route to take. Don't rush from place to place on this book's maps. The most direct route may not be the most interesting one, and as you wander you will find plenty of interesting little places and everyday things on the streets. Instead, stroll, get sidetracked, take your time, take a picture, and stop to rest on occasion. Finally, do not try to hit every sight listed for a neighborhood. Most chapters would take more than a day if you try to see everything. Focus on what seems the most interesting.

My preference is not for the city of the high and powerful: the samurai lords, politicians, financiers, and policy makers. My preference is for the low city rather than the high city: the city of the artisan, the family business, and the laborer; the humble neighborhoods of actors, singers, and street performers. This is one reason I have decied to make these older neighborhoods the subject of many of the chapters in this book. The other reason is that the older neighborhoods often have a higher density of interesting locations.

As I worked on this book, I would occasionally talk to people I know about their preferred activities while traveling and found that many spoke of not being interested in the major sights. Instead they spoke of an interest in the everyday aspects of a city, ordinary neighborhoods, and little things discovered while wandering.

Walks through these neighborhoods will take you past the traditional and modern, the raucous and the quiet, and both large and humble structures, often very close to each other. Is an area too noisy? Are you experiencing too much sensory overload? Just go a short distance on a side street and you will find how quiet a major city can be. Explore all the variety and let the impressions of the city wash over you. It is all the real Tokyo, all the real Japan.

Don't spend valuable trip time and energy hopping around the country. I've spoken to too many people who spent a night or two out and about and barely saw anything, as they were either in transit or too tired upon return. Sit yourself in one place and spend the days enjoying the Tokyo area. On subsequent trips you can explore other parts of Japan, or more of Tokyo. I always advise first-time travelers to spend their trip in Tokyo as it is the most foreigner-friendly city in Japan. A few of the advantages include clear transit signage, locals who are familiar with helping tourists, convenient mass transit, and plenty of information available for visitors.

Style elements

For transliterated text, I use a modified Hepburn romanization. Long vowels are indicated by a macron, as in ō. To aid readers in pronunciation, I am even including macrons in loan words, but not in big-city names such as Tokyo.

In place names, I have followed Japanese pronunciation rather than translating elements of names. For example Kandagawa rather than Kanda River, or Ryōgokubashi rather than Ryōgoku Bridge. This will assist if you have to ask for directions.

In most cases I have avoided the use of hyphens in place names by contracting the phrases. For example, Sumidagawa rather than Sumida-gawa, Eitaibashi rather than Eitai-bashi. The one exception to this is in the names of major boulevards, as signage in Japan uses either hyphens or spaces. I decided to use spaces, so Chūō Dōri rather than Chūō-dōri or Chūōdōri.

For Japanese names, I follow the traditional order of family name first followed by given name. For example, Tange Kenzō rather than Kenzō Tange.

Temple names often have a suffix of -in, -dō, or -ji. I include them as part of the name. For example, Sensōji rather than Sensō Temple.

For shrine names, I use the full Japanese name as in Meiji Jingū rather than Meiji Shrine, Hachimangū rather than Hachiman Shrine, or Inari Jinja rather than Inari Shrine.

An effort was made to provide links to the webpages of the various companies, organizations, and insitutions covered in this book. These links are marked with 🌐 in order to make them easy to pick out in the text. Similarly, don't miss the helpful information contained in the **TIPS** and **NOTES** found throughout the book.

Language

Japanese written in Latin characters has vowels pronounced similarly to Spanish or Italian. American English speakers can use the following guide:

A sounds like the A in *father*

E sounds like the A in *face*

I sounds like the EE in *see*

O sounds like the OA in *oats*

U sounds like the OO in *room*

Acknowledgments

Thanks to Ono Masahiro for checking my kanji and romanization, and for helping identify what to call the Ichikawa Danjūrō IX "Shibaraku" bronze statue in Asakusa. Ono-san, you did far more than I asked for.

Thanks also to Karen G. Anderson, Paul Price, Rick Rudge, and Tom Whitmore for being my test subjects as I guided them through many of the neighborhoods in the book: I learned much from your questions and reactions. Extra thanks go to Paul and Tom for their feedback on the text; those edits were happily made.

Satoshi at Asakusa's Taitō Ryokan for providing a relaxing place to park our stuff and sleep when my friends and I are in Tokyo.

Thanks to Cynthia Olen for her hard work on the maps.

Thanks to Tom Akashi for checking locations in Tokyo during the pandemic to verify shops have not closed or relocated.

Special thanks to my publisher Peter Goodman, who had to wait far too long for this book to reach his hands; Linda Lombardi for her attention to detail in editing the text; and a general thanks to the various writers whose books, essays, articles, and official websites greatly assisted in my gathering information for the entries.

Special thanks to John Sockolov for his diligent work on adding necessary changes during the 2+ years the book was delayed due to Japan restricting entry during the pandemic. Keeping the material up to date was a challenge and his dealing with incorporating my updates is highly appreciated.

Thanks to everyone I met in Tokyo who increased my knowledge of the city: restaurant staff, shop owners, kōban officers, happy drunks, and casual passersby who started up a conversation. It was a delight to learn from you.

Finally, thanks to the Solano Avenue Association, whose annual Solano Avenue Stroll became the inspiration for the title of this book in 2016 when I was beginning my writing.

The maps in this book are based on the data in the maps by the OpenStreetMap creators. OpenStreetMap is an international crowdsourced mapping project. To learn more about OpenStreetMap, and perhaps contribute, see their website at *https://www.openstreetmap.org*.

Introduction

Before there was Tokyo, there was the city of Edo; and before Edo was a city, there was Edo village. The name Edo, "Bay Door," comes from the area located at what was then the mouth of the Sumidagawa river. Fast forward to 1590 when Tokugawa Ieyasu, who would later become shōgun, entered Edo after being granted the Kantō provinces. He then started a massive plan, completed by his heirs, to build the town, with his castle in the center. The construction involved creating an extensive moat and canal system, re-routing rivers, removing hills, and constructing a large, sophisticated fresh water supply. The massive amounts of soil that were removed were used to fill in Hibiya cove as well as marshy areas near the bay. The project not only involved creating the castle area on the highlands but also planning the lower city for the laborers, artisans, merchants, and more that a castle town would need. The city grew at a rapid pace, from a few thousand to 500,000 in less than thirty years. And a century later the population was over a million, easily eclipsing any European city at the time. In 1868 the rule of the shōguns ended and the name of the city was changed to Tokyo after the emperor moved to it and it became the new capital.

From the early days the growth and planning of Edo/Tokyo has been shaped by a significant problem: fire. In the Edo period local fires, nicknamed "the flowers of Edo," often took their toll in a city mainly built of wood and heated by charcoal. Three major fires changed the city dramatically.

In 1657, the Great Meireki Fire, fanned by winds, lasted for three days. It left the majority of the city destroyed and over 100,000 dead. Reconstruction took years and included creating open areas as firebreaks by moving many temples and shrines outside the city center, as well as relocating the Yoshiwara pleasure district to an area north of Asakusa.

The next major fire again changed much of the city. The Great Kantō Earthquake of 1923 struck on September 1 just before noon when many households were preparing lunch. The resulting fires, again fanned by high winds, burned for two days and left an estimated 140,000 dead. The city rebuilt again, this time adding parks as evacuation zones for future disasters and making significant changes to building codes.

The city was mostly destroyed by fire for the third time by the series of firebombings during World War II. The first raid took place on a windy night and was aimed at a densely populated civilian area around Asakusa and Sumida Ward. Estimates of the deaths for that night alone are between 100,000 and 200,000. Over a million survivors were left homeless from this one raid. The other raids left much of the city so thoroughly burned that Allied soldiers who had seen the devastation of the bombings in Germany were shocked when they saw Tokyo.

Today fire is far less of a risk thanks to strict building and fire codes. This means that you will find few buildings that date back more than forty years, as government policies encourage replacing older buildings. It also means that Tokyo is a much safer city to live in.

Things seen and not noticed

There are many details of Japanese cities that may not be apparent to most visitors, and things you may see without knowing what they are. Here is a list of a few you may want to keep an eye out for.

Kōban

Commonly translated as Police Box, a kōban is a small police substation staffed twenty-four hours a day, usually by two or three officers. They include an office, holding cell, and facilities for staff to shower and sleep. You can go to kōban for directions, as many have English-speaking staff.

Daytime versus nighttime

Much of Tokyo either closes for the night, or else opens up for business then. Some areas have a very different feel between day and night, so you may want to visit them more than once.

Fire extinguishers
Public fire extinguishers are found in many neighborhoods. They are usually housed in small upright boxes, often red, or in waist-high columns that may also include a fire alarm.

Fire hydrants and signs
Fire hydrants are usually set into the ground with a cover over them. The most common covers are round or square and marked with a border in yellow paint. Some may have designs cast into the cover with firefighting motifs in bright colors instead of the yellow paint. There is usually a round red sign on a pole nearby to indicate where a hydrant is.

Potted plants
Especially in the older, low-lying areas of Tokyo, if there is space for a potted plant in front of a home or business, odds are there will be one. This is a long-standing tradition: In the 19th century, many Americans and Europeans commented that such neighborhoods were quite green in comparison to cities back home.

Unique street lights in commercial areas
Local merchant associations work to make their shopping districts unique. A common approach is to have street lights that are not found elsewhere. Look up to see these, and perhaps take a picture.

Seasonal and festive decorations
At times you will see small decorations added to doors, utility poles, or other surfaces. Many of them indicate a Japanese celebration. For example at the New Year you may see a rice-straw rope with dried fern and a *mikan* hanging on a door, or a standing bamboo and pine-bough ornament.

Waterways
Edo had rivers, an extensive system of moats around the castle, and canals for moving goods. Streets were mainly for foot traffic—goods traveled by water. Even today, after many canals have been culverted or filled in, there are enough left that Tokyo has over 3,000 bridges. Every bridge in Japan has a name, usually found on a plaque mounted at one end.

Stonework

All the stonework you see in Tokyo is made with stones brought in from outside the city. Tokyo is on an alluvial plain that lacks useable rock, so all of the stone for walls, gravestones, stone items in gardens, and so forth, had to be brought in. When the shōgun's castle was built, the stone was quarried on the Izu Peninsula and shipped to Edo in thousands of boats. Then it had to be transported overland to its final location.

Architectural differences

On my first trip to Tokyo, I was delighted with the variety of architecture. There is no attempt to harmonize styles within a neighborhood. This avoids the cookie-cutter sameness of many American cities. Tokyo's architectural diversity reminds me of the relaxing variety of a forest, compared with the American tendency to uniformity, which is reminescent of cornfields.

Apartments or office building?

Commercial and residential property is often intermixed in Tokyo. How do you tell if a building contains apartments or offices? Simple: Does it have balconies? Apartment buildings have balconies so tenants can hang laundry, dry futons, grow plants, and have a place to step outside. The fact that people live everywhere gives a very different feel to neighborhoods. Unlike office districts that are a wasteland at night and weekends, there are shops, restaurants, convenience stores, and people walking about.

Vertical city

While not unusual in larger cities anywhere, in Japan verticality is taken to a higher level. Homes, buildings filled with different shops, apartments, offices, and more all reach for the sky. Even small villages surrounded by flat land will build up rather than out to preserve farmland.

Vertical shopping

Many buildings will have shops on each floor with a long, vertical sign listing what is on each floor in an easy-to-read fashion.

Vertical dining

When looking for a restaurant or coffee shop for a quick break, see if you can find one that has a second or third story. Having a sweet and sipping tea while looking over the street is a good way to recharge for the next part of your stroll.

Under plastic

On every trip to Tokyo I see buildings undergoing restoration that are covered in scaffolding and enclosed in plastic sheets. My friends and I use the phrase "under plastic" to refer to these. Don't be surprised if a landmark is under plastic when you visit.

Religious sites in Tokyo

Be sure to check the etiquette section on proper behavior when visiting religious sites.

Less than two percent of Japan's population is Christian, Jewish, or Muslim. This means that the majority of religious sites are either Shintō or Buddhist. Shintō shrines and Buddhist temples are popular both among tourists from outside Japan and among Japanese visiting Tokyo. They also make for a pleasant stroll early in the day before stores open, as they often have no gates, so you are free to enter the grounds at any time. If they have a gate that is closed, that means they are not yet open. An easy way to locate medium and large shrines and temples is to look for trees. However, not all areas with trees are shrines and temples, so be careful not to find yourself trespassing on someone's property.

How do you identify the difference between Shintō shrines and Buddhist temples? Shrines often have torii, a simple gate consisting of at least two uprights and a crosspiece. Depending on the shrine, guardian figures such as lions, dogs, and foxes are also common. Temples and some large shrines may have elaborate gates that are more like buildings. It is not uncommon to find guardian figure statues in recesses. In the case of shrines these may be statues of warriors. Temples will also have statues inside the temple hall.

There are also small structures scattered throughout Tokyo, both Shintō and Buddhist. These may not always be on the ground; some may be on rooftops. Some of these are accessible, for example on department store rooftops. Others are private but can be sometimes spotted from the street. There are also free-standing Buddhist statues in some locations, often depicting Jizō.

When you have religious sites, you also have pilgrimages, and Tokyo is no exception. These are usually carried out by small groups or individuals going to a single site or a traditional series of sites. In this book I often refer to sites on routes such as the 33 Kannon Pilgrimage and various Shichifukujin Meguri (Seven Lucky Gods pilgrimages), of which there are several in Tokyo. They also hold festivals, so many that there is a festival every week somewhere in Tokyo. I note major local festivals in the descriptions of many individual shrines and temples.

Preparation and Arrival

Who can travel to Japan? Rather than ask that, let's answer the question: Who cannot go?

A youthful indiscretion resulting in a criminal record may keep you from entering Japan. Several countries, including the United States, share such information with the Japanese government. While Japan is not as strict as some countries, it is a safe bet that any conviction involving drugs, prostitution, or a sentence of a year or more in jail will get you blocked at immigration. Other convictions may also prevent entry.

Depending on the country that issued your passport, you may be able to enter Japan on a tourist visa alone, obtained simply by presenting the passport at the immigration counter upon arrival. There is no need to obtain a special visa. A passport from Canada, the United States, or most European countries allows you to stay in Japan for ninety days as a tourist or on business. This waiver does not apply to the members of the news media or those on government business.

The Ministry of Foreign Affairs has a list of countries that have such visa exemptions.

🌐 *https://www.mofa.go.jp/j_info/visit/visa/short/novisa.html*

Pandemic planning

The Covid-19 pandemic has added many other factors into planning for trips. Even when the current pandemic is over there may be others. Here are items to keep in mind when preparing to go.

1. Before buying your tickets make sure you will be able to enter Japan without a long quarantine, or even able to enter at all.

2. Check the travel and visa section of the website of the Japanese Embassy for your country.
3. For the US this can be found at:
   🌐 *https://www.us.emb-japan.go.jp/itpr_en/travel_and_visa.html*
4. There may be special forms on the website you will need to fill out before the trip
5. If you are transferring flights in a third country make sure you meet all requirements for transiting through that country. You do not want to be stopped and deported back to your beginning point.
6. Make sure you are fully vaccinated before traveling and bring proof of vaccination with you.
7. You may be required to produce documentation of a negative test result taken within a required time limit before your flight. Make sure you are taking the right kind of test, not all are accepted. Currently the limit is usually for a COVID-19 test taken within 72 hours of your flight time. Do not expect the airline to allow you on the flight if you do not have this documentation.
8. You may also be required to take a second test after arrival.
9. Bring extra masks and a small bottle of sanitizer in your carry on, do not assume you will easily be able to obtain masks after you arrive. Be prepared to wear your mask in crowded areas on the street, in closed spaces such as buildings, when in close contact with an individual, and in any public transportation.
10. Remember wearing a mask is not only for your health it is also out of courtesy for others.
11. Remember to follow other precautions, wash your hands properly, use hand sanitizer, maintain a proper distance when you can, etc.
12. All of this information can change so check to make sure you have every requirement covered for your trip.

When to go?

Two major factors are important in deciding when to take your trip: events and weather.

If there are specific events you must see, be aware of the climate during that time and plan accordingly. I also recommend arriving a few days before your event so you can rest and adjust to Tokyo. If you are not constrained by special events, the following section about typical weather conditions may help you decide. Check for festivals around the same time as your trip. In each chapter I list festivals and feast days in the entries for shrines and temples.

Seasonal weather

Spring is cool, especially at night. March and early April are popular for the cherry blossoms; however, the pollen count is high so scope out the pharmacies near where you are staying.

Summer is hot and humid and includes the rainy season, so be prepared. Rain or muggy heat are not the best conditions for walking around, so consider going to a museum or other indoor activities for midday to sundown. The plus side is that there are lots of festivals, including in the evenings. If you have an interest in insects, like many Japanese kids, there will plenty to observe in gardens and parks and near rivers.

Fall weather is mild and there is occasional rain. I often go in October, but November gets you better foliage viewing as the colors change. Another advantage is that evenings are cool but not very cold, so you can see the sights at night in greater comfort. Book early as this is a popular time for tourists.

Winter is cold, although depending where you are from it may be warmer than expected. Tokyo is not as cold as many parts of Europe and the United States, but it does occasionally snow. The New Year holiday is a major event in Japan. To celebrate it like a local, watch the special programs on NHK television and then go to the local shrine or temple at midnight. Almost everything closes for three days or more, but don't be alarmed—restaurants near large shrines and temples will be open, so you won't starve.

NOTE: *Pseudoephedrine (Sudafed) is prohibited in Japan even with a prescription.*

Temperature averages

January	36°F (2°C)–50°F (10°C)
February	36°F (2°C)–50°F (10°C)
March	41°F (5°C)–55°F (13°C)
April	52°F (11°C)–64°F (18°C)

May	59°F (15°C)–73°F (23°C)
June	66°F (19°C)–77°F (25°C)
July	73°F (23°C)–84°F (29°C)
August	75°F (24°C)–88°F (31°C)
September	70°F (21°C)–81°F (27°C)
October	59°F (15°C)–72°F (22°C)
November	50°F (10°C)–63°F (17°C)
December	41°F (5°C)–54°F (12°C)

Money

Cash

Expect to carry cash. Much of Japan operates on cash rather than checks or credit cards. This is especially true of small family businesses. You may be able to use your credit card at businesses in areas frequented by tourists, and at large chains and upscale shops and restaurants. Using cash also ensures the shop gets all the money without the credit card company skimming part of it off. Put some bills—say 6,000 yen worth—in a separate part of your wallet as a reserve to keep from running out. Don't worry about having plenty of cash on you, as Tokyo is one of the safest cities in the world. However, do watch out for pickpockets in crowds. I had one try for my wallet at a crowded festival a few years ago, although they failed.

You will need cash as soon as you arrive. Cash may be required for a transit card, transportation from the airport, taxis, or meals, and some lodgings require prepayment in cash. I exchange cash at the airport when I arrive to have enough to cover costs for several days. Odds are you get a much better exchange rate and pay a far lower fee than you would at your home bank.

To obtain cash on the go, there are now several options for tourists. Post offices have international ATM machines available during business hours, and many convenience stores also have international ATM machines. Be aware that you will need to know your Personal Identification Number (PIN) as a set of numbers rather than letters—Japanese ATM machines do not have letters on their keypads. In a pinch you can check the keypad of a cell phone to find the numbers, as the design is the same. You may want to check your bank's policies ahead of time. I use the post office as they charge a very low fee and my credit union also does not charge international transaction fees. A friend uses his credit card as his US bank does charge fees for using his ATM card in Japan. There are also an increasing number of international exchanges in tourist-heavy areas.

Credit cards

Be sure to notify your bank and credit card company that you will be in Tokyo. Otherwise, you may find your cards blocked.

It is worth having a credit card or two for shops that take them and as a backup in case your ATM card gets blocked by your bank (even if you told them you would be in Japan).

If you are like me and live in a state where you are expected to pay use tax (sales tax for out-of-state purchases), using a credit card is handy as a way to know the cost of the items in dollars rather than having to convert the yen indicated on the receipt.

TIP: *Consider buying a nice coin purse, which will be readily available in Japan. Because the smallest bill is the 1,000 yen note, you quickly end up with a pile of coins. Keep spending the coins to avoid ending up with too many. I put the larger coins in my coin purse and keep the 1-yen coins loose in my pocket for quick retrieval. Save your leftover Japanese funds for later trips, change them at the airport, or drop them into a donation box. Be aware that your bank may not take coins if you plan to do an exchange after returning home. You can also take some sets of coins home as gifts.*

Pasmo and Suica

I recommend getting a Pasmo or Suica card to simplify paying transit fares. These are prepaid smart cards that you simply tap at station gates to enter and exit or when boarding a bus. If you have never done this, observe people using the gates to see how it works. When you tap the card, a small screen will flash the amount you have left. All the transit systems in the greater Tokyo area accept the cards, including buses and some taxis. Both cards have versions for children aged six to eleven, and children aged twelve who are attending school may also qualify for child fare. Children under age six may be able to ride for free depending on the transit system.

A major advantage in using the cards is that you don't end up spending lots of time at ticket machines awaiting your turn. Plus transfer discounts are automatically handled, which means you don't have to spend time and energy buying a transfer ticket.

How to get the cards

Children's cards require proof of age and must be bought at a ticket window. Adult cards can be bought at ticket windows and from station ticket machines. Smaller stations usually do not have ticket windows. All purchases of cards include a 500-yen fee that is refundable at stations before you leave. Suica refunds are handled at JR stations and Pasmo at non-JR subway stations. Or you can keep the cards for later trips to Tokyo—the expiration date is ten years after the last use.

Adding value

You can add value to the cards using ticket machines in any station that accepts them. Ticket machines will have a button for English. Press that button and follow the instructions. If you should find yourself unable to exit, look for machines near the gates that allow value to be added. In smaller stations these will likely be only at the main gate.

Non-transit use

You can also use both cards at many vending machines, convenience stores, coffee shops, and more. I once spent the last of the value on mine at the airport buying coffee and a pastry.

Suica:

🌐 *https://www.pasmo.co.jp/visitors/en/*

Pasmo:

🌐 *https://japanrailpass.net*

Phones and tablets

Cell phones

There is more than one way to use a cell phone. You can use the international plan from your phone company, have the chip changed once you get to Japan, or rent a cell phone from one of several companies. Several companies sell phone chips and rent phones; these often have counters at airports. If you are using your own phone, be sure to know what the roaming fees for data access will be. You may want to turn data off to save money and only rely on wi-fi at your hotel and select hot spots for texting and internet access. If data is off, be aware your voicemail may not be accessible until you return home.

Pay phones

Pay phones are not as common as they used to be in Japan but are still easy to find. The phones are usually green, gray or pink. You can pay in coins or with a prepaid calling card at green or gray phones. Phones with a sign that says "International and Domestic Telephone" accept credit cards.

Costs are usually 10 yen per minute depending on distance, and you can add more money to extend the call. Only 10- and 100-yen coins are accepted.

Portable wi-fi hotspots

It is possible to rent battery-powered pocket-sized portable wi-fi hotspots from the same companies that rent cellphones. These connect via wi-fi to your own phone, tablet, or laptop for internet access.

Line

In Japan the major application for messaging is Line and your friends in Japan may prefer you have it. You need a data connection for it to work.

🌐 *https://line.me/en/*

TIP: *See the navigation section for GPS mapping without data access.*

Airport to hotel

Airport

There are two airports for Tokyo. Haneda is within the city on the edge of Tokyo Bay, and Narita is outside Tokyo. Each have several options for getting to locations within Tokyo and transit time is often about the same. How you get to your destination from either airport will depend on where you are staying in Tokyo. It is best you check the airport's web site to see the current transit options as they have been improving in the last few years.

During your flight you will be given a landing card. Have your passport number and information about your lodging ready to fill out the form.

Before you leave the airport

- Change cash into Japanese yen, you will need some right away.
- If you plan to use public transportation, obtain a Suica or Pasmo transit smartcard if they are available there. See the Pasmo and Suica section below for information.
- If you are renting a phone or wi-fi hub, pick it up.

Hotel

Choosing a hotel in Tokyo is not quite like doing so in other cities. Most cities have one central area where most of the desirable hotels are located. Tokyo, however, has many such areas given the excellent transit system of the city. Find where you plan to go, check the train and subway lines that take you there, and consider basing yourself in an area near such a line. I always stay in Asakusa, a friend always stays near Ueno Station, and another always in Ikebukuro. Choose carefully, as many people I know have ended up in areas that looked good but turned out to have less than desirable features. I know women who ended up near the love hotel district in Kabukichō, and others who stayed in nice hotels in areas with little of interest after dark. Pick a neighborhood that is diverse enough to enjoy for an evening stroll after a day of sightseeing.

Most hotels allow smoking, so if you want a completely non-smoking accomodations consider staying in a family-run inn. More and more of these are going 100% non-smoking, and they are often more affordable than their smoke-friendly counterparts.

Miscellaneous travel essentials

Safety

Tokyo is one of the safest cities in the world. Still one should maintain some degree of caution. For example, Roppongi and Kabukichō have been the scene of drinks being spiked and the victim's bank account being emptied.

Tokyo has operators for several languages. Languages available are

English, Chinese, Korean, Thai, and Spanish. Here are some telephone numbers that are helpful to have on hand:

English non-emergency police hotline:
☎ *03-3501-0110—weekdays, 8:30 a.m. to 5:15 p.m.*

Tokyo Metropolitan Medical Information Center:
☎ *03-5285-8181—daily, 9:00 a.m. to 8:00 p.m.*

Fire and medical emergency:
☎ *119*

Police emergency:
☎ *110*

Carry your passport

Japanese law requires that you carry your passport at all times. The police have the power to arrest you if you don't have it on you. A photocopy of your passport is not an acceptable substitute.

Smoking

Smoking is not allowed on the sidewalks of many major streets, except for designated smoking areas. It is still common in bars and many restaurants.

Accessibility

Train and subway stations are almost all accessible via elevators and escalators. Some stations may have adapted escalators that can handle wheelchairs. Wheelchair users should speak to the station agent who will assist getting on the train with a special ramp. Often there is a difference in height between the train car and the platform. The agent will also contact your destination station and someone will be waiting to assist you there.

Many places are not fully barrier free, but accessibility is improving. I recommend checking the following web sites for up to date information.

Another resource is *Accessible Japan's Tokyo* by Josh Grisdale, a book that goes into detail on planning a trip and what to see. Available on Amazon and Apple's Book app.

Japan Accessible Tourism Center, Tokyo pages:
🌐 *http://www.japan-accessible.com/city/tokyo.htm*

Accessible Japan:
🌐 *https://www.accessible-japan.com*
🌐 *https://amzn.to/2llWmBA*

Power

Electricity is 100 volts AC at 50 cycles. Outlets usually are for two-prong North American style plugs. North American appliances will usually work fine. Travelers from other countries may have to use adaptors.

TIP: *I take lots of pictures and when I get home, I write up a document describing the locations by photo number. Rather than carry around a notebook and write down notes as I wander about, I take photos of location-specific items, such as subway exit signs, landmarks, local maps, and so on. This is much easier than asking your friend, "Where did I take this picture?" and getting a reply like, "I don't know, I think I was hungover that day." This is also useful if your phone or camera does not capture the GPS location.*

Navigation tools

GPS

The directions given by GPS systems such as Google Maps and Maps.Me are generally reliable in suggesting routes including train and subway lines. However, I have discovered that I sometimes do a better job with a detailed atlas or local map, either electronic or printed.

If you are not using a smartphone or tablet with a data plan, which frankly can be quite expensive, a good alternative to Google Maps is Maps.Me, a free app that allows you to navigate with just GPS. If you are using it on a device that does not have GPS, you will still have a very detailed atlas to use. Plus, you can bookmark locations for easy reference.

For more information on Maps.Me and links, see the section title The Maps on page 47.

Apps

I have been very disappointed with most apps for Tokyo. Take your time to evaluate them before spending your money. Those that are just transit maps can often be out of date, and current rail and subway maps can be downloaded as PDF files.

PDF maps

Consider loading PDF maps and informative documents onto your tablet or smartphone for offline use. Many official tourism web sites have such files that you can download. If you have a Mac, or use the Chrome browser on your Windows machine, you can print web pages to PDF files. I organize mine as collections by location on my iPad.

TIP: *In some places you may see large maps at the edge of the sidewalk. On those maps the top is not north but the direction you are facing.*

A compass

This may sound silly to some, but an old-fashioned magnetic compass can greatly assist at times. Given the number of tall buildings in Tokyo, a smartphone compass can often be inaccurate. I found this out on one trip where two different phones showed north to be in very different directions. By the way, smartphones point to true north, which is a little different than magnetic north. Even so, I have successfully used a compass to help me navigate.

Print maps

Folding maps of Tokyo are so general as to be only occasionally useful. Maps of smaller areas can be very handy; this especially includes those available for free at local tourism offices and some subway and train stations.

Address finding

Odds are you will not have to find a place by its address, however if you do, expect it to be different than what you are used to. Most streets in Tokyo do not have names and buildings do not have numbers. This is why business advertisements often include maps.

The Japanese address system for Tokyo works like this:

- First the Chōme (numbered section of a neighborhood): 丁目
- Then the lot number. These numbers are assigned as the lots are developed, so 2 may not be next to 1 or 3.
- Then the Machi or Chō (neighborhood) name: 町
- Then the Ku (ward) name: 区
- Finally the city name, in this case Tokyo.

For example Tokyo Skytree is: 1 Chōme-1-2 Oshiage, Sumida, Tokyo.

Getting directions

There are tourist information centers in larger train stations, and the Metropolitan Government Building has two, one for all of Japan and one for the Tokyo area. Before you exit a station look for free tourism and shopping fliers. Often you will find information that is very local, or as I did in one case, an excellent folding map of the rail system.

As mentioned earlier, one way to get help with directions is to ask at a kōban. The police regularly help Japanese with directions as well, so don't be shy. They may not know English, but will still try to help you.

Even if you know where you are going, if someone offers to help you with directions, let them. This is a great way to interact. Be sure to give a little bow as you thank them.

Station names offer a clue to their location. For example, if you are looking to get to Nakano, check to see if there is a station with that as the name.

Finally: Have fun, get lost, find yourself.

NOTE: *In many entries in this book I will point out the entrance to a location. In some areas you could have to walk some distance to find the entrance.*

Trains and subway

For the areas covered in this book, you will likely rely on the subway and surface train system rather than buses. Tokyo has over 600 train and subway stations, and more are being added. Don't be intimidated—if you can navigate a highway or city streets, or find your way around a small town, you have the skills you need. Tokyo is just a bigger version of what you are familiar with. First find the station near where you want to go. That gives you the line the station is on. Then look for a station near where you are and trace its line to see if it intersects with the other line. At that point you transfer between the two. You may sometimes have to transfer more than once. Directions obtained by Google Maps and Maps.Me will give train, subway, and bus routes. This includes stations and bus stops.

Stations commonly have a map and chart in English, detailing routes and fares above the ticket machines. These maps are usually specific to a train company and their train stations.

Make sure you are on the right platform and that you get on a train for the line you want, as some lines may share tracks. If you find yourself going in the wrong direction, just get off and get on a train back.

TIPS: *Don't rush. The trains run quite often and you are there to enjoy yourself, not to get stressed. If you have the option of taking an aboveground train rather than the subway, consider it. You can view the city as you travel and perhaps spot things to check out later.*

Day passes

Unless you plan to make several trips in one day, passes are not very useful. They do not save you much money and are for only one company, which is impractical given the number of different transit companies in Tokyo.

JR Pass

I also recommend not getting a Japan Rail Pass unless you plan to take long-distance trips well outside Tokyo. The passes are not cheap, are only good for a limited amount of days, and only on JR lines. Though, if you plan to visit places some distance away, such as Kyoto or Nara, the pass can save you money.

🌐 *http://www.japanrailpass.net/en/*

Locating stations

Train stations are relatively easy to locate as they are above ground and the tracks are usually elevated. For subway stations, look for the distinctive logos used by the subway lines. You will also see directional signage in underground walkways between stations, underground shopping arcades, and some large store basements.

NOTE: *Train and subway lines are color coded. In most systems this extends to the color of the cars. Stations are numbered in sequence. On some lines individual stations have their own platform tune.*

Boarding and exiting trains

Expect to line up to get on the train. Just follow the example of other riders. Wait for everyone to exit before boarding the train.

On occasion you may end up on a very crowded train. To exit crowded trains, gently push your way between people to exit. If you are not able to exit in time, get off at the next station and take a train back to the one you want. To avoid ending up in the middle of the train car, stand near the Priority Seats near the ends of the cars.

Exiting stations

Exiting can be as easy as heading to the nearest exit and figuring out where you are once you reach the street. However, in larger stations that have multiple exits, some connect to tunnels that can take you a great distance underground. This is handy in some circumstances to avoid waiting for traffic lights and to keep out of bad weather.

TIPS: *If you are meeting someone at a station, be sure to choose a meeting point. A local landmark is best, or if at an exit, specify which exit.*
If you need to stop in the station to figure out which exit to take, be sure to not block walkways.

Elevators and escalators

In the subways, get used to identifying elevator and escalator signs. A day of walking can be stressful on your body, so using escalators and elevators pays off. Plus some subway stations may be so far underground that you have to take a series of escalators to get to the surface. Be aware that a few of the older stations have yet to have elevators and escalators installed.

Women-only cars

On some lines, there are cars designated for women only for all hours of operation. On other lines they are only for rush hour. The platform will have a sign at the edge of the track indicating where such cars stop. Guys should follow the example of Japanese men as they line up.

Other transit

Walking

First there is the physical reality of your body: Make sure you have comfortable clothing and shoes. Expect to walk much more than at home. For a walker, shoes are crucial. If they are new, make sure the shoes are broken in for comfort. Consider that you may have to take them off in some places, so something you can easily remove and put on is good. You can expect businesses, temples, and shrines that require the removal of shoes to have shoe horns at hand, often ones that are long enough to use standing up.

Some travel books suggest having two pair of shoes so you can trade off to give your feet a rest. I suggest you save space in your luggage and only bring an extra set of insoles; I use the types popular with runners for extra comfort and swap the insoles every couple of days.

I carry good moleskin, the kind that is thin and flexible such as Dr. Scholl's, not the cheap brands that are thick and come off easily. Moleskin comes in sheets, so pack a small pair of scissors in your checked luggage. If you find your feet developing sore spots, put some moleskin on the next day before heading out.

Also expect to climb many stairs. Tokyo has various elevations so stairs and slopes are found in much of the city. You will usually have to use a pedestrian overpass involving stairs for crossing major streets. Elevators and escalators are increasingly common in stations, so take advantage of them to conserve your energy.

TIPS: *Do not jaywalk. Always wait for the light. Look both ways. The Japanese drive on the left side of the road, so traffic may be coming from an unexpected direction; and there are bicycles to keep in mind.*

Buses

Buses have a single fare when travelling within the twenty-three wards; the fare can vary slightly between different companies. Some buses are boarded from the front, others are boarded at the back and exited from the front. Just follow the example of locals getting on the bus or directions from the driver.

Taxis

Taxi drivers usually don't know English and you should expect to give directions or provide a map unless you are headed to a major destination. If you do need to take a cab, you may want to pick a landmark near where you are going and have the driver drop you off there. Don't open the door: taxicab doors open with a switch operated by the driver, and opening it yourself can damage the mechanism.

Bicycle

Renting a bike is an option if you are willing to end up back where you started. Bicycles can be especially useful for places with little auto traffic and where you want to cover a large area. Some of the rivers, such as the Arakawa and Edogawa, are bordered by levees with paved trails on top, making a bike ride an easy way to enjoy the view.

Car rental

Renting a car is only useful in rural areas and for traveling between cities. It is too confusing to drive in Tokyo unless you know the city well, and parking can be expensive and hard to find. In order to rent and drive a car in Japan, you need to be at least eighteen years old and have a Japanese driver's license or an International Driving Permit (IDP).

Water buses

One fun form of transportation is the water bus. These run on major rivers and parts of Tokyo Bay—the Sumidagawa has the most. Some water buses have platforms on the roof so you can stand outside to enjoy the view and take pictures. Particularly popular are the ones designed by Matsumoto Leiji, the manga artist who wrote the *Galaxy Express* and *Captain Harlock* science fiction sagas. These are called Himiko, Hotaluna, and Emeraldus and run on the Sumidagawa.

Shopping

Hours for shops, restaurants, and museums

On the whole you should expect stores to open at 10:00 a.m. and restaurants to open around 11. The exception is convenience stores, which often are open twenty-four hours a day. Museums usually open at 9:00 or 10:00 a.m., and some gardens and parks have similar hours. Most museums accept the Grutto pass, a ticket book that admits you to over ninety museums in the Tokyo area, usually covering full admission. It is available for purchase at any museum that takes it.

Many shops close for a weekday, often Monday, and almost all museums close on Mondays. Family-run businesses are still very common and they need time off. The day a shop or museum is closed may change when that day is a holiday: They often are open and then close the following day. The New Year holiday typically lasts from December 29 to January 4. It is safe to assume that almost all of Tokyo is closed on those days.

Grutto:

🌐 *https://www.rekibun.or.jp/en/grutto/*

Special considerations

At most shops only Japanese will be spoken. Don't let that discourage you. Measurements will be metric, especially for clothing and footwear. Credit cards are not accepted in many small businesses, so you should carry sufficient cash.

Tax-free shopping

For tourists, tax-free shopping is sometimes available. Currently there is a 5,000-yen minimum to qualify, and you will need to show staff your passport. Small stores handle the tax-free process at the register; large stores may have a counter where you take your receipts to have the tax refunded.

For more information on Japan's tax exemption see:

🌐 *https://tax-freeshop.jnto.go.jp/eng/shopping-guide.php*

Department stores

Department stores are often not only one store, as some of the floor space may be leased to individual businesses. Just think of the store as a vertical mall with no walls between the shops. Simply pay for your purchases at the nearest register. Department stores often have a roof area you can access. While most of these do not have a good view of the neighborhood, they often have other items of interest such as a shrine, gardening supplies, food, places to sit and rest, and even beer gardens in the summer. With the increasing number of tourists from Islamic countries, many large department stores now have prayer rooms.

Local shops

You will see many unique items, often handcrafted, that are only sold at the shop that makes them. This includes museum shops, which may have publications only sold there. Keep these in mind as you window-shop.

You may see some goods that are illegal in your home country such as turtle shell and elephant ivory. Be aware of this and avoid such products.

In this book I have focused on shops and restaurants that have been around for some time. Such long-established businesses are called rōho or shi'nise in Japanese. There is even an association, the Tōto Norenkai, for businesses in Tokyo over 100 years old.

The web supplement to this book will include information regarding closures, relocations, and other shops not listed in the book.

Tōto Norenkai:
🌐 *http://www.norenkai.net/en/*

Souvenirs
Prepare a list of who to buy souvenirs for. The tradition in Japan is to buy items that are local to the area. You will have many opportunities to follow this tradition. Dry food items that store well in luggage is always an option if you are not sure what to get.

Ema sold at shrines and temples also make a great souvenir and there is a unique design for each shrine. Some may even have more than one style for sale.

Storage
Picked up too much and still plan to continue shopping? You can store your bags temporarily in coin lockers for a small fee. Lockers are commonly available in stations, often in several locations in larger stations. Lockers sometimes come in more than one size. In some commercial areas you may even find them in shopping malls or right on the street.

Shipping items home
Shopping may result in too many items to pack in your luggage. If you want to ship items home, your hotel may be able to help. The service at post offices is also excellent. They have boxes in several sizes, will assist with paperwork, and their shipping fees are affordable. Do check their list of prohibited items before shipping.

Dining

How do you order in restaurants if you don't know the language? Many smaller eateries will have picture menus or a ticket machine near the door where you can pay for your choice and hand the ticket to staff. Electronic ticket machines usually have English menus. You don't need to speak Japanese and they don't need to know your language. There is no tipping—if you want to show appreciation, eat everything. Always assume that restaurants and coffee shops take the last order a half-hour before closing.

Be aware that few places are open for breakfast. The staff where you are staying can make recommendations for that meal.

I tend to go with small family-run restaurants when I get hungry. I have found smaller businesses are quite patient and accommodating to non-Japanese tourists. They also usually have a relaxed environment; on one trip we had a conversation about food ingredients with an actor from a troupe that was in town.

Another option is convenience and grocery stores, which have bentō, onigiri, sandwiches, and other ready-to-eat foods.

Be aware that you will need to know how to eat with chopsticks in some places. Practice before you go to Japan, even if you are confident of your ability. One test of skill is to take two bowls and transfer dried beans between them.

Smoking

Want to avoid restaurants that allow smoking? Laws now ban smoking in most restaurants, also look for signage regarding smoking at the door.

Taboo foods

If you avoid certain foods because of allergies, or for religious or other reasons, you should study up on what is used to make specific Japanese meals. For example, wheat is in nearly all noodles, broths are often made with fish stock, and eggs are in almost any fish paste product and in some (lower quality) ramen.

If you are vegan, be aware that pretty much anything simmered is cooked in fish stock. Do research and figure out what individual items you can eat. The number of vegan restaurants is increasing but they are still few and far between. There are several websites that cover vegan restaurants, so a web search can help.

If you are Jewish or Muslim, it should be easy to avoid pork. Stay away from Chinese-style dishes like ramen, which often uses stock based on pork bones. Other foods on the Japanese diet should be easy to identify by just looking at them. Many restaurants will have a sign if they serve halal food.

For those with food allergies, check the Essential Japanese page listed under the Accessibility menu on Accessible Japan's web site for handy phrases.

🌐 *https://accessible-japan.com/essential-japanese-phrases-and-words-for-people-with-disablities/*

TIPS: *For variety you can try to avoid eating the same thing twice in your stay, there is plenty of variety to choose from.*
To order food to go, you can say "take out," as the English phrase is used in Japan.

Toilets

Toilets are not hard to find. In stations they tend to be in the area inside the fare gates. Large shopping buildings have them on some floors and they can also be found in public parks. In a pinch, just ask at a convenience store. The Japanese know the meaning of the English word toilet.

TIP: *Park toilets may be out of paper, so carry a pack of tissues with you. Paper towels or hand driers are also not always available. Many Japanese use their handkerchief to dry their hands, not to blow their nose, so do as the locals do and take one along when you go out.*
WARNING: *While they are increasingly rare, there are still traditional squat toilets in Japan. If you are an experienced camper, you will have no trouble using one. Otherwise keep looking.*

Words and a phrase to remember

Sumimasen. Often translated as "excuse me." This is the magic word that is useful in so many situations, from getting a waiter's attention to letting folks know you want to squeeze by when exiting the train.

Hai, pronounced like the English word "hi," is a polite way to say yes.

Toire wa doko desu ka? (the *desu* is pronounced with a silent u). "Where is the toilet" is a very important phrase, so keep it handy.

Some Basic Etiquette

In the spring of 2018, the year thirty million tourists visited Japan, I started seeing articles on "kankō kōgai," or "tourism pollution." The large increase in the number of tourists is having a negative effect on the lives of the residents of many highly popular locations. Some of this is due to rude and disrespectful behavior, but some is just the result of not knowing what is offensive or objectionable. I hope this section helps you adjust your behavior so you are not part of the problem. In other words: people live here. Be polite, and don't lower the quality of life for locals. Observe the Japanese around you and take them as your model.

As this section only covers some basic tips, I strongly recommend a copy of *Amy's Guide to Best Behavior in Japan* for a broader guide to etiquette.

Noise

It is often important to be quiet. When you return from your trip you may be surprised how noisy things seem at home. If you are strolling in a residential area, keep your voice down. If you need to speak to your travel mate, don't do it from several feet away or raise your voice. This is especially true in the early morning or late at night.

Physical contact

Avoid touching unless your Japanese acquaintance initiates it. Expect to bow slightly rather than shake hands in many instances. In situations where contact is unavoidable, such as crowded trains, you don't need to apologize for being pressed against someone, as it is understood this is unavoidable. Be sure to remove any backpacks before boarding trains. Hold them in front of you or place them on an overhead rack.

Shoes off

There will be situations where you will have to remove your shoes, such as in some restaurants and traditional hotels. Be sure you pack socks without holes or stains. Never step on tatami mats with footwear, even slippers. Some restaurants will have raised tatami seating areas, or whole rooms with the floor covered in tatami.

Walking

- On crowded sidewalks walk on the left. This may differ from where you are from, so expect to remind yourself to shift to the left.
- If you need to use your phone in busy areas, move to the curb and do so standing.
- Don't eat and walk. It is considered crude and there are few trash receptacles on the streets.
- Smoking is banned on busy sidewalks in much of Tokyo, with the exception of designated locations.
- If you hear the bell or squeaking brakes of a bicycle behind you, move to the side and let them pass.
- If you are using GPS navigation in a smartphone or tablet while walking, raise your device to eye level to get your bearings, then move the phone back down and continue on.
- Watch your step. There are many small rises and irregularities on sidewalks and other locations.

Roji

The word *roji* is usually translated as "alley," but in reality they are more complex than the English word indicates. Some roji are public, either commercial areas or passageways to places that may be worth exploring. Some are private; these are usually very narrow and only give access to dwellings. Think of them as you would an apartment building lobby. However, I have seen narrow roji (some listed in this book) leading to small neighborhood shrines that are acceptable to pass through. Just remember to be quiet as you do so.

Photos

I tend to avoid photos where the faces of people are clearly visible. This is especially important if you plan to post pictures online. The Japanese tend to be rather private about many things. If you do post photos, obscure any visible faces and license plate numbers before doing so. Also, don't block paths when taking pictures. Make sure people don't have to stop and wait for you to hit the shutter.

Visiting Shintō shrines and Buddhist temples

Even if you do not plan to worship at a shrine or temple, the following etiquette will help you be respectful of the community. There are regional variants in behavior at shrines and temples, but your sincerity is more important than observing strict rules. For behavior at the temizuya and at shrine buildings, I used the instructions on the Meiji Jingū website as the model.

Entering the grounds

When approaching and leaving a shrine or temple, bow once at the gate facing the shrine. Not all Japanese do this, so don't worry if you forget. If there is a heavy wooden bar on the ground at the gate, do not step on it. Treat the area past the gate as sacred, as you would treat a holy building. As much as possible do not walk on the middle of the path leading to the shrine or temple. This portion is reserved for the kami and buddhas. Shintō tradition says you should not visit a shrine if you are sick, have an open wound, or are in mourning.

Purification

Most shrines, and some temples, have a temizuya or chōzuya, a place to ritually purify yourself with water. The practice is considered respectful and is not a religious act of worship. To do this, pick up a ladle in your right hand and fill it with enough water for the following process. Be sure none of the water spills back into the basin. Pour some of the water over your left hand to rinse it, then transfer the ladle to your left and do the same to your right hand. Return the ladle to your right hand and pour some water into your left to use for lightly rinsing your mouth. Politely spit the water on the ground (do not drink it). Finally, hold the ladle vertically so the remaining water flows down the handle, then return it to its place. Often there will be a sign at the chōzuya showing how this is done.

For those who wish to perform a small act of individual worship, the following covers the basics.

Paying your respects at a shrine

- Toss one or more coins into the offering box. Many people use a five-yen coin, as the Japanese for five yen "go en" (五円) is a homophone with goen (御縁), "go" being a respectful prefix and "en" meaning relationship.
- If there is a bell, there will be a rope hanging in front of the offering box. Ring the bell two or three times.
- Bow twice.
- Clap twice, then keep your hands together.
- Make a wish, or pay your respects and thank the kami.
- Bow once before leaving.

Paying your respects at a Buddhist temple

- Bow slightly.
- If there is one, ring the gong one, two, or three times.
- Toss a coin in the offering box.
- Bow slightly. Do not clap but put your hands together in a prayerful pose.
- If you have a Buddhist rosary, hold it while you pray.
- Pay your respects and thank the Buddha.
- Bow slightly before leaving.

General shrine and temple behavior

- Be respectful of worshippers. Do not block walkways or converse loudly.
- While it is OK to dress casually when visiting shrines and temples, leave the shorts and revealing tops at home.
- You may be required to remove your shoes when entering some buildings. There will either be shelves where you can leave them or plastic bags you can carry them in.

- Some temples and shrines do not allow photography as they have had trouble with photographers interfering with worshipers. Look for signs.
- At shrines and temples you will see ema. These are small wooden plaques that people buy and write a prayer on. It is OK to read these if you get curious. You can also buy them as souvenirs.

Bathhouses (sentō) and hot springs (onsen)

If you plan on visiting a sentō or onsen, here are some procedures you should follow:

- You will need shampoo, soap, and towels for sentō. You can bring your own or obtain them for a fee on site.
- Expect to take your shoes off soon after entering.
- Go to the proper side: look for the kanji 男 for male and 女 for female.
- Strip in the changing room, place your clothing in a locker, and enter the bath area with your small towel and locker key. Be modest in your nudity, cover your crotch.
- Sit facing the wall at a faucet and wash first. Do a good job, and rinse well so you don't take any suds into the bath itself. Be sure to not splash water on others. Do not take your towel into the bath. You can place it on the rim so it does not touch the water.
- Think of the bath as a hot tub rather than a place to wash. In fact the hot tub is simply a Western adaptation of the Japanese bath. If there is more than one bath, be careful which one you get into. Different baths may be very hot or cold, so test the water first.
- If you use a sauna on site, rinse before soaking in the bath.
- Be aware there is a thing called denkiburo "electricity bath" 電気風呂 that has a small current running through it. Some folks like it, some don't. If you have a pacemaker or heart condition, avoid these.
- When you are done there may be vending machines and a place to rest a little before heading out.

NOTE: *If you have an open wound or are menstruating, you should avoid public baths.*

The Maps

Each chapter has a large area map at beginning of the chapter. These are followed by smaller detail maps with numbered locations marked on them. Each detail map is followed by descriptions of the numbered items. Note that some numbers are on more than one location on a single detail map—these are branches of the same company. In some cases more than one entry will have the same number; this is the case when different shops are inside one building.

In a few cases there are items listed as Off the Charts. These are nearby features that would not fit on one of the maps. Instead directions are given.

Why have such detailed maps rather than addresses? Most streets in Tokyo do not have names, and buildings do not have numbers. There is an address system, which works for the Japanese, but to non-Japanese it is very complex. Even some Japanese have trouble using it.

On each map, blank blocks are simplifications—these actually have several buildings. Buildings near the numbered items are included to give an idea of the exact location of the specific item; nearby buildings are not part of the numbered item. Buildings on the other side of the block may be left blank to simplify the map. In some cases, such as Golden Gai, a very large collection of small buildings may be indicated as a group of small structures.

Maps.Me bookmarks

I have also created downloadable bookmarks of sites in this book to be used with the Maps.Me app. Green bookmarks indicate items with entries. Red bookmarks are items in the web supplement to this book, as well as some branch locations on different detail maps. Purple indicates useful locations such as kōban, public restrooms, stations, landmarks, etc.

Instructions on how to download Maps.Me, the maps for Tokyo, and the bookmarks list can be found in the web supplement to this book. See page 483 for details.

Tokyo Stroll Supplemental Materials:
🌐 *http://www.koyagi.com/TokyoStroll/TSmain.html*

Maps.Me, Google Maps, Google Earth, and Tokyo Stroll Locations:
🌐 *http://www.koyagi.com/TokyoStroll/TSMaps.html*

Google Maps

Google Maps also has the ability to import the Maps.Me bookmarks. Presently these are in only one color for marked locations, however you can turn a particular set of bookmarks on and off or display all of them. If Google adds the ability to color code locations, either from the Maps.Me bookmarks or its own lists of places function I will include this in the instructions in the web supplement to this book.

Map legend

Major road

Elevated road

Depressed road

Minor road

Mixed vehicle and pedestrian way, alley

Dedicated pedestrian way

Stairway

Surface rail

Elevated rail

Depressed rail

Subway line

Bridge

Unmarked boundary

Tunnel entrance / exit

Fence wall, barrier

Buildings

Statue, sculpture, decorative feature

Artificial water feature

pond

Pond, moat

Shinto shrine

Police

Fire station

Museum

Post office

Hospital

Buddhist temple

Church

Mosque

Onsen

Cemetary

Train

Subway

River River, channel

park Greenspace, park

Descriptive text

Directional marker for off-map feature

1 2 Item numbers

Lavatory

TOKYO STROLL GUIDE

秋葉原・神田

AKIHABARA AND KANDA

Akihabara

This area gets its name from Akibagahar "Akiba Field." Once the location of Akiba Jinja "autumn leaf shrine," it later became the site of a rail yard. Today Akihabara is famous for two things: electronics, and merchandise for fans of anime, manga, and video games. After World War II the area near the Yamanote line train tracks was a thriving black market, stretching from what is now Ameya Yokochō, next to Ueno Station, in the north to the JR Akihabara Station in the south. The illicit goods found there included food, which was heavily rationed at the time, alongside a legal market for electronic components. As rationing ended and the remaining illegal operations were shut down, the market started to specialize. Akihabara became a center for electronics, everything from complete appliances to small parts, and later came to include personal computers and video games, which in turn drew a clientele interested in anime and manga. Today the area contains a diverse mix of shops: Stores may occupy several floors of a tall building or be tucked away on side streets, or even in basements accessible only by walking through another store. The main street is Chūō Dōri, which can be so crowded, noisy, and bustling that you may want to escape due to sensory overload. Head to a side street or enter a shop and you will likely find a quieter environment. At night a profusion of commercial signs light up, making this area truly electric. Chūō Dōri is also closed to vehicles on Sundays to become a broad pedestrian promenade.

Kanda

This is an area spanning both sides of the Kandagawa, including much of Akihabara, and is a mix of the modern and the old. The old includes shrines, temples, and even an Eastern Orthodox cathedral, as well as buildings, scattered here and there, that survived both World War II and the predation of developers. While Akihabara has plenty of inexpensive eateries, this area has restaurants you may want to save your appetite for.

NOTE: *Shops open, relocate, and go out of business at a faster pace in Akihabara than in many other parts of Tokyo, so do not be surprised if there are changes. In fact as I was writing this chapter, two shops moved to another building. I will attempt to track these changes in the online supplement to this book.*

TIP: *Akihabara is often the location of theme cafes focusing on a particular TV show or game. These are often temporary, so keep your eye out for what is open when you go.*

DETAIL 1

❶ Akihabara Station 秋葉原駅

There are actually three stations with this name in close proximity. For rail traffic there is the larger JR station for the Chūō Sōbu, Yamanote, and Tōhoku Main lines. For the subway there is the Tsukuba Express station just to the east of the JR station, and a Tokyo Metro Hibiya Line subway station two blocks to the east of that (and not shown on the map). Which one you exit will affect your initial navigation of the area.

❷ Akihabara Radio Kaikan
秋葉原ラジオ会館

This collection of shops is housed in twelve stories if you count the two basements. The original Radio Kaikan was two stories and opened in 1950. An additional eight-story building was constructed in 1962 on an adjacent lot. In 1972 the original was demolished and another eight-story building was linked with the 1962 building to form a new complex. In 1976 NEC opened a shop here, igniting the microcomputer boom in Japan. Originally the shops mainly sold electronics, but with the growth of otaku culture the building tenants shifted to goods for fans of anime, manga, and PC games. After the 2011 Tōhoku earthquake, Radio Kaikan was closed for safety reasons and it was decided to demolish the building. The current building was built in 2014 and houses over thirty shops.

AKIHABARA AND KANDA WEST

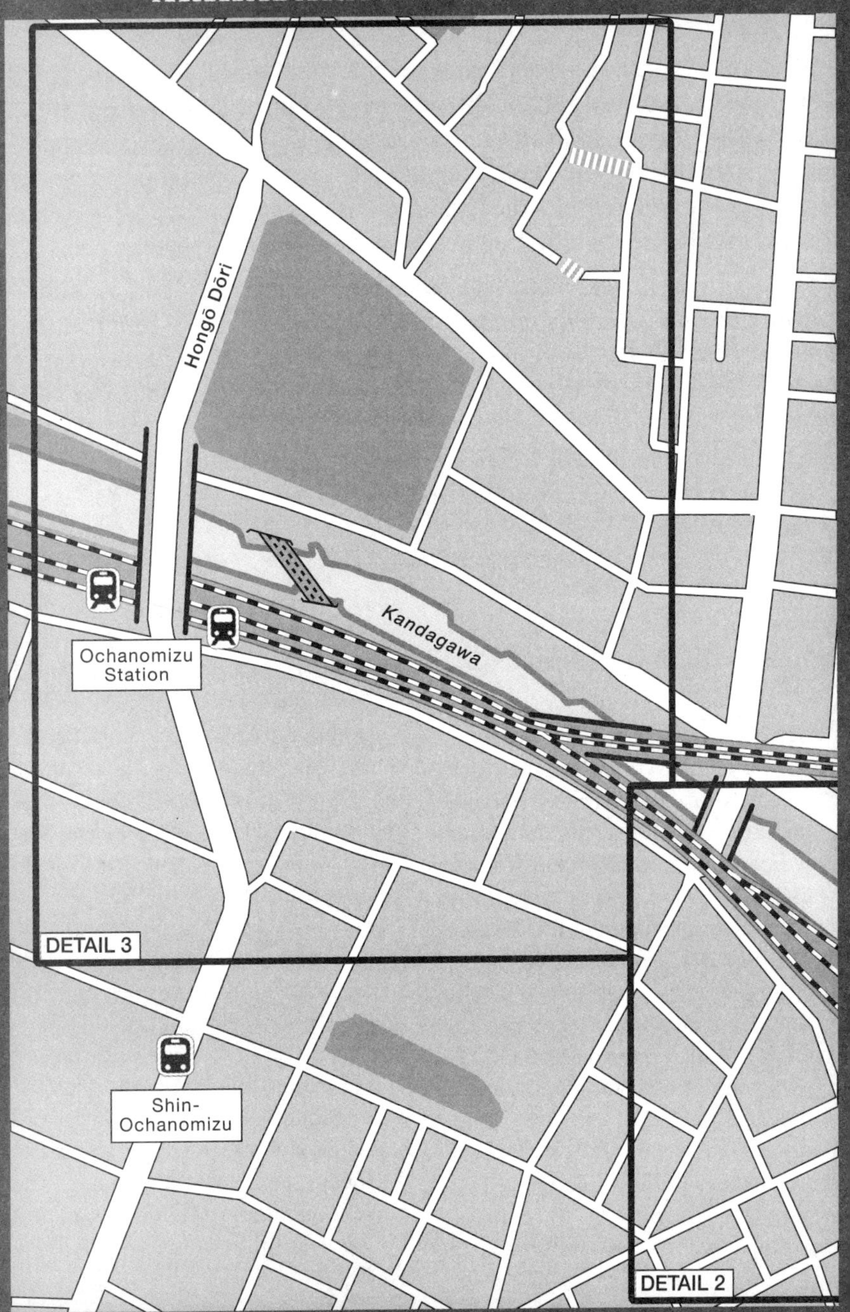

AKIHABARA AND KANDA EAST

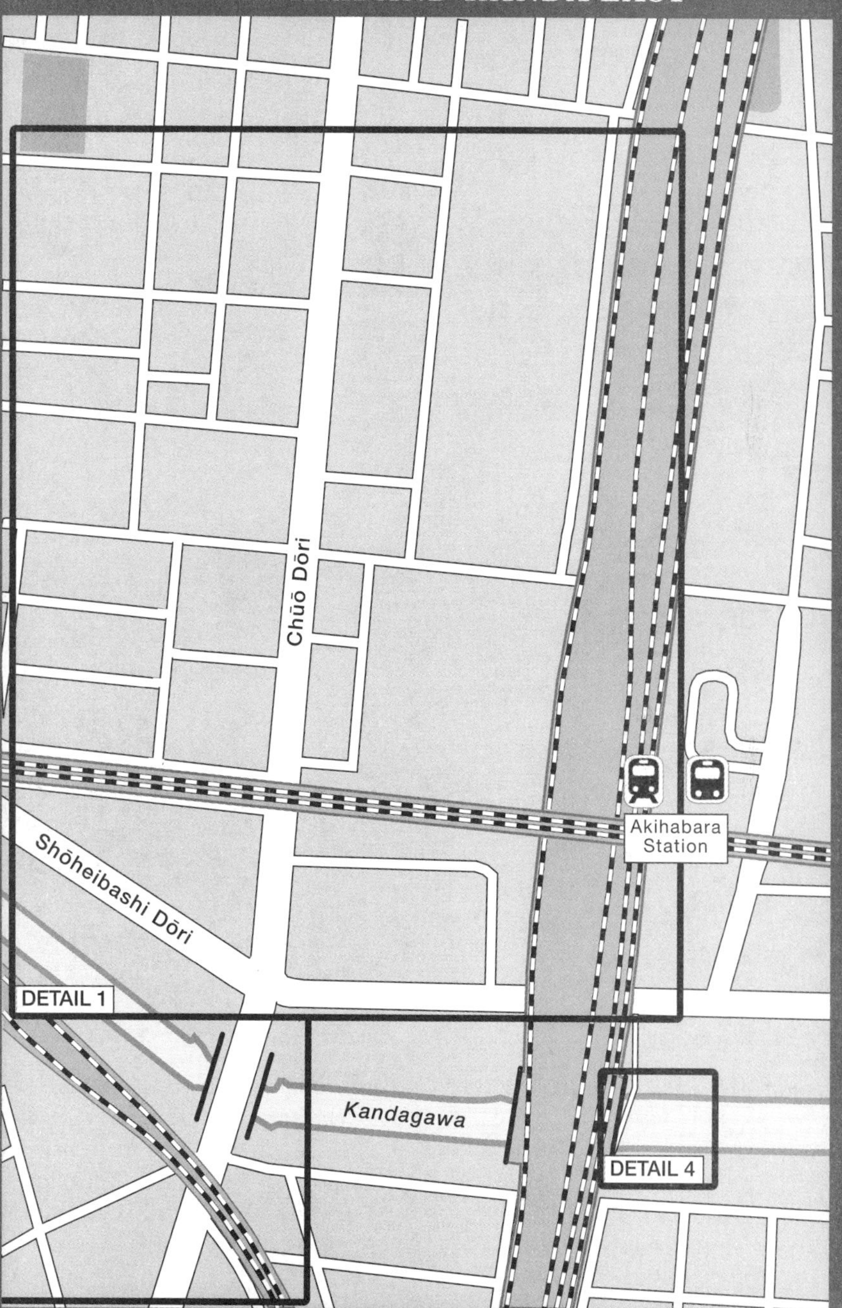

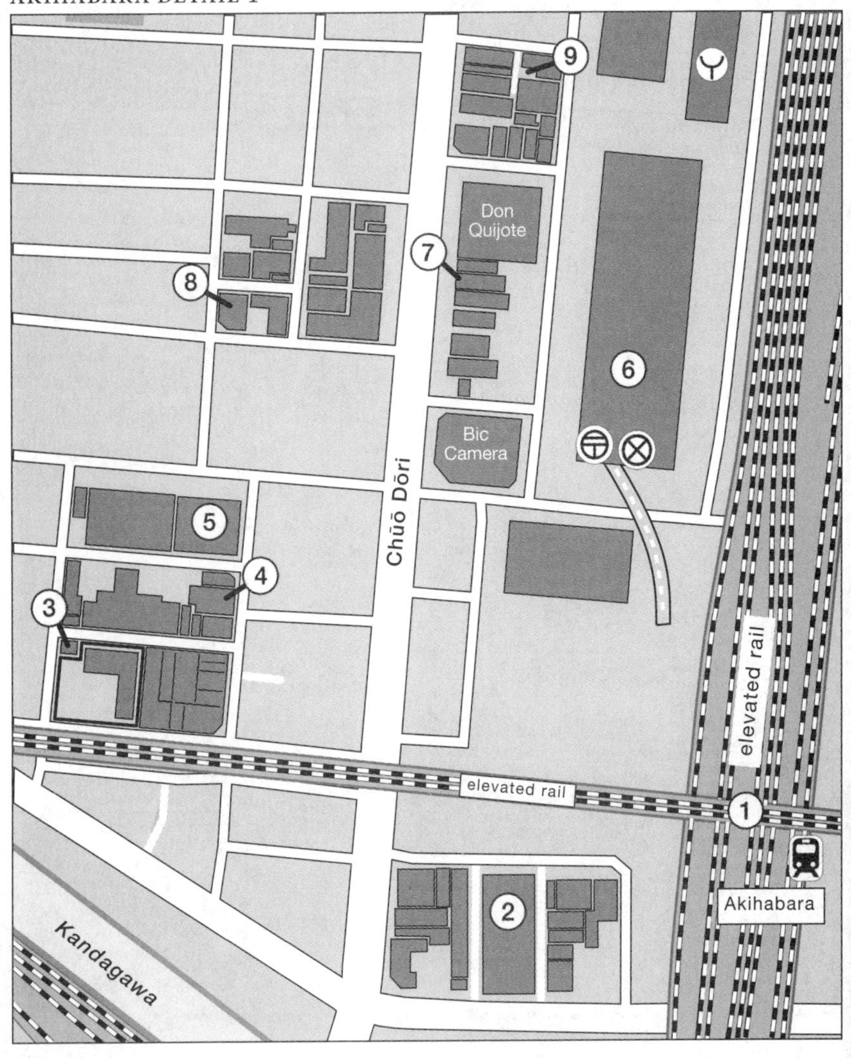

🌐 *http://www.akihabara-radiokaikan.co.jp*

❷ **ASTOP** アストップ

There are two locations for this store established in 2003, one on the second floor of the Akihabara Radio Kaikan building ❷ and the other on the fourth floor of the AKIBA Cultures ZONE ❺ building. Both locations of this shop sell second-hand models, figurines, stuffed toys, and retro games, as well as goods related to anime, manga, and idol singers on consignment. A seller rents a numbered clear display case, and each item in the case is numbered and priced. Buyers find what they want, pick up a purchase card (available near the register), fill out the case and item numbers, then give it to staff who retrieve the desired items. The store then handles the transaction and pays the seller. One major advantage of this kind of shop is that you get to appraise the item in person rather than order online and be disappointed. The Japanese take very good care of their property and I've very rarely seen anything that looks worn in these cases. Often you can find hard-to-obtain items for very reasonable prices. Credit cards accepted for purchases over 3,000 yen.

🌐 *http://www.astop.co.jp*

NOTE: *Purchases are not refundable.*

❷ K-Books

A small chain specializing in new and second-hand goods with a focus on anime, manga, video games, popular music, and related items. Many of their shops specialize in goods for women and girls, especially their stores in the Ikebukuro area. For this reason it is not surprising that the company has a majority of women on the staff and a large percentage of women managers. The first Akihabara store opened in 1996; it is presently located on the third floor of the Akihabara Radio Kaikan building, with several departments including a men's store for ages eighteen and over only. The main store and over fifteen branches are located in Ikebukuro, all east of Ikebukuro Station, with most in the vicinity of the Sunshine 60 building.

🌐 *http://www.k-books.co.jp*

Akihabara Shopping

Many location numbers for the Akihabara maps refer to the building a shop is in. For this reason a few shops have the same number. Shops with more than one location and number are cross referenced to the first entry for that shop. When in a shop, check for stairs and elevators—some shops are larger than they look and spread over several stories, or each floor could be a separate shop. If you plan to hunt for products related to anime, manga, and games, be aware that the focus in Akihabara is the latest and most popular shows. For older materials check second-hand shops like Mandarake and ASTOP or head to the Nakano Broadway Mall in Nakano. If there are specific items you want, bring a printout or screen capture on your smartphone to show staff. When asking about specific titles know the Japanese name and don't assume your pronunciation will be understandable.

❷ Kaiyōdō Hobby Lobby Tokyo 海洋堂Hobby Lobby Tokyo

Located in the Akihabara Radio Kaikan building, this is the Akihabara shop for the internationally famous figure manufacturer. Their figures range from hyper-realistic animals to fictional characters. The company's products also include poseable replicas of Buddhist statues, military vehicles, buildings, historical personages, artworks, and pretty much anything else they think would have a market. They even partner with major museums and other institutions, such as the nearby Kanda Myōjin, to do small replicas of related objects.

🌐 *http://kaiyodo.co.jp*

❸ Kōbu Inari Jinja 講武稲荷神社

An attractive Inari shrine dating from 1858 in the middle of a modern neighborhood of small shops and residences. The red fencing and torii stand out framing a corner plot filled with plants and a shrine. The building is elevated; a short flight of stairs leads to the front of the shrine. This is an excellent example of the little surprises one can find walking down an ordinary street in Tokyo.

❹ Kotobukiya Akihabara コトブキヤ秋葉原館

The Akihabara store for the famous toy, model, and figurine maker. The store is quite large: five stories including an event space. Products are grouped together by show or theme, and some items are unique to this one store. Among other highly popular series, they sell figures for Star Wars, DC Comic characters, Sailor Moon, Studio Gainax shows, and Studio Ghibli movies. They also have display cases, model making supplies, stationery, accessories, plushies, character themed snacks, pillow cases, and—oh, the heck with it—just lots of stuff.

🌐 *http://en.kotobukiya.co.jp/kotobukiya-akihabara-store-floor-guide/*

❺ AKIBA CULTURES ZONE

See ❷ ASTOP アストップ

❻ Akiba-i / Akihabara Tourist Information Center
秋葉原観光情報センター

I recommend going here early on your visit to Akihabara to obtain information. Located on the second floor of the Akihabara UDX building since 2010, this is a good place to pick up a very detailed map of the area in any of several languages, as well as have questions answered and get directions to specific shops. They have some English-speaking staff.

🌐 *https://www.akiba-information.jp/html/multi/multiple/index.html*

❼ Animate

Since the first store in Ikebukuro opened in 1983, Animate has been a major retailer of anime and manga related goods. Today there are something like 120 stores in Asia, although they do have a mail order business in the US. This particular store is one of the largest shops in the neighborhood. At the Akihabara branch there are seven floors plus a basement level with one of the floors reserved for special events. Find the floor you want on the directory or just take the elevator to the top floor and work your way down as you explore. Animate stocks anime, manga, dōjinshi, light novels, photo books, magazines, cards, games, CDs, art supplies, and especially character figures. In fact there are two floors devoted to character goods of all kinds, they even have unique items which are sold only at Animate stores.

Animate is more than retail, subsidiaries of the company include Animate Film and Libre Publishing.

🌐 *https://www.animate.co.jp/shop/akihabara/*

NOTE: *A little of the stock is adult oriented as this shop caters to all ages.*

❽ Mandarake まんだらけ

This is the eight-story flagship store of the famous chain of second-hand shops for fans of anime, manga, and video games. This particular building was built to house the Akihabara branch and opened in 2008. As you approach the store you will see an entrance on the corner; while you can enter that way, it will put you right into the area where people bring items to sell to the store. It may be better to enter through the entrance on the side that places you at both the stairs and elevators. Unlike most shops in Akihabara, this one has many items from older anime and manga.

Shop carefully as there are no refunds or exchanges.

🌐 *https://mandarake.co.jp/dir/cmp/index-en.html*

❾ Hanabusa Inari Jinja 花房稲荷神社

A small Inari shrine completely surrounded by buildings and accessible only by going down a narrow alley and then another, narrower alley. Depending on which route is taken, larger folks may find themselves brushing the walls on both sides. The alley is dark and there are lights with sensors that will turn on as you walk toward the shrine, so don't be startled. The shrine is on a very small but well-maintained plot of land, an example of what can be hidden away out of sight in Tokyo. Around 2014 a building next to this location was torn down, making the shrine visible from the street for a short time, pictured on various websites.

The alley leading directly to the shrine may be private property so be respectful and quiet.

NOTE: I was told of this shrine by popular culture scholar Patrick Galbraith many years ago. I could not find it on that trip but did find it a couple of years later.

DETAIL 2

❶ Mansei 万世

This restaurant specializes in beef. All the beef is wagyu, which simply means any beef from Japan—and Japanese beef is very good beef. Established in 1949, it is housed in a ten-story building with specialties on three of the floors. In 2021, during the COVID pandemic, the company sold the building and is presently leasing space in it, and has scaled down the number of floors the restaurant uses.

As of the time of writing this the selection is:

Third floor: Western-style dishes. Nonsmoking on weekends and holidays.
Fourth floor: Western-style dishes. Nonsmoking.
Fifth floor: Korean-style BBQ.

🌐 *http://www.niku-mansei.com/foreign_language/index.html*

❷ Manseibashi 万世橋

Over the centuries several bridges with different names have spanned the Kandagawa at this location. The bridge that opened in 1903 was to be called Yorozuyobashi, "Ten Thousand Generation Bridge," however the kanji used for that name can also be pronounced Manseibashi and that pronunciation stuck with the local population. The pre-1903 bridge had been nicknamed the Meganebashi, "Eyeglasses Bridge," due to it having two arches. The current bridge, built in 1930, is an attractive single-arch structure made of concrete. If you are there around sundown or after dark, look down toward the river and you may see some of the bats that nest in the area flying about.

❸ Isegen いせ源

This is the only Tokyo restaurant specializing in ankō (anglerfish, monkfish). The previous building was destroyed in the Great Kantō Earthquake and rebuilt in 1932. The lovely wooden structure sits on a corner near the Takemura sweetshop so you can actually photograph both of them in the same shot. Originally the restaurant was known as Iseshō (いせ庄) and opened near the Ginza in 1830. The second-generation owner moved the restaurant to its current location and re-named it Isegen. At first they served a variety of nabe dishes, until the fourth-generation owner decided to specialize in ankō. They still use a traditional method, considered the best, to cut the fish by hanging it from the jaw and slicing off the

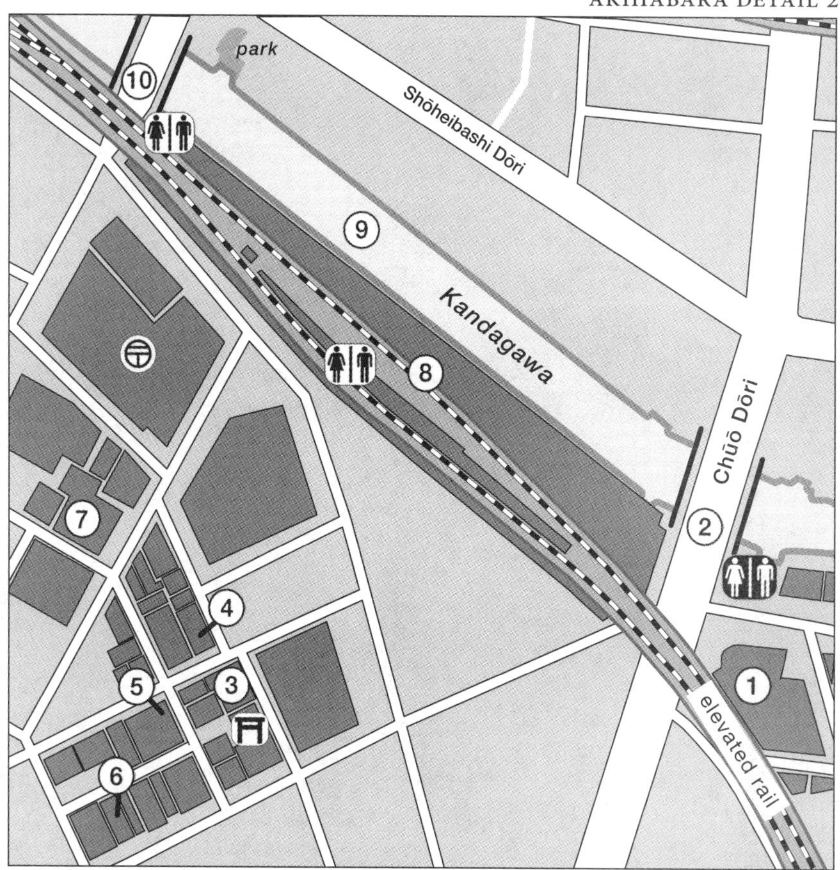

meat. Everything but the bones is used. There is also a seasonality to the menu as some dishes, such as eel, sweetfish, and loach, are only available in the summer. The building has been designated a historical landmark by the Tokyo government.

🌐 *http://www.isegen.com/English/*

🌐 *http://www.norenkai.net/en/portfolio-item/isegen/*

NOTE: *Seating is traditional, on a cushioned tatami mats.*

❹ Takemura 竹むら

This is a traditional sweetshop, a kanmidokoro (甘味処, "sweets place"), that is still operating in the original 1930 building. Takemura has a large menu but is best known for their awazenzai, a cake of steamed millet served

▲The lovely garden on the street side of Kanda Yabu Soba.

▲ A statue of a rather overly endowed male tanuki at Yanagimori Jinja.

▲ Kanda Matsuya stands out as it is surrounded by contemporary structures.

with red bean paste, and agemanjū, a deep-fried bun filled with red bean paste that is served warm. Enjoy the sakurayu, a tea made with dried and lightly salted cherry blossoms. The only non-traditional item on their menu is ice cream, which was available in Japan when the restaurant first opened. Modern and traditional seating are available. Non-smoking.

❺ Botan ぼたん

Botan was established in the late 1890s. The present building dating from 1929 replaces one destroyed in the Great Kantō Earthquake. Their specialty is chicken sukiyaki. The staff prepares and brings you the ingredients for your order. You then do your own cooking at the table in a pot over a charcoal fire. The raw egg provided is for dipping your cooked meat in; you can leave it if you prefer. Expect to take your time—a sukiyaki meal here is in three parts followed by a light dessert. The staff does not speak English but will take your shoes at the entrance and show you a card with a description of the meal written in English. Credit cards are accepted.

❻ Kanda Matsuya まつや

A sobaya dating from 1884 with a relaxed and informal atmosphere. The current two-story building, constructed in 1925, has a narrow garden of plants between it and the sidewalk and is as old-fashioned as it sounds. This popular restaurant is busy at times, so it is not unusual to have to share a table with other customers. The menu is limited to variations on a few items. They serve both soba and udon, and the noodles are made by hand throughout the day so freshness is ensured. If you are not familiar with soba, order morisoba, which is just plain noodles, or zarusoba, which has a little shredded nori seaweed on top. Both are served cold and come with a dipping sauce and a small side dish of sliced onion that you can mix into the sauce. That square pot on the table is filled with sobayu: after you finish your soba, pour some into the remaining dipping sauce and sip it. Kanda Matsuya also has their own brand of various food items you can buy. Seating is Western style at tables.

🌐 *http://www.kanda-matsuya.jp*

❼ Kanda Yabu Soba かんだやぶそば

The oldest operating sobaya in Tokyo, opened in 1880. Vegan and vegetarian dishes are on the menu. The building was rebuilt in 2014 after a fire destroyed the older 1923 structure. The building is wheelchair accessible with an elevator to the second floor. The grounds have a traditional bamboo fence over a low stone wall and the entrance is through an attractive garden. There is an old-fashioned atmosphere with chair seating.

🌐 *http://www.yabusoba.net*

🌐 *http://www.norenkai.net/en/portfolio-item/kanda-yabu-soba/*

❽ mAAch ecute マーチ エキュート

A mall of shops and restaurants arranged around the central passageway of the former Manseibashi Station. The original station, which opened in 1912, was much larger, with a design similar to Tokyo Station. It was destroyed in the Great Kantō Earthquake and replaced with a simpler structure of which all but the first floor was torn down after the station closed in 1943. The present building is the remaining first floor portion that supports the tracks above, which continue to be used by trains. The building housed a transportation museum until 2006, when the much larger Railway Museum opened north of Tokyo in Saitama. There is a deck overlooking the river, a walkway along the Kandagawa side which runs for some distance, and you can take one of two stairways to the enclosed rooftop deck between two sets of tracks on the Chūō Line.

🌐 *https://www.ecute.jp/maach*

❾ Kandagawa 神田川

This river was actually constructed in the early 17th century as part of the creation of a series of moats for the shōgun's castle. The flow of the old Hirakawa was redirected northward by removing most of Kanda hill, excavating a very deep channel, and then connecting the flow to a much smaller river that drained into the Sumidagawa. The displaced soil from the project was used to fill in Hibiya inlet and nearby marshy areas. The name of the river's entire flow was changed to Kandagawa. If you look at the depth of the valley around Yushima Seidō and Ochanomizu Station, you can get an idea of the massive nature of this part of the project to create the moat system around the castle.

❿ Shōheibashi 昌平橋

The original bridge was built in the early 17th century. In 1691 it was given the present name; before then it was variously known as Atarashibashi, Aioibashi, and Imoaraibashi. The present bridge, built in 1927, is in three separate parts: a large central one for vehicles and two narrower ones for pedestrians on either side. All three spans are made of concrete, and the two pedestrian sections are paved in red brick with metal guardrails.

DETAIL 3

❶ Holy Resurrection Cathedral / Fukkatsu Daiseidō 復活大聖堂

On top of a hill in the Surugadai neighborhood is a building commonly known as "Nikolai Cathedral" (Nikoraidō ニコライ堂) after Nikolai

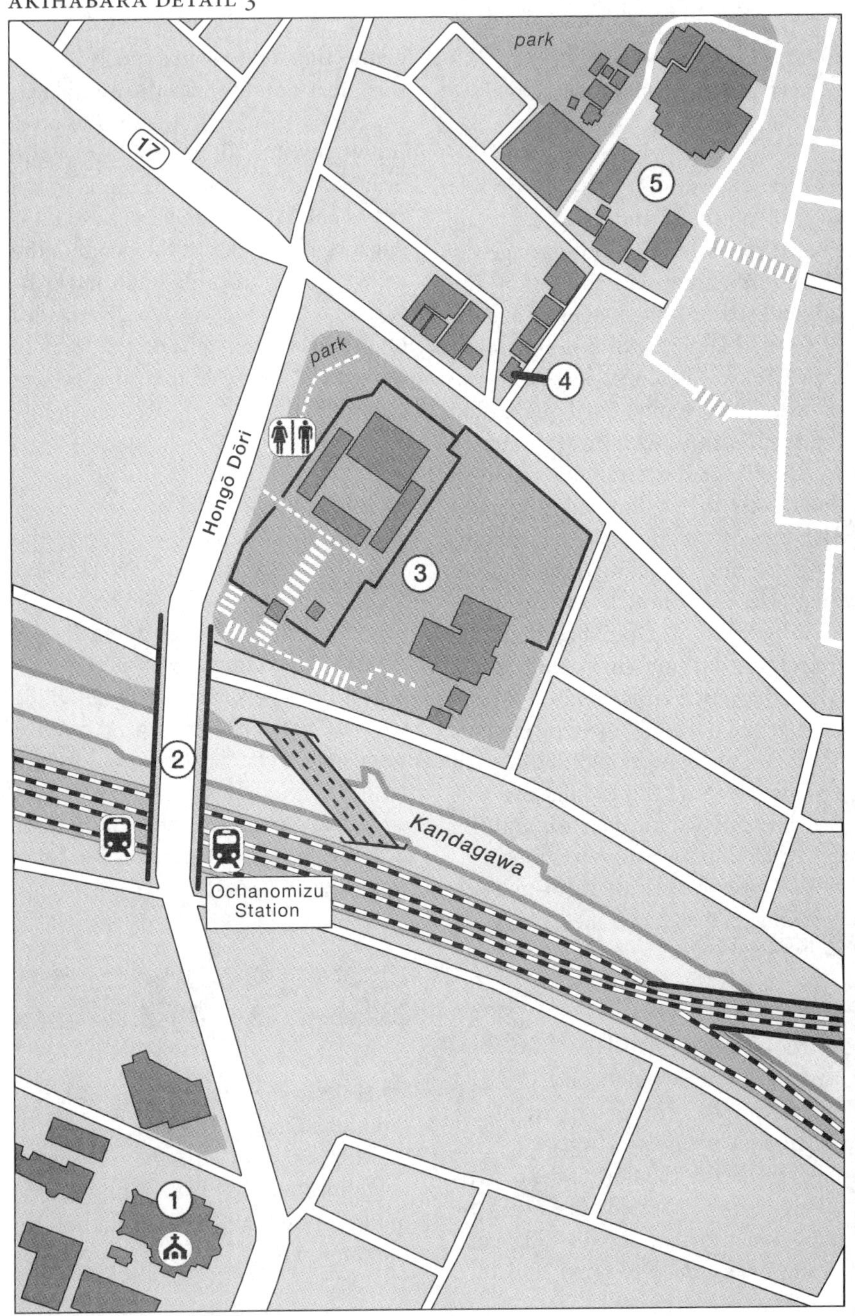
park
17
5
park
4
Hongō Dōri
3
2
Kandagawa
Ochanomizu
Station
1

Kasatkin, the first Orthodox Archbishop in Japan, who raised money to build it. The plans for the building were adapted for the site by Josiah Condor, who supervised the construction, which lasted from 1884 to 1891. After significant damage to the building during the Great Kantō Earthquake, repairs were made and additional changes completed in 1929. In 1962 the government declared the cathedral a Nationally Designated Important Cultural Property.

The entrance is on the north side.

❷ Hijiribashi 聖橋

An attractive single-arch bridge spanning the Kandagawa designed by Mamoru Yamada. A public contest was held to choose the name of bridge. The name Hijiribashi means "Saints Bridge," referring to the nearby Confucian temple Yushima-seidō and the Eastern Orthodox Holy Resurrection Cathedral, which are located on opposite sides of the river. The bridge can be best viewed from the Ochanomizubashi to the west, the roadway on the north bank of the river, or up close from the platform of the Chūō and Sōbu lines Ochanomizu Station on the south bank.

❸ Yushima Seidō 湯島聖堂

Yushima Seidō was founded as a Confucian temple in 1630 in Ueno and then relocated to the present site in 1691 by order of Tokugawa Tsunayoshi, the fifth Tokugawa shōgun. In 1797 it was expanded into a Confucian school for high-ranking samurai and officially recognized by the government. Like many buildings in Tokyo the school was destroyed in the Great Kantō Earthquake and fire. The current structures were rebuilt in 1934 using concrete, but the gate is the original from the 18th century. Today Yushima Seidō is run by a local non-profit and used for lectures on Confucianism as well as other subjects. The site is open to the public and the buildings are open on weekends. The main gate is located on the south side of the grounds, and you can also enter on the west side.

The main festivals are the Confucius Festival on the fourth Sunday in April and the shrine festival on November 23. These festivals and others are celebrated with lectures.

🌐 *http://www.seido.or.jp*

❹ Amanoya 天野屋

The store sells a variety of fermented foods such as miso, nattō, and amazake. These products are prepared in a deep cellar. The shop originally had a much larger system of several cellars, which they had to reduce over time. The amazake is their specialty. It is served cold in the spring and summer and heated in the fall and winter. There is a lounge with a separate entrance where you can sit and enjoy your amazake. The business dates from 1846 and the lounge is filled with many old objects including a surprising number of antique clocks.

🌐 *http://www.amanoya.jp*

🌐 *http://www.norenkai.net/en/portfolio-item/amanoya/*

❺ Kanda Myōjin 神田明神

Founded in 730 near what later became the Edo Castle, this shrine was relocated to near Kandabashi in 1603, then moved again to the present site on Kanda hill in 1616. The current buildings, replacing those destroyed in the Great Kantō Earthquake, are from 1934 and were some of the first in Tokyo to be built of reinforced concrete, although the structures look so nice that it is hard to tell that they are not made of painted wood. The rōmon (main gate) on the south side of the grounds is made of wood and dates from 1975. Enshrined here are Ōnamuchi no Mikoto (associated with Daikoku), Sukunahikona no Mikoto (associated with Ebisu), and Taira no Masakado. The grounds include the EDOCCO Edo Culture Complex, which opened in December 2018 for spiritual exchange and to share information about Shintō and traditional arts.

Kanda Myōjin shrine is popular place to pray for love in marriage, prosperity in business, family well-being, and winning in sports or gambling. The main entrance is on the south side; you can see the torii on the street approaching the shrine off Hongō Dōri.

To the east of the shrine, there is a steep stairway, the otokozaka, "male slope." (When there are two access routes to a shrine, the harder one is referred to as "male.")

🌐 *Kanda Myōjin: http://www.kandamyoujin.or.jp*

TIP: *Enter though the main gates. After exploring the courtyard and shrine, go to the left of the main building where you will find traditional storehouses, and then around to the back where there are small subordinate shrines.*

Kanda Festivals

Kanda Matsuri is held every other year in mid-May, alternating with the Sannō Matsuri of Hie Jinja. This shrine festival is held on a major scale with 200 mikoshi and several floats.

DETAIL 4

❶ Yanagimori Jinja 柳森神社

Founded 1457 as an Inari shrine, this is a branch of the famous Fushimi Inari Taisha Shrine in Kyoto. Today it is more associated with Japan's trickster the tanuki, as the grounds include a small sub-shrine to that animal that was once on the grounds of the shōgun's castle. There are several amusing statues of tanuki near that sub-shrine, with the males having the typical

AKIHABARA DETAIL 4

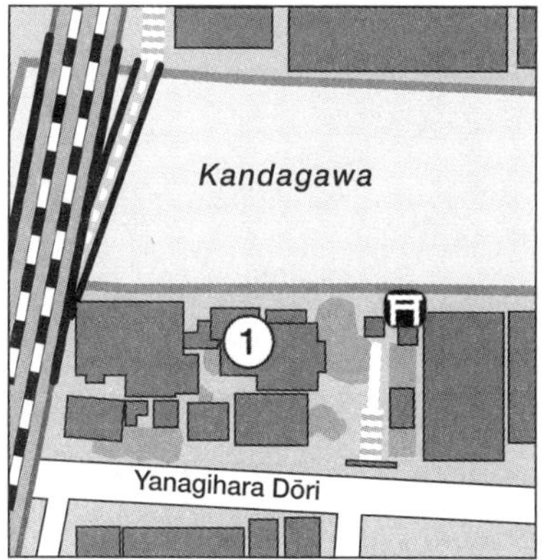

exaggerated scrotums. That association has earned the shrine the nickname of Otanuki Sama. Situated between the roadway and the river, the shrine is far enough downslope to be a quiet spot, with traditional buildings, trees, and a place to sit and perhaps converse with a neighborhood cat. The annual festival is held on the weekend closest to May 15.

浅草

ASAKUSA

My home base when I visit Tokyo, Asakusa is located on the west bank of Tokyo's major river, the Sumidagawa. Several major subway and rail lines provide easy transit to and from this area. Older buildings are common and the atmosphere is laid back, with plenty of small family-run businesses and restaurants. Many of the shops in the Asakusa area date from the 19th century, and some from the days when the Tokugawa shōguns still ruled Japan. Asakusa has been a pilgrimage site since the early 7th century when the famous temple Sensōji was established. In the early Edo period the temple became surrounded with a large variety of shops, and in 1657 the Yoshiwara prostitution red light district was relocated a short distance north of the temple, bringing in a different kind of pilgrim. In 1842 the kabuki and bunraku theaters were moved to the area during a government crackdown on frivolity, likely in the hope the theaters would lose business and fail. The result was the establishment of a lively entertainment district that would produce some of Japan's first Western-style dance halls and jazz clubs; the first movie theater, Denkikan; and in the post-war period, the first strip joints. Today the kabuki and bunraku theaters have relocated to the Ginza and Nihonbashi and the dance halls are gone, but remaining are small-stage theaters, a yose where you can enjoy rakugo, the oldest Western-style bar in Japan, local artisan-run shops that have been in operation for generations, and one strip joint, the Rock-Za. If you go a little north behind the temple, you will find what appears to be just a residential area. Look closer and you will spot ryōtei, those classic restaurants where geisha provide music and dance for private parties. Each summer in August the Asakusa Samba Carnival takes place. This is one of the major summer festivals of Tokyo, with dancers going down the main street for hours.

All of this means that this chapter is the longest in the book, not because of any favoritism on my part, but due to the density of what is there.

KANJI NOTE: *The kanji for Asakusa can be read two ways. The other reading is Sensō, as in Sensōji.*

ETIQUETTE NOTE: *This area is very crowded, so it is very important to not eat or drink while strolling around.*

NAVIGATION NOTES: *Unlike most of Tokyo, the smaller streets near the temple often, but not always, have names. However, they rarely have signs identifying them.*

There are four separate stations named Asakusa Station, so know which one you want. The subway stations for the Ginza Line and the Asakusa Line are blocks apart near the Sumidagawa. The rail stations include one for the Tōbu Railways just north of the Ginza Line station, and one for the Tsukuba Express located underground on Kokusai Dōri several blocks further west.

DETAIL 1

❶ Asakusa Culture Tourist Information Center 浅草文化観光センター

This is a good place to start your visit to Asakusa. Staff can speak Japanese, English, Chinese, and Korean. There is free wi-fi, a nursing room, currency exchange, event rooms, and ticket sales for many events. There is also a restaurant and observation deck on the top floor with good views of both the Sensōji area and across the Sumidagawa. The building was designed by Kengo Kuma and Associates to resemble neatly stacked wooden structures.

❷ Funawa 舟和

A confectioner in business since 1902 with multiple locations: a main shop at the intersection of Shin Nakamise and Orange Street, branches on Kaminarimon Dori, two at the intersection of the Nakamise and Shin Nakamise, and a cafe south of Kaminarimon Dōri (east of the Asakusa Culture and Tourism Center). Their specialty is confections made from sweet potato (imo) paste. At the time they developed their first recipes, traditional sweets were too expensive for many, but imo proved to be an inexpensive ingredient. Today they have a variety of sweets to eat there or to take with you from all the locations.

🌐 *http://funawa.jp*

ASAKUSA WEST

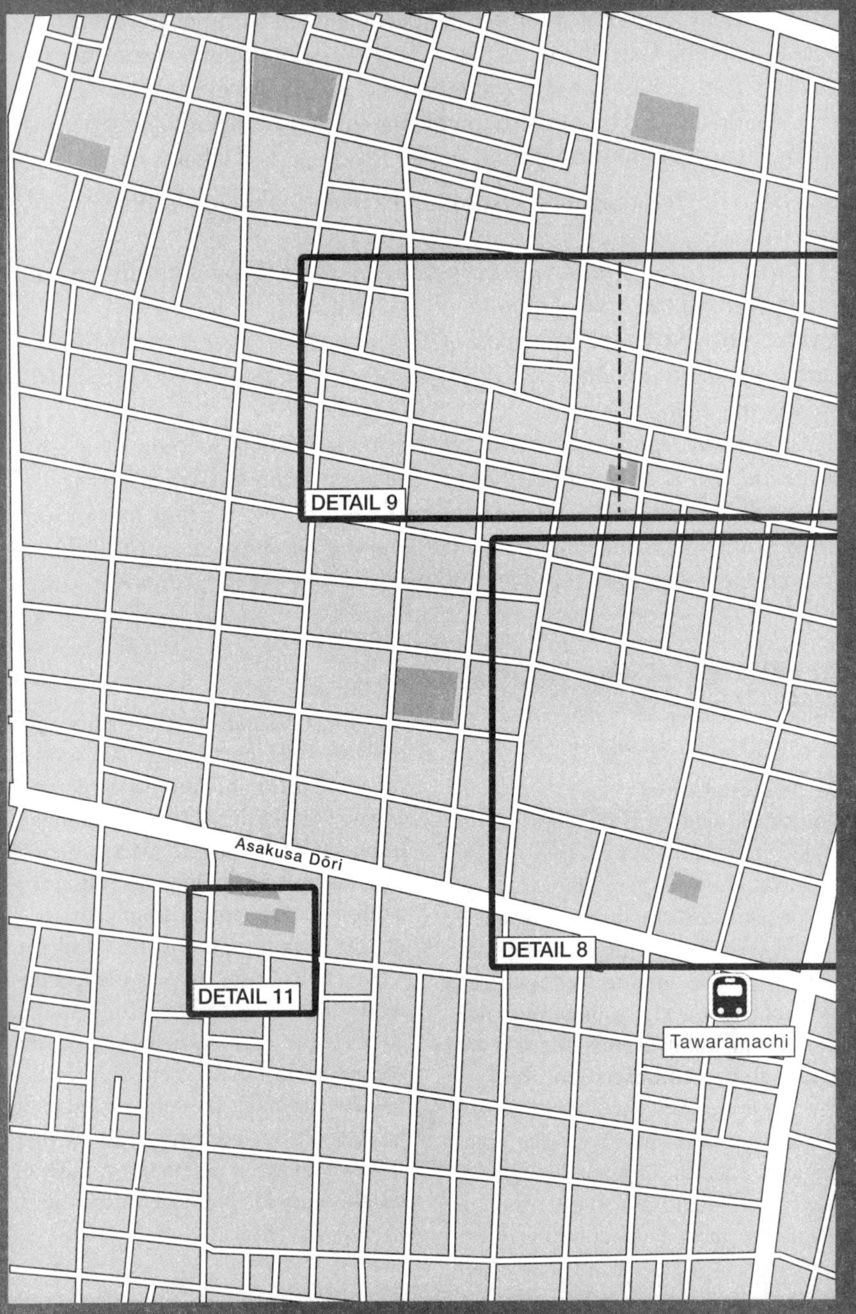

ASAKUSA EAST

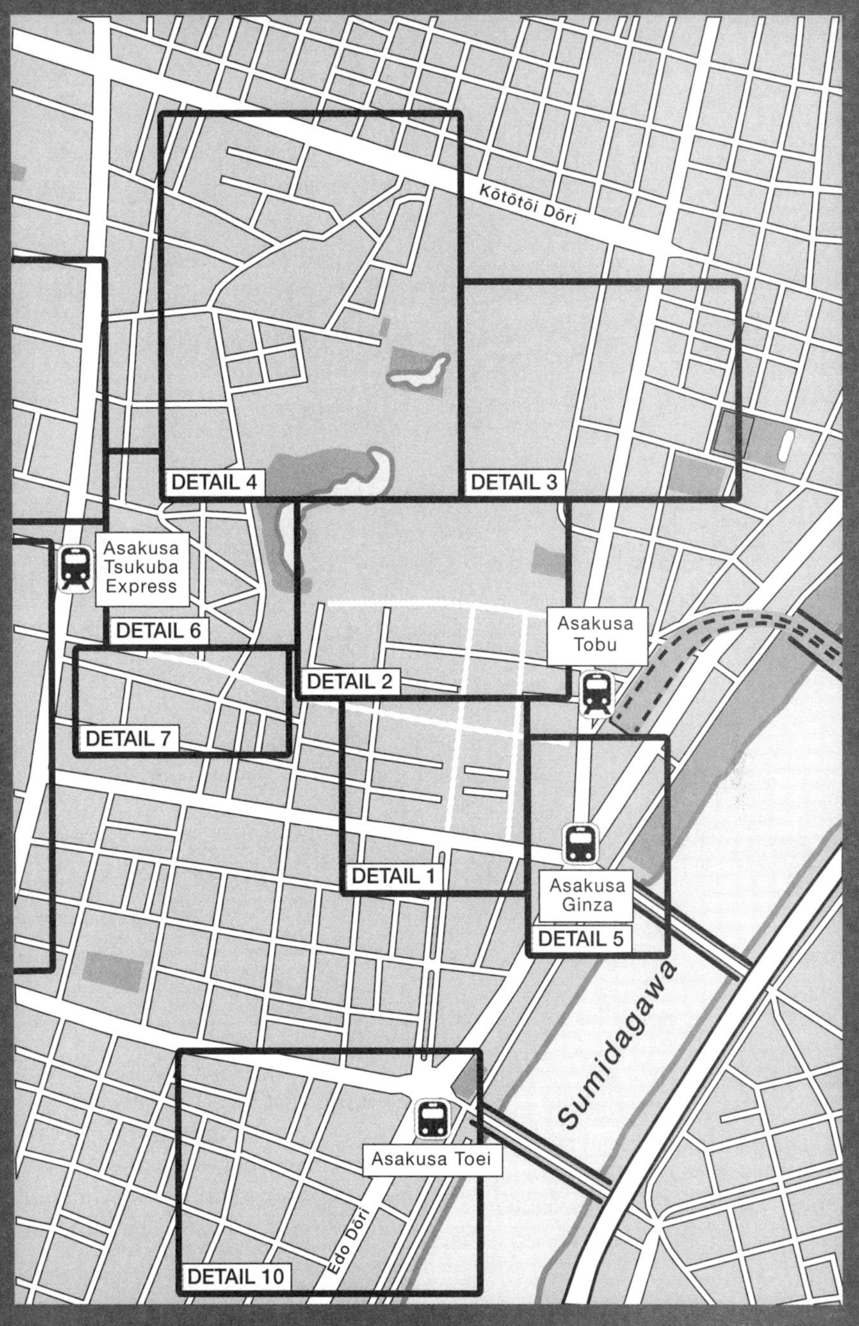

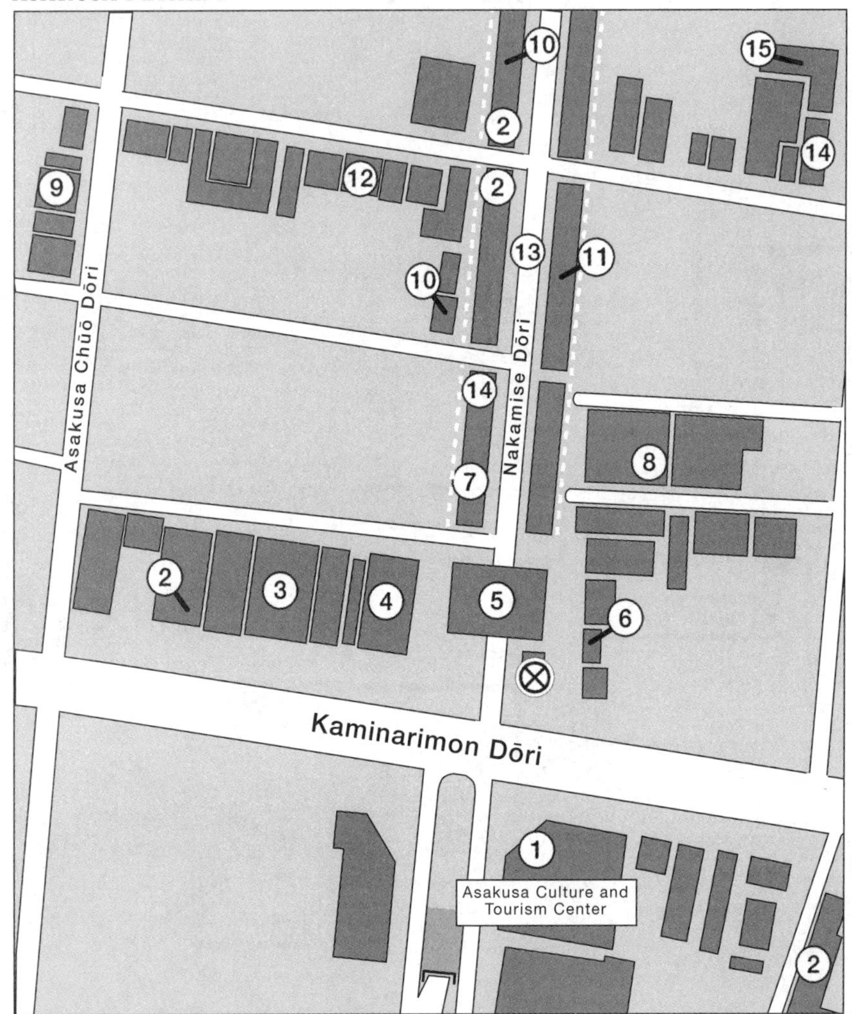

❸ Chin-ya ちんや

Chin-ya was established in the Edo period as a business providing pets and veterinary services to high-ranking samurai and wealthy merchant households. In 1880 the owners changed the business into a restaurant but kept the old nickname, which means "Pekingese Shop" or "Chinese shop." As you enter, remove your shoes and exchange them for a wooden tally with a black number on it. Chin-ya specializes in

high-quality sukiyaki and shabu shabu. You can enjoy your meal in either traditional Japanese- or Western-style seating. When you pay, the staff will exchange your shoe tally for one with a red number, which you can then use to claim your shoes. The original building suffered damage in both the Great Kantō Earthquake and World War II; the brick building dates from 1975.
🌐 *https://chinya.co.jp*

❹ Tokiwadō Kaminari Okoshi Honpo 常盤堂雷おこし本舗

Located to the left of the Kaminarimon of Sensōji, this is the main store, though the company has a few other branches in the Tokyo area. For over 250 years this business has been making confections. They are especially known for their kaminari okoshi, bars made of puffed grain, sugar and, other ingredients for flavor such as peanuts or green tea. You can watch them being made through a window into the shop. The store also makes and sells ningyōyaki with a variety of fillings and shapes, including characters from the popular TV show "Shōten," as well as karintō crackers in various flavors. Products are sold in bags, individually wrapped, and in wood boxes for special items. Okoshi make an excellent tasty lightweight gift to bring home.
🌐 *https://tokiwado.tokyo*

❺ Kaminarimon 雷門

On Kaminarimon Dōri at the entrance to the Nakamise is a massive gate that has come to symbolize the Asakusa neighborhood. Originally built in 941, the gate burned three times: the first in 1642, again in 1767, and it was at last destroyed by fire in 1865. The current gate was constructed in 1960 with donations from Matsushita Kōnosuke, who founded Matsushita Electric, now known as Panasonic. Between 1865 and 1960 people would still speak of the former location of the gate as Kaminarimon. This large gate is easy to spot as it sports a huge lantern over ten feet (3.3 meters) tall. Every ten years a new lantern is put up. Statues of the wind god Fūjin and the thunder god Raijin—who is also known as Kaminari—are in either side of the gate as you face Sensōji. The gate's official name, Fūraijin Mon, is written on the back of the lantern. On the back side of the gate there are statues of two Buddhist deities: Tenryū on the left, and Kinryū on the right. These two statues were donated in 1978.

❻ Kurodaya 黒田屋

Located immediately east of the Kaminarimon—just look for the wooden signboards above the awning at the entrance—this shop has been in business since 1856 selling a large number of paper products. Viewing their selection of sheets of printed paper at first glance gives the impression that you are looking at a display in a fabric shop. You will also find papier-mâché items, stationery goods, traditional and modern Japanese prints, hanging scrolls, beautiful goshuinchō (notebooks for collecting shrine stamps), and more.

❼ Bairindō 梅林堂

A shop selling a variety of snack foods since 1876. These consist of charcoal-roasted rice crackers, ningyōyaki (which you can watch being made), kaminari okoshi, and other treats such as various snacks made of beans and nuts; roasted, fried, or glazed. Most are packaged for convenience, however some you can buy by weight. Such treats are a bit of tradition and are good with tea, beer, or sake. Many are dry and store well so you can bring them home as gifts. Bairindō is very easy to find, being the third Nakamise shop on the left after the Kaminarimon.

❽ Sake no Daimasu Kaminarimon Branch 酒の大桝 雷門店

This combination izakaya and liquor store is a branch of the local Daimasu liquor store, which was founded in 1930. This branch has a focus on sake, with a selection of local beers, and has a small menu of side dishes to enjoy with your drinks. If they don't have the sake you want and their main store does, you can have a bottle brought over for a corking fee, or pick it up yourself. They have an English menu, credit cards are accepted, and Western cutlery is available.

🌐 *http://www.e-daimasu.com/sakebar/index.html*

❾ Some no Anbō 染の安坊

This shop specializes in hand dyed tenugui and other dyed cloth goods. The patterns sold vary with the seasons. Their tenugui are 100 cm long, whereas the usual length is about 90 cm. They also sell Aloha shirts, fans bundled with matching tenugui, kakejikubō mounts for displaying tenugui, and more. They have been in business since 1907 and their products are also sold in various shops across Japan. They will do custom tenugui and aloha shirts based on their designs, but orders take some time to fill so are not an option for most tourists.

🌐 *https://www.anbo.jp/en/*

❿ Arai Bunsendō aka Bunsendō 荒井文扇堂

A handheld fan shop with a history going back to the Meiji period. There are two locations near each other: the original on the west side of the Nakamise in the third block from Kaminarimon, and the branch store, just west of the Nakamise at the first intersection. Their fans range from very high-quality handmade folding fans—which are popular with geisha, professional performers of traditional dance, kabuki actors, and rakugo storytellers—to inexpensive and whimsical non-folding uchiwa fans.

⓫ Kikuya 喜久屋

In operation for over 100 years, Kikuya is located in the second block of the Nakamise, the ninth shop from Kaminarimon. They produce several types of daifuku and dango plus a few other sweets, and sell containers of powdered green tea. This is a good place to get a small sweet and snack on it to give you an energy bump before continuing down the Nakamise. You can also get items to go—use the phrase "to go" and they will understand. If they sell out of stock, they close for the rest of the day.

🌐 *https://www.kikuya-nakamise.com*

⓬ Obigen 帯源

A store specializing in belts for kimono, known as obi in Japanese, since 1920. The many styles for men and women range from narrow to wide, and simple to ornate. The obi on display are changed seasonally depending on their color or printed motifs. Most of the obi are from looms in the Hakata area of Fukuoka and from Nishijin in Kyoto, two places famous for their woven fabrics. It is recommended that you bring in your kimono when selecting an obi to go with it.

🌐 *http://obigen.jp/index.html*

⓭ Nakamise Shōtengai 仲見世商店街

This is a pedestrian shopping street just shy of 980 feet (300 meters) long, divided into seven blocks. The eighty-eight shops located here are all between the Kaminarimon and the Hōzōmon. While you will find some mass-produced cheap toys and souvenirs, several of the shops have high-quality handmade items for reasonable prices. Be aware that the street can be very crowded, so you need to take your time to look at the goods. Who knows, you may discover very unique items for yourself or for gifts. You can also find a variety of locally-made snack foods sold either freshly made or packaged. Two of my favorite shops on the Nakamise include Bunsendō for fans, and Sukeroku for small handcrafted Edo-style toys.

🌐 *http://asakusa-nakamise.jp/e-index.html*

Nakamise Murals

If you wake up early in the morning and go to the Nakamise well before everything opens, you will see the lowered shop shutters painted with murals relating to the Asakusa neighborhood. The murals were added in 1992 at the suggestion of Professor Hirayama Ikuo, president of the Tokyo University of the Arts.

⓮ Umaimon Azuma
うまいもん あづま

This restaurant was founded in 1940 and has been operating in the present location since 1952. The menu includes a variety of Japanese as well as Japanese-style Western and Chinese dishes. Set meals are also on the menu. Seasonal items and Japanese deserts are also served, banquet courses are available by reservation only.

The first floor has Western seating, the second floor is all Japanese seating with horigotatsu. The restaurant has some English speaking staff and an English menu is available.

There is a branch shop on the Nakamise, Kibidango Azuma, at the end of the first block on the left after the Kaminarimon gate. This branch sells kibidango, a traditional Japanese sweet. Both shops are open 7 days a week.

The restaurant is non-smoking, restrooms are on both floors.

🌐 *http://www.aduma.tokyo*

⓯ Yagenbori Nakajima Shōten
やげん堀 中島商店

A shop specializing in shichimi tōgarashi, a blend of seven spices that can be sprinkled over any of several dishes. While this spice mix exists in various forms all over Japan and is now sold in many other parts of the world, it originated at this shop employing Chinese medicinal knowledge to make something both tasty and good for your health. The original shop location was in an area with many doctors and medicine wholesalers; in 1943 the business relocated to Asakusa. They have three different ready-made mixes with varying levels of chili powder, or you can request different levels of heat and watch as they mix your order. They also sell attractive re-useable wooden storage containers in the shapes of a barrel, a gourd, or a length of bamboo, as well as furikake and some individual spices. The shop name Yagenbori comes from a canal shaped like a type of mortar called a yagen that is used to grind medicinal herbs.

There are two stores in Asakusa, the main store on Shin-Nakamise Dōri, and a branch on Metro Street.

🌐 *http://www.yagenbori.jp*

NOTE: *In Kurosawa Akira's film Red Beard, there is a scene early on where you see a yagen being used to grind medicine.*

DETAIL 2

❶ Asakusa Morigin 浅草もり銀

A shop specializing in items made of gold and silver, all handmade in-house since 1927. Items for sale include netsuke, tableware, drinking cups, chopsticks, Buddhist altar fittings, wind chimes, ornaments, earpicks, accessories, and more.

🌐 *https://www.asakusamorigin.com/english/*

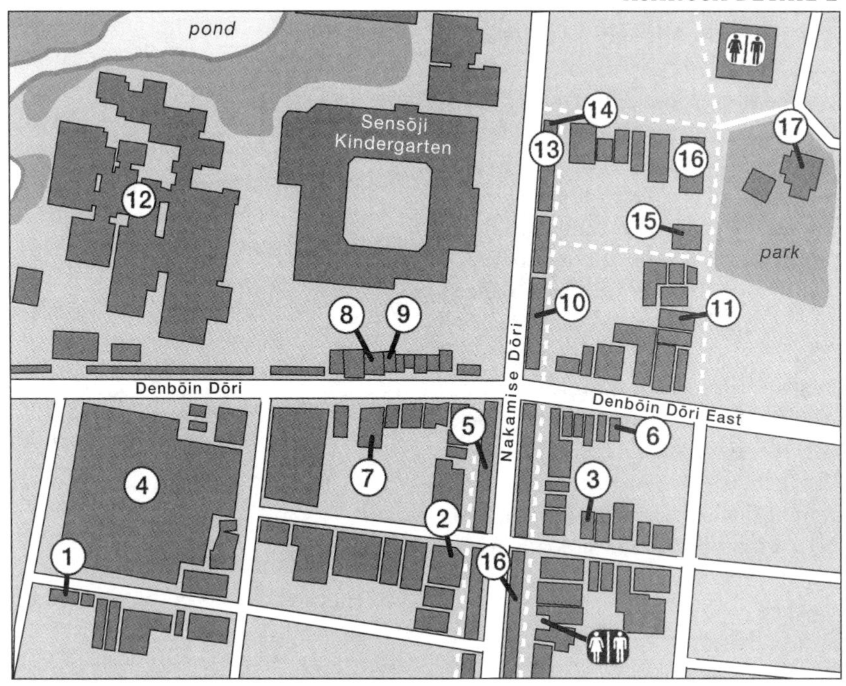

❷ Umezono 梅園

This tea house/cafe, whose name translates as Plum Garden, specializes in Japanese sweets. It first opened in 1854. They have several types of oshiruko, a sweet dessert soup served in a bowl. Anmitsu, made with fruit and other sweets, is also popular. One famous dish is awazenzai, millet cakes covered in sweet azuki bean paste. They also serve ice cream and some dishes come with whipped cream. They have a few take-out items on the menu. Don't be surprised if all the seats are taken, as in Nagai Kafū's novel *The Dancer* where a character is unable to sit because the place is full of customers.

🌐 *http://www.asakusa-umezono.co.jp*

❸ Isekan いせ勘

Isekan was established in 1717 when Tokyo Bay was the major location for nori production in Japan and Asakusa was a major center for its distribution. Several types of nori in sheet form, tsukudani paste made from nori, and a few other items are sold. They have two stores: The main one is on a corner just south of the Nakamise on the cross street between the fourth and fifth blocks, and the branch is on the second block of the Nakamise on the left side.

🌐 *https://www.isekan.jp*

❹ Asakusa Public Hall / Asakusa Kōkaidō 浅草公会堂

A general-purpose event space that opened in 1977, the hall is best known for the Shinshun Asakusa Kabuki (Asakusa New Year's Kabuki) stage performances held in January. Other performances in the theater may include traditional or modern dance, song festivals, jazz, lectures, workshops, and various popular entertainments. The facilities include the large theater, an exhibit hall, and a tea house that serves reasonably priced meals. The Stars' Plaza (Star no Hiroba) in front of the hall consists of metal castings of handprints and autographs of famous entertainers connected with Asakusa.

🌐 *https://asakusa-koukaidou.net/en*

❺ Sanbidō 三美堂

This shop established in 1941 deals in a variety of items including handmade reproductions of traditional woodblock prints; small paintings; Buddhist statuary in wood, metal, or plastic; papier-mâché masks (including lots of yōkai and folk masks); samurai figures, kokeshi dolls; and a changing selection of other small items.

🌐 *http://sanbido.rgr.jp*

❻ Tsujiya 辻屋

Established in 1912, this store is devoted to traditional Japanese footwear for men, women, and children. They make and stock geta, zōri, setta, and all sorts of other traditional footwear. A wide range of materials are used to make them including wood, leather, fabric, bamboo, snakeskin, and hemp cloth. The stock ranges from items for formal kimono wear to many that are suitable for casual wear, for example geta with skull patterns on the straps.

🌐 *http://getaya.jp*

❼ Yonoya Kushiho よのや櫛舗

Yonoya Kushiho was established in the Hongō area of present-day Bunkyō Ward in 1717 and moved to this location in the late Meiji period. Presently located on Denbōin Dōri, this is one of two shops in Tokyo devoted to traditional wooden combs (the other being Jūsanya in Hongō). They also have a selection of traditional handmade hair ornaments. The wood used to handcraft their products comes from Ibusuki in Kagoshima Prefecture and is carefully selected and specially aged for a full year. Such items can last for generations if properly taken care of.

❽ Asakusa Menchi 浅草メンチ

This small shop is easy to find: above the shop you will see a decoration in the form of a ladder with a traditional bell attached to the top, and the shop's sign has the name in white on a red circle. Asakusa Menchi serves only one thing, a classic Japanese street food called menchi katsu that consists of breaded, spiced minced pork and beef, mixed with vegetables and deep fried. Be careful with that first bite as the outside is crispy but the inside is very hot and juicy. I first had menchi katsu here on a snowy morning, when it was a perfect snack to warm me up. There is a bottle of karashi (Japanese mustard) on the counter if you want to spice it up. I advise trying it plain first as it is very tasty by itself.

🌐 *http://www.asamen.com*

❾ Toyofuku 豊福

You can't get more specialized than literally selling just one thing. Toyofuku has been doing this for over 100 years. They sell karēpan (curry bread) made with high-quality kuroge wagyu beef. The only choices on the menu are regular or spicy. Japanese spicy is pretty mild, so don't worry if you don't speak the language. This place is so busy that as soon as they make some karēpan buns, they hand them to waiting customers. Even if there is a line, and there often is, it will move fast. Do note this is a crowded area so don't walk around eating your curry bun.

❿ Asakusa Chōchin Monaka 浅草ちょうちんもなか

This shop sells monaka with ice cream filling between two crispy wafers instead of the usual sweet ankō. The wafers are in the shape of the Kaminarimon lantern. They also sell seasonal ice cream flavors and items such as shaved ice in the summer with seasonal fruit flavors, fruit vinegar juice from March to November, and oshiruko and amazake in the winter. They also sell traditional monaka including boxed sets.

🌐 *https://www.cyouchinmonaka.com*

⓫ Fujiya ふじ屋

A shop located near Sensōji, on the block just southwest of the Bentendō, open since 1946. Look for a blue noren with a repeating fuji flower (wisteria) pattern in white that is put out when they are open. They specialize in traditionally dyed Japanese cotton tenugui, usually translated as hand towel. In Japan these are more than just towels—they are also traditionally used as head coverings, rolled into headbands, for wrapping items to carry, and so on. The different colorful designs are both traditional and modern. Bunraku, kabuki, ukiyo-e, and seasonal motifs all are among the inspirations. I have a lovely one of a woman in the snow that I bought on a cold January day, and the next day it did snow. They have some 200 unique designs made by the store. They are so attractive that some people mount them as art, which costs more than the tenugui but can be worth it. There is not enough room for all the designs, so they periodically change them, often according to the season.

🌐 *http://tenugui-fujiya.jp*

⓬ Denpōin 伝法院

The official residence and office of the head priest of Sensōji. The name is sometimes romanized as Denbōin. The main buildings date from 1777. Denpōin is known for its Edo period garden designed in the 17th century by the tea master Kobori Enshū. The garden features a large double pond shaped like the kanji for kokoro, "heart" or "feelings." The garden is private, however beginning in 2012, to raise money for the victims of the 2011 earthquake, access has been allowed starting in mid-March through early April or May. Pay for entry at the temple office in the five-story pagoda. At other times the garden is partly viewable through the fence at Chingodō.

Photographers inside the garden can get a good view of the pagoda and Tokyo Sky Tree with the garden in the foreground.

⓭ Sukeroku 助六

This very small shop, big enough for only two or three customers at a time, sells handmade traditional toys in the style of the Edo period. In fact they have been in business since 1866 when the Edo period was winding down. Many of these are very cleverly made, such as a tiger made from a sheet of painted paper and small weights that always lands on its feet. The materials vary greatly: ceramic, papier-mâché, wood, bamboo, cloth, plaster, and more are all used depending on the toy. Literally thousands of toys of a wide variety are available: figures of people of various occupations, animals, good luck charms, kabuki actors, street scenes, even wordplays based on the subjects and materials, and much more. There have been so many designs made and sold by this shop over the years that you can buy bilingual hardcover catalogs with color illustrations at the shop.

TIP: *Go on a weekday when the store is less crowded, especially if it is rainy.*

⓮ Kimuraya Honten 木村家人本店

A shop in the seventh block of the Nakamise selling ningyōyaki with several Sensōji-themed designs originated by the store. These include the five-story pagoda, Raijin (whose statue is in the Kaminarimon), one of the gate lanterns, and a pigeon. The pigeon is modeled after a ceramic charm of a pair of pigeons that used to be sold by a nearby shop. One of their sweets is good for a pick-me-up after having strolled the length of the Nakamise. They have been in operation since 1868.

🌐 *http://www.kimura-ya.co.jp*

⓯ Hyakusuke 百助

Popular with kabuki actors, geisha, and traditional Japanese dance performers, Hyakusuke has been selling traditional makeup for over 200 years. It is easy to find as the location is across from the children's playground near the Bentendō. They also sell a variety of handcrafted Japanese makeup brushes and wooden combs. This is apparently the last place in Tokyo to sell a traditional powdered skin cleanser made with nightingale droppings. It is sold in an attractive pink package with a plum blossom decoration.

⑯ Nakaya 中屋

Since 1910 this festival goods specialty store has been making and selling all the clothing supplies one needs to have a traditional matsuri look, as well as various accessories including necklaces, lanterns, kimono bags, and tenugui to roll into a headband. They also sell other garments such as wataire hanten. You can even order tegaki fuda, which are card-sized wood blocks with your name handwritten on them. There are two shops, one located on the east side of block four of the Nakamise and the other directly across from the Bentendō.

🌐 *http://www.nakaya.co.jp*

⑰ Bentendō 弁天堂 **and Bentenyama** 弁天山

A little way southeast of the Hōzōmon of Sensōji, at the edge of the temple grounds, is an ancient burial mound known as Bentenyama. The name of this mound comes from a small red temple to the Goddess Benten located on top of the mound. The statue here is of Rōjo Benzaiten with distinguishing white hair, and it is considered one of the three most famous Benten statues of the Kantō. The statue can only be viewed on special festival days. The present building was rebuilt in 1983. This is also the location of the famous bell of Sensōji. This bell was one of two bells that were used to ring the hours for the city in the Edo period, the other being at Kan'eiji in Ueno. While the bell tower was destroyed in World War II, the bell was unharmed. If you find yourself at Sensōji minutes before the New Year begins, you can see the bell being rung 108 times starting at midnight. It is also struck at 6:00 each evening. The bell itself is a recasting from 1692 and is famously referred to in haiku by Bashō. Illustrations in early 19th-century works such as Matsudaira Kanzan's *Sensōji Shi* and Saitō Gesshin's *Edo Meisho Zue* show that there was once open water at the base of the hill. Water is associated with the godess Benten and usually found near her shrines.

DETAIL 3

❶ Hōzōmon 宝蔵門

An impressive two-story gate just before Sensōji, beyond the far end of the Nakamise. The name of the gate, which is used to house many treasures of the temple, translates as "Treasure

Storage Gate." Many also refer to it as the Niōmon since there are two Niō statues on either side of the gate as you face toward the temple. As you pass through the gate, you walk under the middle of three large lanterns. There are also two huge straw sandals on the back, said to be for the use of the Niō. These are a donation by Maruyama city in Yamagata Prefecture. The original gate was from 942 and burned down many times during the history of the temple. The present gate is a 1964 reconstruction made of concrete.

❷ Sensōji 浅草寺

Sensōji, one of the oldest and most famous temples in the Tokyo area, was founded in 645. It was built to house a small statue of Kannon found nearby by two fisherman brothers, Hinokuma Hamanari and Hinokuma Takenari, in 628. Thinking it was a worthless lump, they threw it back, only to have it turn up in their nets seven times. They then noticed that it was shiny and took it to their village chief Haji no Nakatomo, who recognized it for what it was. The statue is a hibutsu "hidden image" and since about 670 it has been housed in a special sealed case. In time it came to be never viewed, even by the priests. In the 9th century the famous priest Ennin carved a replica of the statue, which is also treated as a hibutsu except on special occasions when the public is allowed to view it. The temple was destroyed in the 1945 air raids and reconstruction was completed in 1958. The present building is in traditional

Sensōji Event Calendar

Sensōji hosts a number of regular events

January 1 through 3: Hatsumōde, the first temple visits of the year. Some 2.5 million people visit the temple in the first three days of the year.

January 18 around 6:30 p.m.: Mōja Okuri, where two men dressed as demons exit the temple bearing large torches and walk a route on the grounds, occasionally striking the torches and scattering burning embers.

February 3: The Setsubun ceremony, roasted soybeans are tossed to cast out demons and bad luck.

March 18: Golden Dragon Dance.

Mid-April: The White Heron Dance.

Mid-May: The Takara no Mai "Treasure Dance."

July 9 and 10: Chinese Lantern Plant Fair.

Early August: Nō performances.

October 18: Golden Dragon Dance.

Mid-October to mid-November: Chrysanthemum exhibition.

November 3: White Heron Dance.

December 17 through 19: Toshi no Ichi, a fair where highly ornamented hagoita (battledores) are sold. (These are paddles used for a game similar to badminton.)

December 31 at midnight: ringing of the temple bell.

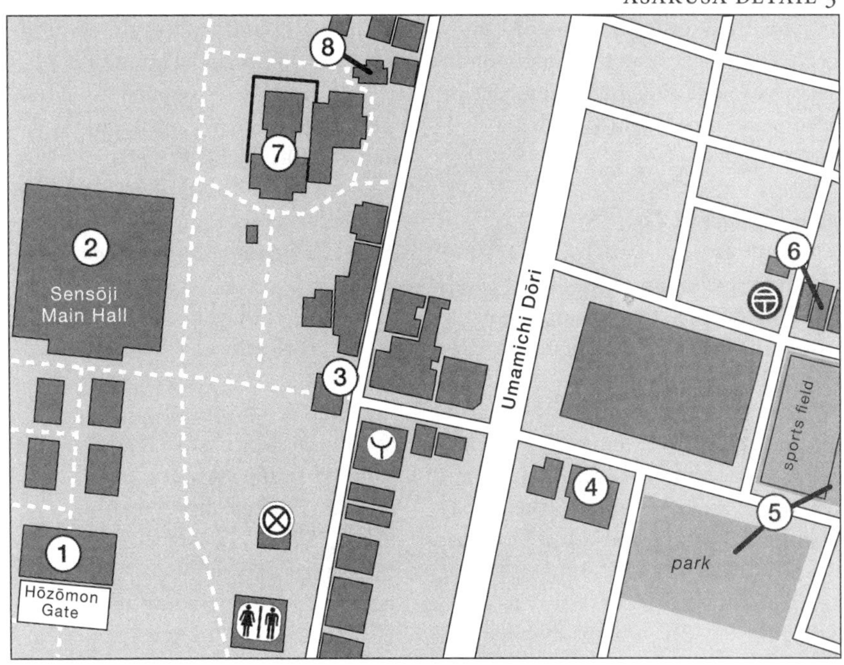

style, made of fireproof concrete with a titanium tile roof. The outer sanctum has beautiful ceiling paintings that are worth seeing.
🌐 *http://www.senso-ji.jp*

TIP: *For disabled access there is an elevator on the left side of the main hall.*

TRIVIA: *The kanji for Asakusa 浅草 is the same as that for the Sensō in Sensōji 浅草寺. The reason for this is that kanji can be pronounced in at least two ways, the Chinese way and the Japanese way. The full name of the temple is Kinryūzan Sensōji 金龍山浅草寺.*

❸ Nitenmon 二天門

A red gate to the east of Sensōji and Asakusa Jinja. This gate dates from 1618 when it was part of Tōshōgū, before it was relocated to Ueno. Originally called Zuijinmon, the gate was given the present name in the Meiji period. The gate escaped the flames of the Meireki Fire, the Great Kantō Earthquake and the firebombings of World War II. However, in World War II the original statues that were in the gate were removed to another location to protect them and that location was destroyed. The current statues date from the 17th century and were relocated from a spot near the monument to shōgun Tokugawa Ietsuna in Ueno. Between this gate and the Hōzōmon is a 600-year-old ginkgo tree that shows burn scars from World War II.

❹ Kaminari Issa 雷一茶

Sometime you just want to get off your feet for a spell, Kaminari Issa is a good place to do just that. Their menu is based around matcha, Japanese green tea, and there is plenty of variety. For beverages there is traditional hot tea—the frothy kind you find at a tea ceremony, chilled matcha, green tea latte, and even matcha beer. Sweets are both traditional Japanese and modern Western style. You can also get a parfait, which pairs Japanese sweets with ice cream. They have a gift shop which sells a variety of sweets made with matcha. They have menus in English, Korean, and traditional and simplified Chinese. The facility is smoke free.

🌐 *https://en.kaminari-issa.com*

❺ Hanakawado Park/ Hanakawado Kōen 花川戸公園

The site of this park was once the location of the Ubagaike "Old Woman Pond," a large pond that was filled in and converted into a park in 1891. The name comes from a legend that dates back to a time when this was an isolated area. There was an old woman who used to murder travelers with a stone pillow to steal their clothes and other belongings. She unintentionally killed her daughter and in despair, committed suicide by jumping into the pond.

The park also contains a monument, inscribed with a poem by famous actor Ichikawa Danjūrō IX, referring to the kabuki play *Sukeroku*, the main character of which is Sukeroku Hanakawado. In mid-December there is a popular weekend shoe market organized by neighborhood retailers and wholesalers.

❻ Amezaiku Ameshin Asakusa main workshop / Amezaiku Ameshin Asakusa honten kōbō 飴細工アメシン浅草本店工房

This shop was founded by Tezuka Shinri in 2013 to make and sell amezaiku, a type of traditional handcrafted sweet quickly sculpted by hand from a piece of hot candy before it cools. There are various shapes sold in the store, including animals such as goldfish, cranes, and rabbits. Natural coloring is used, at times applied with a brush. Tezuka is quite young, having been born in 1989, but already has apprentices working under him. There is a branch store at Tokyo Skytree Town.

🌐 *http://www.ame-shin.com/en/*

❼ Asakusa Jinja 浅草神社 also called Sanja Sama, Shrine of the Three Guardians

A shrine to the spirits of the three founders of Sensōji: Hinokuma Hamanari, Hinokuma Takenari (the fishermen brothers), and Hajo no Nakatomo. There is an area in front of the shrine with many stones commemorating theater people and manga creators. Such commemorative stones are a feature that can be seen at some temples and shrines. The shrine was founded in the 14th century and the present buildings date from 1649, which means they survived the three great fires that destroyed so much of the city: the great Meireki Fire of 1657, the Great Kantō Earthquake, and the firebombings of Tokyo in World War II. People come here to pray for family well-being and business prosperity. The Yano family, descendants of Hajo no Nakatomo, are still priests of the shrine.

The shrine's main festival is the Sanja Festival, which takes place on the third weekend in May. This is the largest festival in Tokyo, drawing about two million people over the weekend.
🌐 *https://www.asakusajinja.jp*

❽ **Hikan Inari Jinja** 被官稲荷神社
Behind Asakusa Jinja is a lovely Inari shrine from 1854. The shrine was built by Shinmon Tatsugoro, the head of the tenth division of the local fire brigade. His wife had fallen seriously ill, so he went to the Fushimi Inari in the Kyoto area to pray for her health. After her recovery he built this shrine. The present shrine is the original, having survived the fires of the Great Kantō Earthquake and the bombings of World War II. The shrine proper is small—most of the area is filled by a protective roof over the shrine.

DETAIL 4

❶ **Hoppī Dōri** ホッピー通り
A street lined with traditional izakaya in older buildings. In the evening, when most of the tourists have pretty much left the Asakusa area, these pubs are filled mainly with locals relaxing in the evening. The atmosphere is very laid back so you may end up in conversation with other drinkers. Since most customers don't just drink in izakaya, many of the places have picture or English menus and some have staff that can speak a little English. One common tasty food is *gyusuji nikomi*, a stew of beef tendon and vegetables. Most of these izakaya open for lunch and stay open into the evening. The street is named after Hoppy, a beer-like carbonated beverage that has 0.8% alcohol that was invented in Asakusa in 1948. It is often mixed with shōchū, a practice that dates from when beer was too expensive for the Japanese working class. These days beer is more affordable but mixing Hoppy with shōchū has a certain nostalgic appeal for many.

❷ **Wasendō** 和泉洞
A small antiques shop selling a variety of unique items from across the

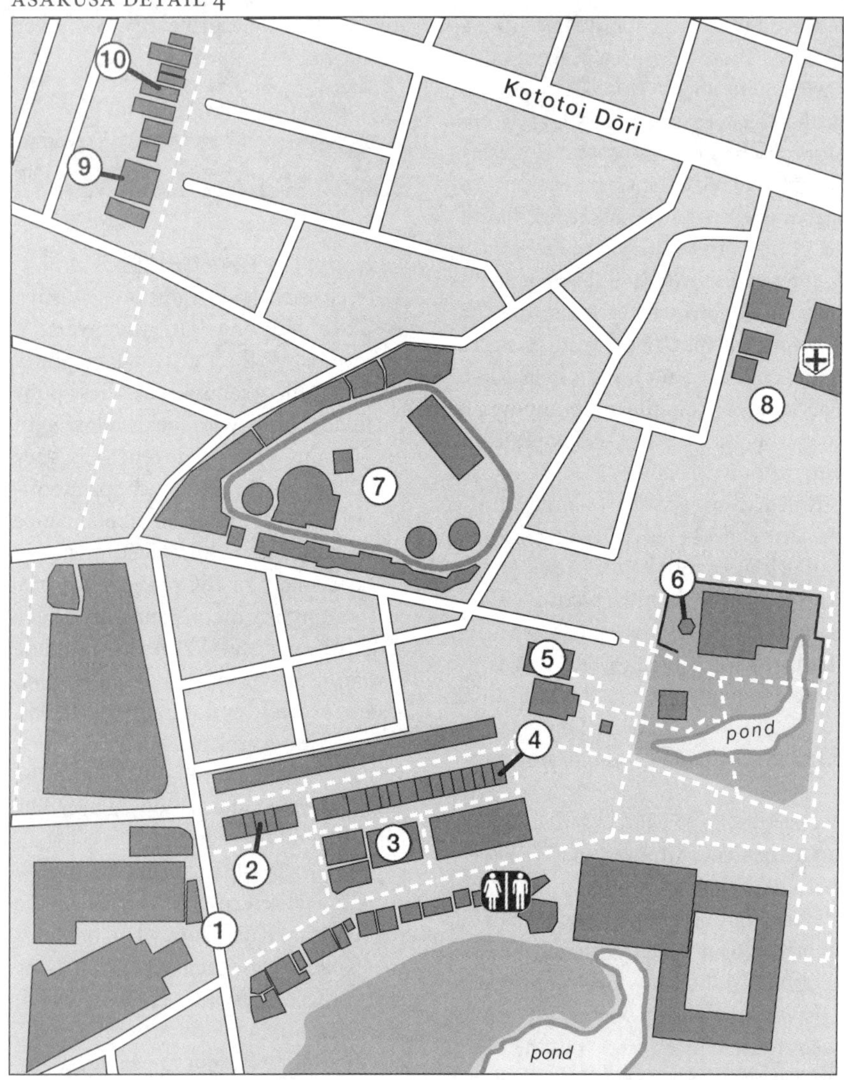

world since 1962. There is a good selection of coins, old paper money, proof sets from the Japan Mint, commemorative medallions, old postcards, jewelry, medals, postage stamps, watches, lighters, and pamphlets about stamps and medallions. You can pick up an unusual souvenir or gift, such as a coin from the Edo period, from the ever-changing stock.

❸ **Asakusa Mokubakan** 浅草木馬館

A small theater only dating back to 1977 where small traveling troupes perform, generally for one month at a time. The performances are in traditional clothing and the makeup, hair styling, costuming, and action are often flamboyant. The actors playing female roles are often young men crossdressing, much to the delight of the older ladies in the audience. This is taishū engeki, theater of the masses; do not expect refined elegance, but do expect a fun show, so sit back and enjoy the program. There are two shows daily that usually open with a dance performance for about a half hour, followed by a play for about an hour, and finishing up with another hour of dance. You never quite know what to expect as the content of a performance is announced just before the show starts. Each day has a different program, so you can go often if you wish. If you read Kawabata Yasunari's novel *The Scarlet Gang of Asakusa,* you will find mention of small theaters like the Mokubakan that existed in the area in the 1920s.

Performances are all in Japanese.

🌐 *https://www.shinohara-engeki.jp/sp/mokubakan.html*

❹ **Asakusa Kagetsudō** 浅草 花月堂

A bakery specializing in Jumbo Melon Pan since 1945. The menu also includes a selection of Japanese sweet deserts and beverages. They have branches in several parts of Tokyo; the one in Asakusa is the headquarters. Their melon pan is uniquely fluffy, made using a process that took over a decade to perfect. The owner majored in fermentation at the Tokyo University of Agriculture and worked as a researcher before focusing on the restaurant. The recipe is adjusted each day in consideration of the temperature, humidity, the condition of the flour, and other factors. When they sell out of the day's production of melon pan, they close shop.

🌐 *https://asakusa-kagetudo.com*

❺ **Awashimadō** 淡島堂

A temple to Awashima Myōjin, a protector of women who cures their health problems and is patron of their crafts such as sewing. On February 8 all over Japan, broken or worn needles and pins are brought to local Awashima temples and stuck into blocks of tōfu to thank them for their service. The idea that is after having been worked through hard things, they now have a final rest in something soft. The tōfu block at the Awashimadō in Asakusa is especially large, and specifically made for the occasion. The temple is painted in red and has a large incense burner in front.

❻ **Rokkakudō** 六角堂

Also known in English as the Hexagonal Temple due to its shape. This small building is the oldest surviving

▲ Near Asakusa Imahan in the Kappabashi neighborhood, a sign includes female kappa.

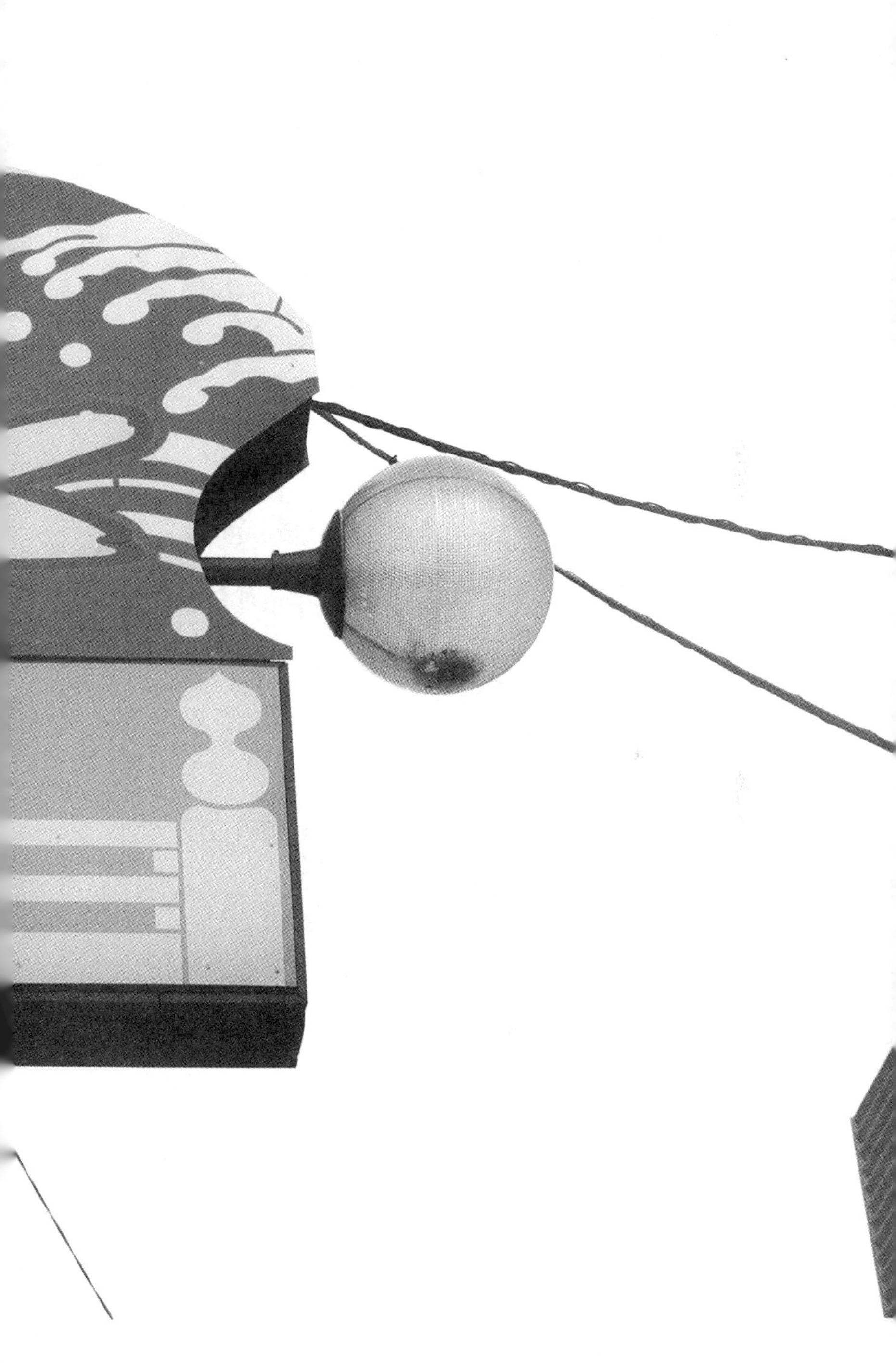

▲ The grave stone of Hokusai at Seikyōji, note that the stone shows signs of fire damage.

▲ ▼ Art symbolizing various festivals on the closed shutter of the Drum Museum.

▼ The Golden Dragon dance held at Sensōji on the 18th of March and October each year.

▲ The bronze statue Ichikawa Danjūrō IX as the hero of the kabuki play 'Shibaraku.'

structure at Sensōji—records indicate it was built in 1618. The hall enshrines Higiri Jizōson. The specific style of the building is not often found in this part of Japan. This is not the original location of the hall as it was moved in 1994 from the original spot about 72 feet (22 meters) from the east.

❼ Asakusa Hanayashiki
浅草花やしき

Japan's oldest amusement park, founded in 1853 and located just west of Sensōji. The name means "flower mansion" and this compact park was originally a botanical garden, with later additions of caged animals and entertainers in booths. Over time the park started adding other attractions, such as a puppet theater, rides, and a movie theater. The park was destroyed in the Great Kantō Earthquake and rebuilt with different attractions. Today the park manages to pack a large variety into a small area with multistory structures. Attractions include rides, small restaurants, shops, a haunted house, a 3D theater, a multistory labyrinth, traditional festival games, an arcade, fortune tellers, rooftop gardens, and even occasional masked wrestling.

🌐 *http://www.hanayashiki.net/en*

❽ Ichikawa Danjūrō IX "Shibaraku" bronze statue
九代目市川團十郎「暫」銅像

This statue is one of several points of interest related to kabuki that are scattered about Asakusa. It depicts the young Kamakura Gongorō, the main character from the famous kabuki play *Shibaraku*, in a classic mie pose. The specific actor depicted in this role is Ichikawa Danjūrō IX (1838–1903). A local legend has it that Sensōji survived the fire after the Great Kantō Earthquake because this statue held back the flames. The original statue was impounded by the Japanese military in 1944 and melted down for armaments, and the temple was destroyed in the firebombings of 1945. Ichikawa Danjūrō XII had the present reproduction placed here in 1986. Each year on the fourth Sunday in April there is a nakizumō crying baby contest in commemoration of the rebuilding of the statue.

❾ Edo Taitō Traditional Crafts Museum / Edo Taitō Dentō Kōgei Kan 江戸下町伝統工芸館

When you hear the name of this museum you may think, as I did, that it is filled with exhibits of musty artifacts from the past. Nope, everything is new: the museum was founded in 1997 to highlight the traditional crafts that are still practiced in the area. On the second floor you will see many excellent examples of such crafts including furniture, dolls, traditional lanterns, hairpins, metalwork, cut glass, woodblock prints, and embroidery, as well as tools. There is an exhibit space on the ground

floor where, if you go on a weekend, one of the local artisans may be giving a demonstration. Today a large percentage of Tokyo's practitioners of traditional crafts live and work in Taitō Ward. The reception desk has a pamphlet of locations of the various studios and shops in the area. You can also buy many small items in the museum shop.
🌐 *https://craft.city.taito.lg.jp/en/kogeikan/*

⑩ Adachiya あだちや
A specialty shop for festival goods such as happi coats, tenugui, pants, tabi socks, and waraji sandals woven from straw cords. They make the products they sell, even doing the cloth dyeing. Sizes range from children's to 3L (US XL or 85-93 cm). The shop is located on Hisago Dōri, between the Traditional Crafts Museum and Kototoi Dōri.
🌐 *https://www.adachiya.co.jp*

DETAIL 5

❶ Amisei あみ清
A company that provides charter services with a traditional type of roofed party boat dating from the Edo period known as yakatabune. Their typical tour lasts about one and a half to two hours and goes down the Sumidagawa, under the Rainbow Bridge, and back. They also have special tours for the annual summer fireworks show and cherry blossom viewing season. The smaller boats seat sixteen on tatami mats, the largest seventy with table seating. Food and drink are part of the packages. Their offices are located one block inland from their docks on the river.
🌐 *https://amisei.com*

❷ Kanmidokoro Nishiyama 甘味処西山
This shop established in 1852 sells a variety of traditional sweets handmade in house. The ice cream is freshly made, as well as the sweet bean paste used in many items they sell. The menu varies a little by season. Some items are available to take out.
🌐 *https://www.asakusa-nishiyama.com/english-top/*

❸ Kamiya Bar 神谷バー
Oldest Western-style bar in Tokyo, opened in 1880, founded by Kamiya Denbe. This was the first bar in Japan to use the English word "bar" in its name. Kamiya Bar has three floors: the first is a bar, the second and third are restaurants. Each floor has a different menu with some overlap. While it is in every English language guidebook I have looked at, you almost never see tourists in the place. Perhaps this is because it is very much an unpretentious neighborhood bar. They serve their signature brandy cocktail Denki

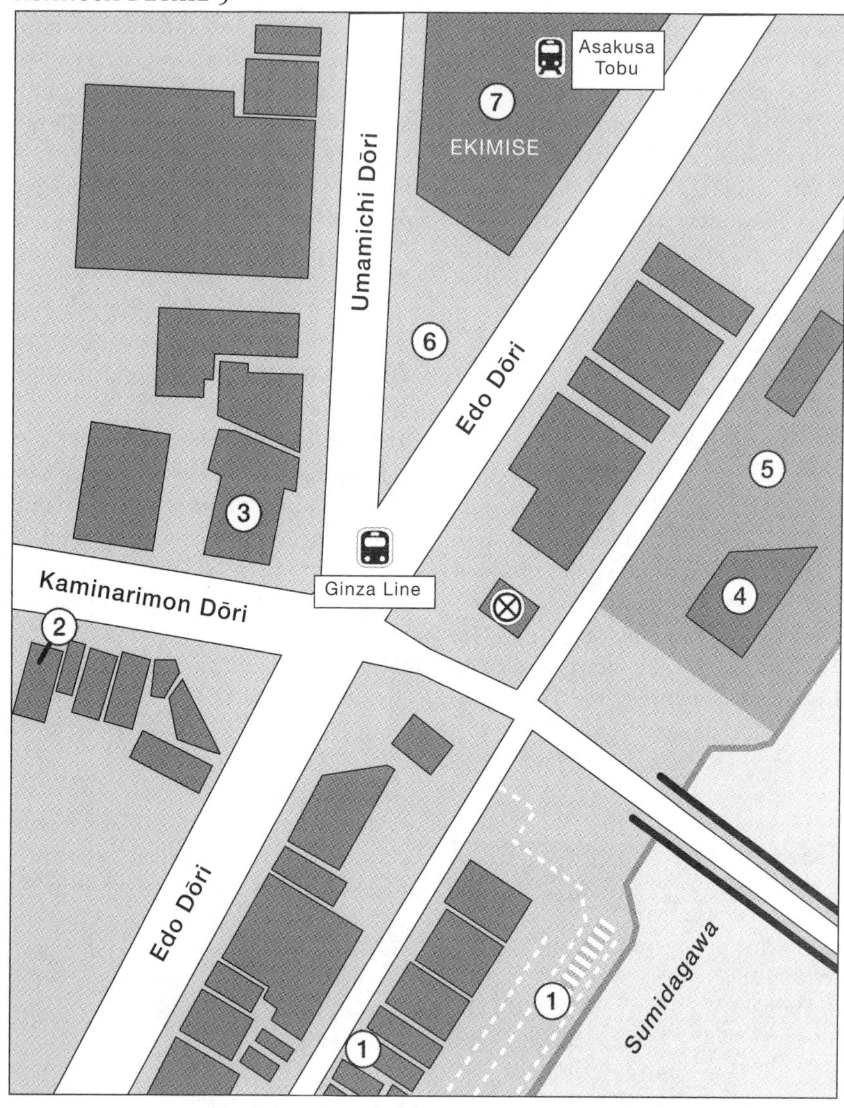

Bran, "Electric Brandy," which can also be purchased in bottles, at night, at a counter on the sidewalk. Denki Bran is a popular and inexpensive souvenir among Japanese who want to take something local home as gifts. You can also buy Chateau Kamiya wine from Japan's first full-scale winery, which

began operation in 1903. The current Kamiya Bar building dates from 1921. In 2011 the building was designated as a National Tangible Cultural Property by the Japanese government.
🌐 *http://www.kamiya-bar.com*

❹ Water Bus / Suijō Basu 水上バス
Several companies depart from this station. Routes either go downstream toward other landings or to Tokyo Bay.

Tokyo Cruise Ship Company operates three futuristic-looking enclosed water buses named Himiko, Hotaluna and Esmeraldas. These were designed by the Japanese science fiction manga writer Matsumoto Leiji. Himiko is the only one that is fully enclosed; Hotaluna and Esmeraldas have rooftop decks for when the weather is nice.

Tokyo Mizube Line is operated by the Tokyo Metropolitan Government Park Association.

Tokyo Water Taxi is available for small groups and as a taxi service.

Tokyo has many docks that are maintained by the government for emergency use, and the government has been opening more of these to water bus and water taxi service as part of encouraging such transportation. I have also noticed new docks along the river, so the system is expanding.

Tokyo Cruise Ship Company:
🌐 *http://www.suijobus.co.jp*
Tokyo Mizube Line:
🌐 *https://www.tokyo-park.or.jp/waterbus/index.html*
Tokyo Water Taxi:
🌐 *https://www.water-taxi.tokyo*
Go Tokyo page on Tokyo Water Taxi:
🌐 *https://www.gotokyo.org/shuun/en/course/020.html*

❺ Sumida Park / Sumida Kōen
隅田公園
This park is on both sides of the Sumidagawa. This entry covers the park on the west bank; for information on the east bank side, see the chapter for Northwestern Sumida Ward. This park was part of mayor Gotō Shinpei's reconstruction plan after the Great Kantō Earthquake. The goal was to create a space both for relaxation and for evacuation in case of future disasters. The park starts at Azumabashi and continues upstream past Sakurabashi. Each spring people congregate here for flower viewing, as the park has variety of cherry trees, camellias, and ume (plum) trees. On the last Saturday in July, the fireworks show packs the park with onlookers.

❻ Asakusa Underground Shopping Street / Asakusa Chika Shōtengai
浅草地下商店街
A shōtengai is a local shopping street. These are found throughout Japan, often close to a train station. This particular one was founded in 1955 and is located between the Ginza subway line's Asakusa Station and the EKIMISE Department Store. This is literally

the Tokyo underground: a subterranean walkway lined with small inexpensive shops, restaurants, fortune tellers, barbers, and so on. When open, many of the businesses overflow onto the narrow walkway to provide a little extra space for their customers and signage. Nothing fancy, but with an old-fashioned ambiance that provides a relaxing environment for those wanting a glimpse of Shōwa period Tokyo.

❼ EKIMISE エキミセ

A shopping mall housed in an art deco building. The name literally means Station Shops. The building opened in 1931 next to the Asakusa station for the Ginza Line and the second floor houses the terminus for the Tōbu Railways Skytree Line. For many years this was a Matsuya department store and they still occupy several floors. The basement has a variety of food shops for takeout, and the seventh floor is mainly restaurants. The building has a rooftop terrace with a great view across the Sumidagawa toward the Asahi brewery and Tokyo Sky Tree. In the summer the rooftop becomes a beer garden. The basement has a connecting passageway that takes you to the Asakusa Underground Shopping Street.

🌐 *http://ekimise.jp/en*

DETAIL 6

❶ Tempura Nakasei 天麩羅 中清

A mid-priced restaurant specializing in Edo-style tempura, meaning only seafood, no vegetables. It was founded in 1870; before the restaurant was opened, the founder sold tempura at a local stall. The architecture is old-fashioned, in the style of a traditional storage building, with a large stone lantern out front. There are twelve private dining rooms around a courtyard garden with a koi pond. To go orders are possible.

There is an English menu. Seating is Western and on tatami. Entrance is off Orange Street.

🌐 *http://nakasei.biz*

❷ Chingodō 鎮護堂

This temple is said to have been founded in 1872 to discourage tanuki (raccoon dogs) from damaging a garden at Sensōji by encouraging people to come to that part of the grounds. This association with tanuki quickly resulted in the temple being referred to as "Otanuki Sama." The shrine was moved to the present location in 1883, and the the shrine was rebuilt in 1913. Tanuki Dōri, a street south of the shrine, is worth a visit for its distinctive streetlamps. This shrine is known for prayers for business success, as well as protection against fire and theft. Festival rites are conducted on March 17 and 18 every year.

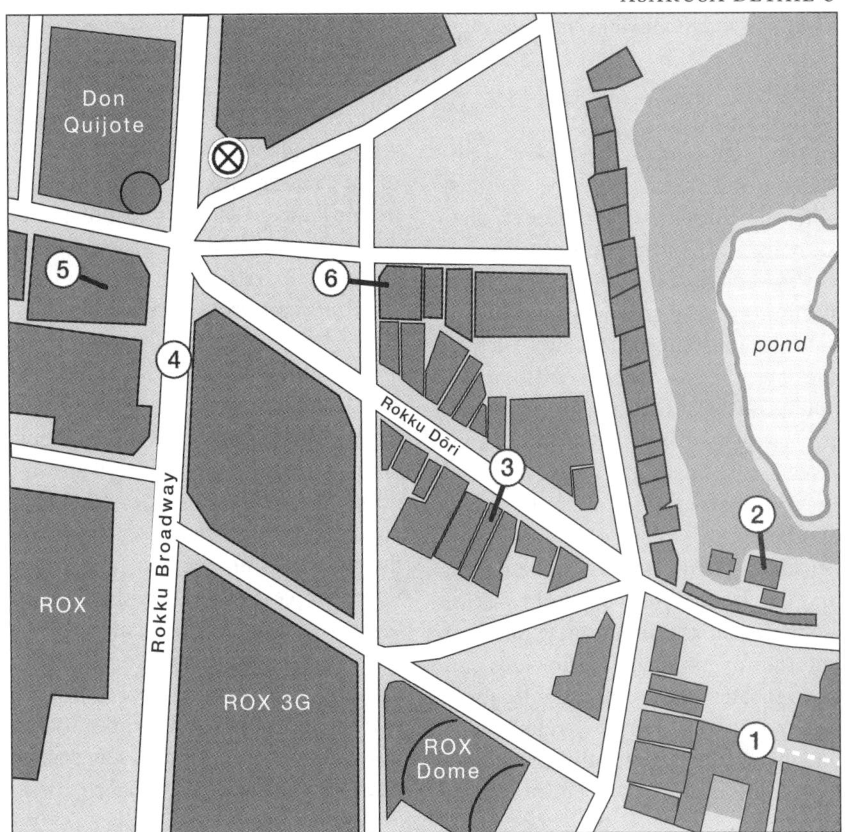

❸ Mokuhankan 木版館

A shop founded in 2014 by David Bull, a carver of traditional woodblocks for-printmaking. Bull has been practicing his craft in Tokyo for decades and strives for perfection. The shop has a staff who produce beautiful and affordable hand-printed works. There is also a broad selection of prints from other printmakers available for purchase. Viewing such prints directly shows details that photos do not reveal, such as the same color printed with shiny and dull finishes, or patterns pressed into the paper creating subtle shadows that add to the impact of the image. At the shop you can sign up to join a Print Party, where you make a simple multicolor print from woodblocks using traditional implements and techniques. Aprons are provided, the inks are non-toxic, and school-age kids can participate. Imagine taking home a souvenir you have printed yourself.

🌐 *https://mokuhankan.com/index.php*

❹ Rokku 六区

In the Meiji period, the rokku (sixth) section of Asakusa Park was the area with the theaters, opera houses, music halls, and, starting in 1903, cinemas. Destroyed during the Great Kantō Earthquake, the area was rebuilt with cabarets and musical reviews such as the famous Casino Follies. In 1929 a young Kawabata Yasunari began writing a series of popular articles about Asakusa in the Asahi newspaper and the number of visitors to this area climbed. After suffering from the heavy censorship of the wartime government and the firebombings of World War II, Rokku again rebuilt and new forms of entertainments such as strip clubs and porn theaters arose and then declined. Today this area is mostly retail shops and bars, but theater still exists here with the continued presence of Asakusa Mokubakan with traveling acting troupes, Asakusa Engei Hall for rakugo, and the Asakusa Kōkaidō with kabuki, among other entertainments.

❺ Asakusa Engei Hall
浅草演芸ホール

One of a few theaters in Tokyo where there are daily performances of rakugo story telling. The building has been the venue for a variety of entertainments since it first opened in 1907. These days it is mainly used for rakugo, even if other types of performances are occasionally presented. I have observed audience members waiting outside that ranged from the very elderly to middle school students, either on a field trip to the area or skipping school to see a performance. Skipping school to see rakugo? If I was their teacher, I would give them extra credit.

🌐 *http://www.asakusaengei.com*

❻ Mizuguchi Shokudō 水口食堂

An old-fashioned Japanese neighborhood diner since 1950. There are two floors, Western seating on the first, Japanese with cushions on tatami on the second. The food is straightforward, simple, tasty, and, with some 100 dishes, quite varied. You can order a la carte or set meals. Their drink menu includes beer, sake, shōchū, wine, whisky, alcopops (soft drinks with a low alcohol content), and soft drinks. Credit cards accepted. English menu available

🌐 *http://asakusa-mizuguch.main.jp*

DETAIL 7

❶ Sushihatsu 寿司初

A sushi restaurant established in 1910, located near the midpoint of Sushiya Dōri. Only seafood in season is used. The menu has a large selection of chirashizushi (scattered sushi), nigirizushi

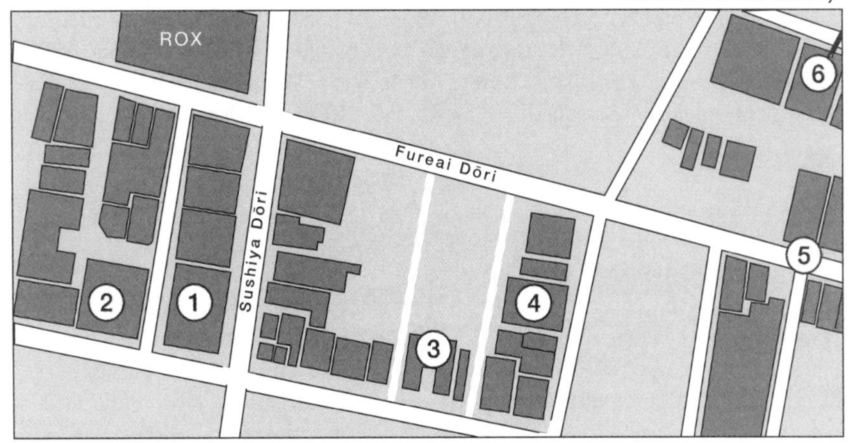

(topping on rice), and zukedon (marinated tuna on rice). They have a broad selection of sake and other alcoholic beverages. There is Western-style counter and table seating. The second floor is has a banquet hall and private rooms with Japanese seating on tatami.
🌐 *http://www.sushi-hatsu.com*

❷ HUB Asakusa shop / HUB Asakusa Ten / HUB 浅草店
Normally I would not recommend a branch of a chain of British-style pubs. However the HUB in Asakusa is an exception. It is a jazz club with music every night, open 365 days a year. There is a cover charge earlier in the evening. The place is popular with locals, the beer varied, seating is non-smoking though there is a smoking booth, and the bands constantly change.
🌐 *https://www.pub-hub.com/index.php/shop/detail/6*

❸ Bujitomi Inari Jinja
無事富稲荷神社
In a mixed commercial and residential area, this is a humble shrine to Inari that is located behind a small gate. Such shrines, many even smaller, are scattered throughout the city, a testimony to the devotion this deity has enjoyed in Japan. If the gate is open, consider visiting the shrine, respectfully take a picture or two, leave an offering, and, perhaps, a prayer.

❹ Kamameshi Haru 釜めし 春
A restaurant operating since 1926, specializing in kama meshi: rice dishes cooked and served in a small wooden-lidded kama, a type of iron pot. Kamameshi Haru is considered the first restaurant to specialize in this cuisine. While rice is the main ingredient, what goes with it can vary greatly, even including uncooked toppings. Seasonal

dishes are also offered. Seating is both traditional and Western style. Take-out orders are possible. English, Chinese, and Korean menus are available.

❺ **Tanuki Dōri** たぬき通り
Located a little way south of Chingodō, this one block long street is easy to identify, as the base of each lightpost has a red enclosure with a different small statue of a tanuki dressed in human clothes. The statues are quite whimsical—you can find Buddhist priests, Shōki the Demon Queller, and more. It is not unusual to see someone photographing each and every statue.

❻ **Yagenbori Nakajima Shōten**
やげん堀 中島商店
See entry 15 for detail map 1.

DETAIL 8

❶ **Butsudan Dōri** 仏壇通り
On Asakusa Dōri from Inarichō to Kokusai Dōri are shops specializing in Shintō and Buddhist home altars, as well as related implements and small outdoor shrines. The shops are mainly on the south side of the street, to prevent direct sunlight from damaging the wooden goods. Some of these shops are just suppliers of Shintō items or specific Buddhist sects; others are more general, serving more than one sect or religion. There also a few shops near the intersection with Kokusai Dōri. The name Butsudan Dōri, appropriately titled "the street of household Buddhist altars," is an informal one often used to refer to this group of shops.

❷ **Kappabashi Street / Kappabashi Dōgugai** かっぱ橋道具街
An entire street devoted to supplies for restaurants and caterers. While a few of the larger shops stock a variety of supplies, almost all of the shops specialize in one type of product. There are shops for chairs and stools, for food replicas, for restaurant stationery, for cloth items, for knives, for signage, for traditional paper lanterns, even a shop for rustic items to give your business a time-worn and rural look, and so on. At least one of the plastic sample food shops has a hands-on workshops. Kappabashi is lined with carved wooden sign holders in the shape of a cute swimming female kappa. If you are in Asakusa Dōri, look for the landmark on top of the Niimi Building at the intersection: a statue of the head of a chef that is 39 feet (11.7 meters) tall.
🌐 *http://kappabashi.or.jp*

❸ **Honzan Higashi Honganji**
本山東本願寺
A Jōdo Shinshū Buddhist temple. Originally in Kanda, it was relocated to Asakusa after the Meireki fire. During

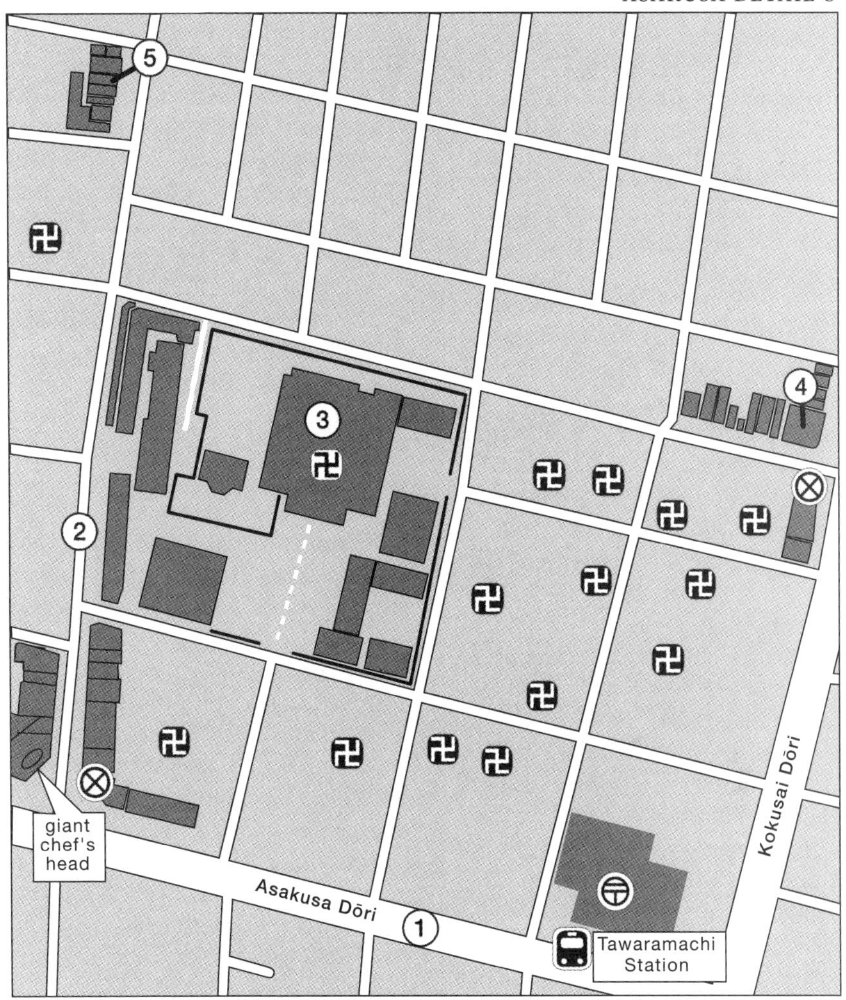

World War I the temple grounds were used to house captured sailors from the German Navy. After the Great Kantō Earthquake the temple again burned down and was replaced with a reinforced concrete structure. The interior of the building was gutted during the March 1945 firebombing of Tokyo in World War II. In the *36 Views of Mount Fuji* by Hokusai, the print titled Tōto Asakusa Honganji captures the rooftop of this temple with a kite and Mount Fuji visible in the distance.

🌐 *http://honganji.or.jp/index.shtml*

OFF THE CHARTS

Ikenami Shōtarō Memorial Museum / Ikenami Shōtarō Kinen Bunko
池波正太郎記念文庫

If you follow the main street of the Kappabashi shopping area north, you will reach a very large building that is home to the Taitō Kuritsu Central Library and Taitō City Lifelong Learning Center. On the first floor is a museum devoted to the writings of Ikenami Shōtarō (1923–1990). The museum was planned as a part of this new library and opened in 2001. Displays include photographs he took for reference, a large collection of books, his manuscripts and paintings, maps he drew to aid in plotting scenes in stories, and a reconstruction of his study filled with items he owned. Ikenami Shōtarō was born and raised in the Asakusa area and early on worked scripting plays for the Shinkokugeki theatrical company. To date, the only works translated in English are two: *Master Assassin* and *Bridge of Darkness,* from his *Shikakenin Fujieda Baian* series. The Baian series was adapted into more than one TV series; the one starring Watanabe Ken was released in the United States on subtitled DVD in 2006.

🌐 *https://www.culture.city.taito.lg.jp/bunkatanbou/culture/ikenami/ikenami_e.html*

❹ **Drum Museum / Taikokan** 太鼓館
This shop was founded in 1988 by the Miyamoto Unosuke Shōten company, makers of traditional musical instruments and mikoshi. The ground floor is a shop; the museum is upstairs, accessible by elevator. The museum houses a collection of hundreds of drums and percussion instruments from around the world. There are even some props used for sound effects in kabuki. Several drums in the museum are marked to let you know you can play them.

❺ **Kamata Hakensha** かまた刃研社
A shop specializing in knives located on Kappabashi Dōri. They sell over 800 different Japanese and Western knives, Japanese whetstones, and a selection of kitchen gadgets. Operating since 1923, they originally just repaired or sharpened knives and later they expanded into sales. They still do knife repair and sharpening, and now offer knife sharpening classes. Free hand engraving on knives purchased there is available.

English-speaking staff are on site.
🌐 *https://www.kap-kam.com*

DETAIL 9

❶ **Kappadera** かっぱ寺
A shrine dedicated to the mythical kappa on the grounds of Sōgenji. The

roof's end tiles have kappa faces on them and there are several kappa statues near the shrine. According to one legend, a local merchant wanted to improve drainage in this marshy area. At one time he had saved a kappa from a trap, so various kappa helped with the project. You may be able to arrange to go inside the shrine if you have Japanese-speaking friends call and make an appointment. Allow a week or two for this, as the temple staff may be busy. Do this properly and have a modest gift of some paper money in an envelope to give thanks—be a little generous. When you are inside, or just peeking through the glass, you will see several objects. These include an altar with offerings, panels on the ceiling painted by famous manga artists, and a glass case with small items including a mummified kappa arm. As this is a religious shrine, do be respectful.

The entrance to the grounds is on the south side.

❷ Fukuzendō Sakai Kanbanten 福善堂坂井看板店

This business has been run by the Sakai family since 1924, producing traditional carved signs such as kanban (business signs), signs for Shintō shrines and Buddhist temples, sponsors' placards at kabuki plays, and mon (crests) for businesses, schools and families. They did the restoration work on the large sign for the Mistukoshi Department Store in Nihonbashi. Their clients are found in all parts of Japan, so they may be working off site and closed at times.

🌐 *http://www.interq.or.jp/tokyo/fukuzen/*

❸ Kama-asa 釜浅

This shop has been in operation since 1908 and specializes in finely crafted traditional and modern cooking supplies such as knives, charcoal grills, and pots and pans. Many items are made from wood, bamboo, or natural fibers. Knife repair and sharpening are also handled by the store. The knife selection is impressive, including not only highly specialized blades but regional variants of knives used for the same task. For example, they have four different knives designed for fileting eels. Free engraving of knives purchased is available on request. English- and French-speaking staff are on hand.

🌐 *http://www.kama-asa.co.jp/en/*

❹ Dojō Iidaya どぜう飯田屋

A restaurant serving dishes based around the humble dojō (loach) since 1903. Seating is traditional or Western style in chairs. Be aware that in some of the nabe dishes the fish are cooked whole, bones, guts and all; be sure to chew it well. You can also order boneless and gutless dishes, such as kabayaki, in which the fish are cut open lengthwise and grilled.

🌐 *http://dozeu-iidaya.com*

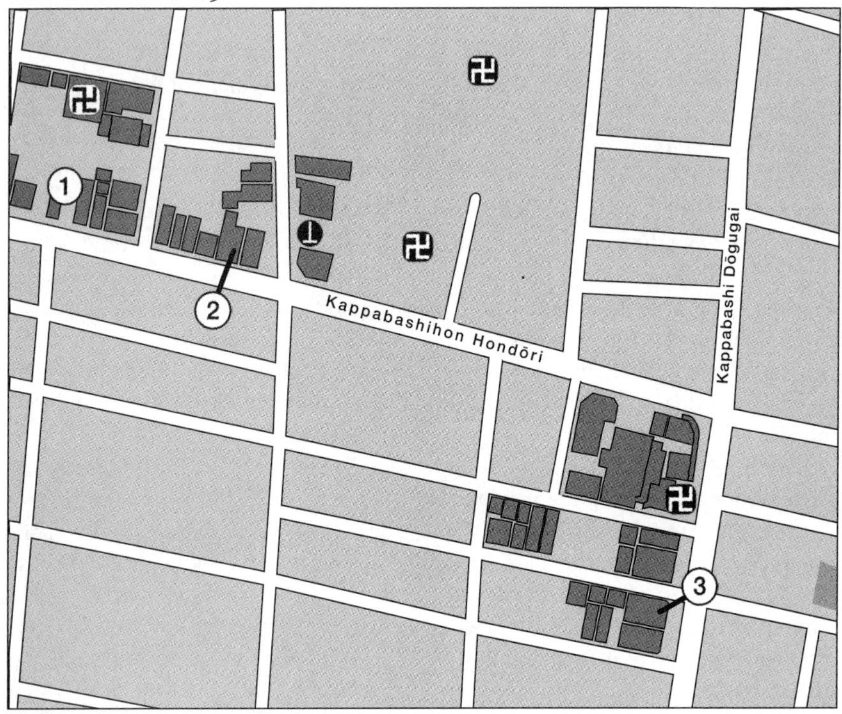

❺ Asakusa Imahan 浅草今半

This sukiyaki restaurant originally opened in the Honjō Azumabashi neighborhood in 1895 as Imahan; in 1913 the Asakusa location opened near the Kaminarimon. The restaurant changed its name in 1928 to Asakusa Imahan and moved to the present location on Kokusai Dōri. The current three-story building dates from 2008, with both Western and traditional seating. They use wagyu beef in their products and since 1945 have made tsukudani from beef in their own sauce. They also sell beef tsukudani, and various cuts of meat in boxes, which are available at many department stores.

🌐 *http://www.asakusaimahan.co.jp/english.*

DETAIL 10

❶ Bandai head office building
バンダイ本社ビル

The offices of the internationally famous toy and hobby division of Bandai Namco are easy to spot, with its sculptures of characters from famous

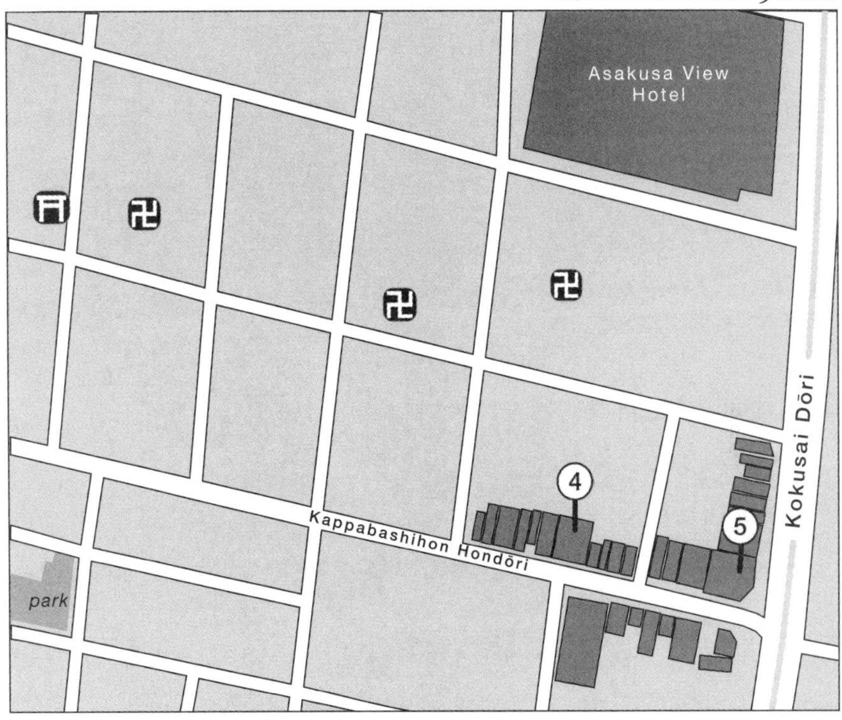

animated and live action shows. Just look for a street with full-sized statues of Doraemon and Kamen Rider, and a smaller Ultraman. The lobby of the building is filled with display cases of toys and other products sold by the company. If they happen to be closed when you wander by, you can still see a large portion of the exhibits through the windows on the street.
🌐 *http://www.bandai.co.jp/e/*

❷ Ōshimaya Onda 大嶋屋恩田
A shop that makes and sells all sorts of traditional lanterns with a large variety of shapes, sizes, and designs. They have been in business since 1854. They produce lanterns for shrines, temples, restaurants, and ryokans, as well as for ceremonies, gifts, homes, shops, and any other use. They stock lanterns to be hung, mounted, handheld, and for special purposes. Some of the Edo period designs include those for use on horseback, on boats, and while walking at night. The majority of lanterns are handmade from traditional materials such as bamboo and washi paper. In some types, modern materials may be preferred, such as metal, Western paper, or vinyl. Also stocked are

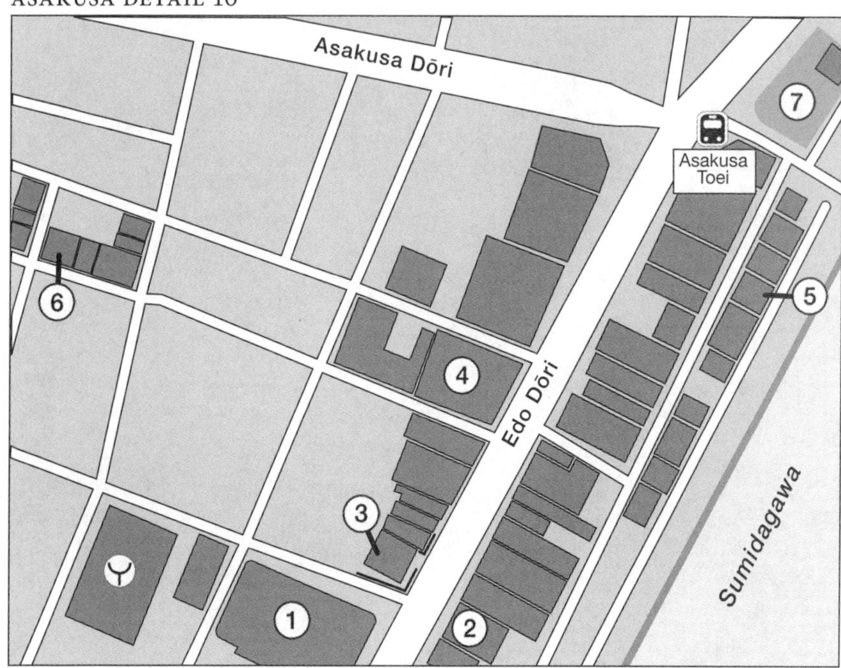

accessories including gift boxes, electric lights in the shape of candle flames, hanging lights, clear vinyl covers, special long poles for raising the lantern high, and floor frames for free-standing display. Custom-made lanterns are a regular part of the business.
🌐 *http://www.chochin-ya.com*

❸ Komakata Dozeu 駒形どぜう
A restaurant with a menu centered around dojō (loach), a small freshwater fish found in many parts of Japan. As the fish are small and sometimes cooked whole, some dishes may include soft bones, so you may need to chew those well. The building, modeled on the original wooden structure from 1801, has two floors above ground and a basement level. There is both traditional Japanese floor seating and Western chair seating depending on the floor. Komakata Dozeu is very proud of its history and every other month they host a presentation, in Japanese, on Edo period culture; in 2011 they were granted a MECENAT Award for this work. One traditional element you will see is small dishes at the entrance filled with purifying salt.
🌐 *https://www.dozeu.com/en/*

❹ World Bags and Luggage Museum / Sekai no Kaban Hakubutsukan 世界のカバン博物館

A unique museum operated by luggage maker Ace. The humble bag—may it be a purse, pouch, backpack, attaché case, suitcase, or other means of carrying items—has various forms and uses throughout the world. The collection is well displayed in cases with good lighting. For decades Ace founder Shinkawa Ryūsaku collected hundreds of such items from around the world for this collection, which he made available for public viewing in 1975. The range of materials used to make them is as interesting as the bags themselves.

🌐 *https://www.acejpn.com/about/csr/museum.html*

❺ Maekawa 前川

Originally Maekawa was a wholesaler of river fish. The founder then turned it into an eel restaurant in the early 19th century. Located on the Sumidagawa, its name can be translated as "river front." The second and third floors have tatami rooms with Japanese-style seating. The season for wild Japanese eel is generally May through November; at other times, they use high-quality farmed domestic eel from the Tone River area. Farming eel in Japan has been going on since 1879 and they have found good sources.

🌐 *http://www.unagi-maekawa.com*

🌐 *http://www.norenkai.net/en/portfolio-item/maekawa/*

❻ Sōshū 宗舟

A workshop and gallery focusing on traditional woodcarvings for shrines, temples, and households since the Meiji period. They also make and sell the small ornamental sculptures called netsuke, as well as do restoration and repair. The first floor is a gallery of their work.

🌐 *http://so-syu.jp/index.html*

❼ Komakatadō 駒形堂

A small temple to Batō Kannon "Horse-headed Kannon" next to the Sumidagawa, originally built in 942. Tradition has it that this was the location where the fishermen brothers Hinokuma Hamanari and Hinokuma Takenari found the famous Kannon statue that is at Sensōji. This place was also where boats carrying people to the temple would dock, so pilgrims would first pray here before traveling on. Now prayers for traffic safety are offered here. The nearby bridge, called Komagatabashi, and the Komagata neighborhood are named after this temple. The temple is also seen in several ukiyo-e prints including some by such famous artists as Hokusai and Hiroshige. The present building dates from 2003, replacing the 1933 structure that replaced the one destroyed in the Great Kantō Earthquake.

There is a festival each April 19.

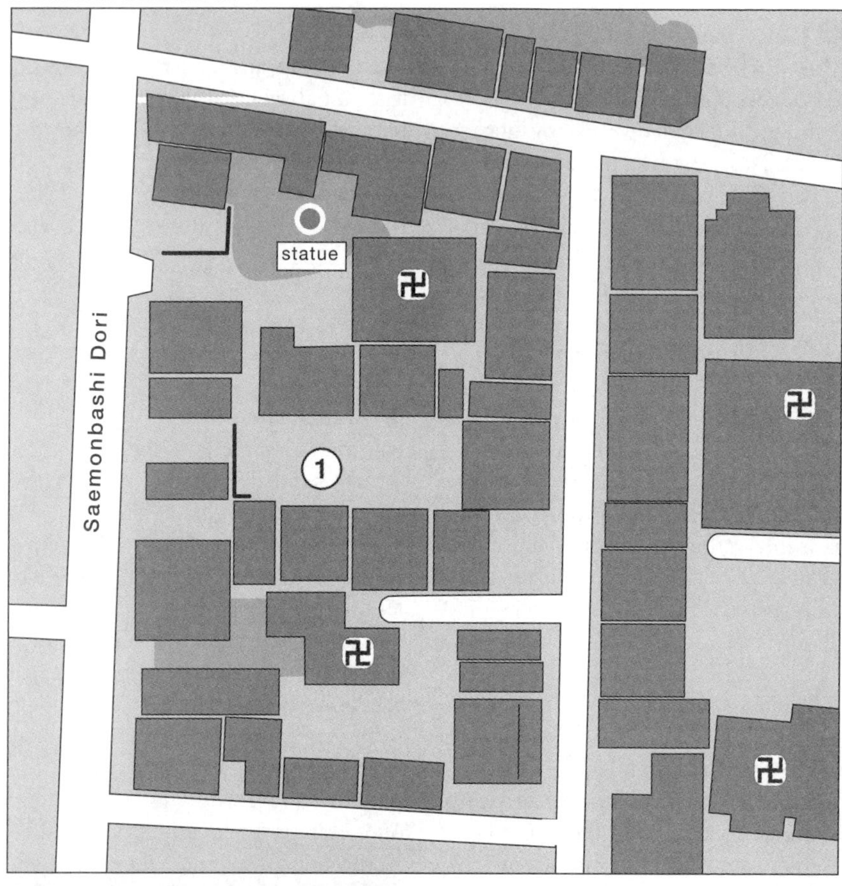

DETAIL 11

Seikyōji 誓教寺
Located in Moto-Asakusa, four blocks west of Kappabashi Dōri and south of Asakusa Dōri on Saemonbashi Dōri, is a small Buddhist Temple of the Jōdo Shinshū sect. At the entrance there is a sign—the same kind you see around the neighborhood for various landmarks—with the temple name and a note that Katsushika Hokusai's grave is located here. The connection with Hokusai is what will interest most tourists. Enter the grounds from the west and look a little to the left: You will see a bust of Hokusai that is placed facing in the direction of Mount Fuji. If you turn right and go along the side of the temple priest's residence, you will reach the graveyard. Hokusai's grave is

easy to identify as it has a wooden roof over it. There is a small box with a slot in it and some postcards in Japanese. If you want a postcard, leave a small offering in the box.

NOTE: *When I visited, the priest pointed out that the inscription on the gravestone says "Crazy Old Man."*

深川

FUKAGAWA

This area has undergone many changes over the past few centuries. After the Meireki Fire of 1657, the Edo lumberyards were moved away from their original location in Nihonbashi to the Fukagawa marshlands located on the other side of the Sumidagawa. During the 17th and 18th centuries the lumberyards and docks of Fukagawa prospered. As the area was developed, canals were dug to both drain the low-lying land and to aid transportation. As a result this area had, and still has, a great many historical bridges. The importance of these bridges has contributed to the wealth of stories about them. Today many of those canals have been either replaced by culverts or filled in. Even so, several still exist. These remnants of the past are still used for the transport of goods and, more recently, boat tours. In the Meiji period the area became a factory district for Japan's rapidly growing industrialization. During the postwar period the factories were replaced with the office buildings and apartments of today.

DETAIL 1

❶ Former Fukagawa red light district 深川岡場所・花街跡

The area south of Tomioka Hachimangū between Eitai Dōri and the Ōyokogawa was once a famous red-light restaurant and brothel district dating back to 1655. The Fukagawa geisha, also called tatsumi geisha, who provided entertainment at parties here were famous for being high spirited, independent, and very stylish with

FUKAGAWA

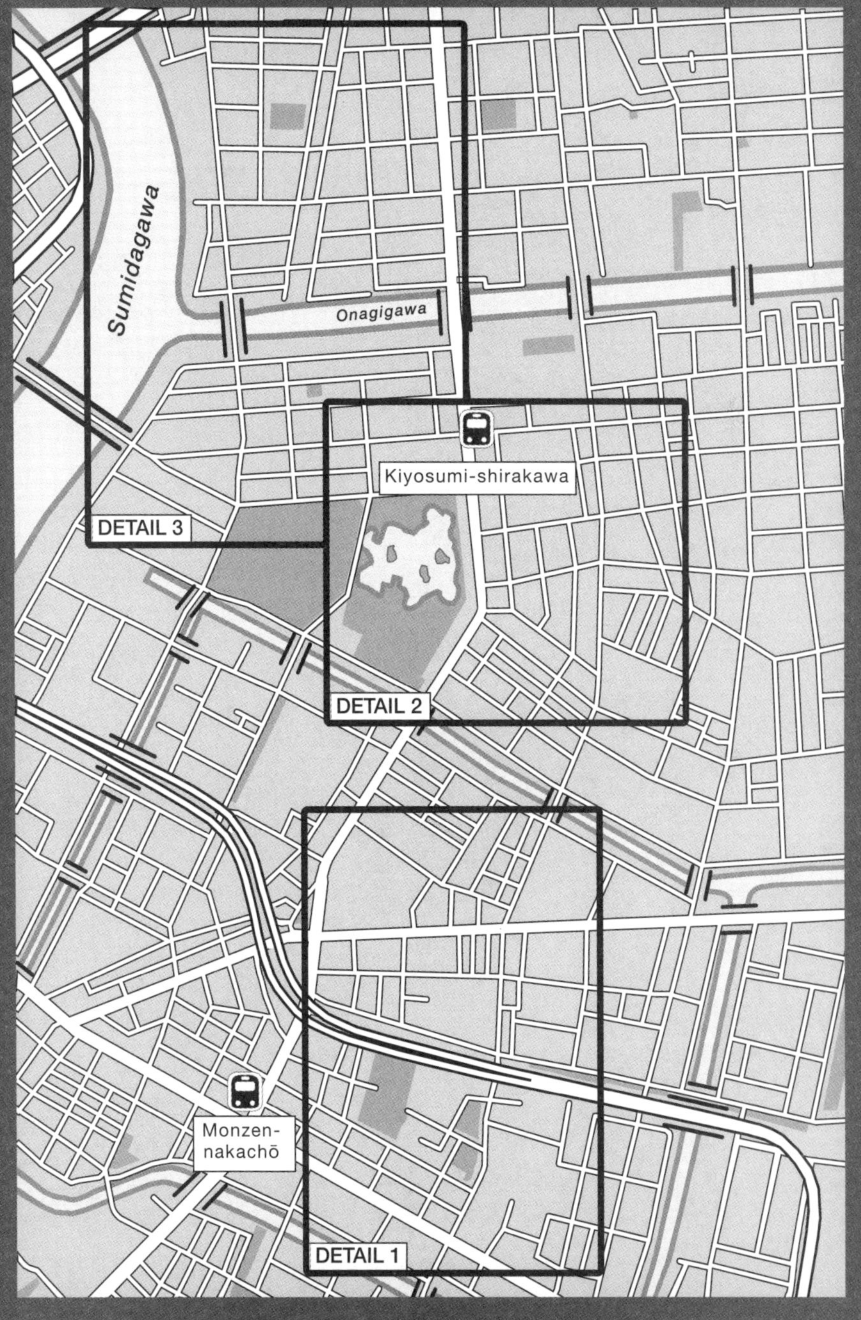

Sumidagawa
Onagigawa
Kiyosumi-shirakawa
DETAIL 3
DETAIL 2
DETAIL 1
Monzen-
nakachō

FUKAGAWA DETAIL 1

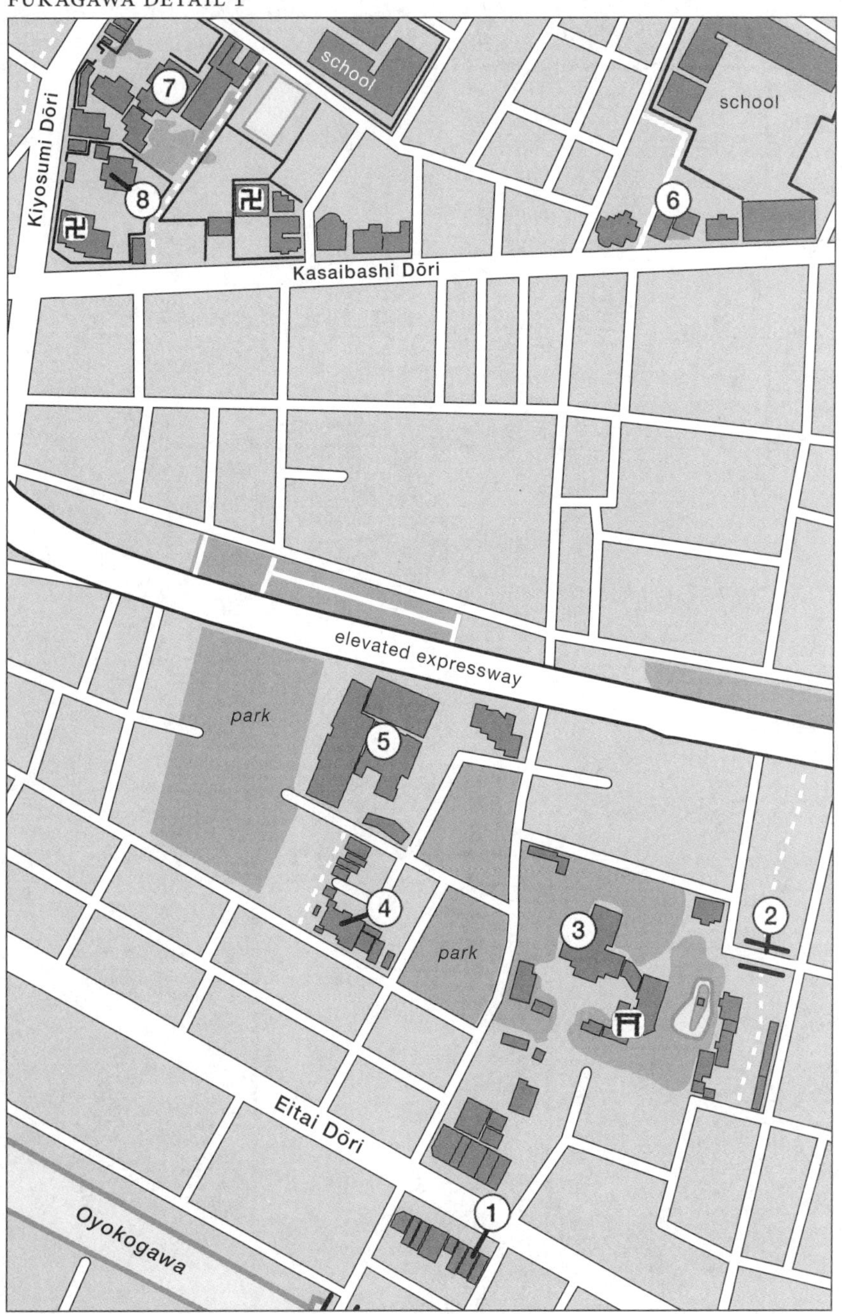

their understated kimono and haori. Today the area is home to many bars and traditional restaurants, often with the owner's residence and apartments on the same lot. There still are some geisha in Fukagawa practicing their trade of traditional music and dance. The appreciation of traditional musical performance, such as with shamisen, and dance, with fans in kimono, has declined all over Tokyo, so the number of geisha is probably much lower than it was just forty years ago when company accounts would still cover the cost of geisha entertainments for clients.

❷ Hachimanbashi 八幡橋

Formerly called Danjōbashi and built in 1878 using a design by noted American engineer Squire Whipple, this was the first iron bridge in Japan. Originally located close to Nihonbashi, it was relocated to Fukagawa in 1929 and renamed Hachimanbashi. The canal it once spanned was filled in but the bridge remains, now spanning a pedestrian pathway in a park. In 1977 it was designated an Important Cultural Property, and in 1989 it received the Honor Award from the American Society of Civil Engineers.

❸ Tomioka Hachimangū 富岡八幡宮

This shrine was founded in 1627 at what was then the edge of the bay. The current reinforced concrete buildings are from 1956, replacing those bombed in World War II. Hachiman and eight other kami are enshrined at Tomioka Hachimangū. There is so much on the shrine grounds that I'll only cover a few highlights here. This shrine is considered the birthplace of modern sumō, as many of the elements of today's version of that sport started here. At the entrance, just past the torii, is a monument to ōzeki, the second highest rank in sumō. If you go well around to the right of the main building, there you will see massive stones with inscriptions of the names of all the yokozuna, the highest rank in sumō. Near the yokozuna monuments is an Inari Shrine as well as Nanawatari Jinja, which is a shrine to Benten with a pond. The path to this shrine leads over a bridge. If you instead go around the left of the main building you will see several large round stones used in Edo period longshoreman's weight lifting contests. Keep going down some steps to three small shrines, one of which is a sub-shrine to Ebisu that is on the Shichifukujin circuit for Fukagawa.

There is also a museum on the grounds that has a variety of objects, artworks, and photographs related to the shrine, its connection to sumō, local history, and more.

The ennichi holy days are held on the first, fifteenth, and twenty-eighth of each month. There is also a flea market on the fifteenth and twenty-eighth of each month and an antiques market on the first (Western goods) and second

(Asian goods) Sundays of each month.

Main Festival: Fukagawa Matsuri is held on the weekend closest to August 15. A larger grand festival with over fifty mikoshi is held every three years (2020, 2023, 2026, etc.). As it is the hottest time of the year, water is thrown on mikoshi bearers to cool them down.

The main entrance to the complex is on the south side; you can also enter on the west and north sides.

🌐 *http://www.tomiokahachimangu.or.jp*

❹ Eitaiji 永代寺

Founded in 1627, this Shingon sect Buddhist temple originally shared land and administration with Tomioka Hachimangū. In the Edo period, Eitaiji was the main Buddhist temple for Fukagawa. Starting in 1703 the famous statue of Fudō from Narita would be shown here annually to raise funds. In the Meiji period the government enforced a strict separation of Shintō shrines and Buddhist temples, and most of Eitaiji was destroyed in 1898. Any buildings that still existed did not survive the devastations of the 20th century. These days a commemorative stone at its former location and a small temple of the same name with a unique cupola are all that is left. Its role as the main Buddhist temple for this area is now filled by another Shingon temple, Naritasan Fukagawa Fudōdō. The entrance to Eitaiji can be found on the west side.

❺ Naritasan Fukagawa Fudōdō
成田山 深川不動堂

Also referred to as Fukagawa Fudōson, this is a Shingon Buddhist temple enshrining Fudō Myōō. The temple was built in 1881 and destroyed in the Great Kantō Earthquake and again in the firebombings of Tokyo in World War II. The grounds contain the oldest building in Koto Ward: Ryūfukuji, a disused temple from Chiba Prefecture built in 1862, was relocated here in 1951 to serve as the temple. In 2012 a very modern square structure became the new hondō (main hall). This is a large and impressive black cube covered in Sanskrit text from a Fudō Myōō mantra. You can enter the hall after removing your shoes and hat and silencing your cell phone. Note that photographs are prohibited inside the hall. A large portion of the hall with stepped seating for worshipers contains the altar. Every two hours starting at 9:00 a.m. a priest performs the elaborate goma fire ritual. Afterward worshipers may have objects blessed over the smoldering ashes. The ritual takes place five times a day, except on the ennichi holy days when it is performed six times. The ennichi for the temple are on the first, fifteenth and twenty-eighth of each month. On those days there are many stalls in the vicinity of the temple selling a variety of goods, giving the place a festive air.

The old hall has an inner portion where you can take an elevator to the first, second, and fourth floors, where artwork is displayed. One interesting work is a mural painted on the ceiling of the fourth floor by contemporary artist Nakajima Chinami. Photography is also prohibited inside this hall.

The main entrance to the temple grounds is on the south; you can also find entrances from the east and west sides.

🌐 *http://fukagawafudou.gr.jp*

❻ Fuyuki Bentendō 冬木弁天堂

This temple to Benten is one of the Shichifukujin shrines on the Fukagawa pilgrimage route. Today it is located on a large street of tall apartments and office buildings. Fuyuki Bentendō was originally built in the 18th century as a private shrine for a wealthy family of lumber merchants. The Fuyuki family left, but their name remained in the names of the shrine and the neighborhood. This Bentendō is raised above the street level with a garden in the front. The building is of subdued colors offset with a bright red railing for the stairs and veranda.

The entrance to the shrine is on the south side.

❼ Shingyōji 心行寺

I am including this temple not for itself but as it is also on the Shichifukujin route. Fukurokuju is enshrined in the small hexagonal building to the left of the main building. There is also a statue of him with his high-domed head next to it.

The temple entrance is on the west side.

❽ Hōjōin 法乗院

This Buddhist temple, which was founded in 1629, has an interesting mix of modern and traditional in its design. Contemporary staircases and a balcony rail combine harmoniously with traditional temple architecture. The first floor has wall paintings of heaven and hell that date from 1784. Hōjōin is famous for a sub-temple containing a large statue of Enma; for this reason the entire temple is sometimes referred to as Fukagawa Enmadō (深川えんま堂). The Enma statue is seated, measures 11.5 feet (3.5 meters) tall, and dates from 1989. When I visited, the Enmadō was dark inside, so I slid open the glass partition in front of the offering boxes to get a better view. Usually temples have one offering box, but this has nineteen, each with a small kanji sign indicating its purpose. When you toss a coin in one, the lights come on and you hear a short lecture from Enma.

The entrance to the temple is on the west side.

DETAIL 2

❶ Enjuin 円珠院

A small temple located on a corner

▲ Hachimanbashi, originally called Danjōbashi, was the first iron bridge in Japan.

lot, which I am including as it is a Shichifukujin temple, this time for Daikoku. This is a sub-temple of the larger Jōshinji on the other side of the street, so head to the humbler building if you are doing the pilgrimage route.

❷ Kiyosumi Garden / Kiyosumi Teien 清澄庭園

Originally this was the site of the villa of the wealthy merchant Kinokuniya Bunzaemon before his extravagant lifestyle bankrupted him. Then the samurai lord Kuze Shigeyuki obtained the land and laid out the basic garden. In 1878 Iwasaki Yatarō, founder of Mitsubishi Group, bought the land and had the present garden constructed, which measures almost 3.8 hectares. The design is what is called a chisen kaiyūshiki teien, "pond stroll garden," intended to be enjoyed from numerous angles as one walks around it. There are many interesting features and structures. The Ryōtei is a traditional-style building built out over the pond to entertain General H.H. Kitchener on his 1909 state visit to Japan. It was damaged in the Great Kantō Earthquake and the firebombings of Tokyo in World War II. Near the entrance is the Taishō Kinenkan, which was originally the funeral hall for the Taishō emperor and later relocated here. Destroyed in World War II, the rebuilt hall employs used materials from the funeral hall for Empress Teimei. While much of garden was damaged in the Great Kantō Earthquake, it still sheltered thousands who took refuge here. In 1924 the Iwasaki family donated the garden to the city.

🌐 *https://www.tokyo-park.or.jp/teien/en/kiyosumi/index.html*

❸ Fukagawajuku 深川宿

You can identify this restaurant by their large wooden sign with the name of the restaurant in green kanji. Fukagawajuku's specialties are local dishes that were originated by local fishermen in the Edo period who needed a quick and nutritious meal. The dishes then became popular with other occupations such as carpenters as this kind of food could be easily carried to work. The restaurant is especially known for their Fukagawa meshi made with asari clams, negi, and miso cooked together then poured over rice; and takikomi gohan, which is rice cooked with asari clams and negi with crushed roasted nori sprinkled on top. They have a variety of other seafood dishes. They also have food packages you can take home and bentō to take out.

There are two locations: the main in front of the Fukagawa Edo Museum, and the branch east of the road to Tomioka Hachimangū.

🌐 *http://www.fukagawajuku.com*

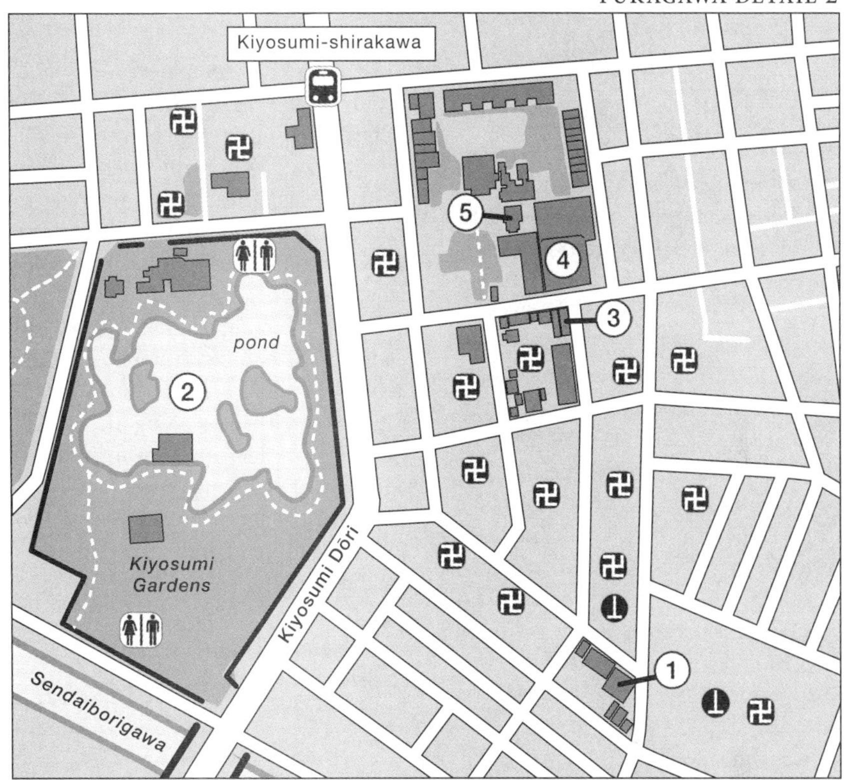

❹ Fukagawa Edo Museum / Fukagawa Edo Shiryōkan 深川江戸資料館

The permanent exhibit of this museum consists of full-sized replicas of the types of buildings that used to be common in this part of Tokyo in the late Edo period. The replicas are underground, so that when you enter, you are looking down on a reconstructed neighborhood. The variety of buildings ranges from prosperous businesses to the humble backstreet dwellings of the poor. The lights shift from morning to dusk and dark, and there are seasonal sound effects and decorations. You can enter many of the buildings and handle some of the items on display. They have a small theater and often hold special events. The museum publishes a book in English also titled *Fukagawa Edo Museum* that is a useful guide to the objects you see displayed and life at the time.

🌐 *https://www.kcf.or.jp/fukagawa/*

OFF THE CHARTS
Eitaibashi 永代橋

Follow Eitai Dōri, the major road in the south of the area, west to reach the Sumidagawa and this bridge.

The first bridge called Eitaibashi "Bridge of Eternal Ages" was built in 1698 to celebrate the fiftieth birthday of shōgun Tokugawa Tsunayoshi and link the neighborhoods of Fukagawa with Nihonbashi. Originally this area had a busy ferry, so the bridge must have been welcome to the residents on both sides. Bashō even wrote a poem about crossing the bridge. The first two Eitaibashi bridges shared a similar fate. During the highly popular Fukagawa Matsuri of Tomioka Hachimangū, both of the bridges collapsed from the crowds, the first in the 18th century and the second in 1807 with roughly 1,000 dead and injured. Kaifukuji in Meguro has two stone memorial pagoda to the victims of the second incident; that temple had originally been in Fukagawa when the pagodas were dedicated and was later moved to Meguro. There is even a late Edo period rakugo story dealing with the incident in a darkly humorous way. The third bridge was destroyed in the Great Kantō Earthquake. The current, and fourth, bridge was built in 1925 just south of the original site and is the oldest existing bridge on the Sumidagawa. It is modeled on the Ludendorff bridge near Bonn.

❺ Reiganji 霊巌寺

This attractive temple on spacious grounds was established in 1624 at Reiganjima, near the mouth of the Sumidagawa. After the Meireki fire, Reiganji was moved across the river to Fukagawa, helping draw more visitors to what until then had been a somewhat isolated location. On the street south of the complex you will see old walls on the path into temple grounds, as well as small ornaments on top of the guardrail posts along the street. Inside to the left of the gate is a seated statue of Jizō that is 9 feet (3 meters) tall. This is one of the Six Jizō of Edo that were placed here and at five other locations along major roads leading to Edo between 1708 and 1720. The back of the temple compound has a row of six Jizō that date from the Edo period.

The entrance is to the south.

DETAIL 3

❶ Kiyosubashi 清洲橋

An eyebar chain suspension bridge built in 1928 as part of reconstruction projects after the Great Kantō Earthquake. The Kiyosubashi was modeled after the Deutz Suspension Bridge in Cologne on the Rhine in Germany. The structure is an attractive blue with older-style streetlights. On March 9, 1945, during the firebombings of Tokyo in World War II, thousands took refuge

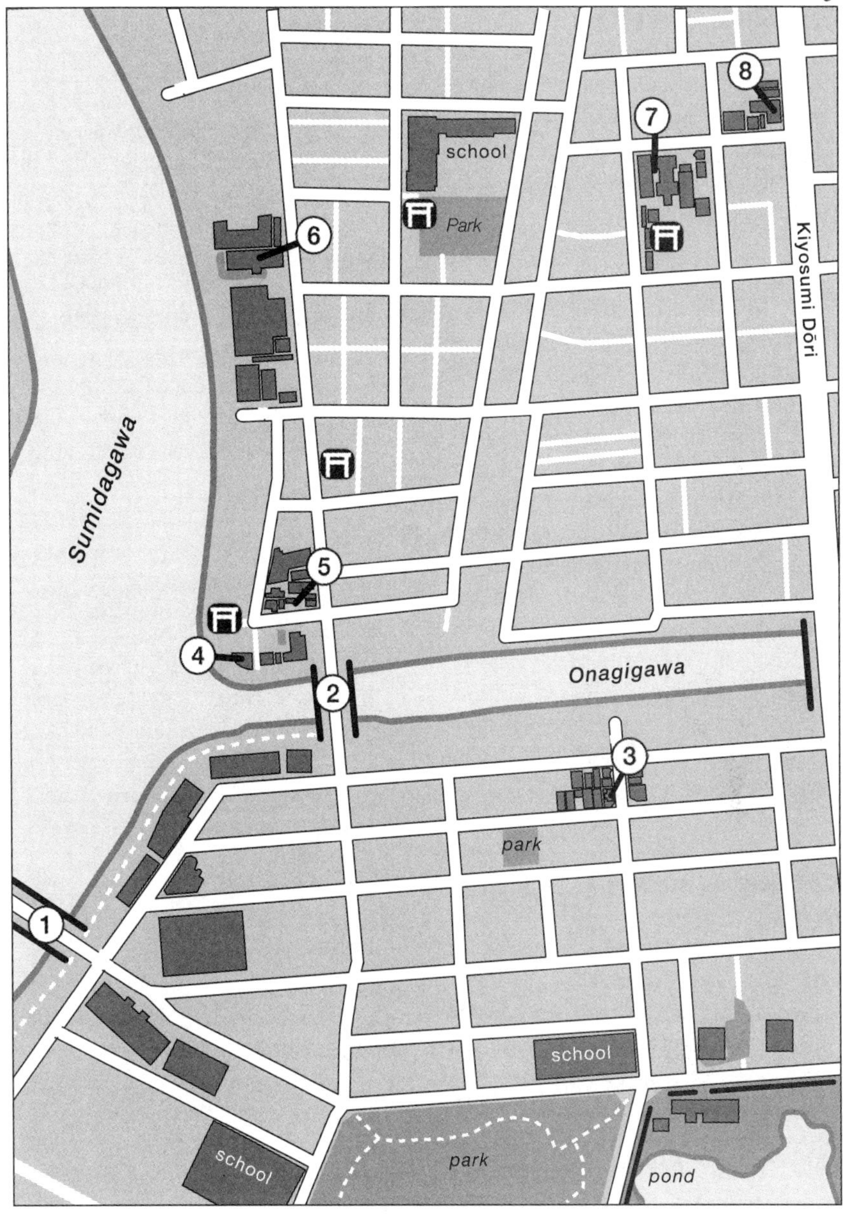

8
7
school
Park
6
Kiyosumi Dōri
Sumidagawa
5
4
2
Onagigawa
3
park
1
school
school
park
pond

on the bridge to escape the flames. The name of the bridge (清洲) comes from combining parts of the kanji of the names of either bank, Kiyosumi (清澄) and Nakasu (中洲) to form Kiyosu (清洲) and then adding the kanji for bridge (橋).

❷ Mannenbashi 萬年橋

Spanning the Onagigawa, the original bridge was built of wood in the 17th century. Today it is an attractive green steel bridge of bowstring design. In the Edo period turtles were sold near the bridge for the devout to release, an act of mercy according to Buddhist teachings. Many ukiyo-e print designers produced works featuring the dramatic arched bridge. Hiroshige's print from his series of views of Mount Fuji shows a turtle suspended on a string in the foreground. "Ten-thousand-year bridge" is the translation of the kanji used to write Mannenbashi.

❸ Fukagawa Inari Jinja 深川稲荷神社

A small shrine founded in 1630 and located on a street corner. Unlike many Inari shrines, this one has no bright red torii. However the shrine sign on the stone torii is very ornate, with carvings of dragons on the frame. This shrine is also dedicated to Hotei and is part of the local Shichifukujin pilgrimage.

The entrance is on the southeast corner of the block.

❹ Bashō Heritage Garden / Bashōan Shiseki Tenbō Teien 芭蕉庵史跡展望庭園

A small park on a hill with a view of the junction of the Onagigawa and the Sumidagawa. Also in view are two local bridges, the Kiyosubashi and the Mannenbashi. The park contains a bronze statue of Bashō, the Edo period master of haiku poetry, as well as art and plants related to his poetry. This garden is also often referred to as the Matsuo Bashō Memorial Park and the Bashō Heritage Historic Sites Outlook Garden.

OFF THE CHARTS: Shin-Ōhashi 新大橋

Located on the Sumidagawa at the northeast corner of the area map. This was the third bridge to be built across the Sumidagawa in the Edo period. The original timber bridge was constructed in 1693. Bashō wrote a poem mentioning the crunch of frost underfoot while crossing this bridge. It was replaced by an iron bridge in 1885, and then that bridge by a third that was completed in 1977. There are bas-reliefs of the earlier bridges along the pedestrian walkways at the bases of the cable towers.

❺ Bashō Inari Jinja 芭蕉稲荷神社

A small Inari shrine at what is believed to be the location of Bashō's residence in the neighborhood. No one knows for sure where Bashō's hermitage was; however, a possible location was identified in 1917 when a stone frog believed to have been owned by Bashō was uncovered by a typhoon. The local community then established the shrine in the poet's honor. The shrine was destroyed in the firebombings of World War II and the current structure dates from 1975. The shrine can easily be spotted from the street by a large red torii at the entrance. As you enter you face the small shrine and a memorial stone.

❻ Bashō Museum / Bashō Kinenkan 芭蕉記念館

Established in 1981 as a museum devoted to Bashō. Usually referred to in English as the Bashō Museum, Bashō Memorial Museum, or as the Bashō Memorial Hall. The square building is easy to identify with its white walls, rounded roof edges, bashō palm, and traditional gate. The museum collection consists of some original manuscripts by Bashō plus other items related to him, such as a replica of his travel garb.

❼ Fukagawa Shinmeigū 深川神明宮

A gray concrete torii on the street followed by double rows of trees and shrine storehouses line the walkway leading to this shrine. Fukagawa Shinmeigū was founded in the late 16th century by Fukagawa Hachiroemon, a local leader and the man who the Fukagawa area is named after. The shrine is on the location of his former residence. The chief kami of the shrine is Amaterasu Ōmikami; also enshrined are Inari and Jurōjin, so this is one of the Shichifukujin shrines on the local circuit. The shrine's great festival is held every three years in August on a weekend near the seventeenth.

🌐 *http://www.fukagawa-shinmei.com*

❽ Cattlea カトレア

A small neighborhood bakery where, in 1927, the owner combined two non-Japanese foods, bread and curry, to make karēpan. Today this particular inexpensive fast food is popular all over Japan—you can even find cheap versions in convenience stores. Cattlea, with its generous portions of curry, is considered one of the best places for karēpan in Tokyo. After all, they have had nearly 100 years to hone their skill in making it.

銀座

THE GINZA AND NEARBY AREAS

Tourists usually think of the Ginza area as only an expensive upscale shopping district. It surely is that and a great deal more. Many of the shops are not all that expensive, and most restaurants have reasonably priced lunches. I once gave a friend, who had less-than-no interest in the Ginza, two tours of the area. The first tour was shortly after sunrise: winding through empty side streets and alleys showing him small lanes of bars, Shintō shrines nested in niches between buildings, and unusual architecture on the main and side streets, as well as just finding interesting places to photograph tucked away here and there. The second tour focused on the interiors of various department stores and their rooftops. Several of the buildings in the Ginza have rooftops where you can sit, eat, and enjoy planted areas and small shrines dating back centuries. These shrines were often relocated to the roof from the ground when the modern building was constructed. Given the high price of real estate in the area such rooftop shrines are not unusual, but many are company or family shrines and not generally accessible, so I will not list those here. My friend ended up with a very positive view of what can be found in the Ginza.

Originally this area had been mostly underwater where the Hibiya inlet met the bay. It was filled in early in the 17th century as part of the work to establish the castle town of Edo. The neighborhood became the location of a silver mint (Ginza). Then, after the Meireki Fire of 1657, it developed into a community of artisans. In 1869 and 1872 much of the Ginza area was again razed in a fire. It was redeveloped with brick buildings and wider

THE GINZA AND NEARBY AREAS

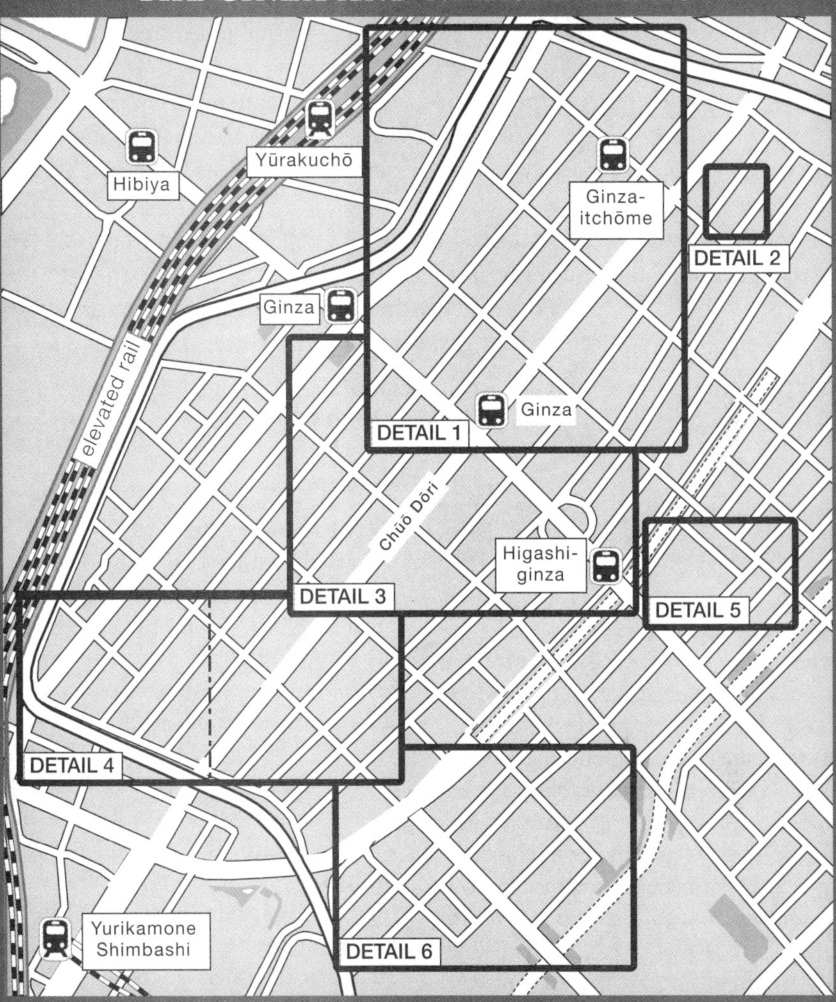

streets to not only reduce risk of fire, but also to make the area a model of modernization.

For fans of cinema, some famous sequences featuring the Ginza are in Ozu's *Tokyo Story*, when Noriko takes her in-laws to the roof of one of the department stores for a view of the city, and several shots in Naruse's *When a Woman Ascends the Stairs*.

And yes, some of the shops can be very expensive—for this reason I left a few out that I was thinking of including. This is out of courtesy to the shops; after all, if you produce a custom-tailored product that costs about $2,000–$3,000, you really don't need casual tourists wandering in.

NOTE: *Some stores have Japanese names and use Roman letters in their signage and advertising; these will not have kanji listed.*

DETAIL 1

❶ Asahi Inari Jinja 朝日稲荷神社
The entrance to this shrine is located next to an intersection. On the street level, you will see a red torii in front of a small shrine with an offering box and bell. However, the main shrine is on the roof. To reach it, take the elevator to the eighth floor and then climb the stairs. The shrine is technically connected to the earth via a pipe filled with soil. There is also an empty pipe—look up when you are at the ground level shrine to see it—and a speaker on the roof, both of which are there to convey the sounds of worshipers on ground. People pray here for prosperous business, the well-being of one's family, and better fortune.

The roof is not accessible on Sundays and holidays.

❷ Mitsukoshi Ginza 三越銀座
This is the Ginza branch of the main Mitsukoshi store in Nihonbashi. There are fifteen floors, four of which are underground. Two of those are devoted to food sales, with refrigerated coin lockers on B3. B1 has a variety of services for tourists. The top two floors are for restaurants. The ninth floor terrace is a good place to rest when the weather is nice. The terrace has a Mimeguri shrine—these are on the rooftops of all Mitsukoshi stores. There is also an interesting statue known as the Shusse Jizō, which in the early Meiji period was found by construction workers in the filled-in Sanjukken canal. The name Shusse can be translated as "appearing in the world." When the store was constructed in 1970, the Jizō was moved to the present location.
🌐 *https://www.mistore.jp/store/ginza.html*

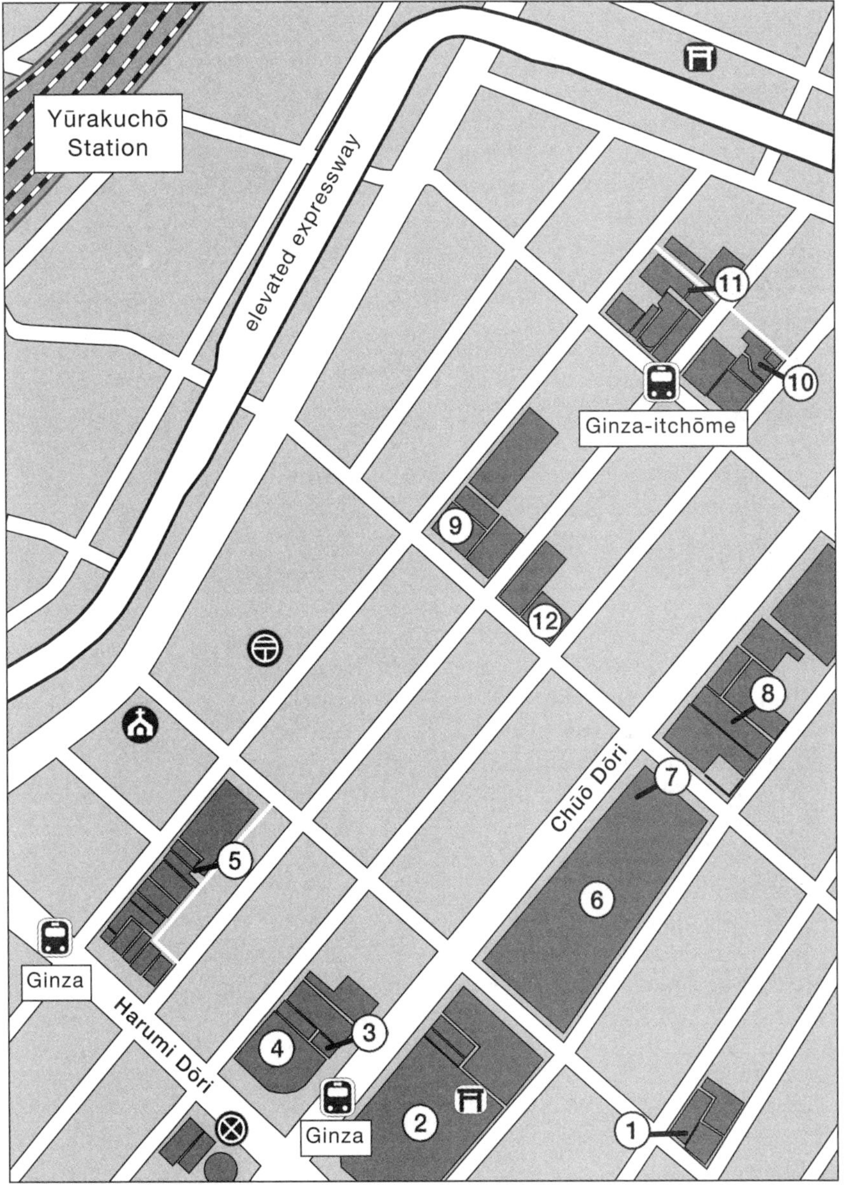
Yūrakuchō Station
elevated expressway
Ginza-itchōme
Chūō Dōri
Harumi Dōri
Ginza
Ginza
1
2
3
4
5
6
7
8
9
10
11
12

❸ Kimuraya 木村屋

This is the main branch of the first bakery in Japan, which was established in 1869 when the country was opening up to the West. Their Ginza shop opened in 1874 directly across the street from its current location. This confectionery owns the honor of having been the originator, also in 1874, of the popular treat anpan, a bread roll filled with sweet bean paste. The Emperor Meiji was fond of anpan, which greatly helped promote the product. These days they produce many different types of anpan, so you may want to try more than one. A special strain of yeast cultured from rice, which has been maintained since the beginning of the company, is used for many of their products. Besides anpan, they also bake several types of breads, melon pan, rolls, and a variety of sweet and savory treats. The bakery produces about 130 different types of products in all, some of which are only available seasonally.

There are eight floors to this location: the first is for selling baked goods, the second is the cafe, the third is the grill, the fourth is a French restaurant, and the remaining floors are offices and the bakery. Kimuraya products are also sold in many branch shops, department stores, supermarkets, and convenience stores.

🌐 *http://www.kimuraya-sohonten.co.jp*
🌐 *http://www.norenkai.net/en/portfolio-item/kimuraya-sohonten/*

❹ Wakō Department Store 和光

This building was constructed in 1932 as the Hattori Building by Hattori Kintarō, who made watches under the brand name of Seiko. There are seven stories if you count the basement. The building was constructed to be fire resistant and survived the firebombings of Tokyo in World War II. It was used as a PX for the occupying forces until 1952. As you enter, the first thing you notice is a large counter area for Seiko watches. With its iconic clock tower, the store is a landmark often used in movies to indicate that a scene is set in the Ginza, for example in *Gojira* (*Godzilla*).

🌐 *https://www.wako.co.jp/en/*

❺ Hōdō Inari Jinja 宝童稲荷神社

Originally erected sometime during the Edo period in the shōgun's castle for the protection of his children, Hōdō Inari is now a neighborhood shrine where people come to pray for protection from fire as well as for the health and education of children. Its present location is on a small pedestrian walkway with an entrance so narrow that you could easily miss it. From Renga Dōri, look for the black and gold sculpture of a monkey pointing into the walkway to the shrine. You will see a pair of monkeys once you start walking toward the shrine. The walkway is nicknamed En Musubu Sandō "Happy Monkey Avenue." The monkeys are by the sculptor Watanabe Motoka, who is known for his works with animal motifs.

❻ Matsuya Ginza 松屋銀座

Originally established in Yokohama as the Tsuruya Gofuku in 1869, the company expanded into Tokyo in 1890 with the purchase of the Matsuya Gofuku store in Imagawabashi. The word gofuku in this case refers to clothing, which is what they originally sold. The Tokyo store expanded to become the first department store in Japan 1907. In 1925 the Ginza store was opened with new features including a cafeteria and a tourist bureau, and customers no longer had to remove their shoes at the entrance. It also sadly was the location of the first highrise suicide in Japan on May 9, 1926. In 1926 the Ginza store would become the flagship store for the company. In 1929 the Ryūkō Fudōson (龍光不動尊) was enshrined on the roof. Feast days for this Fudō are the twenty-eighth of January, May, and September. Given its location, people offer prayers for success in the fashion world.

❼ Louis Vuitton Ginza

This is the main store of three LV stores in the Ginza. I am including this one for those interested in architecture. After all, why shop in a store found all over the world? The building was designed by Jun Aoki and Associates and built in 2004. The structure is basically a cube, but the exterior is truly interesting. Originally it had a different design, but in 2013 Jun Aoki and Associates was hired to redo the facade and it now sports a shell said to be inspired by the brand's Damier pattern. The edges of the pattern warp outward and inward in a series of panels of varying size that add a texture during the day and allow light out at night.

❽ Itōya 伊東屋

Itōya is one of the most famous stationery stores in Japan, in business since 1904. Look for the large red paperclip over their sign. Itōya stocks products from all over the country. Two whole floors are devoted to paper: in one area you can custom design a notebook, and another floor is themed for communication, with seats and a counter for writing letters. You can buy or borrow a pen, write, buy stamps, and mail your letter or postcard right there. An entire floor is devoted to high-quality fountain pens, including some that are hand lacquered with various traditional designs. There is even CAFE Stylo on the twelfth floor, which grows some of its vegetables on the site. Services include printing, custom engraving, repair of fountain pens, and more. There are branch stores in other parts of Tokyo and Japan as well as stands within other businesses.

🌐 *https://www.ito-ya.co.jp*

❾ Mikimoto Ginza 2 / MIKIMOTO 銀座2

A branch of the Mikimoto Ginza main store that focuses on casual pearl accessories. The building was designed by Toyo Ito and Associates and opened in 2005. The walls consist of concrete sandwiched between two layers of steel plate. There are 163 asymmetrical windows scattered across the smooth surface of the structure. The slightly pinkish walls provide the support for the entire nine-story building. Mikimoto Ginza 2 contains retail space, multipurpose floors, and restaurants.

🌐 *https://www.mikimoto.com/jp_en/ginza2-store-en*

❿ Dear Ginza

A nine-story commercial building for shops and offices designed by Amano Design Office and completed in 2013. The texture of the front of the building resembles crumpled wrapping paper. Photographers will be tempted to return several times a day since the shadows change constantly as the sun moves across the sky. At night, lights behind the perforated aluminum facade panels can be different colors, changing with the season and making the apparently opaque facade seem transparent.

⓫ Saiwai Inari Jinja 幸稲荷神社

Saiwai Inari Jinja was founded sometime in the Edo period. The current building dates from 2014 as part of a redevelopment of the area. It is a neighborhood shrine of attractive plain wood construction in a niche between buildings, located about mid-block on a narrow street between Namiki Dōri and Ginza Renga Dōri. At each entrance to the street are the New Yorker store on Namoiki Dōri and GINZA Global Style on Ginza Renga Dōri. People come here to pray for business success and domestic harmony.

⓬ V88 Building (formerly the De Beers Ginza Building)

Designed by Jun Mitsui & Associates for De Beers, the building was completed in 2008 and consists of eleven floors and two basement levels, with interior decoration done by CAPS Architecture Interior Design. The structure curves on its front very much like a wave. On the side street, alternating long windows divided by stone create a "glitter" effect on sunny days. In 2009 the building won the Japan Stainless Steel Association Prize.

DETAIL 2

❶ Okuno Building 奥野ビル

This building was designed by Kawamoto Ryōichi and completed in 1932, with a new wing added in 1934. Originally there were six stories, making it

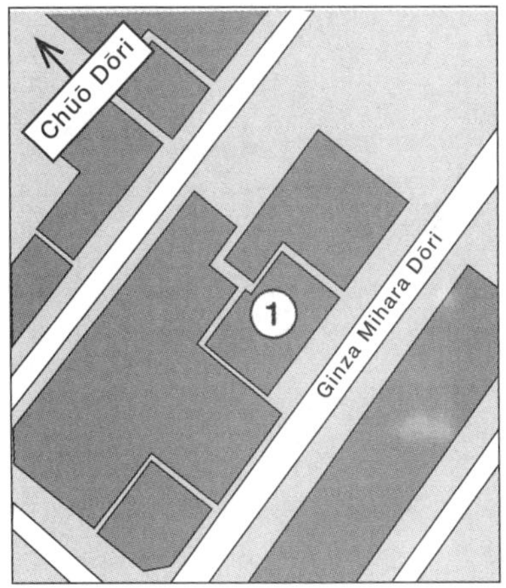

one of the tallest buildings in the area. A seventh story was added later. This was the first apartment building in the Ginza to have an elevator. The elevator is manually operated and still in service—be sure to pay attention to the instructions if you use it. Today the building consists of small shops and galleries. One interesting detail is that the original flooring is still in use, making it something of a time capsule. The building survived the firebombings of Tokyo in World War II and is the second oldest building in the Ginza. The building shows its age, being rather worn; repairs are done when they need to be. I find the Okuno Building to be a pleasant contrast to the polished shiny Ginza of the other buildings.

DETAIL 3

❶ **Ginza Six / G Six** ギンザシックス
This massive complex, designed by Taniguchi Yoshio, was built in 2017 by merging two blocks, one quarter of which had been occupied by the Matsuzakaya department store. The resulting building houses some 240 shops, making this the largest commercial complex in the Ginza. Of note is the shop of Jotaro Saito, the famous kimono designer, who produces gorgeous works. His shop, on the fourth floor, also has a cafe. Fine kimonos are something you rarely buy off the rack, so the store has great displays of fabrics to choose from. For serious photographers, the fifth floor has a Leica camera shop. Browsing the tastefully displayed items for, it feels like you are in an art gallery, or perhaps a high-end jewelry shop. There is also an exhibit space for photographs. The sixth floor has what is most dangerous for my pocketbook: Tsutaya Books. Unlike some bookstores, English and Japanese books are shelved together by topic, so browse and ask the helpful staff. I plan ahead and bring printouts of titles published in Japan that I am looking for. There are so many books that not everything is on the shelves. The whole building is bracketed between the 480-seat Kanze Nō theater in the third basement and a large rooftop garden, which is accessible on most days from 7:00 a.m. to 11:00 p.m. The rooftop garden has

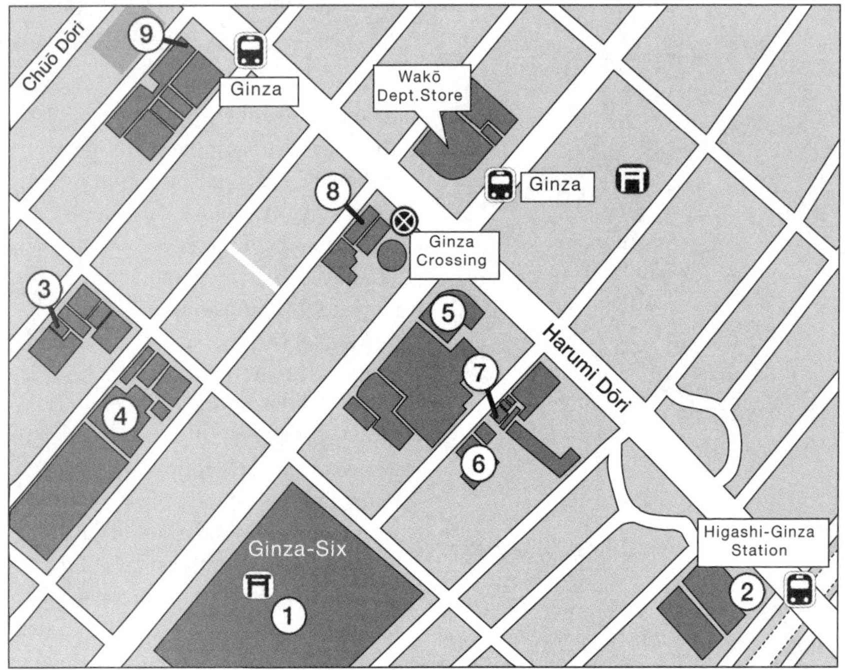

great views of that part of the Ginza. The roof also houses Kakugo Inari Jinja (霍護稲荷神社). This small shrine was established in 1815 and had previously been on the rooftop of the Matsuzakaya department store. People pray there for protection from fire.

Ginza 6:

🌐 *https://ginza6.tokyo.e.abf.hp.transer.com*

Jotaro Saito:

🌐 *http://jotaro.net/ginza/*

Leica:

🌐 *https://en.leica-camera.com/Stores-Dealers/Leica-Stores-Worldwide/Leica-Store-Ginza-Six*

Tsutaya Books:

🌐 *https://store.tsite.jp/ginza/english/*

❷ Ōnoya 大野屋

A maker and seller of custom-made traditional tabi socks established sometime in the 1770s. They also sell tenugui and clothing items. They moved to the current location in 1849, and the present building dates from the Taishō period. Their location near the Kabukiza is a good one for them, as tabi are worn by kabuki actors and by many audience members who attend the theater in kimono.

🌐 *https://www.oonoyasohonten.jp*

❸ Kūya 空也

A maker and seller of only one type of traditional confection: monaka, sweet azuki bean paste sandwiched between two crunchy oval wafers. Everything is made in the shop and there is no mail order service. This product is so popular that at times you need to pre-order a week or so in advance to get a box of this inexpensive treat. Usually it is possible to buy without a pre-order, but it is best to do so early in the day. The first store opened in Ueno in 1884, where it quickly gained fame by being mentioned in many literary works of the time. After the first store was burned out in World War II, they reopened in the Ginza in 1949.

❹ Ginza Komatsu Miwa Jinja 銀座小松三輪神社

In 1992, a branch of Ōmiwa Jinja in Nara was installed in a rooftop garden of the Komatsu West building. This shrine is sometimes referred to as Tenkū Jinja "Shrine in the Sky." Originally it was installed as a shrine for the business; around 2011 the shrine and garden were renewed and made publicly accessible. To access the shrine you have to go to the seventh floor of the building and take an external stairway to the roof. The wood, stones, and plants for the shrine and garden were carefully chosen to have connections with religious and Feng Shui traditions.

🌐 *http://www.ginza-komatsu.co.jp/en/blog/archives/466*

🌐 *http://www.ginza-komatsu.co.jp/en/blog/archives/118*

❺ Nissan Crossing

Designed by Eight Inc. for Nissan and completed in 2016. The exterior has a white mesh-like pattern that curves and elongates as the building rises. At night moving patterns are projected on the windows adding to the unique visuals of the building.

The street level has regularly changing displays of concept cars as well as classic and racing models. The second level has a digital touch screen wall where you can explore Nissan's history. It also has the Crossing Cafe, where you can choose to top off your latte with an image from a variety of a Nissan vehicles or from your own photo. That level also has the Nissan Boutique, where Nissan-themed goods are sold along with detailed miniature replicas of cars. They even have tenugui and face masks available for the health conscious.

❻ Kikunoya 菊廼舎

Operating since 1890, the main store is now located one block east of Chūō Dōri on the first floor of the Ginza Azuma Building. Kikunoya is a maker of finely crafted dry and moist tea sweets in both old and modern styles. As is traditional with tea sweets, many items and designs are changed seasonally. While the moist sweets need to be

▲ The approach to Toyoiwa Inari Jinja, accessed by narrow walkways between buildings.

▲ The large Shusse Jizō on the roof of Mitsukoshi Ginza.

▲ The morning lights plays on the exterior of the main Louis Vuitton store in the Ginza.

▲ The iconic Wako department store and the Ginza Crossing intersection seen from the rooftop garden of the Ginza Six building.

consumed in a day or two, the many dry treats would make great gifts with their attractive packaging. The wrapping papers used by the store are seasonal, or one can get a general design for congratulatory gifts in traditional white and red.

There are also branch stores in various parts of the Tokyo area.

🌐 *https://www.ginza-kikunoya.co.jp*

❼ Azuma Inari Daimyōjin あづま稲荷大明神

After World War II, this part of the Ginza suffered from several fires. The neighborhood determined that there had once been an Inari shrine here and built this shrine on Miharakōji (三原小路), an alley just off Mihara Dōri. This stone-paved pedestrian street is lined with potted plants and has bamboo and wood construction along much of it. Since the shrine was established, there have been no fires in the area. An association of twenty-eight shops along the street supports the shrine, where people pray for protection from fire.

❽ Ginza Akebono 銀座あけぼの

A small confectionery that has been making and selling a large variety of modern and traditional sweets and rice crackers since 1948. You can purchase packaged items or choose freshly made ones from the counter. Some products, like the ichigo daifuku (strawberry mochi), are very perishable, so you should eat them the day you purchase them. Go ahead and be a little greedy and get extra. There are also seasonal items and packaging, so if you are a frequent visitor to Tokyo you may find things you have not seen before. Most depachika (department store basement food halls) have branches selling their products, so you can also find them outside the Ginza.

🌐 *http://www.ginza-akebono.co.jp*

❾ Maison Hermès メゾンエルメス

Of course this French high fashion line has a store in the Ginza, this one in a building built in 2001. The front is narrow but the lot is very deep, with additional entrances on the side. The eleven-story building, designed by Renzo Piano, is encased in large glass bricks. At night, the entire building lights up like a lantern. The main entrance is framed by two display windows, and the artists commissioned for the displays are given credit on the store's website. The building is directly accessible from Ginza Station. The first four floors are devoted to retail space. The eighth floor houses Le Forum for art exhibits, which, while usually free, may have an admittance charge. The tenth floor houses Le Studio, a private forty-seat cinema; reservations are required but admission is free.

DETAIL 4

❶ Kumagaya Inari Jinja
熊谷稲荷神社

This neighborhood shrine was rebuilt in early 2018 and moved to the present location. Historical records indicate this was the fourth location of this shrine in the immediate neighborhood. The small shrine proper is older than the rest of the site. It has a black roof, and the stand, offering box, walls, and torii are newer and made of plain wood. Two old stone foxes guard the shrine area just inside the torii, and two smaller ones are on either side of the shrine.

❷ Cheepa's Cafe チーパズカフェ
Cheepa's Gallery チーパズギャラリー

Two parts of the MYS Ginza building:

Cheepa's Cafe occupies the first two floors. The second floor is available for parties and is therefore not always accessible. The cafe is a simple spot to take a break. Well, not so simple—on both floors there is a large display of toys from the Shōwa era to the present.

Cheepa's Gallery on the third floor is famous for hosting exhibits dealing with literature, manga, anime, and other visual arts. Depending on the exhibit, the cafe may even do related designs in chocolate on your cappuccino: imagine being handed an ephemeral artwork with an image of Godzilla or Captain Harlock.

🌐 *http://mys-ginza.com/cafe/*

❸ Café de l'Ambre / Kafe do Ramburu カフェ・ド・ランブル

You may have not heard of this lovely small coffee shop, but it is famous among those in the industry. It was founded in 1948 by Sekiguchi Ichiro, who had been told by his coworkers that his coffee was so good that he should open his own shop. Each cup is individually brewed. While this is not that unusual in Japan—they even individually brew chilled coffee—what makes this shop different is the dedication they put into it. They not only grind the coffee for each cup, they even roast their own beans. The owner continued to do this himself until he passed away at 104. Café de l'Ambre breaks many rules of coffee making, rules that apparently had little basis in reality, as the resulting beverage is wonderful. For example, they age beans, long considered a very bad thing to do. Just after the war, they were able to get a batch of five-year-old beans on the black market, and the coffee made from it turned out to be excellent. Through experimentation they found which coffees age well and which do not. The owner was originally an engineer, so he modified his coffeemaking equipment, and even patented some designs, to produce a better cup.

Warning: smoking is allowed here.

🌐 *http://www.cafedelambre.com*

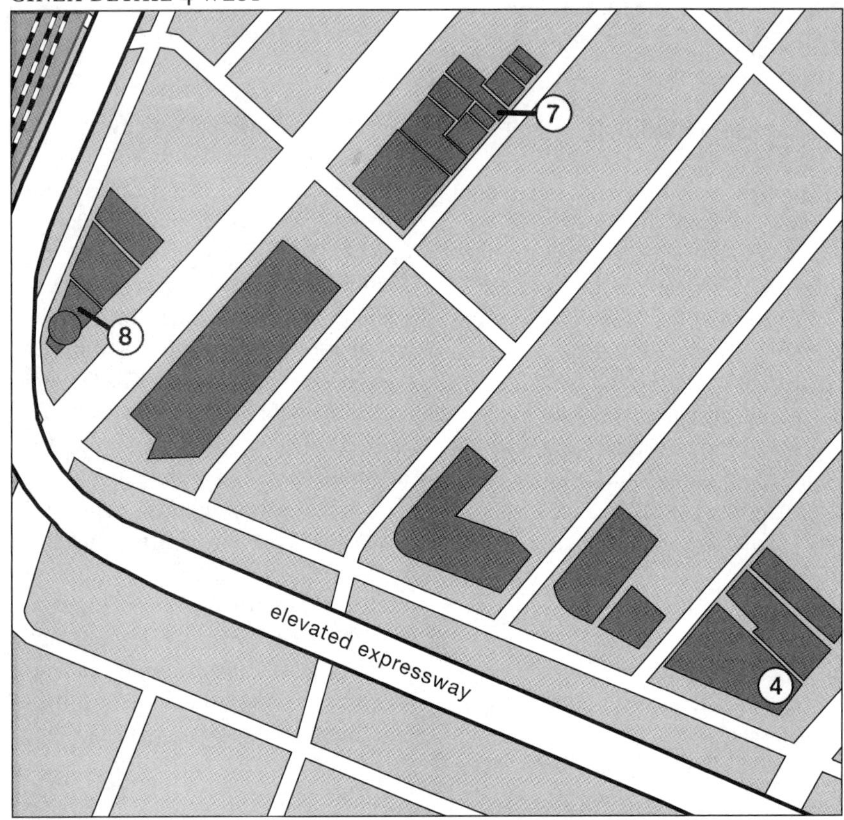

❹ Hakuhinkan Toy Park
博品館トイパーク

An excellent multistory toy shop in business since 1982. There are eight floors in the building, four for the retail space and the eighth for a theater. The merchandise ranges from the most modern high-tech toys to traditional wooden ones. They carry more than just toys for kids, though there is a massive amount of those to choose from. Adults can find unusual smartphone cases, accessory cases with amusing designs, an excellent selection of hanafuda cards, and more. The selection of dolls is large, and there are stuffed toys, character goods, educational toys, board games, puzzles, and even a slot car racetrack. I picked up a couple of interesting things there: a hanafuda card deck with yōkai designed by famous manga artist Mizuki Shigeru, and a cell phone strap in the shape of a Kewpie doll dressed up as Lum from the Urusei Yatsura manga and anime.

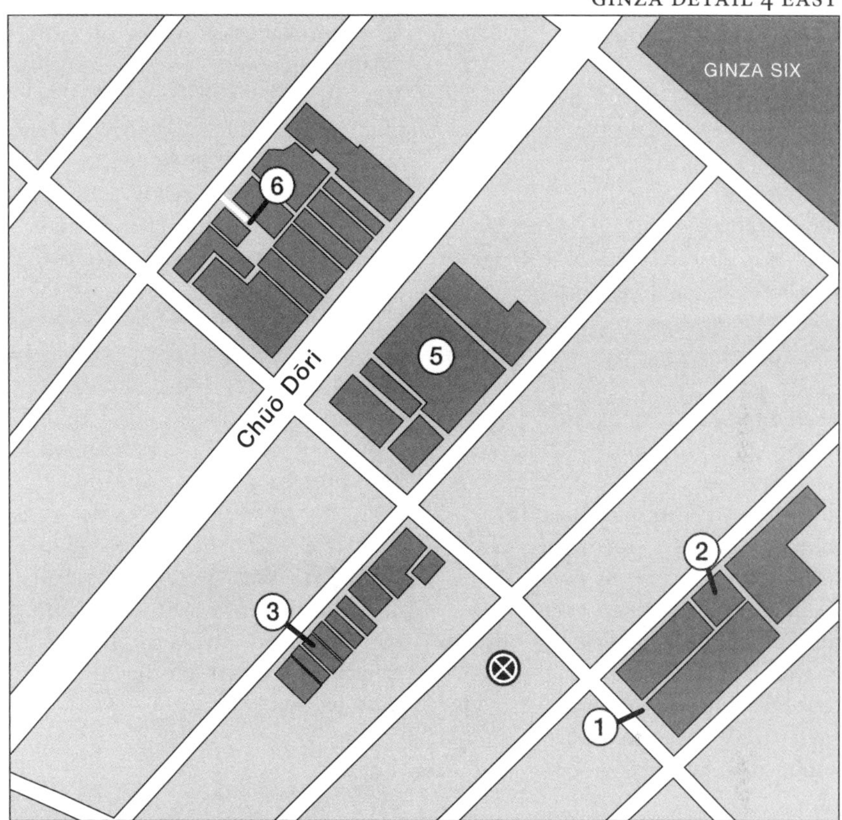

They also have branches at several airports in Japan. Show your passport for tax-free purchases over 5,000 yen.
🌐 *http://www.hakuhinkan.co.jp/toypark/*

❺ **Yamaha Ginza** ヤマハ銀座
This entry is for music lovers and musicians: Yamaha Ginza is a music department store. The flagship store of the Yamaha music company has fourteen stories devoted to musical instruments, sheet music, books, CDs, a music academy, concert hall and concert salon, and in the basement, a live house (a club for live music). Designed by the Nikken Sekkei company, the gold leaf laminated glass of the facade reflects light in a series of panes in a diagonal grid. This diagonal pattern is repeated inside the store in several places. There is direct access from the Ginza subway line's Ginza Station.
🌐 *https://www.yamahamusic.jp/shop/ginza*

❻ Toyoiwa Inari Jinja 豊岩稲荷神社

While the dates of the founding are unclear, legend has it that this shrine dates back to the 16th century and was established by a vassal of Akechi Mitsuhide shortly before he had his home built here. Located in a narrow walkway between buildings, it can easily be missed. Even in the middle of the day the area is in deep shadow, and as you look deeper into it, you see it is lit by a series of traditional hanging lanterns. In the late 19th century, kabuki actor Ichimura Uzaemon would pray here for success in his productions. This tradition continues, as many people from the theater do so even today. People also come here to pray for luck in romance and marriage. The best way to approach this shrine is from the northwest off Suzuran Dōri. Look for an upright stone with red lettering at the entrance to the alley.

❼ Hachikan Jinja 八官神社

In the late 17th century this shrine was moved to this location by the Lord of the Akashi castle in Banshū. At that time the shrine was called Kokuhō Inari Jinja. In 1869 the kami of another local shrine, Kagahime Inari, was moved to Kokuhō Inari, so the shrine became the tutelary shrine of the Hachikanchō neighborhood. The present name was given to the shrine in 1924.

❽ Shizuoka Press and Broadcasting Center / Shizuoka Shinbun Shizuoka Hōsō Biru 静岡新聞静岡放送ビル

Built in 1968, this is another unusual building for those interested in architecture to appreciate. It houses the local offices of a news company in Shizuoka.

This is a famous work designed by the architect Tange Kenzō, who was a mentor to the Metabolist movement and incorporated some of their ideas in the structure. The building is an unusual one, with its central column containing elevators and a stairwell. The thirteen offices then protrude from this central mass. The design is such that additional office modules could be added; however it still has the same number as when the building was completed. The vertically-oriented structure makes effective use of its small triangular lot.

DETAIL 5

❶ Kabuki Inari Jinja 歌舞伎稲荷神社

Sometimes referred to as Kabuki Inari Daimyōjin, originally this shrine was in the Kabukiza garden and not accessible to the public. When the Kabukiza theater was rebuilt, the shrine was moved to the present location to the right of the building, close to exit 3 of the Higashi Ginza Station. While taking photos one day, I waited for when there were no worshipers in front of the shrine; then a group of theater people came out of the subway station to pray. I just waited a few minutes longer.

❷ Kabukiza 歌舞伎座

Japan's principal kabuki theater. The Kabukiza opened in 1889 in a Western-style building that reflected the modern sensibilities characteristic of the time. In 1911 it was redecorated in an elaborate traditional Japanese style. The theater burned down in 1921, and the partially-rebuilt structure again burned down after the Great Kantō Earthquake. The theater was again rebuilt in 1925, only to burn again in the firebombings of World War II. Rebuilt in 1951, it provided a place for performances until 2010 when it was demolished and rebuilt due to concerns regarding the stability of the foundation. The new theater, which strongly resembles the old one, opened in 2013.
🌐 *http://www.kabuki-za.co.jp*

***TIPS:** If you plan to watch a play, consider renting a G-marc Guide for captioning of the performance.*
For a short taste of kabuki, you can buy a ticket for a single act near the entrance shortly before the play begins. It is best to bring binoculars or rent a pair in the theater, as the one-act seats are in the nosebleed section, high up in the upper balcony seating.

❷ Kobikichō Square / Kobikichō Hiroba 木挽町広場

Located in the B2 level of the Kabukiza basement since 2013, this is an underground shopping arcade with a variety of restaurants, shops, and stalls selling kabuki-themed items and souvenirs. You can find T-shirts, tenugui, postcards, cosmetic face masks, sweets in kabuki-themed tins, cloth shopping bags, and more. The last time I was there with a friend, we picked up a couple of English-language books on kabuki and looked over the video selection in one of the shops. The square is directly connected to the Higashi Ginza subway station—use exit 3.

❸ Kabukiza Gallery
歌舞伎座ギャラリー

The reconstruction of the Kabukiza theater also involved the construction of the Kabukiza Tower behind the theater. On the fifth floor there is the Kabukiza Gallery, where for a small fee you can see special exhibits, view costumes, and sit on a stage. You can also look at and handle some of the props and sound effect devices. Also on the fifth floor there is a terrace garden with a view of the theater's roof, a store with various kabuki related items including video discs, a photo studio, and a tea shop to sit and rest.
🌐 *https://www.kabukiweb.net/about/service/kabukiza_gallery.html*

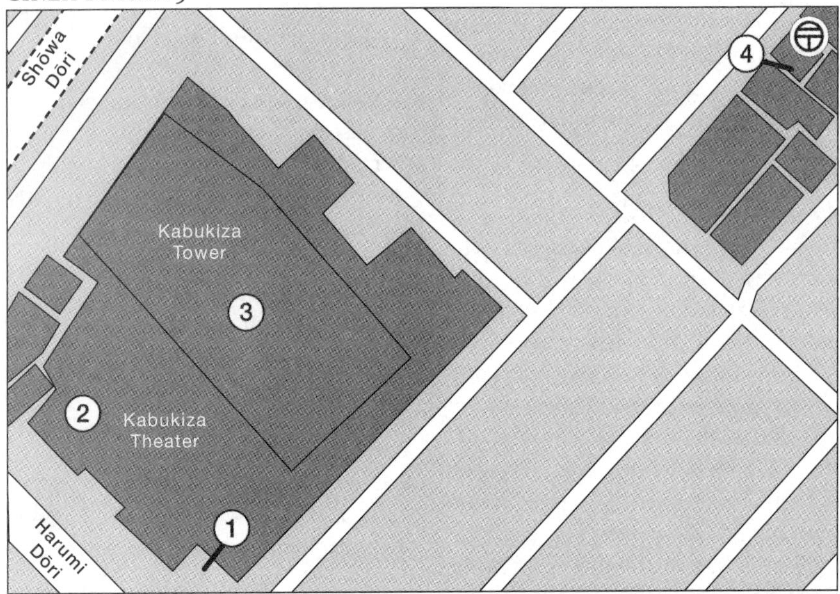

❹ Hōju Inari Jinja 宝珠稲荷神社
Established in 1706 as the home shrine for the daimyō Itakura Shigemasa, today this is one of the larger shrines in the Ginza area and is the tutelary shrine of its neighborhood. It is easy to spot as it is a full-fledged shrine with priest's residence and office. It is not far from the Kabukiza, near a post office, with stone komainu and a red torii marking the entrance.

DETAIL 6

❶ Shōwadōri Ginza hodōkyō / Showa-dori Ginza Pedestrian Bridge (Tokimeki Bridge)
昭和通り銀座歩道橋(ときめき橋)
This entry is for a pedestrian bridge built in 1997. Now, such bridges are found all over Tokyo to allow people to cross major roadways above the flow of traffic, so why include such a structure? This one is a little different, most such bridges are utilitarian structures with one set of stairs on each side, crossing from one side of a busy boulevard to another and about the width of a regular sidewalk. This bridge is much wider than most, crosses a major

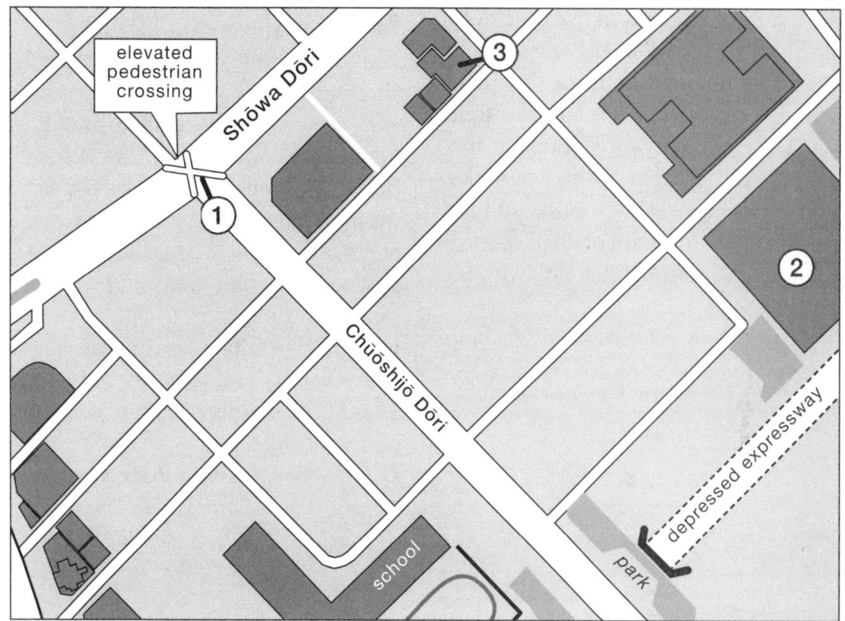

highway and a side street, and has an X shape with stairs at four corners of an intersection allowing pedestrians to cross in several directions including diagonally, it also has elevators and escalators that operate during the day. The corners even have areas which are planted with some shrubs adding a bit of greenery to the structure. The unique design of this bridge makes it a landmark, and it has been a location for scenes in movies and TV, both on the bridge and from street level. The bridge is nicknamed the "Ginza Tokimeki-bashi": "Ginza Heartthrob Bridge."

❷ Shinbashi Enbujō 新橋演舞場
Originally run by the Shinbashi Enbujō Joint Stock Corporation, this theater was built in 1925 as a place to allow geisha to perform in public. The police had banned such performances in 1905, so permission had to be sought before the theater was built. When the spring and autumn dance performances were over, the theater would be rented out for other events. In 1934 the theater was leased to Shōchiku for kabuki performances, and in 1940 it was taken over by Shōchiku. The theater burned down in the World War II bombings and was rebuilt in 1948 for kabuki and geisha dance performances. In 1981 the Nissan New Building

with sixteen stories and five basements opened on the site. This new building still contains the theater, which is mainly used for performances of shinpa, a Meiji-era style of dramatic theater. It is also used for kabuki, bunraku, and traditional dance. Geisha still put on an annual program of dance performances, maintaining that link with the past.

🌐 *https://www.kabukiweb.net/theatres/shinbashi/*

❸ **Yasuda Shōkeidō** 安田松慶堂

The main shop of a small, prestigious chain specializing in making, selling and repairing handcrafted Buddhist home altars since 1792. They also sell Buddhist statues, incense, sect-specific rosaries, memorial tablets with name engraving, and items for the altars. Designs range from traditional to very modern. There are usually between 150 and 170 altars on display, made with a variety of woods. They also have branch operations in many major department stores.

🌐 *http://www.yasuda-shokeido.co.jp*

🌐 *http://www.norenkai.net/en/portfolio-item/yasuda-shokeido/*

白山・小石川

HAKUSAN/KOISHIKAWA AREA

Koishikawa was a separate ward of Tokyo until 1947 when it was merged with Hongō to form Bunkyō Ward. The principal attractions here are the large gardens that were once daimyō property and variety of temples and shrines with interesting historical connections. The area is hilly. Arriving at Hauksan station, you may want to start your stroll with the Koishikawa Botanical Garden, moving southward so that the rest will be mainly downhill.

DETAIL 1

❶ Enjōji 圓乘寺

In *Five Women Who Loved Love* by Ihara Saikaku, there is an account of an unfortunate young woman connected with this temple. Oshichi was the daughter of a greengrocer whose family had temporarily evacuated to the temple after a fire. There she fell in love with a young novice priest. Later, in the hope of being reunited with him, she tried to set fire to the family home and was caught. The punishment for arson at that time was being burned alive and she was duly executed by that means. Next to her memorial stone is a statue of Jizō, where flowers and incense are commonly left. She gained much sympathy and her story can be found in plays, stories, and woodblock prints. In Hiroshige's print series *The Hundred Poets Compared*, poem number 45 by Fujiwara no Koretada is accompanied by an image of Oshichi.

❷ Hakusan Jinja 白山神社

This shrine was established in 948 and moved to this location in 1655. It is not particularly flashy; rather this is the

HAKUSAN/KOISHIKAWA AREA

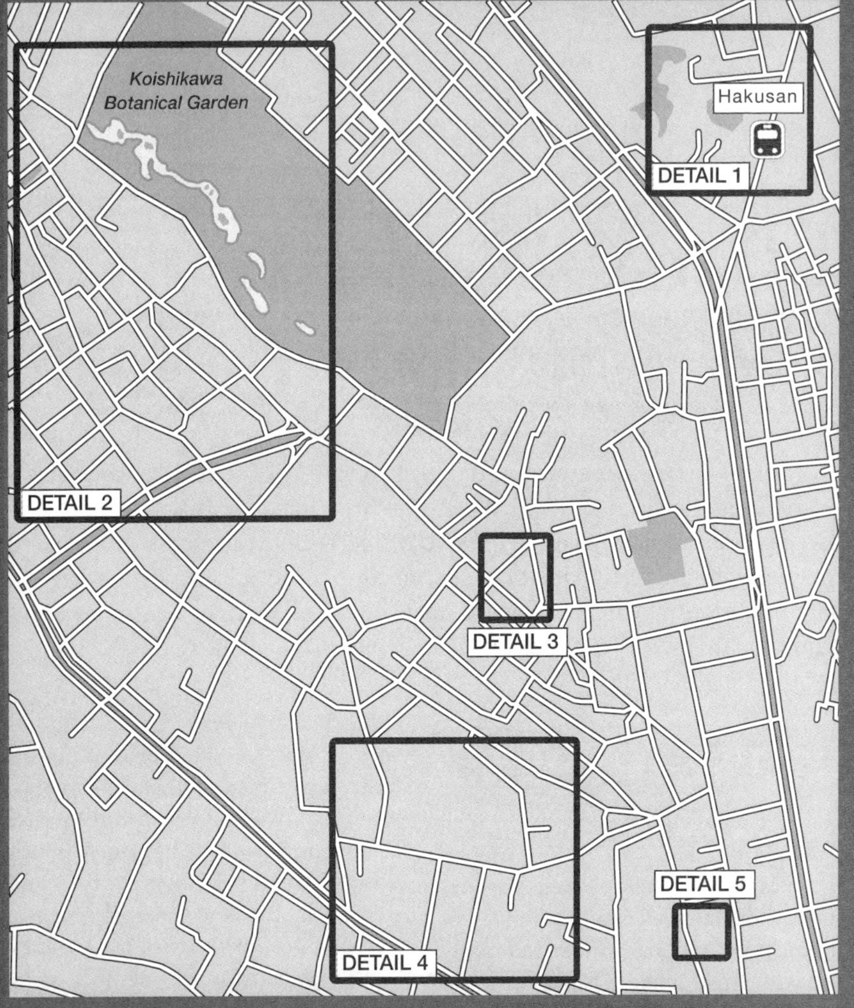

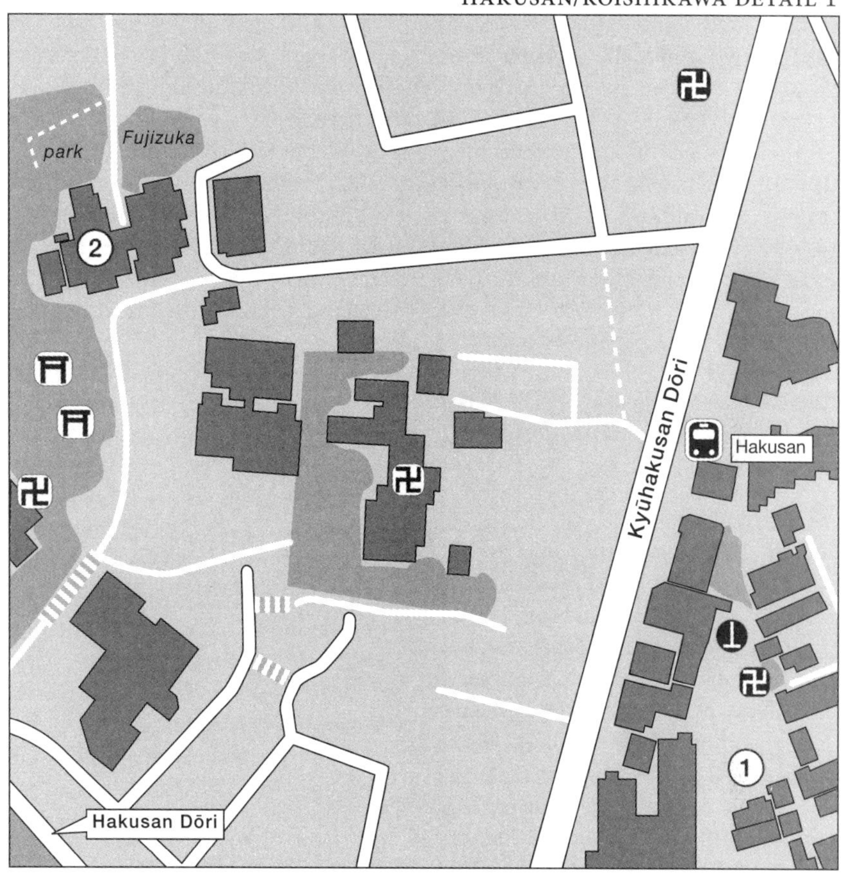

kind of simpler place with a certain elegance that I enjoy visiting in Japan. The main hall has some nice carvings. It is particularly known among flower lovers for its hydrangeas and in mid-June holds a major hydrangea festival. Behind the shrine, next to Hakusan Park, is a nice fujizuka in a gated enclosure. When I first visited, the gate was locked and other visitors had left coins as offerings on the gate. Kikurihime is enshrined here and people pray here for luck in marriage. For some reason, during the Edo period the shrine also became a place to pray from relief from toothaches. Even now, people can leave their old toothbrushes in a box during the hydrangea festival and a memorial service will be held for them. A non-religious point of note is that the shrine is popular with neighborhood cats (well, for some it could be religious). There is also a statue of Sun Yat-sen, who is said to have seen Halley's comet from the shrine and been inspired in his revolutionary ideals.

The shrine is in the middle of a dense neighborhood with many small streets and walkways. Main access is from the east and south. You can also enter from the small park just north of the shrine.

DETAIL 2

❶ Sōkeiji 宗慶寺

This Jōdoshū temple lies in a white, three-story building with red trim on the beams and a green roof, placed very close to the street. This was the family temple of Chaa no Tsubone, a concubine of Tokugawa Ieyasu who gave birth to his sixth son, Matsudaira Tadateru. As would be expected, Chaa no Tsubone is buried here. There is a famous spring, no longer flowing, on the grounds, known as Gokurakusui "Water of Paradise." Jurōjin is also enshrined here and it is on the local Shichifukujin pilgrimage.

The entrance is on the southeast side.

❷ Harimazaka 播磨坂

A wide sloping section of road with a large center divider that has twin pedestrian pathways running down it. Harimazaka is famous for its cherry blossoms: the road has roughly 150 trees on either side and a third row in the middle of the center divider. These were planted in 1960 as part of a works project on the slope. During the cherry blossom season, one of the pathways on the center divider becomes an area for people to place mats and have viewing parties. At the top end of the slope you are one block from the Koishikawa Botanical Garden. The name comes from when the lords of Harima had a compound nearby.

❸ Tarō Inari Jinja 太郎稲荷神社

A very small Inari shrine located in the Koishikawa Botanical Garden, slightly up slope from a pond and along a path in the southwest portion of the garden. The shrine is wooden with a tile roof. There is an easy-to-spot stone torii along the trail, at the head of the stone-lined pathway that leads up to the shrine.

❹ Koishikawa Botanical Garden / Koishikawa Shokubutsuen 小石川植物園

This garden was originally a tsukiyama-style (hill-style) garden established by the Mito-han branch of the Tokugawa family in 1629. The Koishikawa Medicinal Herb Garden was established on the grounds in 1684 by Tokugawa Tsunayoshi to study the cultivation and extraction of medicines.

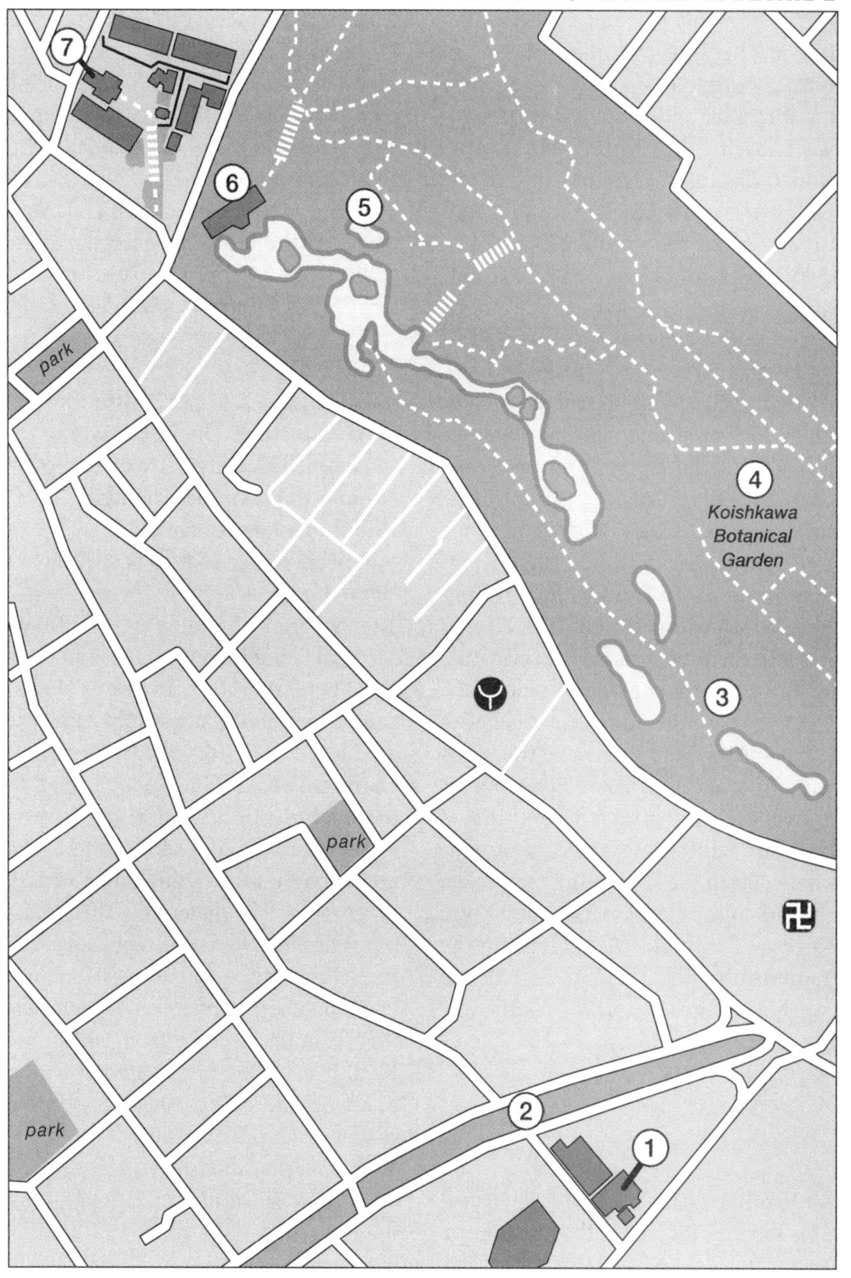
7
6
5
park
4
Koishkawa
Botanical
Garden
3
park
2
park
1

It had been his place of residence before he became the fifth shōgun. In 1722, a hospital was established here for the poor upon the urging of Ogawa Shōsen. This is also where Aoki Konyō did his successful experiments with sweet potatoes in the 18th century to see if they could be grown in colder parts of Japan. In 1877, the administration of the garden was transferred to the University of Tokyo; it is presently operated as a research facility by the Graduate School of Science. There are some 4,000 species of plants growing in the garden. You can purchase an English map at the entrance. Just past the garden office is an apple tree that was a gift of the United Kingdom in 1964. The tree was grown from a graft of Newton's famous tree. Next to it is a trellis with a grapevine propagated from the rootstock of a plant used by Gregor Mendel in his plant genetics experiments. That grapevine was a gift from Austria-Hungary in 1913. There is a Japanese garden with a pond that is popular with painters and photographers. Given the large number of trees, the fall colors are worth checking out. Kurosawa's film *Red Beard* is set in the garden's hospital.

The entrance is near the south-west corner of the gardens.

🌐 *http://www.bg.s.u-tokyo.ac.jp/koishikawa/eng/*

❺ Jirō Inari Jinja 次郎稲荷神社

This shrine is located in the Koishikawa Botanical Garden, upslope from the Japanese garden—cross the bridge, turn left, and head uphill. The shrine placed against the hillside is very small and made of metal. It is filled with small ceramic foxes left as offerings by worshipers. The shrine itself is hard to see from the trail—look for the stone torii at the head of the path made of stepping stones that leads to it.

❻ Koishikawa Annex, Museum of Architecture, The University Museum, The University of Tokyo / Tōkyō-daigaku sōgō kenkyū Hakubutsukan Koishikawa bun'in 東京大学総合研究博物館小石川分館

The old main building of the Tokyo Medical School, built in 1876 and relocated here from the University's Hongō campus in 1969, is next to the Japanese garden of the Koishikawa Botanical Garden. The building was not open to the public until 2001. Starting in 2013 it was reorganized to house miniature architectural models and and a variety of ethnological materials. The building is designated as an Important Cultural Property. Admission is free and it is possible to enter the museum either from the street or from within the Koishikawa Botanical Garden via a one-way gate. There is no access to the garden from the museum.

🌐 *http://www.um.u-tokyo.ac.jp/architectonica/index_en.html*

NOTE: The museum is closed Mondays, Tuesdays, and Wednesdays unless those are national holidays. It is also closed during the summer and year-end holidays.

❼ Hikawa Jinja 簸川神社

The roof of the worship hall of Hikawa Jinja is ornamented with chigi—crossed beams at the ends of the rooflines—and katsuogi, which resemble logs laid perpendicular to the ridgeline. These are older architectural elements that trace back to the Jōmon period. Hikawa Jinja shrines are popular—there are fifty-nine in Tokyo. The main shrine is located in Ōmiya, north of Tokyo. The slope Hikawazaka (簸川坂) runs on the west side of the shrine grounds. The honden of Hikawa Jinja is close to the slope, so you can get a view of the back and one side of it from the street. This Hikawa Jinja is not to be confused with the one in *Sailor Moon*. Actually I should say the two, as the shrine in the manga is based on a different Hikawa Jinja than the one in the anime; both of those are in Minato Ward.

The kami enshrined here is Susanoo no Mikoto. The entrance is to the south.

DETAIL 3

❶ Nensokuji 念速寺

The temple itself is rather ordinary; however the graveyard includes the grave of an interesting woman. Mikijo was the first person in Japan to will her body for medical research. Years earlier her father was ill and to make ends meet, she signed a contract to become a prostitute, something considered a self-sacrificial act of filial piety in the past. As a result of her trade she contracted syphilis, and shortly before her death she donated her body to medical science. At the time such a thing would have been unheard of and we have no idea why she did this. The back of the gravestone has a message of thanks from the Tokyo Medical School doctors who studied her body. The grave is in the middle of the back wall of the graveyard; the only characters you can still read on the front are 美幾, Miki. The gravestone is protected in a plastic case and there is a signboard behind the stone indicating that it is her grave. The plastic case is open at the lower end of the front so flowers, incense, and offerings can be left.

The entrance to Nensokuji is to the east.

▲ The Koishikawa Annex of the University of Tokyo Museum, standing since the Meiji.

▲ The main gate of Denzūin, with the triple hollyhock leaf crest of the Tokugawa clan.

▼ Hakusan Jinja on a quiet weekday morning still has worshipers visiting.

▲ The Zenkōjizaka Mukunoki Tree: There are stone benches nearby to stop for a rest.

HAKUSAN/KOISHIKAWA DETAIL 3

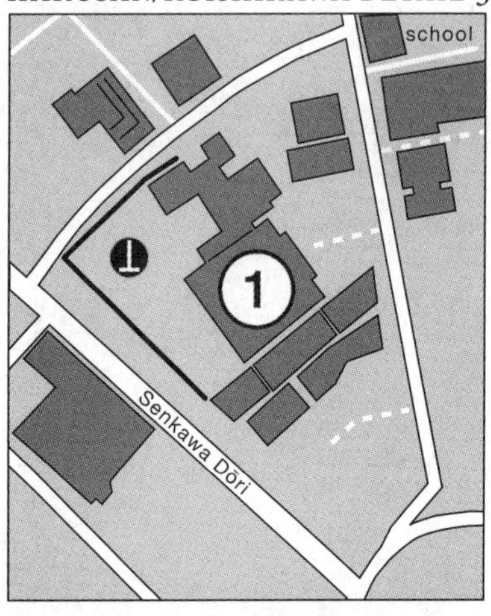

DETAIL 4

❶ Mansei 萬盛

This sobaya goes back to at least the early 17th century. The entrance is located between a convenience store and an apartment building entrance. The sign has the same symbol of a wish-granting gem flanked by stylized, curved rice stalks as Takuzōsu Inari Jinja. There is a legend that the monk Takuzōsu was fond of soba and regularly visited Mansei. The shopkeeper became curious as to why there would often be a leaf in the cash box at the end of those days. He followed the monk after a meal and saw him disappear into the Inari shrine. The story has been passed down in the family to this day, and they offer a fresh portion of each day's first soba at Jigenin, the temple that the shrine is part of.

❷ Zenkōjizaka Mukunoki Tree 善光寺坂のムクノキ

This tree is estimated to be about 400 years old and is said to be visited by Inari from Takuzōsu Inari Jinja. At one time the tree was set to be cut down for road expansion, but the objections of the neighborhood resulted in it being spared. The tree was damaged in World War II but has survived. Nearby was the former residence of two well-known 20th-century novelists, Kōda Rohan and his daughter Kōda Aya.

❸ Takuzōsu Inari Jinja 澤蔵司稲荷 and Jigenin 慈限院

This shrine was established in 1620 and is part of the same complex as the Jōdoshū temple Jigenin. The two are under the same administration, a rare example of a Buddhist temple and Shintō shrine that were not separated in the Meiji period. The main temple hall was last rebuilt in 1956 and houses an Eleven Headed Kannon statue. On the grounds there is a stone with inscription by Bashō, who once rested at the temple when he was involved with maintenance of the Kanda waterworks. Enshrined in Takuzōsu Inari Jinja are Inari and Takuzōsu. Takuzōsu was a brilliant monk who had studied at the nearby Denzūin, mastering many teachings in only a few years. At

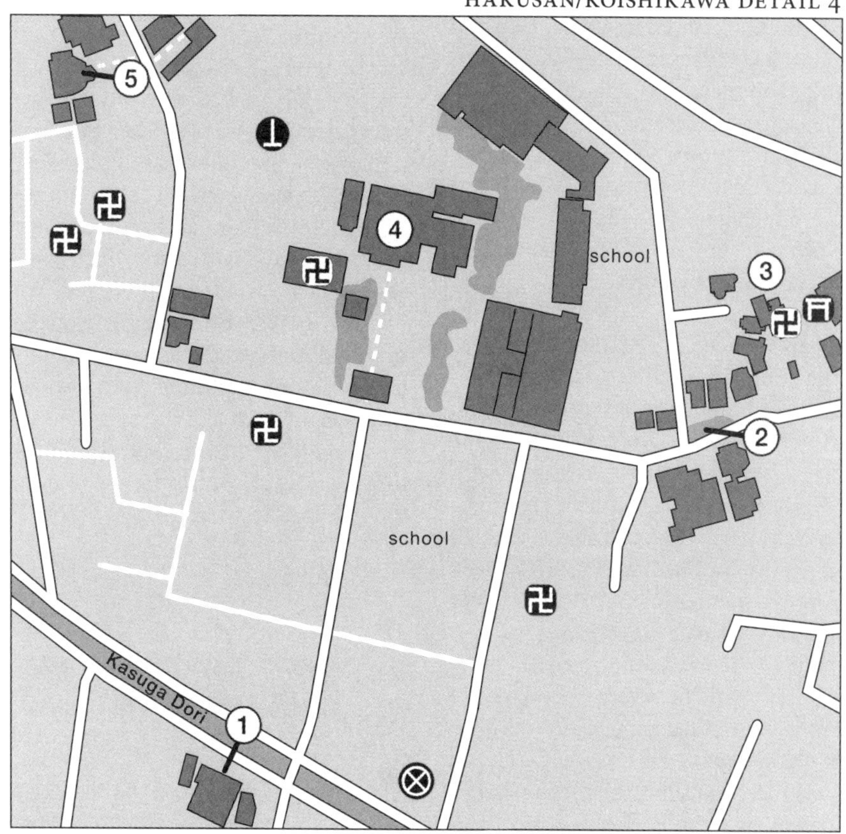

one point Takuzōsu appeared to the head priest of Denzūin in a dream and explained that he was an incarnation of Inari, and so the shrine came to be built.

The shrine, or cluster of shrines, is on a hillside to the right of the temple and includes a small cave where a white fox is said to have a den. The site has a good number of trees and is often in shadow; it must be a cool place to visit on hot summer days. Nagai Kafū also mentioned Takuzōsu Inari Jinja in his story "The Fox."

The entrance is to the south.

🌐 *http://takuzousuinari.com*

❹ Denzūin 傳通院

A Jōdoshū temple founded in the 14th or 15th century. Tokugawa Ieyasu had the remains of his mother, Odai no Kata, moved to this temple in 1603. The temple was then nicknamed after her posthumous Buddhist name, Denzūin Den. Her grave is the tallest in the cemetery and there is a memorial tablet on the right of the main altar. Many other Tokugawa graves are here, such as the grave of Senhime, daughter of Tokugawa Hidetada and wife of Toyotomi Hideyori. Other women connected to the Tokugawa buried here include Takatsukasa Takako, the wife of Iemitsu, and concubines of several shōguns. The complex was devastated in World War II; the main building was rebuilt in 1988 and the main gate in 2011. The main statue is Amida Buddha, with two Bodhisattvas on either side: to the left is the main Kannon statue, and left of that is another Kannon with many arms, a memorial to the dead from the 2011 Tōhoku Earthquake and tsunami. There is a small tearoom on the grounds with literature about temple events. The three large statues in front of the bell tower are known as Yakushi Sanzon, "Yakushi trinity." The sculpture of two hands is called the Yubizuka and is a monument to the good done by practitioners of shiatsu, a Japanese bodywork technique.

A Kannon ceremony is held at 10:30 a.m. and 2:30 p.m. on the eighteenth of every month. On the weekend closest to July 20 there is a morning glory fair at the temple. Denzūin is one of the temples on the Tokyo 33 Kannon Pilgrimage.

The entrance is to the south.

🌐 *http://www.denzuin.or.jp*

❺ Shinjuin 真珠院

The hondō (main hall) at this Buddhist temple is an interesting round modern structure. The courtyard has a collection of several statues mainly along the left side as you enter. If you go around to the left of the main hall and down the stairs, you will reach the graveyard, which includes some impressive daimyō tombs. Just to the left of the main hall and before the stairs is a multisided stone sculpture mounted about head height, with a different Bodhisattva or Buddha on each side. The sculpture rotates so a worshiper can choose the one they wish to address a prayer to.

The entrance is to the east.

DETAIL 5

❶ Genkakuji 源覚寺

A Jōdoshū temple founded in 1624. Konnyaku Enma, one of the three great Enma of Edo, is located here. The statue was carved in the Kamakura period with some restoration work done in 1672 and is designated a Cultural Property of Bunkyō Ward. The right eye of the statue is a solid color, much like that of a blind eye. Prayers to this Enma are said to help cure eye diseases. There is a legend of an old woman who prayed to Enma and was cured of her eye disease. In thanks, the woman gave up eating konnyaku, which was

HAKUSAN/KOISHIKAWA DETAIL 5

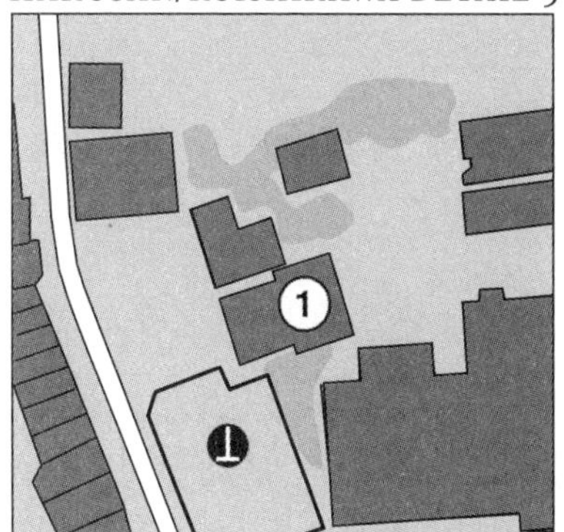

her favorite food, and instead offered it to Enma. Giving something up as an offering is an old tradition in Japan. Since then, konnyaku offerings have been common at this temple.

At the entrance, the stone under a small roof is a hyakudoishi. There are also two headless Jizō statues in a small shelter collectively known as the Shio Jizō "salt Jizō." People pray here for relief from a health problem and then put some salt on the corresponding body part of the statue. These Jizō are considered especially good at dealing with toothaches. There is also an interesting bell on the temple grounds. The bell was placed in storage after a fire in 1844; in 1937 it was transferred to a temple in Japanese-controlled Saipan, where it went missing during the war. In 1965 it was found in Texas—the assumption is that a GI took it home as souvenir—and the bell was returned to the temple. Next to the temple is a bodhisattva statue as a memorial to those who died in the South Pacific. People who travel to Saipan bring back shells and place them in front of this statue.

The sixth of every month is the temple fair. On the weekend closest to July 20 there is a Hōzuki Ichi "Chinese Lantern Plant Fair" at the temple.

The entrance is to the east.

🌐 *http://www.genkakuji.or.jp*

本郷

HONGŌ

Hongō was a separate ward of Tokyo until it was merged with Koishikawa to form Bunkyō Ward in 1947. In the Edo period, it was the location of many samurai residences. In the Meiji period, several schools of higher education were founded in the area. These were merged to form what is today the University of Tokyo. The area included a brothel district that was moved to Fukagawa in 1888 as it was proving distracting to the students. It was also the location of the Hongō Congregational Church, one of the first churches in Japan not under the control of foreign missionaries.

DETAIL 1

❶ University of Tokyo / Tōkyō Daigaku 東京大学

The main campus of Japan's most prestigious university is a mixture of recently built and older structures. As would be expected on such a busy campus, much of the space is taken up by buildings, but even so there are plenty of open areas with greenery. It is often near these where one sees the older buildings. This is especially the case on the west side of the campus near the main gate.

🌐 *https://www.u-tokyo.ac.jp/en/*

❷ Akamon 赤門

Dating from the 1820s, this gate was originally built for Yasuhime, the twenty-fourth daughter of shōgun Tokugawa Ienari, on the occasion of her marriage to Maeda Nariyasu, the daimyō of Kaga. The formal name of the gate is actually Goshudenmon, as

HONGŌ

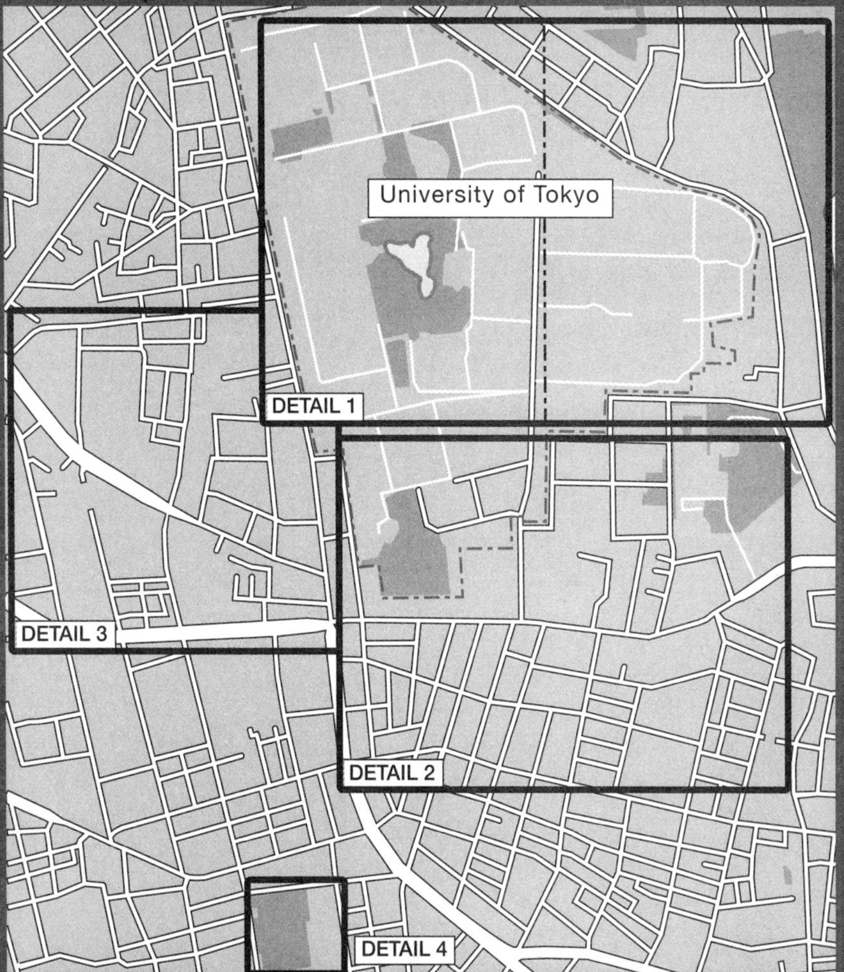

HONGŌ DETAIL 1 WEST

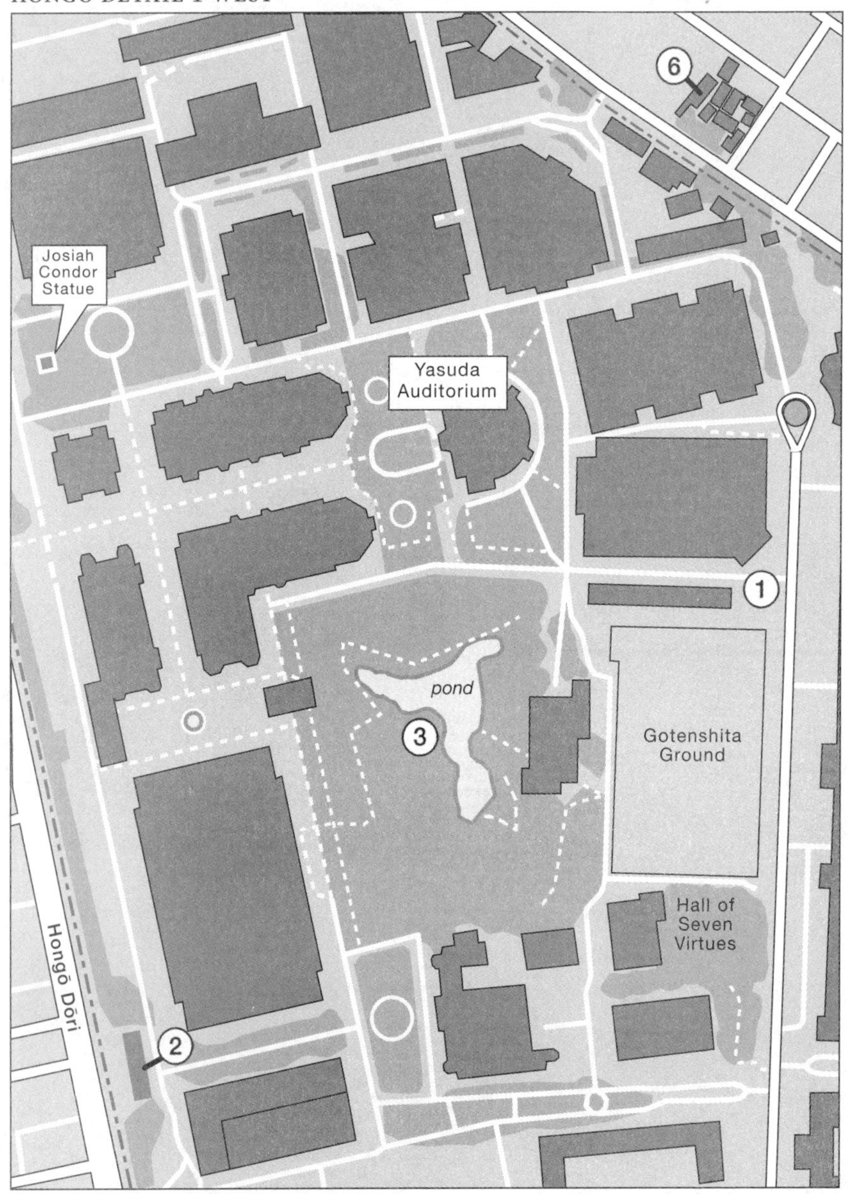

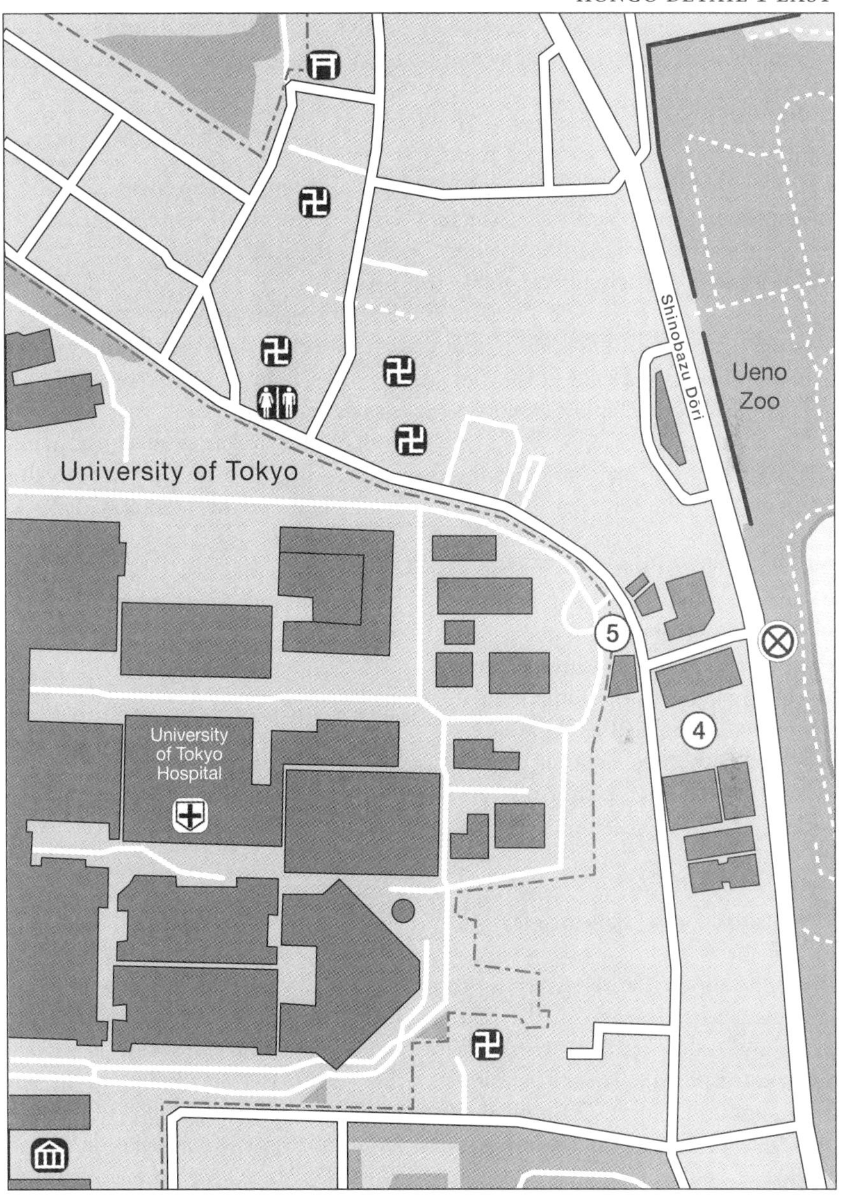
Shinobazu Dōri
Ueno Zoo
University of Tokyo
5
4
University of Tokyo Hospital

daughters of shōguns who married into families of a certain rank would be given the honorific title of Goshuden. The aka in Akamon means red, referring to the color of the gate. There are small guardhouses on each side of the gate with namakokabe walls, which have a black background and a white lattice pattern. The circular roof tiles are capped at the ends with the Maeda family crest of an ume flower, and the large tiles have a wild ginger motif for the Tokugawa family. One interesting addition made after the Great Kantō Earthquake are some end tiles that have the kanji for gaku (learning) on them. These replaced tiles that had fallen in the earthquake. The gate is located on the western edge of Tokyo University on Hongō Dōri and is classified as a national treasure. Its function as a major entrance to the campus makes it a symbol of the University. It is one of only three such major gates in Tokyo that survive from the Edo period.

❸ Sanshirō Pond / Sanshirō ike 三四郎池

This pond on the University of Tokyo campus is what remains of the Maeda daimyō estate garden, which was constructed in 1638. The official name of the pond is Ikutokuen Shinji Ike (育徳園心字池). The commonly used nickname comes from the Natsume Sōseki novel *Sanshirō*, where a famous scene takes place at the pond. The pond is surrounded by a small forest and has trails leading down to it, making it a peaceful location in the busy campus.

❹ Yokoyama Taikan Memorial Hall / Yokoyama Taikan Kinenkan 横山大観記念館

Yokoyama Taikan was a major figure in the Nihonga art movement of the early 20th century. This building was his home for many decades. The building was destroyed in World War II and rebuilt in 1954. Taikan lived here until his death. After his wife died in 1976 the house became the memorial hall. It contains works by Taikan and by other artists associated with him.

The entrance is on the east side of the grounds.

🌐 *http://taikan.tokyo*

❺ Sakai Inari Jinja 境稲荷神社

This shrine is located on a small plot of land between a wall of the University of Tokyo and a busy side street. Be careful crossing here as the street curves, so visibility is limited for both drivers and bicyclists. The location is marked by a large red torii and red picket fence. The shrine was likely founded in the 15th century. Behind the shrine is a well that legend says was found by the famous warrior monk Benkei in the late 12th century. After the firebombings of World War II this well provided water for many of the locals. There is an old hand pump at the well that still works.

❻ Yayoi Museum / Yayoi Bijutsukan 弥生美術館 and the Takehisa Yumeji Museum / Takehisa Yumeji Bijutsukan 竹久夢二美術館
Two museums devoted to two famous illustrators of the Taishō and Shōwa periods. The museums share a common entrance and access to each other. The Yayoi Museum was established in 1984 by Kano Takumi, a friend of Takabatake Kashō, whose art works are displayed here. Not much later the Takehisa Yumeji Art Museum was established by Kano to display Yumeji's works. The two museums also display illustrative art from other artists of the Taishō and early Shōwa period. Both artists did extensive work for magazines aimed at young women and were highly popular for their illustrations of slender young women stylishly dressed in kimono or modern styles. Their work would influence illustrative art down to the present. Such magazines played a major role in establishing a certain autonomy in girl's culture and published several famous writers such as Kawabata Yasunari. There is a small gift shop with some interesting materials and books. As you hunt for the museums keep a sharp eye out—it is easy to miss the entrance since it is slightly away from the street.
🌐 *http://www.yayoi-yumeji-museum.jp*

DETAIL 2

❶ Reiunji 霊雲寺
Reiunji was established in 1691 by fifth shōgun Tokugawa Tsunayoshi as a Shingon temple for offering prayers for peace. The temple was destroyed in both the Great Kantō Earthquake and the firebombings of World War II; the present building dates from 1976. A magnificent tree survived and adds beauty to the grounds. The grounds are spacious but rather barren, with a large parking lot taking up a significant portion. The gate at the south end of the enclosure is impressive, as is the main hall. You can also access the grounds from the west.

❷ Yushima Tenmangū 湯島天満宮
Also referred to as Yushima Tenjin (湯島天神), this shrine was founded in 458. The current buildings date from 1995. They are built from 250-year-old cypress and employ a special fire suppression system to be exempt from certain fire codes. The kami enshrined here when the temple was founded was Ame no Tajikarao, and in 1355 the spirit of Sugawara no Michizane (Tenjin sama) was added. Students come here to offer prayers to Tenjin for success in entrance exams. Other popular subjects to pray for are success in the entertainment business and good fortune. Depending on when you visit, you will see large numbers of ema with

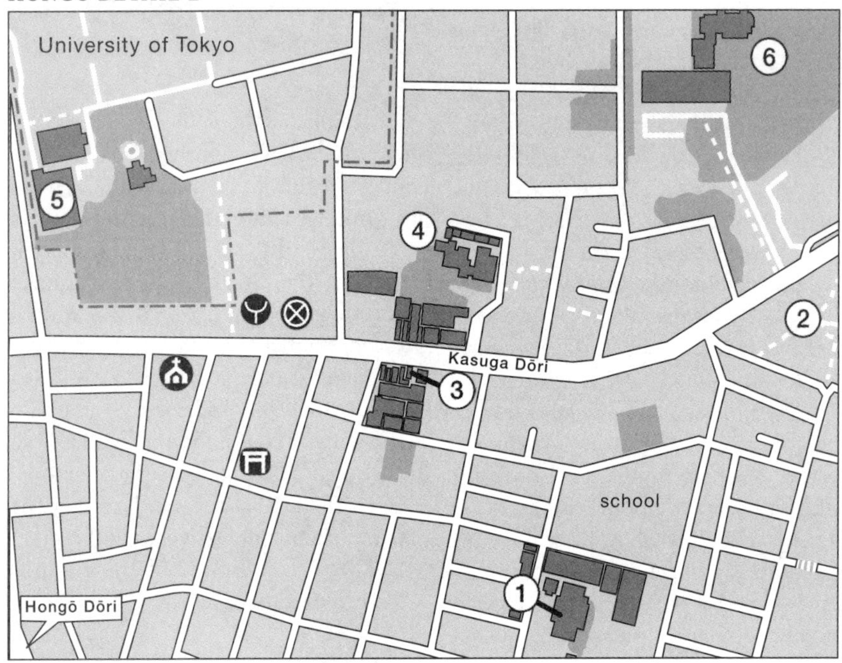

prayers written on them tied to special racks. The temple is also famous for its grove of some twenty varieties of ume trees, which were planted around 1355. This is considered the best spot in Tokyo to see flowering ume in the spring. The grove is the location of the most famous scene in the 1908 play *Onna Keizu* (*A Woman's Lineage*) by Kyōka Izumi. A memorial, where Kyōka's writer brushes are buried, is located in the grove.

Festivals are held here on the following dates: November 1–23, Chrysanthemum Festival; February 8–March 8, Ume Matsuri (Plum Festival); May 25, including the weekend before or after, Reitaisai (Annual Festival), in which you can view mikoshi being brought out.

Access is from the south, east, and north.

🌐 *http://www.yushimatenjin.or.jp/*

❸ Tsuboya 壺屋

It is said that this small pastry shop established some 400 years ago was planning to close in the Meiji period when Katsu Kaishū asked them to try to stay open. They took the advice of this national hero and the shop is still with us today. When you are facing the counter, look up and you will see a framed piece of calligraphy by Kaishū. The shop does not permit photography, but if you ask they will allow you to take a picture of the calligraphy. I recommend the monaka, a confection shaped like a jar and filled with sweet bean paste.

❹ Rinshōin 麟祥院

A Rinzai Zen temple also known as Karatachidera "Orange Tree Temple" after a hedge made of karatachi. Lady Kasuga, the wet nurse of the third Tokugawa shōgun Tokugawa Iemitsu, requested that the temple be established. After ten years she took Buddhist vows and was given the religious name of Rinshōin Den Ninen Ryōgini Daishi. She passed away at the age of 64 and is buried here. Her grave is marked with an impressive gravestone that has holes bored all the way through it. The holes were done at her request so that she could watch over the land of Japan. The temple was originally called Tentakuji; the name was changed using the Rinshōin from her Buddhist name. As with many of my wanderings in Tokyo, I only knew the name and location of the temple when I first visited. The young woman at the office near the gate spoke excellent English and gave us some directions. My fellow traveler was an amateur photographer with a love of cemeteries. Both of us felt the one here was especially lovely and impressive.

Please be very quiet when you visit, as people are often practicing meditation at this temple. The early morning meditation is open to the public. If you wish to practice, you should contact the temple for more information.

🌐 *https://www.rinshouin.jp*

❺ The University Museum, The University of Tokyo / Tōkyō Daigaku Sōgō Kenkyū Hakubutsukan 東京大学総合研究博物館

This museum grew out of the University Storage Center for Research Materials, which was founded in 1966. The present museum was established in 1997 and is the main building; there are branches and other museums in the university system, such as the Koishikawa Annex in the Koishikawa Botanical Garden. Exhibits cover a wide range, with many on the natural sciences and history.

🌐 *http://www.um.u-tokyo.ac.jp/index_en.html*

❻ Kyū Iwasaki-tei Garden / Kyū Iwasaki-tei teien 旧岩崎邸庭園

Built on the location of the Echigo Takeda clan's Edo residence, this garden is the former estate of the Iwasaki family, the founders of Mitsubishi. The house was built in 1896 as a complex of Japanese- and Western-style buildings by order of Iwasaki Hisaya. The Western-style mansion and Swiss-style billiard house were designed by Josiah Conder. The Japanese section was designed by Ōkawa Kijūrō. The paintings in the tokonoma and on the fusuma are

▲ In front of Hōshinji is this statue of Higuchi Ichiyō as a young girl enjoying a book.

▲ Tsuboya a small shop with a long history, buy a sweet for a later snack.

▲ A tree-lined path alongside the Law and Letters Building at the University of Tokyo.

▼ There so many ema at Yushima Tenmangū that the frame holding these is made of steel.

mainly the work of Hashimoto Gahō, a major artist of the time. The garden is a mix of Japanese and Western styles; apparently it was originally a Japanese-style garden that was changed by later generations. The present grounds are only one-third of the original size and most of the Japanese-style buildings were destroyed some time ago. The family lived in the Japanese residence, and the Western-style building was for guests and special events. After World War II, the site became the property of the Japanese government and housed the Judicial Research and Training Institute of the Supreme Court. In 1994 the Agency for Cultural Affairs took over management of the grounds, and then the city of Tokyo took over management in 2001. Expect to remove your shoes at the entrance.

- 🌐 *https://www.culture.city.taito.lg.jp/bunkatanbou/history/iwasaki_tei/iwasaki.html*
- 🌐 *http://teien.tokyo-park.or.jp/en/kyu-iwasaki/index.html*
- 🌐 *http://www.kensetsu.metro.tokyo.jp/content/000007565.pdf*
- 🌐 *http://www.kensetsu.metro.tokyo.jp/content/000026924.pdf*

DETAIL 3

❶ Kaneyasu かねやす

A drugstore founded by dentist Kaneyasu Yūetsu that became famous in the Kyōhō period (1716–1736). The store's renown came from its popular Nyūkōsan "frankincense" toothpowder. Any possible documents regarding the toothpowder formula were lost when the store burned in the firebombings of World War II. Today the store still exists and is run by the same family, but now sells cosmetics and clothing. A well-known senryū shows how famous the store was: Hongō mo Kaneyasu made wa Edo no uchi (本御もかねやすまでは江戸の内), "Hongō up to Kaneyasu lies within Edo." The store displays this poem on their front wall to the left of the windows. Another factor adding to the fame of the store was its signboard. The calligraphy on the sign was done by Horibe Yasube, one of the famous Forty-seven Rōnin.

❷ Bunkyō Historical Museum / Bunkyō Furusato Rekishikan 文京ふるさと歴史館

This two-story museum established in 1991, also referred to simply as the Bunkyō Museum, focuses on local history from prehistory to today. There are exhibits on Jōmon and Yayoi pottery, as the first Yayoi ceramics were found in Bunkyō Ward. Dioramas of life from the Edo period to recent times help the visitor to understand the many changes in the area. There is also a collection of everyday items from the Meiji period to the present. Another section exhibits famous writers from the area.

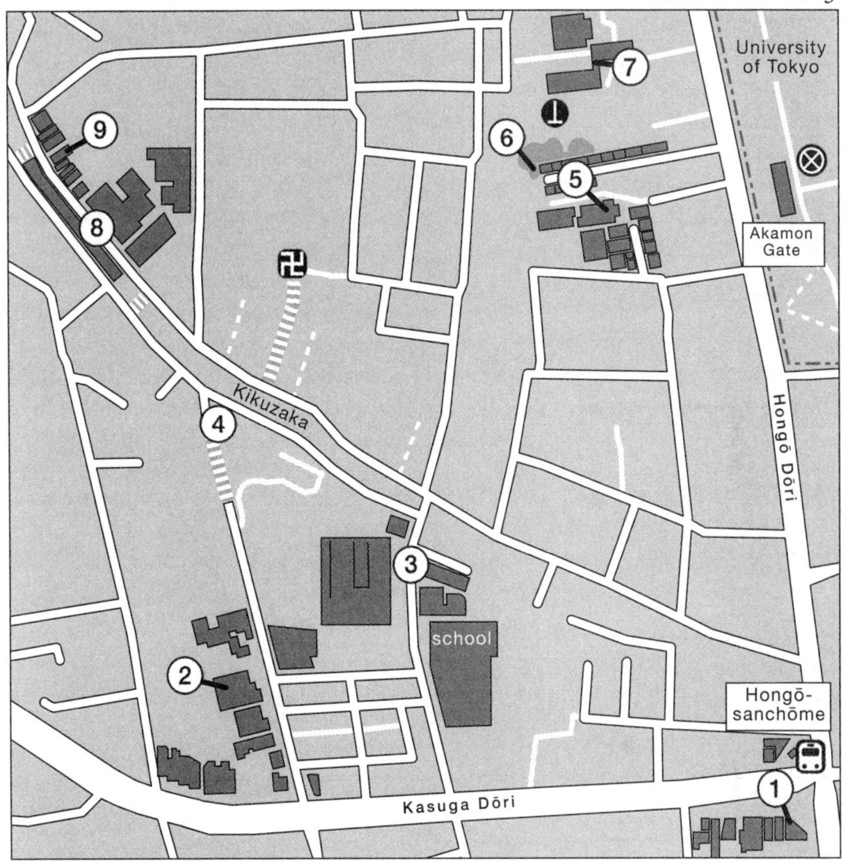

🌐 *https://www.city.bunkyo.lg.jp/rekishikan/*

❸ Honmyōjizaka 本妙寺坂

This slope and the neighboring side streets have a number of older two-story wooden buildings, especially in the area between the Hongō Elementary School and the Bunkyō Historical Museum. Such buildings were once common in Tokyo. Government programs encouraging reconstruction in accordance with stricter safety codes have almost eliminated such structures. Who knows how much longer these buildings will continue to exist?

❹ Tadonzaka 炭団坂

The name of this slope translates as "Charcoal Slope." At one time there were no stairs and people would sometimes lose their balance and roll down the slope. In the Edo period, tadon were an inexpensive type of charcoal made into balls from charcoal powder. The slope is steep and long enough to warrant three flat spots along the climb, where the flower beds add a nice touch. Note that there is a flat area on one side of the stairs. This is so people with bicycles can walk while rolling their bike on the incline. You will see this feature in many places in Tokyo.

❺ Hōshinji 法真寺

A Jōdoshū temple. While the date it was founded is unclear, the temple is mentioned in documents from 1596. The main statue of Amida Buddha was brought to this temple in the early 18th century and is said to be the work of Eshin Sōzu. The main hall also contains a statue of Enma from the late Edo period, which is on the Tokyo Enma Pilgrimage route. Outside and to the left of the hondō is a Koyasu Jizō that tradition holds was carved by Kūkai. There are also two Niō statues in front of the main hall. The courtyard in front of the temple contains a small pond with walkways. Two other statues were added in 2015: a statue of a Taishō period girl who would have lived in the upper-class neighborhood of Hongō, and a statue of the famous Meiji period writer Higuchi Ichiyō as a young girl reading a book. Ichiyō had spent happy years next to the temple as a child and mentioned it in her stories *Yukukumo* "Passing Clouds," *Takekurabe* "Child's Play," and *Jūsanya* "The Thirteenth Night." Next to Hōshinji is a small museum devoted to Higuchi Ichiyō that is operated by the temple. The museum contains a collection of everyday items from the Meiji period. This museum is not to be confused with the larger museum mentioned in the Asakusa chapter. There is also the Ichiyōzuka, "Ichiyō mound," with a rectangular stone pillar with her name in red. For more about her, see the Ichiyō Memorial Museum section in the Yoshiwara and Sanya chapter.

The temple is accessible from the east off of Hongō Dōri.

🌐*http://www.hoshinji.jp/abouthoshinji/*

❻ Fujinomori Inari Jinja 藤之森稲荷神社

A small, very humble shrine at the end of a pedestrian walkway between residences. This is a good example of a neighborhood shrine continuing to exist in the modern city. There is the stump of a large tree just past the torii and some old stone basins at the base of the tree. The street is also interesting as an example of the narrow lanes (roji) that were once far more common in the city. Do be quiet when accessing the shrine to avoid disturbing the local residents.

❼ Wadatsumi no Koe Museum / Wadatsumi no Koe Kinenkan わだつみのこえ記念館

A small museum devoted to the memory of students who died in World War II. In 1949 *Kike Wadatsumi no Koe* "Listen to the Voices from the Sea," a best-selling collection of letters and writings by students who died in the war, was published by a group who had survived. The collection was translated and published in English by the University of Scranton Press. The group later formed the Nihon Senbotsu Gakusei Kinen-Kai, an association partly organized with the goal of establishing a memorial, and in 2006 the museum opened. The exhibits are in chronological order and include many items donated by families. Toward the end is a section on the Korean student soldiers in the Japanese army who were sent to the front lines when the Japanese troops pulled back.

🌐 *http://www.wadatsuminokoe.org*

🌐 *Listen to the Voices from the Sea: https://www.press.uchicago.edu/ucp/books/book/distributed/L/b03757809.html*

❽ Kikuzaka 菊坂

Kikuzaka means "chrysanthemum slope" and refers as much to the neighborhood as to the slope itself. This area still has some old wooden buildings that have not been replaced with modern structures. Some date back to the Taishō period, when two-story buildings replaced the older one-story tenements. Even the modern buildings have a certain traditional quality with their potted plants and modest height. Do quietly explore while the old buildings remain, and enjoy some of the narrow pedestrian passageways and old walls, which are likely to still be here when the buildings are gone.

❾ Former Ise Pawnshop / Kyū Iseya Shichiten 旧伊勢屋質店

An old pawnshop that is owned by Atomi University and, in cooperation with Bunkyō Ward, is open for viewing. The reception area, store, and storehouse are accessible. The building is two stories with a passageway to the storehouse on the second floor. Noted Meiji period author Higuchi Ichiyō was an occasional customer of this pawnshop when her funds ran low.

DETAIL 4

❶ Tokyo Waterworks Historical Museum / Tokyo To Suidō Rekishikan 東京都水道歴史館

This museum is a must for anyone interested in Edo/Tokyo history. The establishment of waterworks early in the creation of the city of Edo was crucial for providing clean water to the residents and was an innovative feat of engineering. The system originally used

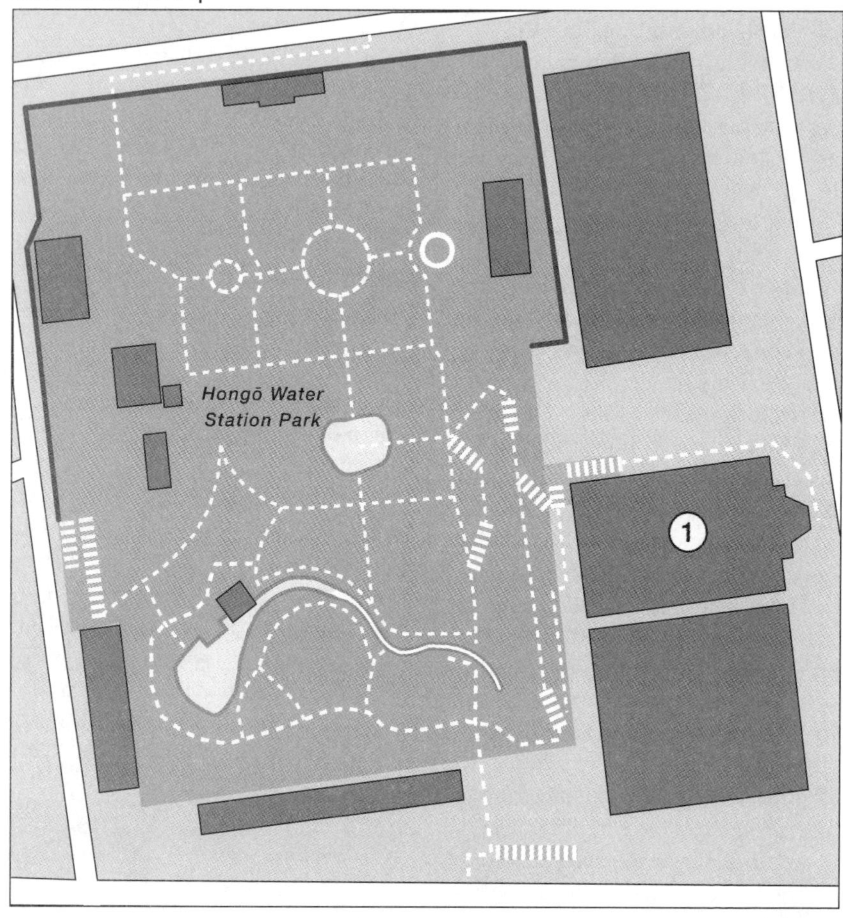

stone, wood, and bamboo conduits to carry the water to each neighborhood; examples from the period are on display. The system expanded as the city grew into one of the largest in the world. In the Meiji period, the modernization of the water system began, as the older system was showing its age. Included are exhibits on access to water in daily life in the Edo period as well as items from the Meiji era to the present day.

🌐 *http://www.suidorekishi.jp*

皇居

KŌKYO (IMPERIAL PALACE)

Most of the central portion of this area is off-limits, as it is the Imperial Palace Grounds. The accessible portions of the grounds, though, are large enough that you may want to plan a full day if you are in good shape, or return later to finish your stroll. There is enough of a continuous slope from north to south that I recommend a route this time. For the area west of the palace, you can go downhill by starting at Kudanshita Station and walking along the moats to your left, taking small detours to view interesting sights. Then you can return to your starting point via the East Gardens, which contains a good place to stop and rest in the Honmaru Rest House.

You can also start at the same station and enter Kitanomaru Park via the Tayasu Mon. This route would bring you to areas north and east of the palace. You could also start at the south at Sakuradamon Station but expect that much of the walk will be uphill.

DETAIL 1

❶ National Shōwa Memorial Museum / Shōwa Kan 昭和館

A seven-story museum designed by Kikutake Kiyonori and opened in 1998. The building is windowless, often looking much like a squat pillar depending on your viewpoint. The museum was proposed by the Japan Association of Bereaved Families, a group that was founded to represent the relatives of war dead. There was considerable disagreement during the planning process about how the

KŌKYO (IMPERIAL PALACE)

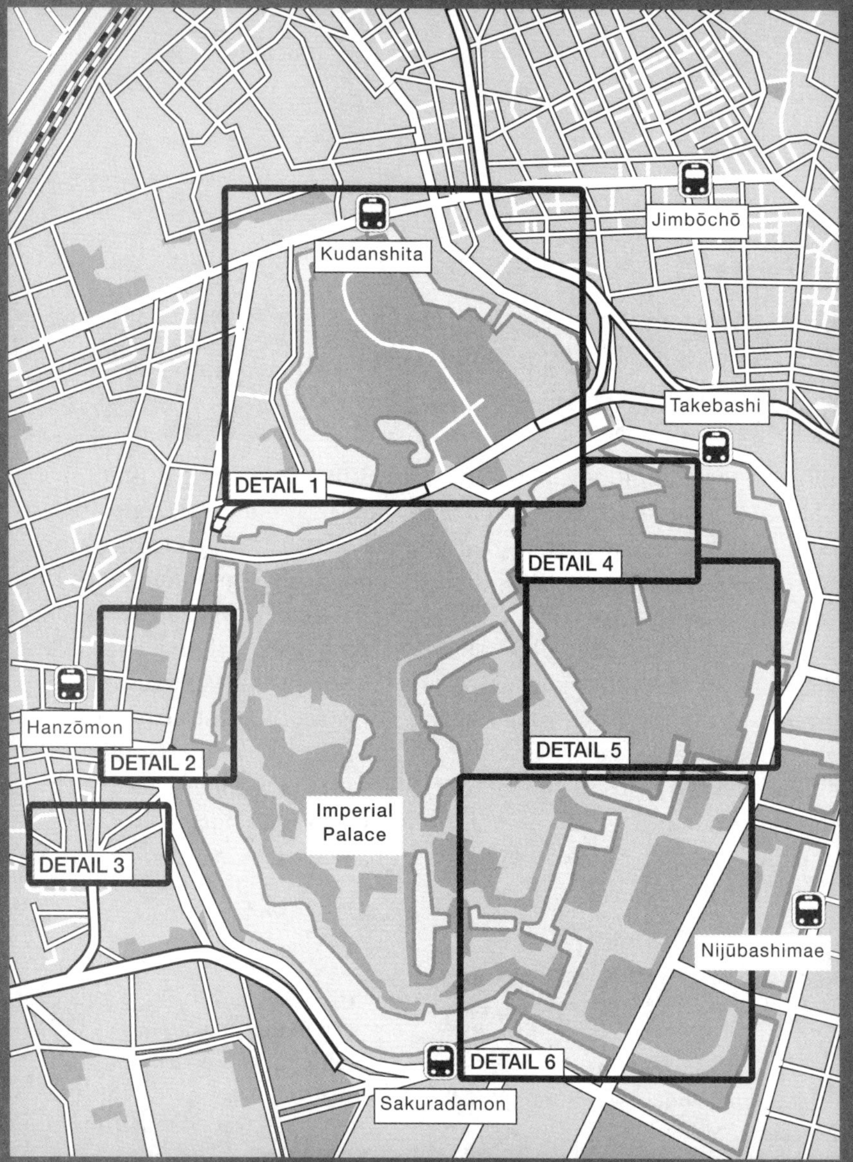

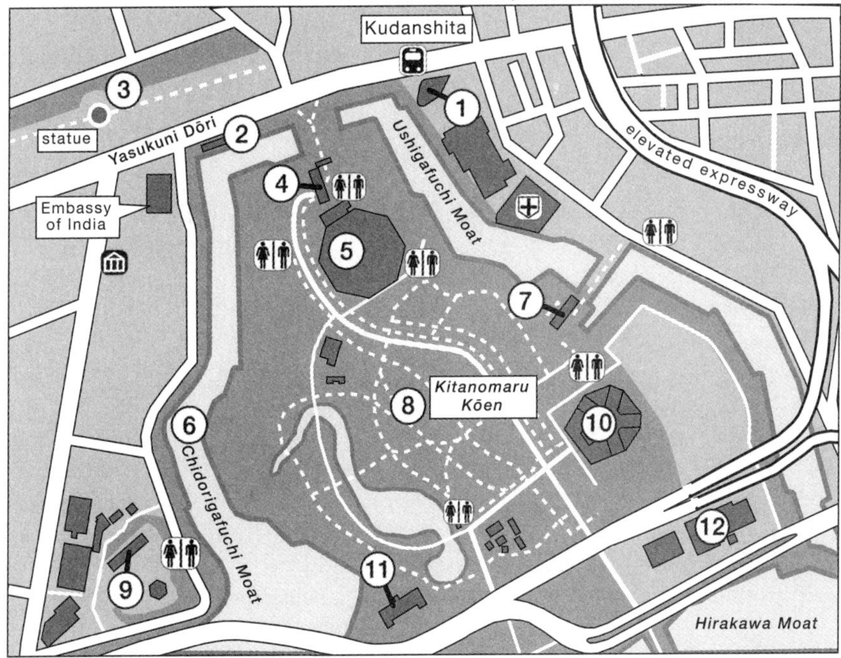

war period should be remembered. The museum avoids many points of controversy in the exhibits. It focuses on the depiction of life during a significant portion of the Shōwa period, from 1935 to 1945 when Japan was at war, and then the period of occupation and reconstruction up to 1955. Many of exhibits are about everyday life, and ordinary objects from the period are displayed. In addition to the exhibits, there is an audio-visual room and a library. There are English-language audio guides you can get from the receptionists to use in the museum. Taking video or photographs without permission is prohibited.

🌐 *http://www.showakan.go.jp*

❷ Statue of Ōyama Iwao 大山巌像

This statue was sculpted by Shinkai Taketarō in 1918. Originally from Satsuma Han, Iwao would study gunnery and later military science in France. He was an official observer during the Franco-Prussian war, went to Switzerland to study languages, and became fluent in Russian. In the Meiji period he became one of the founders of the Imperial Japanese Army. In the Sino-Japanese War he led the Second Army, for which he was made a marquis. Not long after that, he became a field marshal, and he commanded the Manchurian Army in the Russo-Japanese War. After the Japanese victory, he was made a prince of the empire. He died in 1916.

❸ Yasukuni Jinja 靖国神社

Japan's most controversial shrine was established in 1869, the Tokyo Shōkonsha, dedicated to those who had died in the restoration of power to the emperor. In 1879 the name was changed to Yasukuni Jinja. After World War II the shrine no longer received support from the Japanese government and became an independent institution. It now is dedicated to all who have died fighting for Japan. The names of some 2.5 million enshrined are listed in official records. Fourteen Class-A war criminals were added to the rolls on October 17, 1978, a decision which greatly disappointed the emperor as names are not automatically added. Since then, no emperor has visited the shrine. Many consider the shrine a right-wing symbol and when politicians visit, there are usually formal objections by nations that suffered under the Japanese military in World War II. It is not only ethnic Japanese who are enshrined; Koreans and Taiwanese who died while in the Japanese military are also included, as those nations were part of Japan until the end of the war. The first torii at the entrance is 82 feet (25 meters) tall and made of steel; it dates from 1974. There is also a museum, the Yūshūkan, which was established in 1882 and is known for its nationalistic portrayal of World War II.

The main entrance is to the east. Additional entrances are to the south and north.

🌐 *http://www.yasukuni.or.jp/english/*

❹ Tayasu Mon 田安門

This gate was initially built in 1607. In 1636 it was reconstructed into the masugata-style gate it is today. The Tayasu Tokugawa family, one of the three branch families of the Tokugawa, had their residence inside this gate. The upper story of the yaguramon was destroyed in the Great Kantō Earthquake and restored in 1963. It has a stone drop that can be seen when you are close to the gate. The moat here is called the Ushigafuchi, meaning "Ox Depths." During one of the festivals of Kanda Myōjin, an ox lost control of the large float it was pulling and they both sank into the moat, never to be seen again.

❺ Nippon Budōkan 日本武道館

The octagonal Budōkan was designed by Yamada Mamoru and completed in 1964 for use in the Tokyo Olympic Games judo competitions. It is still used for a variety of martial art competitions and for other events. When martial arts tournaments or championships are being held, there is often free admission. These usually take place on weekends. One of the most famous events at the Budōkan was the first rock and roll concert held there on June 30, 1966, which was heavily opposed by conservative groups. While the Beatles are often said to have been the first rock band to play the Budōkan, they were not. There were six bands that opened for them at their famous concert. They were Bitō Isao, Mochizuki Hiroshi, Uchida Yūya, Jackie Yoshikawa and His Blue Comets, Sakurai Gorō, and The Drifters. This means that the Beatles were in fact the seventh rock and roll band to play the Budōkan.

🌐 *http://www.nipponbudokan.or.jp/english*

❻ Chidorigafuchi Moat 千鳥ヶ淵

Originally Chidorigafuchi was a lake in the Kōjimachi heights to the west of the castle. It was the fortification building project started by Tokugawa Ieyasu that made it part of the present-day moat system. It is the largest moat for the palace and being on a hill, the sides slope down for some great distance. Depending on the time of year, rowboats can be rented for relaxing on the moat itself.

❼ Shimizu Mon 清水門

This gate gained its name by being the gate to the Shimizu Tokugawa residence. The Shimizu Tokugawa were one of the Gosankyō, the three branch families of the Tokugawa. This gate was built around 1620 and rebuilt in 1658 after burning in the Meireki Fire. The larger yaguramon was repaired in the Meiji period and fully restored in 1965. When you are very close, look up and you can see the stone drop that could be used by defenders.

❽ Kitanomaru Park / Kitanomaru Kōen 北の丸公園

This park was established in 1969. It was originally the northern (kita) citadel (maru) part of the former Edo Castle. There are several structures in the park including the Budōkan, the Science Museum, and remnants of the shōgun's castle. Close relatives of the shōgun and some high-ranking officials resided in this area. Today several hundred people, mainly Imperial Guard staff and their families, are counted in census records as living in the same district as the park, in a separate area behind the Science Museum.

❾ Chidorigafuchi National Cemetery / Chidorigafuchi Senbotsusha Boen
千鳥ヶ淵戦没者墓苑

This cemetery was established in 1959 for the remains of hundreds of thousands of unidentified war dead, not only soldiers but also civilians who died away from Japan. The green-roofed hexagonal pavilion in the cemetery is the Tomb of the Unknown Soldier. Underground vaults hold the remains of unidentified dead and the cemetery is visited each August 15 by the emperor. Part of the structure is a five-ton ceramic coffin made with stones gathered at the various battlefields of the war. It contains an urn donated by the Shōwa emperor. The park also has two square stones, each inscribed with a poem, one by the Shōwa emperor and one by the Emperor Emeritus.

🌐 *http://www.env.go.jp/garden/chidorigafuchi/english/index.html*

⓾ Science Museum / Kagaku Gijutsukan 科学技術館

This museum was founded by the Japan Science Foundation to promote knowledge of science and technology. It opened in 1964. The building consists of five floors with a basement restaurant. The exhibits are mainly interactive, and are popular with families with children. There are English guide sheets at the entrances to the exhibits.

🌐 *http://www.jsf.or.jp/eng/*

⓫ Former Imperial Guard Headquarters / Kyū Konoe Shidan Shireibu 旧近衛師団司令部

This Gothic Revival building dates from 1910 and was the headquarters of the Imperial Guard, a branch of the Japanese Army. The Guard was reorganized in 1947 under the control of the National Police Agency. In 1968 it was announced that the old building would be demolished; architects organized to save the building. In 1972 it was decided that the building would be preserved. Restoration work was carried out to reinforce the building and restore the original slate roof, which had been replaced with copper after the Great Kantō Earthquake. It then functioned as an annex for the National Museum of Modern Art displaying crafts from around the world with a research library. The museum closed in early 2020 and reopened in Kanazawa City, Ishikawa Prefecture in October.

⓬ National Museum of Modern Art MOMAT / Tōkyō Kokuritsu Kindai Bijutsukan 東京国立近代美術館

The museum was established in 1952 by the Ministry of Education in Kyōbashi. It relocated to the present location in 1969 in a building designed by Taniguchi Yoshirō. The interior has been remodeled twice to accommodate changing needs. The buildings were given to the public as a gift by Bridgestone founder Ishibashi Shōjirō, who was a member of the museum board. The exhibits are changed periodically as the collection contains over 13,000 items, with a focus on works created after 1907. There is a museum shop, a library, and the restaurant L'Art et Mikuni, which closes later as it has an outdoor terrace entrance.

Photographs are generally allowed within the posted guidelines. There is free wi-fi.

Museum:

🌐 *http://www.momat.go.jp/english/am/*

Restaurant L'Art et Mikuni

🌐 *http://lart-et-mikuni.jp*

Night at the Guard Headquarters

A dramatic event took place in the building around midnight of August 14 and 15, 1945. Army officers killed the Imperial Guard commander Lieutenant General Mori Takeshi and his chief of staff Lieutenant Colonel Shiraishi Michinori. This was a failed attempt to prolong the war by taking control of the guards, staging a coup to isolate the Imperial Palace, and preventing the broadcast of the emperor's statement of surrender.

DETAIL 2

❶ Chidorigafuchi Park / Chidorigafuchi Kōen 千鳥ヶ淵公園

Today this area is known for having one of Tokyo's most famous sets of cherry trees on both sides of the moat. The first of these were Yoshino cherry trees planted in 1898 by the British diplomat Ernest Satow. Many were destroyed in the bombings of World War II and in 1953 replacement trees were planted. The trees have grown to be quite large, reaching almost to the water in some places. There are some 260 trees in the area with several varieties of flowering cherry represented among them. If you look across Uchibori Dōri from the park, you will see an institution connected with Ernest Satow, the British Embassy.

❷ JCII Camera Museum / Nihon Camera Hakubutsukan 日本カメラ博物館

A small museum devoted to cameras and the history of photography. The museum was founded in 1989 by the Japan Camera Industry Institute, which tests Japanese cameras for quality before they are placed on the international market. Besides exhibiting some 300 of the thousands of cameras in the museum collection, they also collaborate with the JCII Photo Salon, which is located next door, for exhibits of photography, and with the JCII Library (closed weekends).

🌐 *http://www.jcii-cameramuseum.jp*

❸ Hanzōmon 半蔵門

This gate is named after the famous samurai Hattori Hanzō, whose home was just inside it. Hanzō was in charge of a prestigious unit of men from Iga who guarded this gate. Another name for Hanzōmon is Kōjimachi Gomon, as it faces the Kōjimachi neighborhood to the west. Today the gate is an entrance into the Imperial Palace grounds and can only be viewed from a distance. There are guards posted both at the gate itself and in a kōban by the street.

A note on Hattori Hanzō: he is often described as a ninja from Iga. He was from Iga, but there is absolutely no historical evidence from his time that he was a ninja. For an excellent analysis of the ninja myth see *Ninja: Unmaking the Myth* by Stephen Turnbull.

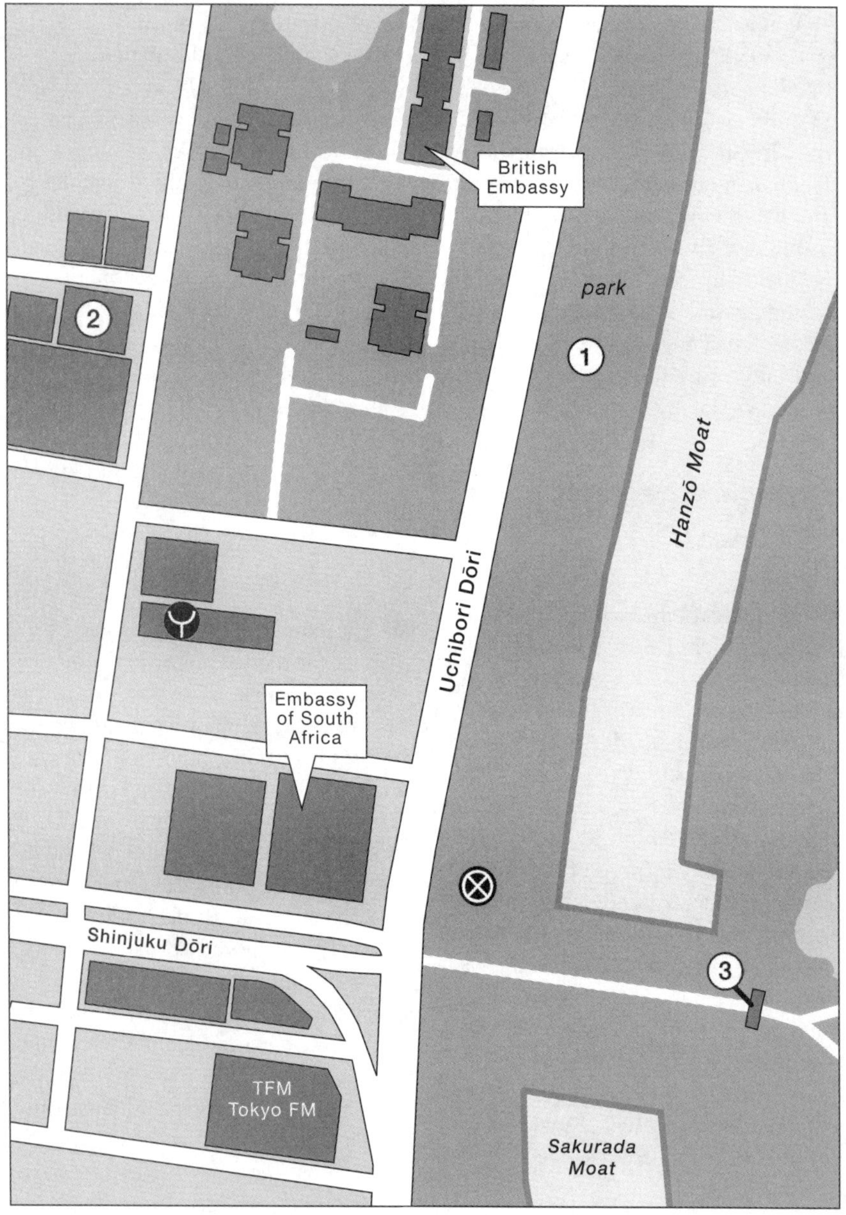
British
Embassy
park
1
2
Hanzō Moat
Uchibori Dōri
Embassy
of South
Africa
Shinjuku Dōri
3
TFM
Tokyo FM
Sakurada
Moat

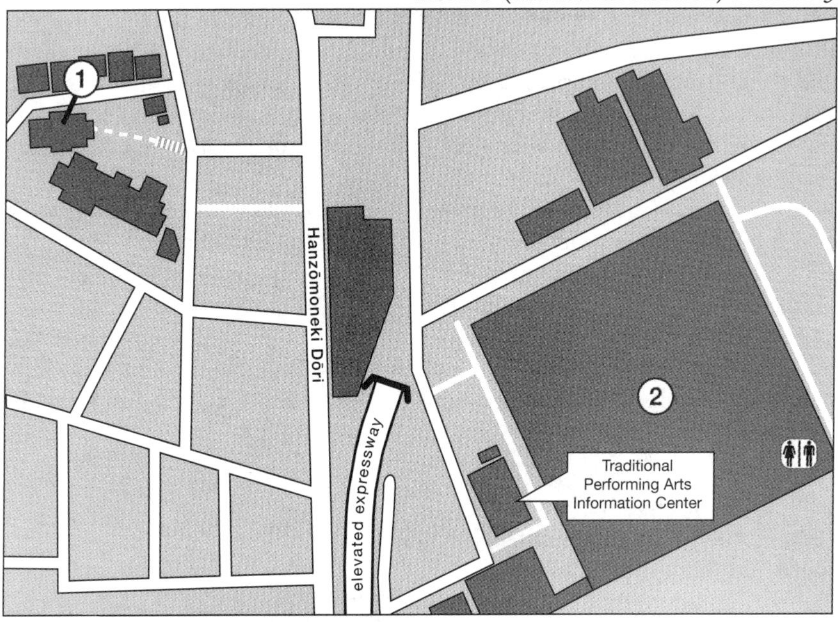

DETAIL 3

❶ Hirakawa Tenmangū 平河天満宮
Hirakawa Tenmangū, also referred to as Hirakawa Tenjin, was founded in 1487 by Ōta Dōkan at the present location of the East Garden. Later it was moved to outside Hanzōmon, and then moved again to the current location on the orders of Tokugawa Ieyasu when his design of Edo Castle was being carried out. The kami enshrined here is Sugawara no Michizane. There is an attractive small Inari shrine on the grounds. A hyakudoishi for doing 100 pilgrimages is next to the bend on the path to the Inari shrine. The main entrance to Hirakawa Tenmangū, with an impressive copper torii, is located on the east side of the shrine. Festival days are the first and twenty-fifth of every month.
🌐 *http://hirakawatenjin.or.jp*

❷ National Theater of Japan / Kokuritsu Gekijō 国立劇場
Designed by Iwamoto Hiroyuki, this theater opened in 1966 and is operated by the Japan Arts Council. The ferroconcrete building is built in the style of traditional azekura storehouses, which drew criticism from advocates of a more modern style. The building has two theaters, the large with 1,610 seats and the small with 590. There is also an exhibition room that is accessible

without charge. The focus is on national theater, including kabuki, bunraku, traditional dance and music, nō, kyogen, gagaku, various folk performing arts, and the traditional variety-hall entertainments known collectively as engei. The land in front of the theater is heavily planted with trees and shrubbery, both echoing the greenery of the Imperial Palace across the moat and contrasting with the taller modern buildings in the neighborhood.
🌐 *https://www.ntj.jac.go.jp/english/*

Familiar Sights

Proof that you can never anticipate what you will see: As I was walking in front of the National Theater on one of my trips, I spotted a familiar sight. It was one of those motorized tour buses made from an old San Francisco cable car. This one had a poster on the side of the two girls from the *Pop Team Epic* manga flipping the bird.

DETAIL 4

❶ Hirakawa Mon 平川門

This gate is located where the Hirakawa Moat and the Ōtebori Moat meet. The Hirakawa Moat is a vestige of the old Hirakawa that was redirected north and east to create the Kandagawa in the early 17th century. This was the gate used by the women of the inner portion of the castle on those very rare occasions when they left the grounds. It was nicknamed the Otsubone Mon due to its location near the Ōoku.

Next to the main gate is a smaller gate called the Obikuruwa Mon, also known as the Fujōmon "the unclean gate." This gate is where criminals and the dead exited the shōgun's castle. Hirakawa Mon is connected to a wooden bridge with Edo period metal caps on the posts.

❷ Kita Hanebashi Mon 北桔橋門

The name Kita Hanebashi Mon is a rather straightforward one: it translates as "Northern Drawbridge Gate," and this was the location of a drawbridge in the Edo period. The drawbridge was torn down in the Meiji period and the present bridge is ferroconcrete. However, you can still see the metal fixings that were part of the drawbridge system attached to the gate. There are no masugata or yaguramon here; they were destroyed some time ago. What is left is the kōraimon, the outer gate. There was also a tower next to the bridge that overlooked the moat, which is also gone.

❸ Tenshudai 天守台

This is all that remains of the base of the castle donjon. It is the base for the fourth tower. The first tower was built

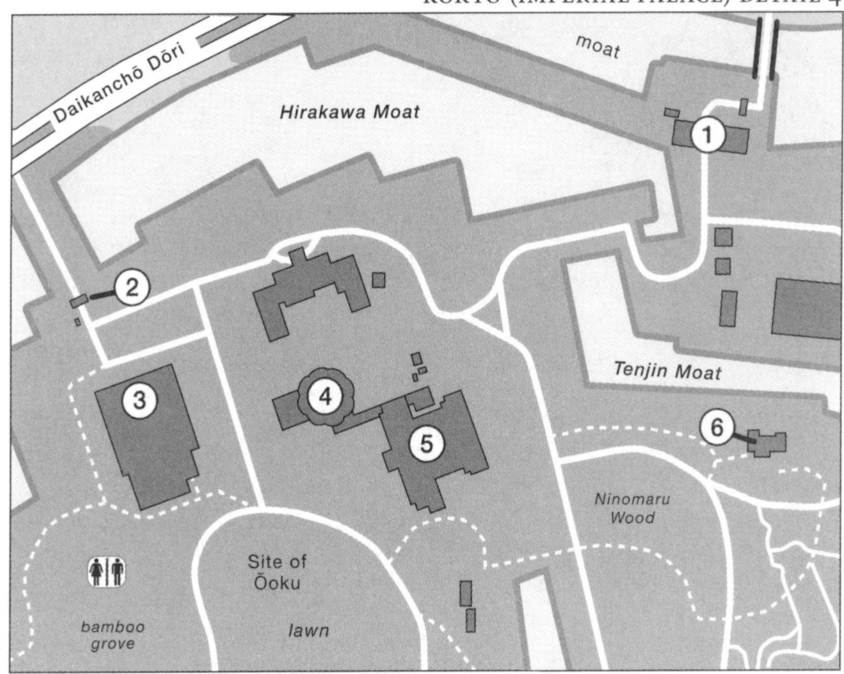

by Tokugawa Ieyasu in 1606 and was five stories high. His son Hidetada had it demolished and replaced in 1623 with a taller one. The third was built by the third shōgun Tokugawa Iemitsu and burned down in the Meireki Fire of 1657. A fourth tower was planned—the base we have today was built for it—however it was then decided that such a fortification was no longer needed in times of peace and that the funds were better spent on restoring the city. The present base is a good place to look over the area. In front of the tenshudai is a well to supply water for those in the tower, which has never dried up.

❹ ❺ Tōkagakudō and the Kunaichō Gakubu 桃華楽堂 **and** 宮内庁楽部

The Tōkagakudō, "Peach Blossom Music Hall," was completed in 1966. It was designed by Imai Kenji as part of the sixtieth birthday celebrations for Empress Kōjun. The building consists of an entrance and performance hall. The walls of the octagonal portion are covered in mosaic murals. Each year, graduates of various music schools hold performances here in March.

The copper-roofed building nearby houses the Kunaichō Gakubu, usually translated as "Music Department of the Imperial Household Agency"

▲ Meganebashi or "Spectacles Bridge" is named for the reflection of the arches in the water.

▲ The contrast between the stone walls of the palace and the modern city is striking.

▼ The Suwa no Chaya is a tea house from the Meiji Period in the Fukiage Garden.

▲ The base is all that remains of the main tower of the shōgun's castle.

or “Imperial Music Department.” The Kunaichō Gakubu was founded in 1870 to perform traditional court music for ritual occasions and special events. They also do occasional public performances and have released several recordings.

❻ **Suwa no Chaya** 諏訪の茶屋
In the Edo period there was a teahouse with this name on the grounds of the shōgun’s castle. The present Suwa no Chaya was built in 1912 in the Fukiage Garden of the Imperial Palace and later moved to this location for the opening of the East Gardens. The building is in the style of the Meiji period and has an attractive copper roof.

DETAIL 5

❶ **Tatsumi Yagura** 巽櫓
A two-story tower overlooking the Kikyōbori moat, this is the only remaining corner tower of Edo Castle. In the Edo period this tower was called the Sakurada Nijū Yagura. Many of the castle towers were given names relating to the cardinal directions or the East Asian zodiac—in this case, tatsumi means southeast. This yagura was destroyed in the Great Kantō Earthquake and soon rebuilt.

❷ **Kikyō Mon** 桔梗門
Also called Uchi Sakurada Gate, “Inner Sakurada Gate,” Kikyō Mon translates as “Bellflower Gate.” During the Edo period the gate was used exclusively by government officials. It is now used by visitors on special occasions, by officials, and for deliveries to the Imperial Palace. It has been depicted in ukiyo-e and in early shin hanga prints on more than one occasion.

❸ **Fujimi Yagura** 富士見櫓
This three-story tower was built in 1659 to replace an older structure on the site that was destroyed in the Meireki Fire. It was heavily damaged in the Great Kantō Earthquake and repaired. The name translates as “Fuji viewing tower” as it once was possible to see the mountain from here. Fujimi Yagura is best viewed from outside the garden, as you can then see it towering over the moat and nearby wall. At one time there were twenty-one such towers on the grounds of the shōgun’s castle. Today three remain. This one has three stories, while the others have only two. It also has a stone drop to help repel attackers scaling the wall of the moat. The wall in this area has a carved design of three circles on several stones.

❹ **Hyakunin Bansho** 百人番所
An Ōte Mon guard post near the remains of the Nakano Mon. Only the walls next to that gate remain; the gate,

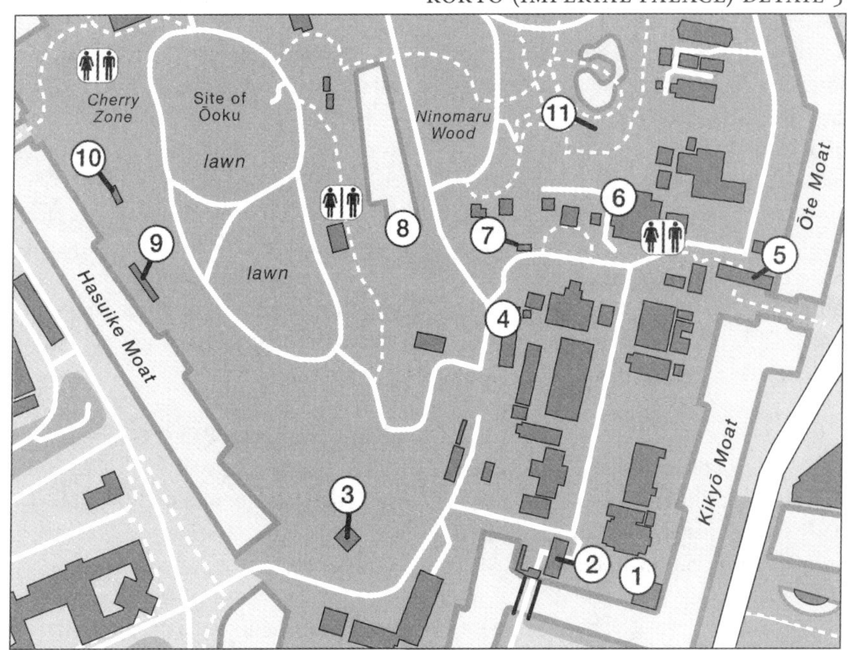

towers, and other buildings are long gone. The Hyakunin Bansho "100-man guardhouse" still exists, where the Teppō Hyakuningumi "100 riflemen" kept watch around the clock. There were several rifle units from families closely related to the Tokugawa that shared this duty, each taking turns at this post. Behind the Hyakunin Bansho is an area that includes the Imperial Guard Headquarters.

❺ Ōte Mon 大手門

When the palace area was still the shōgun's castle, daimyō had to use either this gate or the Kikyō Mon to enter on their visits. This gate was also the one used by visiting nobility. The entire structure contains more than one gate, a common feature in castle defenses. Ōte Mon is the traditional name for the main gate of a castle. Those visiting entered the first gate, kōraimon, then turned 90 degrees to pass through the second gate, yaguramon. This turn was intended to slow down running attackers. There is a square, called a masugata, between the gates to confine attackers if they broke through the first gate. You can see the gun ports above the wall of the larger gate where the guards could fire rifles and arrows into the masugata. The original gate burned down in the Meireki Fire and was rebuilt in 1659. It was again damaged in several earthquakes, especially the Great Kantō Earthquake, after which it was repaired in 1925. The larger yaguramon was burned in the firebombings of World War II and reconstructed in 1967. Inside the masugata you can see a shachi, a fish-like ornament that often graced the roof of larger buildings. Shachi are often referred to as dolphins, but actually they are stylized orcas. This one was placed on the yaguramon in 1659.

❻ Museum of Imperial Collections / Sannomaru Shōzōkan 三の丸尚蔵館
This small museum began as a collection of some 6,000 items donated to the Japanese Government by the imperial family in 1989. The museum was then constructed and opened in 1993. Since that time many items have been added to the collection, including donations in 1996 from the collection of Prince Chichibu, in 2001 from the collection of the late Empress Kōjun, and in 2005 from the collection of Prince Takamatsu, bringing the total to about 9,500. The present collection consists of artworks from around the world from ancient to modern times.

🌐 *http://www.kunaicho.go.jp/e-event/sannomaru02.html*

❼ Dōshin Bansho 同心番所
This was the guard station just past the Ōte Mon where visitors had to undergo inspection before proceeding further. Only the Owari, Kii, and Mito families were allowed to stay in their palanquins, as they were major branch families of the Tokugawa. All others, no matter how high their rank or hereditary status, had to disembark. The end of the shōgun's rule and the relocation of the emperor to Tokyo is reflected in the roof tiles, where you can see both the hollyhock crest of the Tokugawa and the crest of the imperial family.

❽ Imperial Palace East Gardens / Kōkyo Higashi Gyoen 皇居東御苑
This area was opened to the public in 1968. In the Edo period, the East Garden was the inner portion of the shōgun's castle. Most of this space was the Ōoku, the inner palace, which included the quarters of the women including the shōgun's mother, wife, and concubines, and their servants. This was the most secure part of the castle and was almost entirely filled with buildings and small gardens. In the Edo period the walls at the moats were all topped with defensive fortifications, a few of which remain.

The East Garden is rich with flowers and foliage. Some of the major ones, and the best times to view, them are: plums in February, camellias from October to March, Magnolia kobus in March, some thirty-five different kinds of cherries from late March to early April, Kurume azaleas around mid-April, Satsuki rhododendrons in June, irises in mid-June, lilies in July, bush clover in September, and maples in early December.

There are three gates into the gardens, the Ōte Mon, Kita Hanebashi Mon, and Hirakawa Mon. There is an excellent illustrated guidebook that you can purchase at the Honmaru Rest House near the restrooms in the center of the map. I recommend that you buy this early in your visit, as it has many more details than this book.

Should you visit the gardens at a busy time you may be given a numbered tag; turn that tag in as you exit.

🌐 *http://www.kunaicho.go.jp/e-about/shisetsu/higashigyoen-map.html*

❾ Fujimi Tamon 富士見多聞

This is the last tamon (arsenal) that remains on the grounds. During the time of the shōgun there were fifteen of these around the honmaru. There are loopholes on the moat side to allow observation and for firing on attackers. In front of it are hydrangea and roses. The roses are mainly wild Chinese and Japanese varieties, most of which were cultivated from seed by the Shōwa emperor and later transplanted to this location.

❿ Ishimuro 石室

The exact use of this cellar is not known. The most likely theory is that it was for the emergency storage of valuables and documents. The exterior shows fire damage. The entire building, even the ceiling, is made of stone from the Izu Peninsula.

⓫ Ninomaru Garden / Ninomaru Teien 二の丸庭園

Originally the location of a secondary residence for the shōgun and for his heir. The original garden was designed by Kobori Enshū, a famous garden designer and tea master. The garden fell into disrepair in the Meiji period; the present garden is a 1968 reconstruction of the original design. The garden contains the Ninomaru Grove, which was designed by imperial request in the early 1980s and expanded in 2003. This grove contains a wide variety of Japanese trees, providing a sanctuary for several species of birds. Not only was the area seeded but insects were introduced as part of the planning. In the northwest portion of the garden is a collection of thirty-one trees, one from each of Japan's prefectures. Near the Ninomaru Grove are hedges of azalea, near the pond is an iris garden with some eighty-nine different varieties, and the pond itself is home to a variety of plants including the pygmy water lily and the endangered floating heart. The carp in the pond are an unusual long-finned crossbreed that was suggested by the Emperor Emeritus.

DETAIL 6

❶ Imperial Palace / Kōkyo 皇居

In the 12th century fortifications were built here by a chieftain named Edo Shigenaga. In the 15th century Ōta Dōkan, a vassal of the Uesugi clan, built a new castle on the same location. In 1486 Dōkan was suspected of plotting treachery and assassinated by orders of his lord. Castles at that time were mainly made of wood and the castle was left to decay until Tokugawa Ieyasu was granted control of the Kantō area in 1590. Ieyasu began an ambitious building program for a new castle, which would not be completed during his lifetime. The program included the large-scale rerouting of local rivers, creating new moats, moving entire hillsides, filling in part of the bay, constructing a large series of walls and fortifications, and laying out the plan for a new city. In 1868 the emperor moved from Kyoto to his new palace; a few years later there was a fire, so the emperor lived offsite until the new palace was ready in 1888. In May and June 1945 the palace suffered significant damage from being bombed by the Americans. New buildings were completed in the 1960s. Little of what is in the Imperial Residence portion can be seen from outside—mostly Edo period structures and administrative buildings. As you look at the palace grounds from the outside, remember that every piece of stone used had to be brought from a great distance, from Izu, by boat, and then transported overland. Tokyo lies on an alluvial plain, so there were no local stone quarries to draw from.

In March 2018, the Imperial Household Agency began giving free tours of part of the Imperial Palace grounds in English. You have to book a tour in advance.

Book a tour at:

🌐 *http://sankan.kunaicho.go.jp/english/guide/koukyo.html*

❷ Sakashita Mon 坂下門

In the Edo period this gate faced north; in the Meiji period it was rebuilt to face east. The name translates as "Slope Bottom Gate." Presently it is the side entrance to the Imperial Palace. Since it leads to the Palace, you cannot cross the moat to the gate for a close view. There is a guard station and a formidable moveable barrier to prevent people from approaching. The gate is used as a public entrance for special events and as service entrance for staff members. In 1862 Andō Nobumasa, one of the shōgun's council of elders, was assassinated outside the gate by six rōnin who each carried a letter opposing policies he was advocating.

❸ Fushimi Yagura 伏見櫓

This tower was built in the early 17th century, or rather rebuilt, as it was originally a part of Fushimi castle in

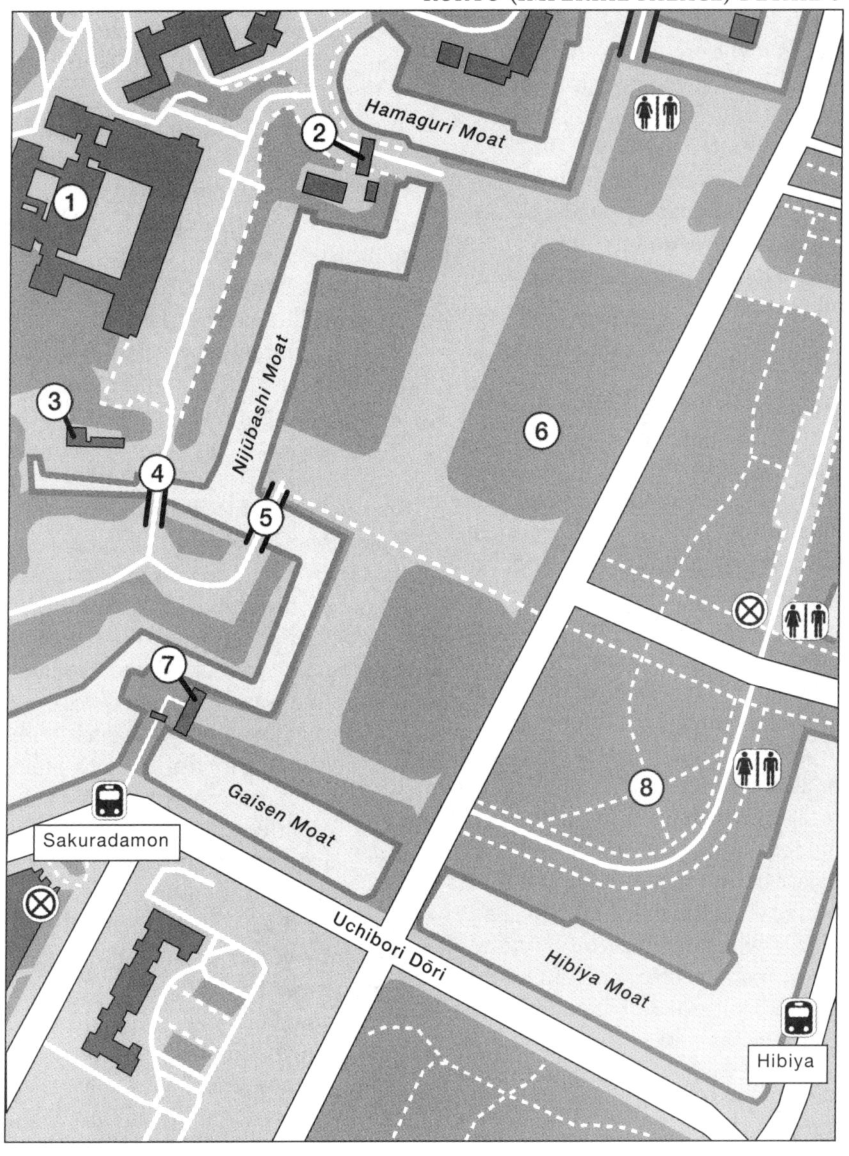

Hamaguri Moat
Nijūbashi Moat
Gaisen Moat
Uchibori Dōri
Hibiya Moat
Sakuradamon
Hibiya
1
2
3
4
5
6
7
8

Kyoto and had been dismantled and moved to the present location. It is one of three surviving towers from Edo Castle. Given its position high above a moat with attractive bridges below, it is one of the most photographed parts of the Imperial Palace grounds. Needless to say the tower and its tamon (galleries) no longer perform a military function, but it sure looks nice.

❹ Imperial Palace Main Gate Iron Bridge / Kōkyo Seimon Tekkyō 皇居正門鉄橋

This bridge carries the nickname of Nijūbashi "double bridge." The original was a wooden bridge that had extra supports, since the gates at each end were situated far above the water of the moat. This structure gave it the appearance of an upper bridge built on top of a lower bridge. In 1888 the wooden bridge was replaced with an iron one designed by Wilhelm Heise. The new bridge had some of the first electric outdoor lights in Japan, as the Imperial Palace had its own power plant. Heise's bridge was dismantled in 1946 and replaced with a steel reconstruction in 1964. Today people often mistake the nearby Ishibashi as the Nijūbashi because it has two arches, or use the term to refer to both collectively. Both bridges are closed to the public except on special occasions, as they are past the security checkpoints for the palace.

❺ Imperial Palace Main Gate Stone Bridge / Kōkyo Seimon Ishibashi 皇居正門石橋

The original Edo period bridge located here was the wooden Nishinomaru Gejo Bashi. It was replaced in 1887 with the present stone bridge, which is said to have been designed by Kawai Kōzō. The bridge is also called the Shakkyō bridge, and nicknamed Meganebashi "Spectacles Bridge," because the reflection of the double arch in the moat resembles a pair of round glasses.

❻ Imperial Palace Frontal Plaza / Kōkyo Mae Hiroba 皇居前広場

This is the public plaza at the southeast corner of the Imperial Palace grounds. It provides excellent views of several palace gates, moats, bridges, walls, and towers. The plaza is an open space consisting mainly of lawns planted with roughly 2,000 well-tended black pines and a large area covered in gravel. In the Edo period this was the location of residences of high-ranking retainers of the shōgun. In the Meiji period it was filled with buildings, until they were removed in 1888 and the present plaza started to take shape. While the plaza was officially opened to the public in 1949, the area had been the site of many demonstrations since 1946 when 250,000 people celebrated May Day, giving the plaza the nickname of "the people's plaza." In 1952 the government banned the use of the plaza for the May Day rally. The courts overturned the ban so the people had a right to gather there but another location had already been arraigned. Some ten thousand marched to the plaza from the official rally site. When the police tried to stop them, fights broke out and tear gas and shots were fired by the police, killing one and wounding many.

❼ Sakurada Mon 桜田門

When Tokugawa Ieyasu arrived to take control of Edo, the area south of this gate to Atago Hill was called Sakurada, "field of cherry trees," and contained thousands of such trees. The official name of the gate was Soto Sakurada Mon, "Outer Sakurada Gate," as Kikyō Mon was once referred to as the inner gate. Sakurada Mon is an excellent example of a double gate with a masugata. As you stand in the center, you can see how an invading force could be boxed in to be fired upon from above.

In 1860 a bloody incident took place in front of the gate when the great elder Ii Naosuke was assassinated by a band of former Mito Han rōnin who opposed his policies. That assassination is depicted in the 1965 movie *Samurai Assassin*.

❽ Statue of Kusunoki Masashige 楠木正成像

Kusunoki Masashige was a samurai who fought for Emperor Go-Daigo against the Kamakura government. Masashige was killed by the Ashikaga when they betrayed the emperor to take power for themselves. In the Edo and Meiji periods he was considered a model of loyalty and in 1880 was posthumously awarded the Senior First Rank by the government. The statue by Takamura Kōun was given to the imperial family by the Sumitomo family in 1890 on the 200th anniversary of the founding of their Besshi copper mines. This statue is the first known depiction of Masashige astride a horse. Great attention was played to making the armor, fittings, sword, and horse as historically accurate as possible.

丸の内・永田町

MARUNOUCHI TO NAGATACHŌ

This chapter covers the areas east and south of the Imperial Palace grounds. In the Edo period this area was filled with government offices and the residences of the daimyō closest to the Tokugawa family. Marunouchi specifically means "within the moats," while Nagatachō was on the higher ground adjacent to it, just outside Sakurada Mon. A suggested route here is to start at the top of detail map 1 and work your way south to where detail map 2 is.

DETAIL 1

❶ Masakado no Kubizuka
将門の首塚

This is a mound that was raised over the head of Taira no Masakado. Masakado was a 10th-century samurai leader who, due to conflicts with relatives and his inability to obtain legal support, attacked a government outpost, which led to his being declared a rebel. After a period of warfare he was defeated and killed. Masakado's head was taken to Kyoto and hung on a tree as a warning against rebellion. However, the head disappeared and legend has it wandering the Kantō looking for its body. Eventually it landed near the village of Shibasaki where the locals buried it, raised a mound over the burial spot, and asked the spirit of Masakado to become a guardian of the area. The mound collapsed in the Great Kantō Earthquake and what remains is a well-cared for monument on the location. The first time I visited, a man in a business suit came, placed a few offerings, and prayed. Then a young man in worker's overalls arrived, put down bags of rice, bottles of tea, and other items, and then prayed in a very

MARUNOUCHI TO NAGATACHŌ

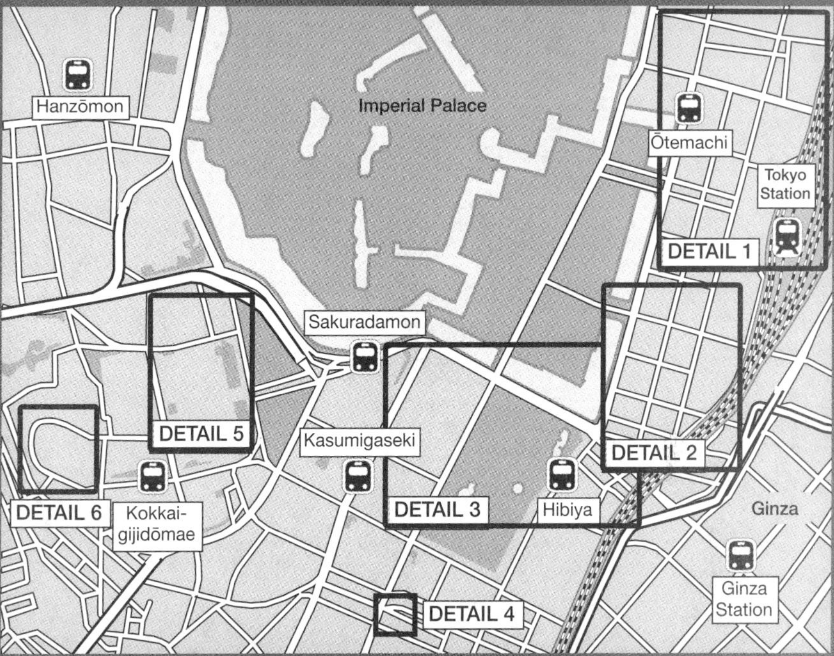

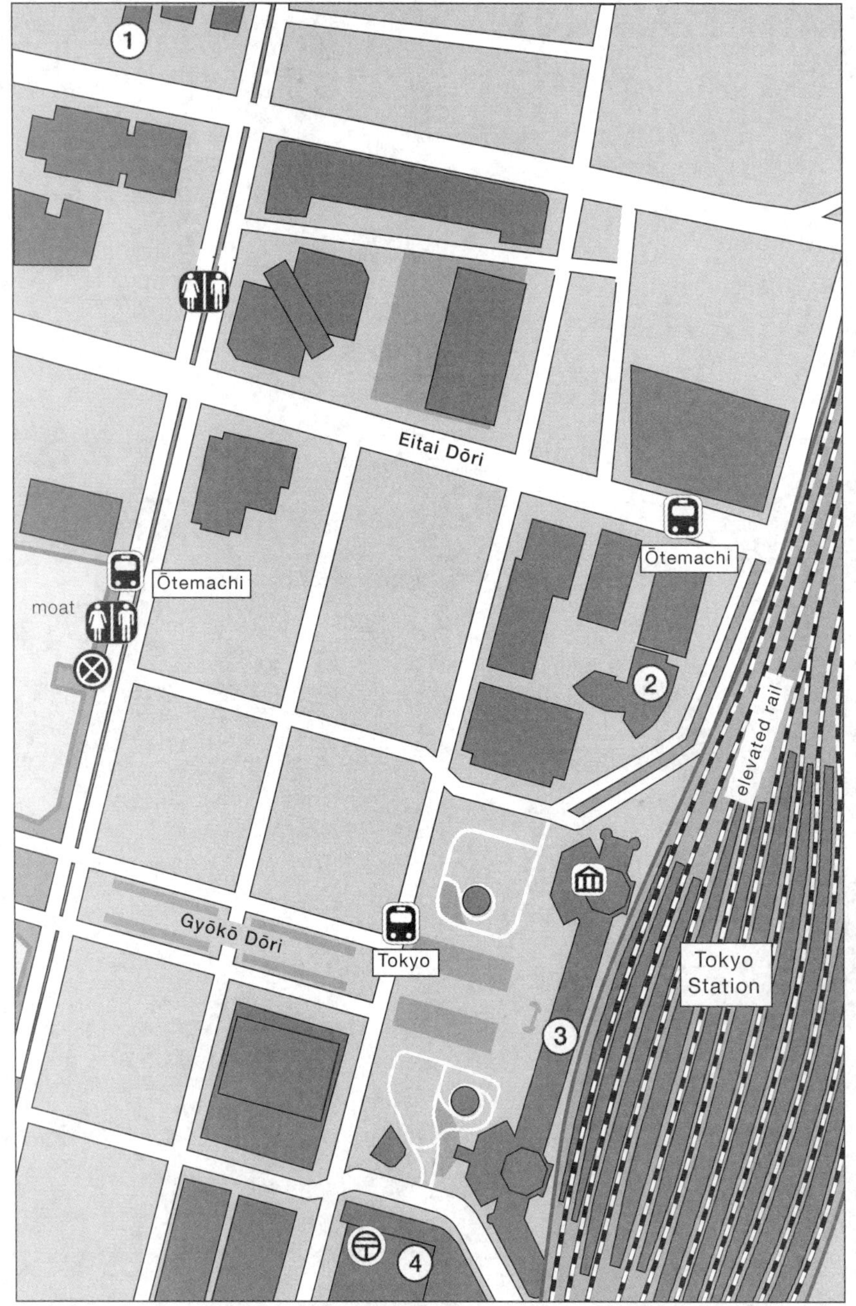
1
Eitai Dōri
Ōtemachi
moat
Ōtemachi
2
elevated rail
Gyōkō Dōri
Tokyo
Tokyo Station
3
4

ritualistic manner. A tradition from the Edo period is that if you visit the mound, or Kanda Myōjin where Masakado is also enshrined, you never visit the temple Narita Fudōson, as the main statue there was brought to the region for rituals against Masakado.

An account of Masakado's rebellion was written not long after the events and is available in English as *Shōmonki: The Story of Masakado's Rebellion*.

❷ Maruzen Marunouchi 丸善丸の内

This bookshop located in the Marunouchi Oazo building is one of my favorite in Tokyo and my favorite Maruzen bookshop. There are four stories of books and magazines to be found here, and the English language section is very large. There is a subsection devoted to English books about Japan, where you will find most of the non-fiction and translated Japanese fiction. A strength of this store is its selection of books in English published in Japan, which are often difficult to get in other countries. If you don't find what you want, ask the staff. The large selection of English books is to be expected, since this bookstore started in Yokohama in 1869 first as an importer of foreign books, mainly in English, and seller of translated foreign books as well as medical supplies.

❸ Tokyo Station / Tokyo Eki 東京駅

This red brick station, which is 1,099 feet (335 meters) long, was designed by Tatsuno Kingo, who also designed the Bank of Japan, and opened in 1914. The bombings in World War II caused extensive damage, destroying the two domes and top story including much of the hotel. After the war a redesigned roof was put into place without the domes or the top story. In 1968 Tokyo Station was greatly expanded on the east side with a very modern building. This entry focuses on the older Marunouchi wing on the west side.

Restoration work to bring back the old design took five years and was finally completed in 2012 in time for the centenary of the building. The restoration involved artisans from many parts of Japan who repaired, and in some cases completely replaced, damaged and lost portions of the building. If you go in through the central Marunouchi wing entrance and look up, you will see the restored beauty of the ceiling.

Tokyo Station serves the largest number of trains of any station in Japan.

🌐 *http://www.tokyostationcity.com/en/*

❹ KITTE キッテ

The former Tokyo Central Post Office is a Shōwa period modernist building designed in 1931 by Yoshida Tetsuro for Japan Post. Presently it consists of seven floors of shops, restaurants, and a museum. It is still administered by Japan Post. The food retailers here serve items from all over Japan. There is a rooftop terrace on the sixth floor with a view of Tokyo Station.

The museum is Intermediatheque (open 11:00 a.m. to 18:00 p.m. and closed Mondays), a museum operated by Japan Post and the University Museum of the University of Tokyo. Exhibits cover a wide range of subjects—there is always something different here. Included is a theater where lectures and events are held. Their publications and other works are sold in the museum boutique. No photography is allowed.
KITTE:
🌐 *https://marunouchi.jp-kitte.jp*
Intermediatheque:
🌐 *http://www.intermediatheque.jp/en*

Station Assassination

Inside the station are two markers where two progressive prime ministers were assailed by right-wing attackers. Next to the southern ticket machines of Marunouchi is a plaque on the wall and a spot on the floor indicating where Hara Takashi was stabbed to death on November 4, 1921. On November 14, 1930, Hamaguchi Osachi was shot; that place is marked by a special tile on the floor at the base of a set of stairs. He died the following year from complications due to the shooting.

DETAIL 2

❶ Meiji Mutual Life Insurance Building / Meiji Seimei Kan
明治生命館

Designed by Okada Shinichirō and completed in 1934, the building is an eight story, steel framed, reinforced concrete structure in the Greek Revival style. In 1941 the government had the building stripped of metal ornamentation so the metal could be used for military purposes. A survivor of the firebombings of World War II, it was requisitioned by the Americans during the Allied occupation to become the headquarters for the Far East Air Force. It was also where the Allied Council for Japan held its bimonthly meetings. Much earlier, this was where the shōgun's firefighting brigade was housed. One of the firefighters had a son who did not follow in his father's footsteps; instead, Hiroshige would become one of Japan's most famous ukiyo-e print designers.

❷ Mitsubishi Ichigōkan Museum / Mitsubishi Ichigōkan Bijutsukan
三菱一号館美術館

The original 1894 three-story Queen Anne structure was designed by Josiah Condor for Mitsubishi and was the first Western-style office building in Japan. As the original was showing its age, it was demolished in 1968. The present building is a detailed reconstruction of

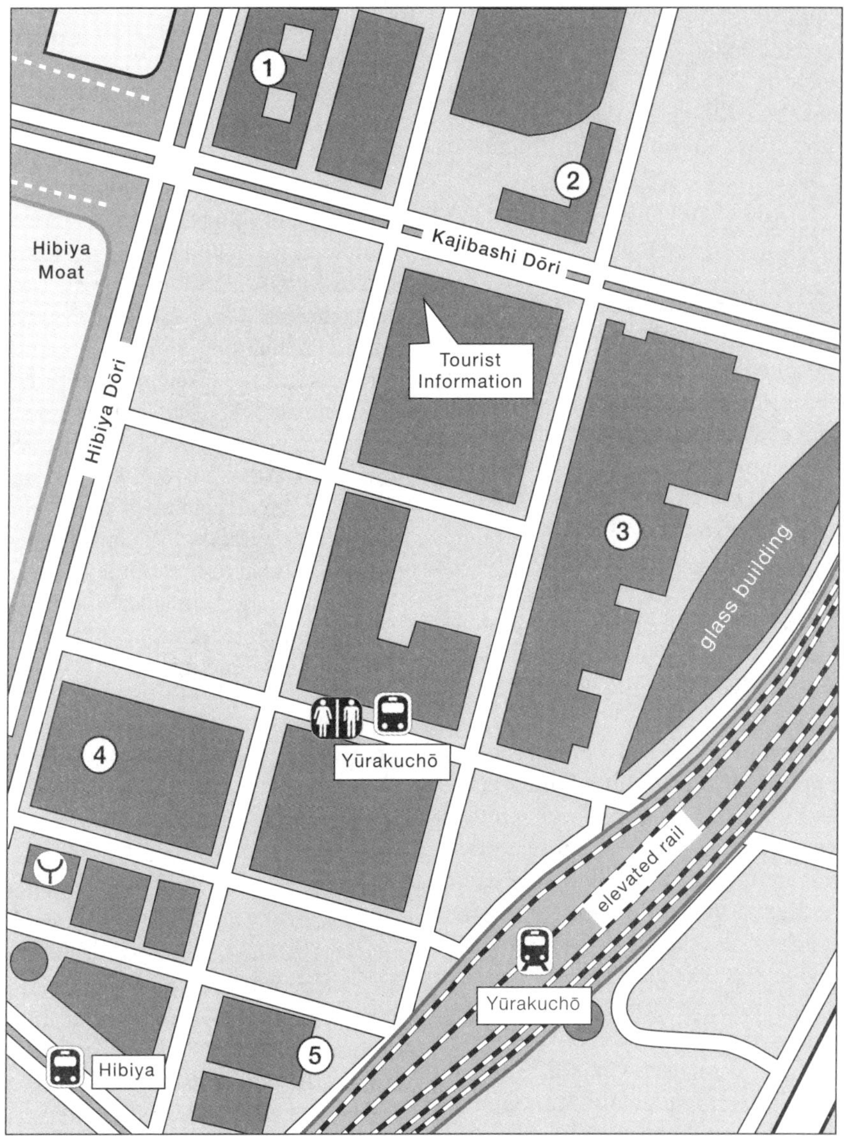

the original and was completed in 2010 using Conder's plans, as well as reusing many of the original interior parts such as handrails, which had been saved. Today the building is a museum whose exhibits are mainly of 19th century European art. Many consider the building itself to be a work of art. There is a park behind the building, and the building houses a cafe and a shop. These do not require a ticket to enter.

🌐 *http://mimt.jp/english/*

❸ Tokyo International Forum 東京国際フォーラム

Designed by Rafael Viñoly and completed in 1996, the Forum is a multi-use complex used for conventions, tradeshows, receptions, performances, and meetings. It was commissioned at a cost of 1.5 billion dollars in the late 1980s when the city of Tokyo had plenty of money to invest in such projects. There are five buildings, four squarish halls, a plaza, and the leaf-shaped Glass Building next to the elevated train tracks. The seven-story Glass Building is an impressive structure to walk around in with its many levels and large central atrium crossed by several bridges on upper stories; the entire structure follows the curve of the nearby train tracks. There is not much to see other than the atrium and public exhibits, but it is worth a stroll. The plaza is the location of the famous Ōedo Antique Market on most first and third Sundays. The site was the location of the previous Metropolitan Government Building of Tokyo.

🌐 *http://www.t-i-forum.co.jp*

🌐 *https://vinoly.com/works/tokyo-international-forum/*

🌐 *https://www.antique-market.jp/english/*

❹ DN Tower 21 / DN タワー 21

This 1995 structure designed by Kevin Roche and John Dinkeloo is based on two previous buildings: the Nōrin Chūkin Bank Building, which was completed in 1933, and the Daiichi Seimeikan building from 1938. Both were designs by Watanabe Hitoshi. The Daiichi Seimeikan building was where Douglas McArthur had his offices during the postwar occupation of Japan. What remains of these two buildings is three facades and a portion of the western part of the Daiichi. The clean, vertical design of the Daiichi building is reflected in the design of the present building.

❺ Yūraku Inari Jinja 有楽稲荷神社

Established in 1859 on the grounds of the Takatsuki han residence, this shrine survived the fires of the Great Kantō Earthquake. It was rebuilt in the 1970s as part of the construction projects for the Yūrakuchō Electric Building. Today this shrine sits in a plaza at the south end of Yūrakuchō Station on the side of the tracks opposite the Ginza. The shrine itself is nested in a square of greenery planted just for it.

DETAIL 3

❶ Yūrakuchō 有楽町

While most of the Yūrakuchō neighborhood consists of modern office buildings, there is one special portion that has survived since the end of World War II. This is the section under the train tracks, the gādoshita, literally "under the girder bridge." Here you will find a handful of small businesses, mainly small, cozy retaurants to grab a bite to eat or drink. These are mostly old and well loved by their regular clients. During the postwar period the neighborhood was quite different than it is today. As the area near the tracks was located not far from the Post Exchanges established for the use of the occupying troops, as well as not far for the GHQ offices, it took on a certain flavor. This part of Yūrakuchō became the site of one of the largest black markets, often selling goods from the PX shops. It was also known for some 500 streetwalkers, called pam pam girls, who congregated there picking up soldiers. Today I recommend strolling the area, perhaps a taking few photographs, and enjoying some yakitori and beer.

❷ Gojira (Godzilla) Statue ゴジラ像

This plaza has long been known among fans of Japanese special effects movies for its Gojira Statue that was in this location since 1995. In 2018 a new statue of Gojira was unveiled, based on the monster from the 2016 movie *Shin Gojira* (*Shin Godzilla* is the English version of the title). The new statue is the largest full-body Gojira statue in Japan, standing at 9.8 feet (3 meters) including the pedestal. The old statue was moved to the lobby of the Tōhō Cinemas Hibiya theater (TOHOシネマズ日比谷), which is a short walk away. When I first visited the old statue many years ago, I put my hands together in prayer and bowed, much to the delight of some office workers taking a break in the plaza.

❸ Tokyo Takarazuka Theater / Tōkyō Takarazuka Gekijō 東京宝塚劇場

The Takarazuka Revue is increasingly famous around the world. Founded in 1913 in the hot spring town of Takarazuka, it has grown to include five troupes of actors. All the actors are women who have undergone two years of rigorous training at the Takarazuka Music School, a private boarding school run by the theater. Applicants are as young as fifteen and no older than eighteen. Most apply straight out of middle school and only about forty out of well over a thousand applicants are accepted each year. The Tokyo theater was completed in 1934 as the second Takarazuka Theater. During the postwar occupation the theater was requisitioned for allied use and renamed the Ernie Pyle Theater until

▲ The west side of Tokyo Station was restored for the 2014 centenary of the building.

▲ Old movie posters and eateries line this passageway under the tracks in Yūrakuchō.

へそでズバリ身上
アノ話題の
長脇差あらし!
FT
Festival/Tokyo

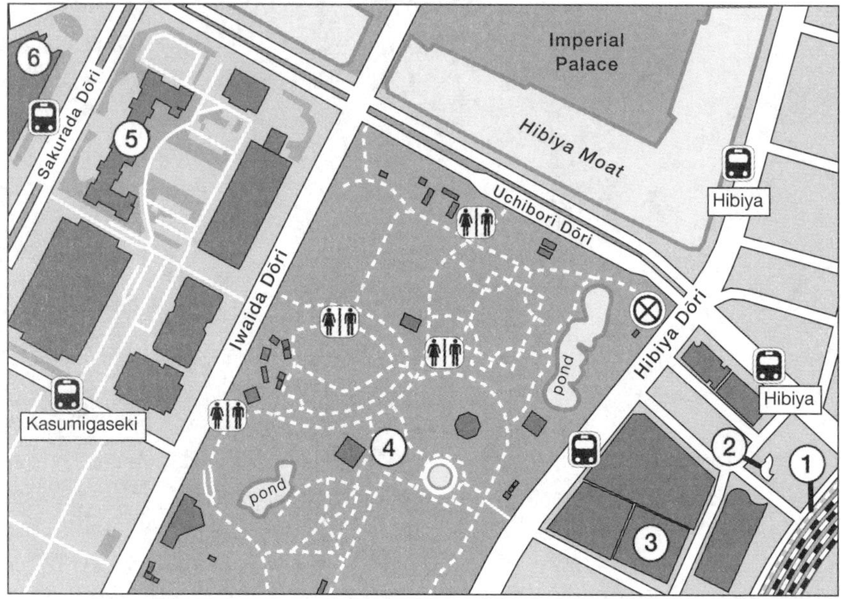

1952. The old building was demolished in 1998 to be rebuilt and reopened in 2001. Audiences are well over ninety percent women and tickets are said to sell out very quickly. The theater has a gift shop just to the left of the entrance that does not require a ticket for access. The shop sells books, magazines, photographs, CD recordings, videos, and other items.

🌐 *http://kageki.hankyu.co.jp*
🌐 *http://www.tms.ac.jp/english/*

❹ Hibiya Park / Hibiya Kōen
日比谷公園

When Tokugawa Ieyasu entered Edo, this area was an inlet off the bay. As part of his building of Edo Castle, the inlet was filled in to reduce the risk of warships approaching within cannon range. Later in the Meiji period this area was considered as a location for government ministry buildings. However, excavations showed the soil was unfit for heavy modern construction so the government gave the land to the city to use as a park. In 1903 it opened as Tokyo's first Western-style park, which came to be surrounded by Western-style government buildings. In 1905 some 30,000 protesters gathered in the park in a rally against the conditions of the Treaty of Portsmouth, which ended the 1904–05 Russo-Japanese War. Many saw the treaty as very unfair to the victorious Japanese. In World War II the metal ornaments of the original park were stripped by the Japanese government to be melted down and made into military hardware. After World War II, GIs looking to relax would head to Yūrakuchō for movies at the Ernie Pyle Theater or for the pam pam girls; others would head in the opposite direction to Hibiya Park to pick up young Japanese men. Needless to say GHQ did not approve of such behavior and the MPs would periodically catch violators, who would then be transferred back home. The famous 1951 novel *Forbidden Colors* by Mishima Yukio has mention of Hibiya Park as a gay pickup spot.

Today the park is known for other kinds of colors, having a famous rose garden and a tulip garden. Each November the park is host to the Tokyo Metropolitan Chrysanthemum Exhibition.

🌐 *https://www.tokyo-park.or.jp/park/format/index037.html*

❺ Ministry of Justice Museum / Hōmu Shiryō Tenjishitsu
法務史料展示室

The exhibits in the Ministry of Justice Museum cover historical materials on Japanese law from the Meiji period to the present, as well as items related to the construction and restoration of the building. The museum is located on the third floor of the Old Ministry of Justice Building; admission is free.

🌐 *http://www.moj.go.jp/ENGLISH/mojm-01.html*

❺ Old Ministry of Justice Building / Hōmu Shōkyū Honkan
法務省旧本館

This building was designed by the German architects Hermann Ende and Wilhelm Böckmann, with modifications to the plans by Kawai Kōzō. Built in the German neo-Renaissance style, it is one of the few large buildings of this style remaining in the world, as Germany's were destroyed in World War II. Construction of the building was begun in 1888 and completed in 1895. High standards insisted on by the Germans, such as steel reinforcement and a solid foundation in the soft soil, allowed it to survive the Great Kantō Earthquake. The building was heavily damaged in World War II, losing the roof and interior floors. Extensive work was done starting in 1991 to restore the building to its original look. Today, one half houses the Research and Training Institute of the Ministry of Justice, the Ministry of Justice Library, and the Ministry of Justice Museum; the other half is the Public Prosecutors Offices.

❻ Tokyo Metropolitan Police Department / Keishichō 警視庁

Designed by Okada Architect and Associates and completed in 1980, the headquarters building is on a V-shaped plot of land and has twenty-two stories, four of which are below the ground level. The Tokyo Metropolitan Police functions as the local police for Tokyo and also handles security for national government facilities, the imperial family, and visiting dignitaries. They have advanced rescue teams for disasters, a unit to fight organized crime, an anti-terrorism unit, and much more. The building is a major landmark often seen in police dramas. As the building's location is in front of that gate, it is often indirectly referred to as Sakurada Mon.

DETAIL 4

❶ Japan Sake and Shōchū Information Center / Nihon no Sake Jōhōkan 日本の酒情報館

This is a center devoted to sake, shōchū, and awamori, Japan's major native alcoholic beverages. There are informational displays on the history of these beverages in Japan, manufacturing techniques, and a variety of implements used in drinking and storing them. About fifty different beverages are available for tasting. They also provide tourist information on breweries that can be visited, sake events, recommended shops, and more.

🌐 *https://japansake.or.jp/sake/en/*

MARUNOUCH TO NAGATACHŌ 4

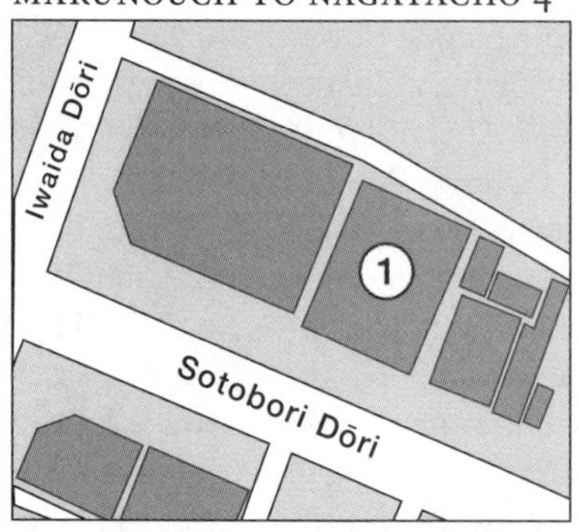

DETAIL 5

❶ National Diet Building / Kokkaigijidō 国会議事堂

Designed by Ōkuma Yoshikuni and Yabashi Kenkichi, this steel-framed granite structure took seventeen years to complete, starting in 1920. It is located on the site of the former estate of daimyō Ii Naosuke, who was assassinated at the Sakurada Mon of the palace grounds in 1860. Visitation to the building is restricted; the web sites of the House of Representatives and the House of Councilors each have instructions on how to visit arrange a visit to their respective portions of the building.

In the iconic 1954 movie Gojira (known in the United States as Godzilla), the title character is seen walking through part of the Diet building, leaving it in ruin.

House of Representatives:

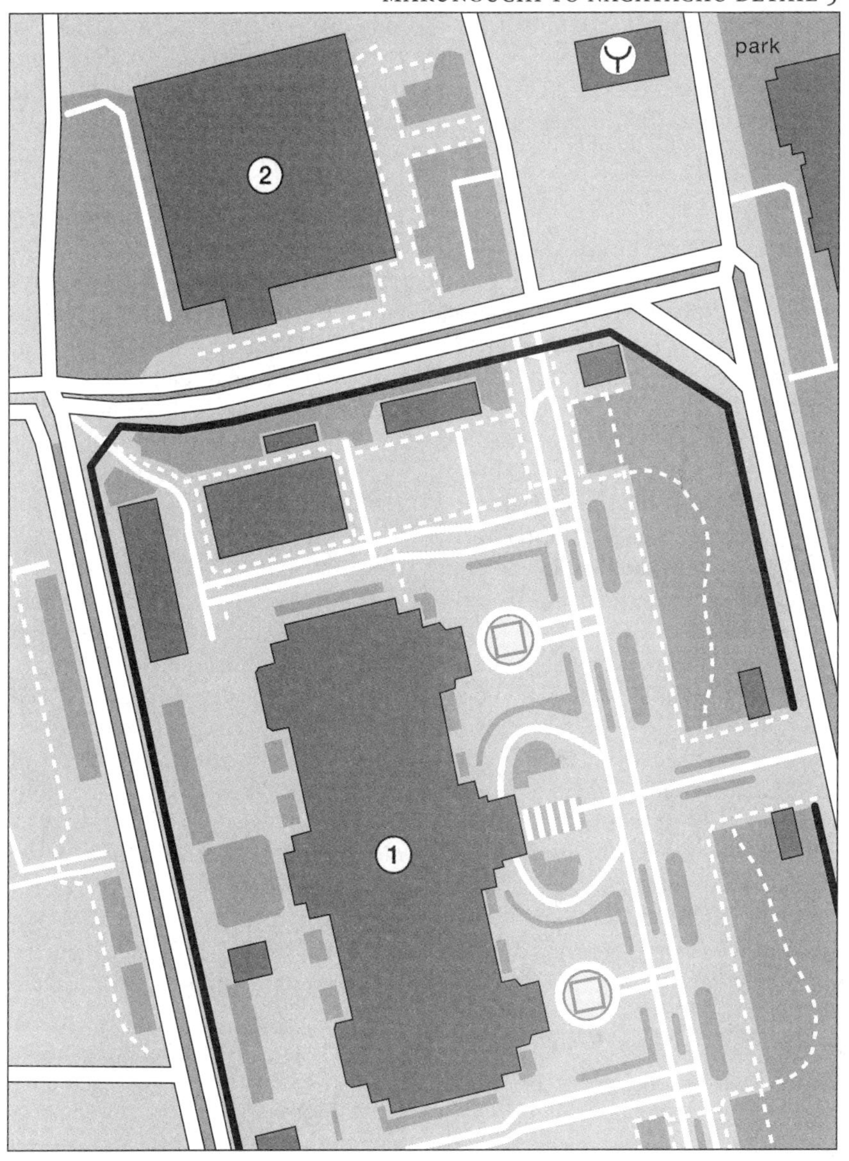
park
2
1

🌐 *http://www.shugiin.go.jp/internet/index.nsf/html/index_e.htm*
House of Councilors:
🌐 *http://www.sangiin.go.jp/eng/index.htm*

❷ **National Diet Library / Kokuritsu Kokkai Toshokan** 国立国会図書館
In 1948 the collection of the National Diet Library was established by merging the collections of the Imperial Library, the library of the House of Peers, and the library of the House of Representatives. The functions of the library are modeled after the United States Library of Congress and perform a variety of services for the Diet, in addition to collecting and cataloging material published in Japan and about Japan. The current central building dates from 1961. The annex addition was completed in 1986. Members of the public over the age of eighteen can visit the library and gain access to the materials after registering. The library also has exhibits, free wi-fi, a cafeteria, a coffee shop, and a kiosk to purchase stationery and food.
🌐 *http://www.ndl.go.jp/en/*

DETAIL 6

❶ **Hie Jinja** 日枝神社
The founding date of this shrine is unclear. Edo Shigenaga built a Hie Jinja in the Kamakura period, as Ōta Dōkan did later when he built his castle in 1478. Some scholars think it is the Sannō Jinja mentioned in a document from 1362. Before the separation of Buddhism and Shintō in the Meiji period, Hie Jinja was also referred to as Sannō Sama. The reason for this is that Ōyamakui no Kami, the kami enshrined there, was also referred to as Sannō Gongen. In any case, it is an old shrine that has long been considered the protector of Edo castle, and after the shōgun left, the protector of the Imperial Palace. Tokugawa Ieyasu had the shrine moved to the southwest, where the Supreme Court is now. After the shrine burned down in the Meireki Fire it was rebuilt on the hill where it now resides. The shrine was last destroyed in the firebombings of World War II; the present buildings date from 1958. As the messenger of Sannō Gongen is the monkey, there are statues of monkeys at the main entrance and in front of the main hall. During the Sannō Matsuri, held in June every other year, the procession is allowed to enter the palace grounds, a tradition that dates back to the Edo period. There is a shrine museum to the right of the main hall.

The main entrance is to the east via a stairway with an impressive torii. There is also a steeper, narrower stairway on the west side.
🌐 *https://www.hiejinja.net/english/index.html*

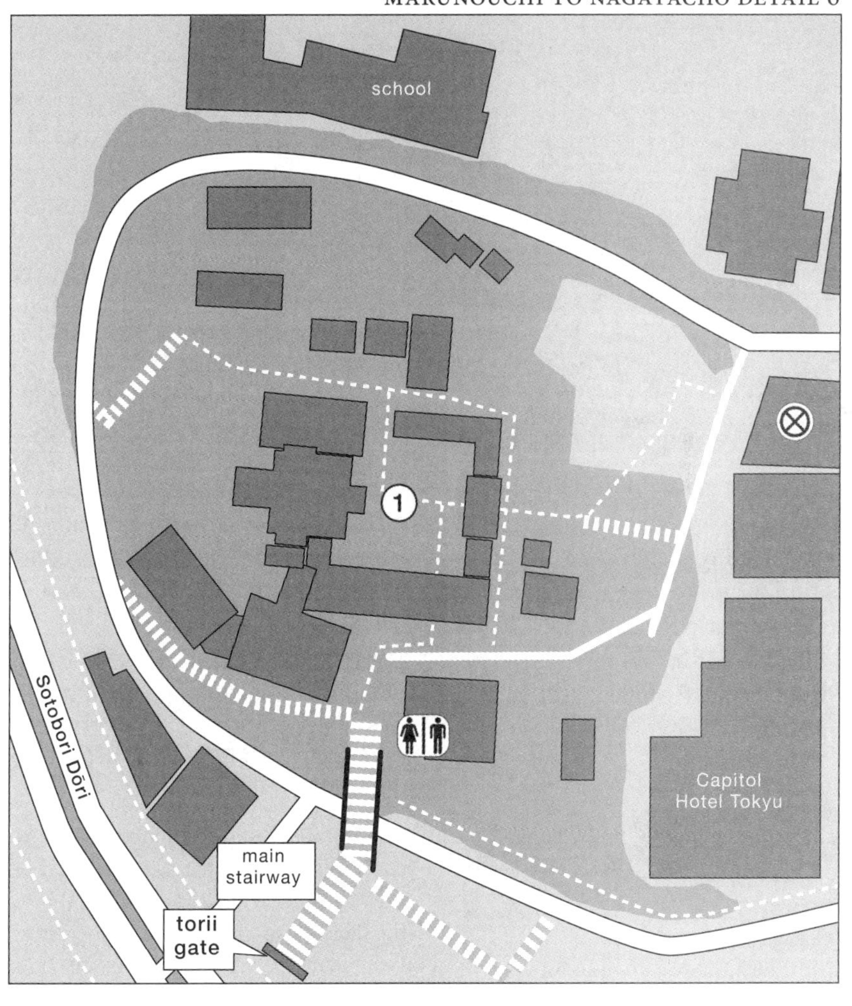
school
1
Sotobori Dōri
main stairway
torii gate
Capitol Hotel Tokyu

目黒駅

MEGURO STATION AREA

I have a suggested route for the west side of the river: Go toward Ryūsenji via Gajoen and the temples in between. There are plenty of restaurants in the shopping district near Ryūsenji if you get hungry. Then, perhaps *after* eating, visit the Meguro Parasitological Museum and work your way back to the Meguro Station area and beyond to the Teien Museum.

If you are in Tokyo in September, check for the dates of the Meguro Pacific Saury Festival, a festival inspired by the famous rakugo tale *Meguro no Sanma*.

DETAIL 1

❶ Kita Roppeita XIV Commemorative Nōgaku Theater / Jūyonsei Kita Roppeita Nōgakudō
十四世喜多六平太記念能楽堂

A theater for the Kita Ryū style of nō. The Kita Ryū was in serious trouble in the Meiji period: the twelfth head had passed away and the thirteenth spent his time in pleasurable pursuits, even selling many of the valued costumes and masks of the Kita Ryū to do so. It was then decided that the grandson of the twelfth head would be adopted into the family to carry on the lineage. After years of training from various instructors, he became the head of the lineage when he was ten years old, going on to become a major performer.

The theater holds performances as well as workshops on dance, chant, and music.

🌐 *http://kita-noh.com*

MEGURO STATION AREA

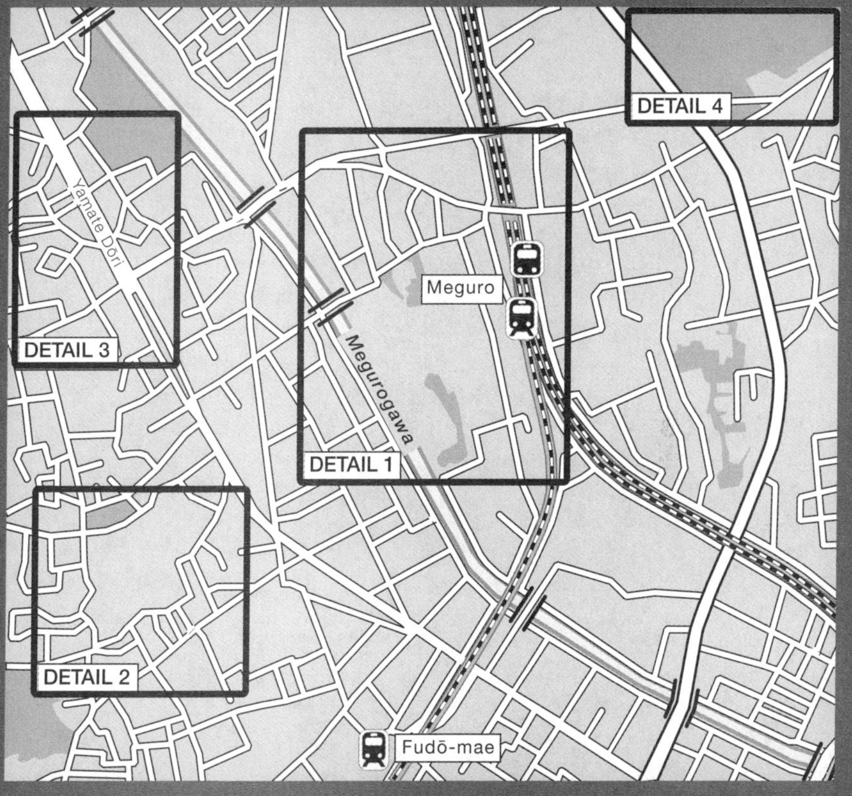

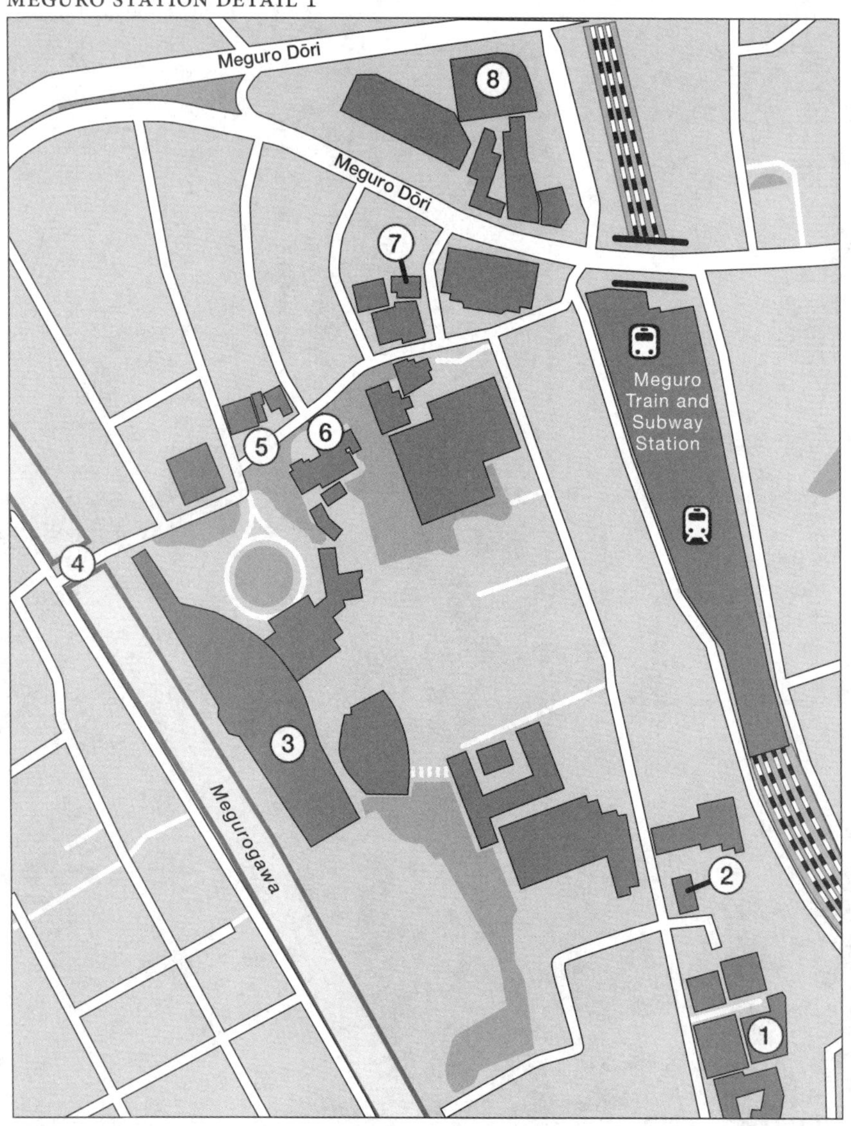

❷ Sugino Costume Museum / Sugino Gakuen Ishō Hakubutsukan
杉野学園衣裳博物館

This specialized museum was founded in 1957 to promote and study the development of clothing with an

emphasis on Western garb. The collection has 1,400 articles of clothing, including non-Western items, as well as art works that are illustrative of what people wear. The museum has four floors and each year it displays a new theme. Many years ago my inner trickster came forth as I was walking nearby with friends and commented that the young Japanese sure dressed well. My friends looked around and agreed; I never did mention to them that we were near the Sugino Fashion College.
🌐 *http://www.costumemuseum.jp*

❸ Meguro Gajoen 目黒雅叙園

Gajoen means "garden of elegance" and the original building earned the nickname of Ryūgūjō "the dragon king's palace." The gift shop sells a book on what the hotel looked like before the 1991 rebuilding. Meguro Gajoen is filled with some 2,500 pieces of art and crafts from around Japan, which at the time of the original building's opening in 1928 included Korea and Taiwan. As you enter, go down the long hall to your right to view much of the art, some of which is on the ceiling. Also check out the restrooms off this hall for their impressive decor. Not all the art is viewable, as much of it is in rooms and halls that are used for private events. There are seven restaurants and cafes, serving Chinese, Japanese, Italian, and American cuisine, and a French patisserie. One of the restaurants consists of an entire traditional building with its own garden within the spacious atrium. Gajoen also has an exterior garden with a waterfall, the stream of which runs through parts of the building. For wedding services there is a Christian chapel, a Shintō shrine, and enough banquet halls to accommodate as many as twenty-four celebrations at once. Meguro Gajoen also hosts special dinners, exhibits, concerts, stage shows, and special events for hotel guests. The interior artwork was a major influence on the design of the bathhouse in Miyazaki Hayao's movie *Spirited Away*.

Warning: Meguro Gajoen hosts many wedding receptions, so be very discreet as you look around to avoid disturbing the guests.
🌐 *https://www.hotelgajoen-tokyo.com*

❹ Taikobashi 太鼓橋

Near Daienji, on the site presently occupied by Meguro Gajoen, there used to be a temple called Myōōin. One of the head priests of Myōōin was named Saiun. Before he became a priest his name had been Kichisa—the same Kichisa from the tragic story of Oshichi (see the entry for Enjōji on page 153 in the Hakusan/Koishikawa chapter). To pray for Oshichi, every other night he chanted while walking to Sensōji in Asakusa, making 10,000 trips over fifty-four years. When people heard of this, they started making donations, which he used to pave Gyōninzaka. He had enough left over to build Taikobashi in 1794. This bridge got its name from its shape, which was round like a drum. Taikobashi was also the subject of many ukiyo-e prints. During a flood in the Taishō period the bridge washed away; in any case it would have eventually been replaced with a flat bridge for automobile traffic like the one that is there today.

❺ Gyōninzaka 行人坂

Gyōnin is a term for a class of Buddhist monks that was at times applied to yamabushi. The slope in front of Daienji gained this name because a great number of yamabushi would walk it to the temple where they received training in Buddhist mikkyō (esoteric) practices.

❻ Daienji 大圓寺

A Tendai sect Buddhist temple founded in 1624 by Taikai Hōin, a yamabushi of Mount Yudono. The Shakadō houses a statue of Shakyamuni from 1193. To the right of the main hall is a hall with a statue of Amida Buddha enshrined in 1712 by Kichisa, the young monk who Yaoya Oshichi had been enamored of. This temple is famous for its stone Rakan (Arhat) images; while there are 500 Rakan, the temple has 519 statues on display. The statues were carved to console the spirits of those who died in the Gyōninzaka Fire. The Gyōninzaka Fire, also called the Great Meiwa Fire, one of the great fire disasters of Edo, started here in 1772. The temple was punished by not being allowed to rebuild until 1848. The Shakadō and the main hall are opened only on January 1 through 7, on April 8, which is the traditional birthday of Shakyamuni Buddha, and on the feast of Daikokuten, which is held every sixty days. On the first Sunday of each month, a copying of the Heart Sutra is held. The temple is on the Yamate Shichifukujin pilgrimage.

The entrance to the grounds is on the north side.

🌐 *http://www.tendaitokyo.jp/jiinmei/6daienji/*

❼ Tonkatsu Tonki とんかつ とんき

A famous tonkatsu restaurant established in 1939. Only tonkatsu, a deep fried cutlet usually made with pork, is on the menu, served as set meals with rice and soup. The set meals are: rōsukatsu (roasted tonkatsu), hirekatsu (tonkatsu fillet), and kushikatsu (skewer tonkatsu). This is simple, robust food rather than fine gourmet fare. Expect to wait for about twenty minutes to be served, as this place is busy. Best to enjoy your wait, savor the meal, catch your breath and head out to make room for others. There are two floors: counter seating is on the first and table seating on the second. The kitchen is on the first floor and open so you can see the staff at work. There are some English-speaking staff, and credit cards are accepted.

❽ Kume Museum of Art / Kume Bijutsukan 久米美術館

Established in 1987, this museum is devoted to a father and his son and the artists and events associated with them, and is built on land that the family owned. Kume Kunitake was an educator, historian, and a participant in the Iwakura diplomatic mission to the United States and Europe in the 1870s. His son Kume Keiichirō was a Western-style painter, professor, and movie pioneer. The father and son each have separate galleries dedicated to their work.

🌐 *http://www.kume-museum.com*

DETAIL 2

❶ Kaifukuji 海福寺

An Ōbaku Zen temple originally built in Fukagawa by the Chinese priest Ingen in 1658. It was moved here in 1910 after being damaged in floods. Kaifukuji was the first Ōbaku temple in Japan; it was not until 1661 that Manpukuji in Uji, the headquarters of the sect, was established. There are two stone pagodas to the left about half way up the stairs that are memorials for those who died when the Eitaibashi collapsed in 1807 during the Fukagawa Matsuri. When the temple was relocated, the pagodas also moved to the new location. The temple bell has an unusual shape—the base of the bell is not round but rather undulates, a Chinese design feature that reflects of origin of the sect.

❷ Gohyaku Rakanji 五百羅漢寺

A Buddhist temple founded originally in Honjō in 1695 to house 500 life-sized wooden statues of Rakan (Arhats). 305 of the statues survive to this day and are on display. Half of the statues are in a curved hall, and the other half in the temple's main hall. In the Edo period a tradition arose of finding the statue that most resembled a dead loved one and praying. Some people continue to do this. A strange statue of the nightmare-eating creature the Baku can also be found here. The statue is hard not to notice as it is a mix of human, cow, and lion, with nine eyes.

The temple was moved to the present location in 1908 where it was neglected and fell into decay. In 1938 the temple was taken over by a woman named Okoi. Okoi had a rather dramatic life. She was a geisha who married and divorced a famous actor, went back to being a geisha, and then became the lover of Prime Minister Katsura Tarō. After his death she owned a fashionable cafe in the Ginza. In 1934 she became involved in a political scandal and walked away from her past life to become a nun. Then she discovered this temple and proceeded to take care of it. After her death in 1948, others took over and eventually the temple was reconstructed in 1981.

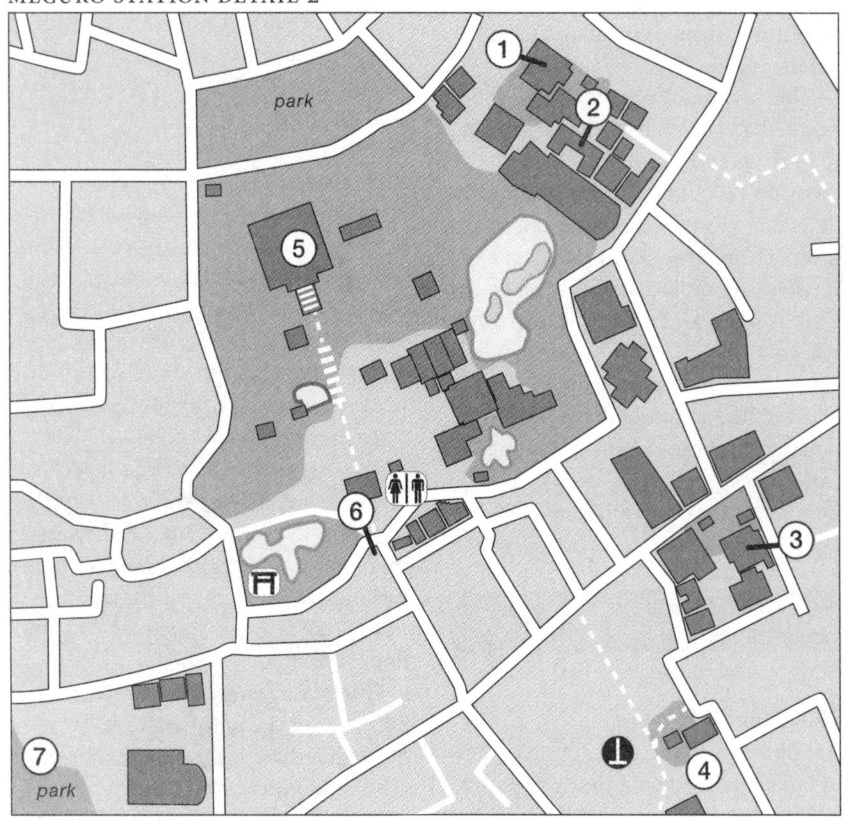

Gohyaku Rakanji was affiliated with Ōbaku Zen until 1948 when it became independent.

The temple has a tea house, the Rakan-jaya, for casual visitors, and upstairs a restaurant, Rakan-tei. Rakan-tei requires reservations at least three days in advance.

Unusual for Tokyo, though common in many other cities, this temple charges an entrance fee to casual visitors. The temple is open 9:00 a.m. to 5:00 p.m. each day.

No photographs are allowed inside any of the buildings, or of any statues outside.

On the fifteenth of each month starting at 1:00 p.m. there is sutra copying.

Access is on the southeast side.

🌐 *http://rakan.or.jp/en*

❸ Jōjuin 成就院

When the famous Buddhist priest Ennin made his trip to T'ang China, he carried an image he had made of Yakushi Nyorai, the Medicine Buddha, as protection. On the return voyage there was a fierce storm and Ennin offered the image to the god of the sea—or in another version of the story, it fell overboard and reached land on the back of an octopus. Years later when in Meguro, he carved another image in the hopes of ending a disease outbreak. This one, which is the main image of this temple, depicts Yakushi riding on the back of an octopus, "tako" in Japanese. The temple is sometimes called Tako Yakushi after this image. The Tako Yakushi is a hidden image, only shown on January 8 and sometimes on May and September 8. One of the things Ennin was said to have learned in China was how to give the power of healing to stones. The temple has such stones considered especially good for getting rid of things that protrude, such as warts or hemorrhoids. One must recite a certain chant, rub the stone for over an hour, and refrain from eating octopus until healed. There is a bit of wordplay here as tako, written with different kanji, can mean a callus or a corn.

The entrance is to the north.

🌐 *http://www.jyoujyuin.jp*

❹ Anyōin 安養院

If you approach this Shingon Buddhist temple from the north, you will see a large stone with red lettering at the intersection of the road leading to it. At the base of the stairs there are two very unusual large komainu that give a hint as to what is ahead. There is a small portion of the grounds filled with sculptures. The most famous aspect of this temple is a five-story burial chamber with an automated system designed by Toyota that retrieves burial urns when someone wants to visit a person interned there.

You can also approach the temple from the west or south.

❺ Ryūsenji / Meguro Fudōson 瀧泉寺 目黒不動尊

When the not yet famous Buddhist priest Ennin was fourteen years old, he headed to Kyoto to study under the already famous priest Saichō. He stopped to rest in the village of Meguro and had a dream of Fudō Myōō. He then carved a statue of Fudō and left it with the villagers. Fifty years later he returned and founded this Tendai Buddhist temple to house the statue, which is still in the main hall. It was the first temple to Fudō in eastern Japan.

In the Edo period, the Tokugawa shōguns became patrons of the temple and in 1634 an impressive new main hall and other buildings were constructed. In World War II most of the temple complex was burned in the firebombings.

The main gate is south of the temple complex. As you pass through the main gate, to your right are the Kannondō, Amidadō, Jizōdō, and temple

▲ The 519 Rakan images at Daienji take up one whole side of the temple plaza.

office. The Amidadō is on the Tokyo 33 Kannon Pilgrimage. To the left and beyond the pond are the only original buildings remaining, the Main Fudōdō and the Seishidō. Near them are seven Jizō statues dedicated to the victims of the 2011 earthquake and tsunami. The pond is fed by natural springs; for centuries ascetics have purified themselves there by standing under the waterfall in the winter.

The main entrance is to the south; one can also enter from the north by way of the nearby park.

🌐 *http://park6.wakwak.com/~megurofudou/*

❻ Hiyokuzuka 比翼塚

Here is a tale of lovers who were the subject of popular of kabuki plays, which have overshadowed the actual history. However, we do know a few details that are likely to be true. Shirai Gonpachi was a young man who had to leave home and make his way to Edo. On the way, he was warned by a beautiful young woman that bandits were holding her prisoner and planning to kill him. The two of them escaped and he returned the woman, Komurasaki, to her home. In time, he discovered that she was now a very expensive prostitute who had entered that profession to help her impoverished family. He went to see her and they fell in love. He then turned to crime to be able to afford to visit his lover. Gonpachi was eventually captured, tried, and executed, and his remains were buried at a small temple near the entrance to Ryūsenji. Komurasaki heard of this, went to his grave, and there committed suicide. The locals, taking pity, buried her with him and erected a stone carved with the word hiyokuzuka, which means a common grave for lovers. The small temple is no more, but the stone is still there, located in a small enclosure just outside and to the left of the main gate of Ryūsenji.

Ryūsenji Festivals

Some of the ceremonies, feasts and festivals at Ryūsenji:

The main temple hall is open from 6:00 a.m. to 5:00 p.m. each day. There is a daily Fudo Myōō goma fire ritual in the main hall at 3:00 p.m.

Each month other halls on the grounds have ceremonies during which the buildings have their doors opened so you can look inside.

Fifteenth of the month: Amidadō ceremony at 2:00 p.m.

Eighteenth of the month: Kannon ceremony at the Kannondō at 2:00 p.m.

Twenty-fourth of every month: Jizō ceremony at the Jizōdō at 2:00 p.m.

There is a temple fair on the twenty-eighth of every month. The Main Fudōdō hall is open then.

Every October 28 there is a sweet potato festival in memory of Aoki Konyō, who is buried at the temple.

❼ Rinshi no Mori Park / Toritsu Rinshi no Mori Kōen 都立林試の森公園

A large well-forested park that can be a good place to take a break. Originally this was a forestry experimental station established in 1900. When the research facility was moved out of Tokyo to Tsukuba, the land became available for a park, which opened in 1989. There are streams and ponds as well as a large variety of birds. If you visit in the fall, you can enjoy the changing of the leaf colors.

🌐 *http://www.kensetsu.metro.tokyo.jp/content/000007587.pdf*

DETAIL 3

❶ Meguro Parasitological Museum / Meguro Kiseichūkan 公益財団法人目黒寄生虫館

The Meguro Parasitological Museum is a private research facility and educational museum established in 1953. Exhibits include video, photographs, and lots of specimens. There is a tapeworm on display that is 28.87 feet (8.8 meters) long; next to it is a box with a cloth tape the same length. There is an English translation of the museum guidebook that you can purchase in the second floor shop. The guidebook makes for an interesting—or disturbing—souvenir or gift. The museum shop also sells the usual T-shirts, postcards, books, and so on. Interestingly this museum seems quite popular with couples. Warning: You likely will want to avoid eating raw salads for some time after visiting.

🌐 *https://www.kiseichu.org/e-top*

❷ Ōtori Jinja 大鳥神社

Ōtori Jinja is said to have been established in the Heian era. This shrine with its pleasant grounds was burned in the firebombings of World War II and rebuilt in 1963. The shrine festival is in September and each November a Tori no Ichi festival is held here.

The main entrance is to the east; you can also access the shrine on the north side.

🌐 *http://www.ootorijinja.or.jp*

❸ Meguro Museum of Art / Meguro Ku Bijutsukan 目黒区美術館

Designed by the Nihon Sekkei architectural firm and opened in 1987, this museum has a focus on modern and contemporary Japanese artists, especially emerging trends. The building has three floors plus a basement level, and includes a gallery where local residents can exhibit their works. Besides exhibits, the museum hosts educational presentations and hands-on workshops, and publishes exhibition catalogs.

🌐 *http://mmat.jp/index.html*

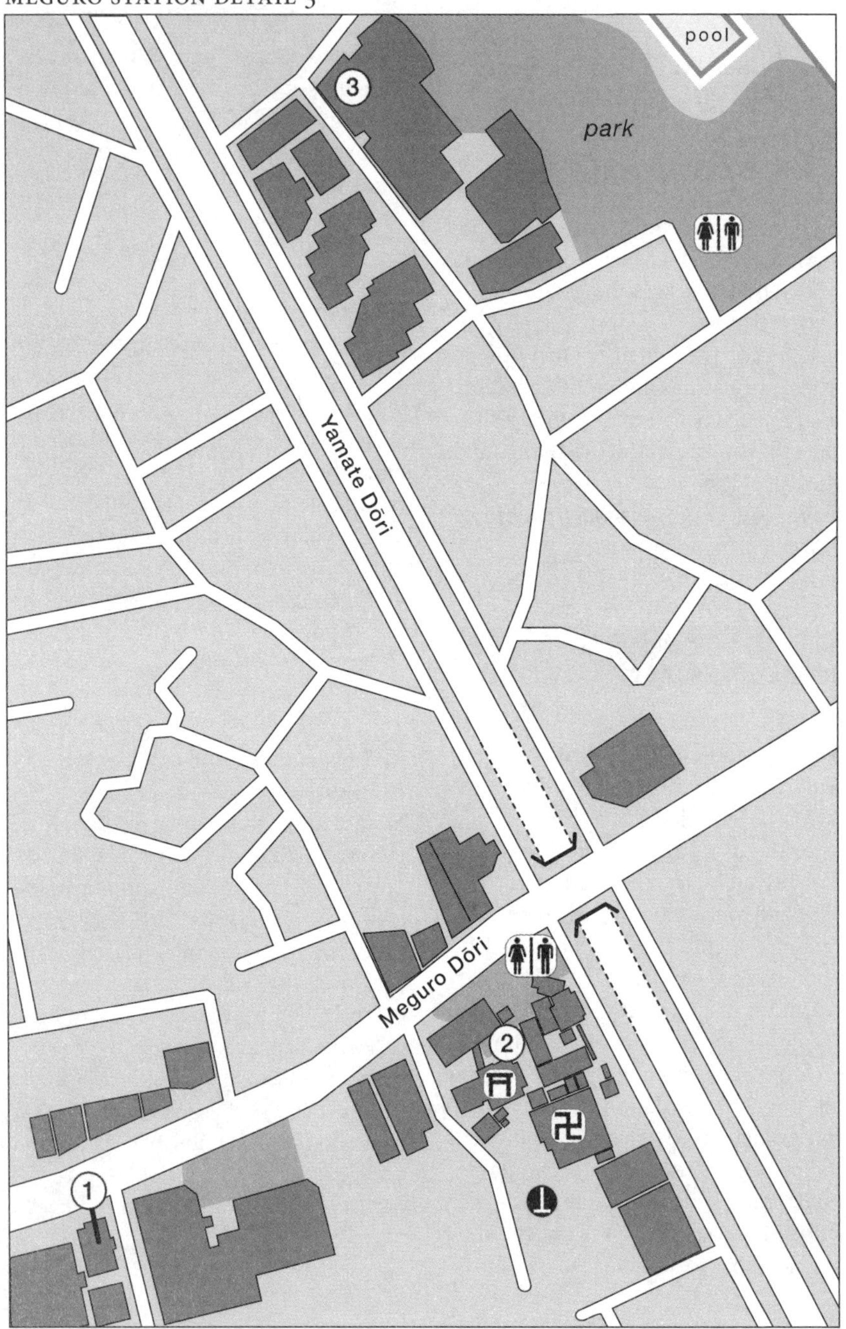
pool
park
Yamate Dōri
Meguro Dōri
1
2
3

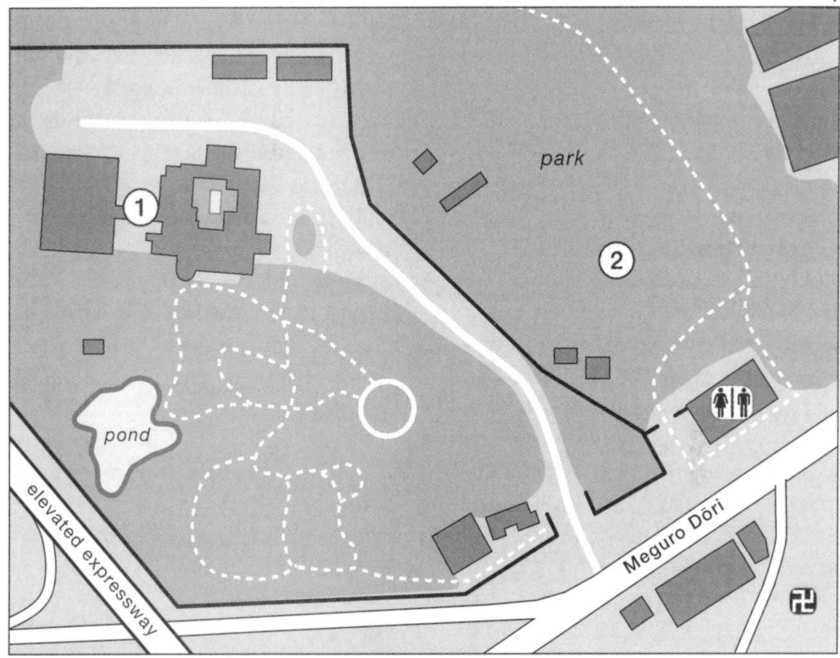

DETAIL 4

❶ Tokyo Metropolitan Teien Museum / Tokyo To Teien Bijutsukan 東京都庭園美術館

The former residence for the Asaka no Miya collateral branch of the imperial family. Prince Yasuhiko studied in France for a few years and his wife, Princess Nobuko, joined him for the last two years of that stay. There they discovered the new style known as art deco. A few years after returning to Japan, they began designing a new home with Gondō Yōkichi as the architect and Henri Rapin doing interior design for seven of the rooms. Ivan-Léon Alexandre Blanchot did the relief sculptures on the dining room walls, Raymond Subes did ironwork, and René Lalique and Max Ingrand designed some of the glasswork. The building was completed in 1933. The family moved out in 1947 after the Imperial Household Law of 1947 abolished the collateral branches, at which point the government took over the grounds. The building was then used as a residence for the foreign minister, then for the prime minister, and later as the state guesthouse. It was opened to the public as a museum in 1983. There is also a museum annex that opened in 2013 for art exhibits.

The former residence is one of the

finest examples of art deco in the world and a must for those interested in that movement.

🌐 *https://www.teien-art-museum.ne.jp/en/*

❷ Institute for Nature Study / Shizen Kyōikuen 自然教育園

The Institute for Nature Study is a research facility and educational park with a forest, meadows, ponds, and marshy areas covering 49.5 acres (19.8 hectares). In the early Edo period this area was under the control of the Buddhist temple Zōjōji. In 1664, it became a residence of Matsudaira Yorishige, daimyō of Takamatsu Han. In the Meiji period the army and navy used the location to store gunpowder. In 1917 the Imperial Household Agency took over administration of the land and renamed it the Shirokane Imperial Estate. In 1949 it became a park, and, finally, in 1962 the park became the Institute for Nature Study of the National Museum of Nature and Science. According to the website, the facility is home to 1,080 species of plants, 2,100 species of insects, and 130 species of birds.

This is a good place to view colorful autumn foliage before the winter approaches.

🌐 *http://www.ins.kahaku.go.jp/english/index.html*

日本橋地区 北部

NIHONBASHI NORTH

Here we are getting into one of the oldest parts of the city. When Tokugawa Ieyasu first planned the laying out of the town, he reserved most of the high city for the samurai and the low city for the commoners. Nihonbashi was designated as the central market area in the low city, close enough to the shōgun's castle to be a food distribution point for both the high and low cities. While the market moved to Tsukiji after the Great Kantō Earthquake, one can still find several stores that continue to deal in products from that period. Nihonbashi as a name will crop up here in more than one context. It is the name of a major bridge in the district, which gave its name to the district on either side of it, and to the local river, the Nihonbashigawa. In Nihonbashi you will find temples, shrines, long-established shops, historical landmarks, museums, government offices, plenty of places to eat, and more.

This section covers the northern portion of Nihonbashi in the vicinity of the bridge. See the following chapter for the portion south of the bridge and nearby areas.

DETAIL 1

❶ Nihonbashi 日本橋
A bridge originally built of wood in 1603. In 1604 the location of this bridge was designated as the zero point in measuring distances from the city. Modern signs that state the distance to Tokyo still refer to this location. The current Western-style granite bridge with its large brass lanterns sporting

NIHONBASHI NORTH

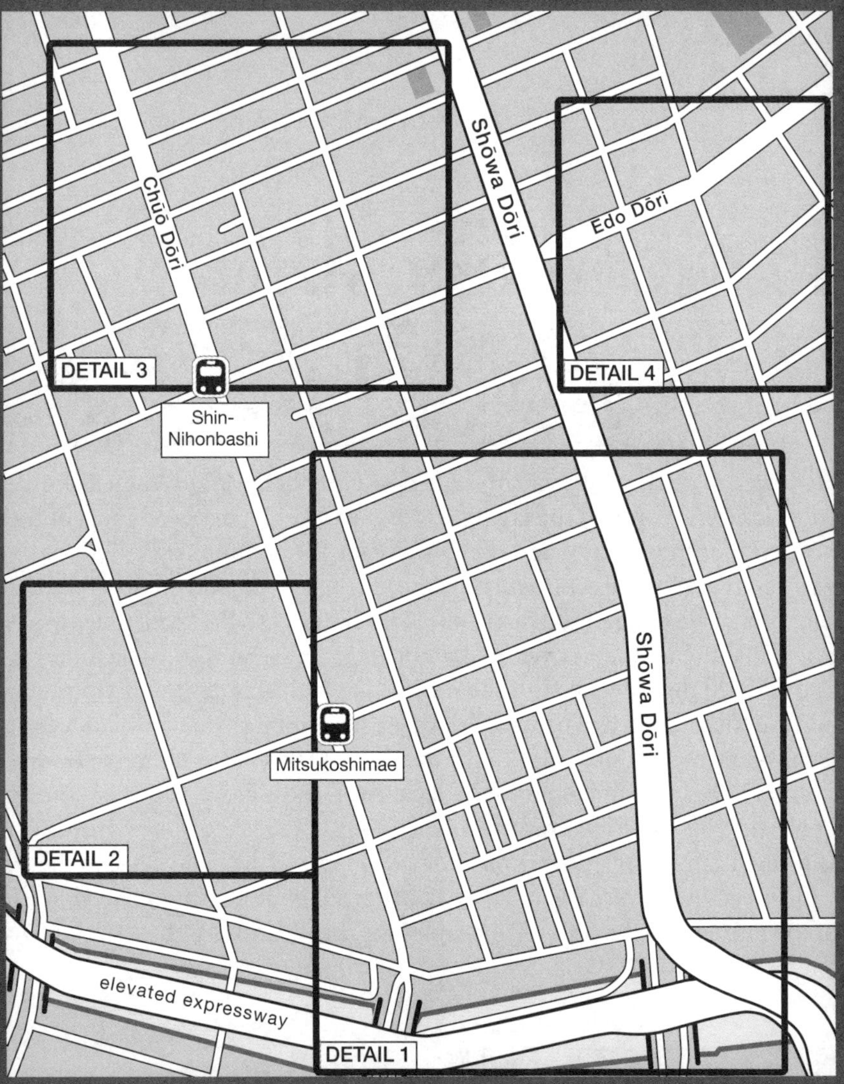

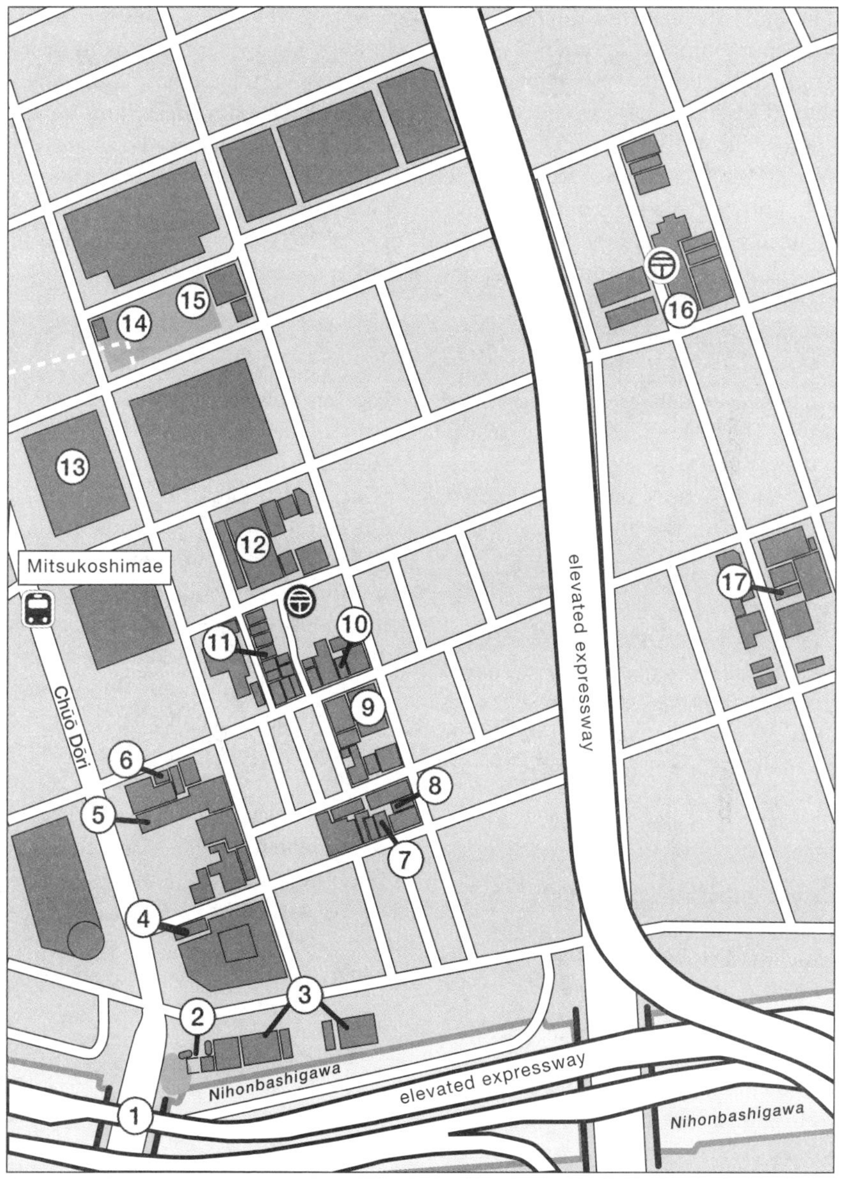
Mitsukoshimae
Chūō Dōri
elevated expressway
elevated expressway
Nihonbashigawa
Nihonbashigawa
1
2
3
4
5
6
7
8
9
10
11
12
13
14
15
16
17

lions and winged kirin dates from 1911. A cleaning in preparation for the centenary of the current bridge intentionally left visible damage from the Great Kantō Earthquake of 1923 and the World War II firebombings, as a relic of important parts of its history. Above the bridge, following the Nihonbashigawa, is an expressway built shortly before the 1964 Tokyo Olympics. Plans to remove the roadway are being developed, eventually replacing it with a massive tunnel system to carry the traffic. The large calligraphy on the expressway above the bridge says Nihonbashi and is based on that of the last shōgun, Tokugawa Yoshinobu.

NOTE: *Since 1971, the bridge is closed to traffic for one day and cleaned by a team of volunteers from the Meikyō Nihonbashi Hozonkai, "The Famed Nihonbashi Bridge Preservation Society." Only members of the organization can participate; the public is not allowed to join in.*

❷ Nihonbashi Fish Market Monument / Nihonbashi Uoichiba Hasshō no Chi-hi 日本橋魚市場発祥の地碑

From the days of the founding of Edo, this was the location of the fish market for the city. During that time, fish from Tokyo Bay would be freshly delivered to the market by boat on the Nihonbashigawa and available for the citizens to buy. Along with the market grew a variety of other businesses, including places where merchants or laborers could rest and have a cup of tea or a snack. The 1923 Great Kantō Earthquake severely damaged the market and it was decided to move it to another location. In 1935 the new fish market opened at Tsukiji and the Nihonbashi market closed.

❸ Kite Museum / Tako no Hakubutsukan 凧の博物館

This museum was founded by the late Motegi Shingo, the owner of the Taimeiken restaurant, who had amassed a large private collection of kites. It is located a few doors west of the restaurant on a second floor. While focusing on Japanese kites, it also contains kites from around the world. Only a few hundred of the thousands of kites in the collection are on display at any one time, due to limited space.

❸ Taimeiken たいめいけん

Established in 1931, Taimeiken serves Western-style Japanese dishes in a relaxed atmosphere. Beef stew, croquettes, omelet rice, hamburger steak, and pasta are some of the dishes offered. If you have seen the movie *Tampopo,* you will recognize the omelet rice served here. This version of omelet rice is apparently based on a recipe developed for the movie by the restaurant. That scene was filmed in the second floor kitchen, and the hands you see in the close-up shots were those of the owner.

This is located near the Kite Museum, which is on the second floor a few doors west of the restaurant. This place is popular, so you may have to wait.
🌐 *https://www.taimeiken.co.jp*

❹ Yagichō 八木長
Founded in 1737 as a store specializing in dried ingredients for dashi, the ubiquitous Japanese stock used in soup, stews, and cooking. This means of course katsuobushi, in both the solid and various flake forms, premixed dashi powder, bottled dashi, shiitake from various parts of Japan, a variety of seaweed, dried beans, furikake, dried noodles, and more. The dry nature of many of these products means they are lightweight and perfect to bring home for those who love to cook.
🌐 *http://www.yagicho-honten.jp*

❺ Yamamoto Nori Ten 山本海苔店
This nine-story building is the main store of the chain specializing in one thing: nori, those sheets of seaweed used in a variety of ways in Japanese cuisine. In business since 1849, they sell not only plain nori but also certain product lines of seasoned nori, nori-based furikake, nori tsukudani, and various nori snacks. Hello Kitty seaweed chips anyone?
🌐 *http://www.yamamoto-noriten.co.jp*
🌐 *http://www.norenkai.net/en/portfolio-item/yamamoto-nori-ten/*

❻ Yūbendō 有便堂
Established in 1912, Yūbendō sells supplies for calligraphy and traditional painting: everything from brushes and paper to a large variety of pigments. They also handle items made with traditional paper, and do picture framing.
🌐 *https://www.yubendo.com*

❼ William Adams' House Memorial / Miura Anjin Kyū Kyo Ato
三浦按針旧居跡
Englishman William Adams was the navigator for a group of Dutch ships that sailed across the Pacific, via the tip of South America, from Europe to Japan. Only one ship, the De Liefde, made it all the way, landing in 1600. Adams so impressed shōgun Tokugawa Ieyasu that he not only made him and the second mate Jan Joosten samurai, but also gave them the high rank of hatamoto. Adams was to spend the rest of his life in Japan, with the exception of a few trading voyages, and died there in 1620. He worked to improve shipbuilding, assisted in expanding trade with the Dutch and British, and advised the shōgun on many topics. The monument to his home is next to Tagawa Jewels on Anjin Dōri. The word anjin means navigator. The monument stone first put up in 1930 was destroyed in World War II; the present

stone dates from 1951. Many English speakers will be familiar with Adams as the character John Blackthorne in the highly fictionalized and historically inaccurate account in the novel *Shogun*.

❽ Nihonbashi Benmatsu 日本橋弁松

This was Japan's first take-out bentō shop. Established as an eatery in 1850, the clientele were mainly people who worked at the Nihonbashi fish market. The busy customers often had little time to eat at the restaurant, so they would often take the rest of their meal with them. Offering takeout seemed a good choice to the owner, so he changed the business to takeout only. The food has a good old hearty Edo-style flavoring, which some find rather strong. The disposable boxes are still made of folded thin wood rather than cardboard or plastic.

🌐 *http://www.benmatsu.com*

🌐 *http://www.norenkai.net/en/portfolio-item/benmatsu/*

❾ Kanmo 神茂

Kanmo has been making and selling processed seafood products since 1688. The most famous products are their hanpen and kamaboko. These two products are made with ground shark (hanpen) or fish (kamaboko) made into a paste and then mixed with other ingredients such as yam or eggs (or both) to thicken, then steamed or boiled until set. Hanpen is sometimes eaten grilled, and both can be ingredients in other dishes such as oden or ramen.

🌐 *https://www.hanpen.co.jp*

🌐 *http://www.norenkai.net/en/portfolio-item/kanmo/*

❿ Muro Ichi Ramen 室壱羅麺

A small ramen restaurant, the type of place businessmen go to for a quick lunch. They have a nice variety of ramen dishes and use whole-wheat flour in their noodles. At the entrance there is a ticket machine where you make your selection. Open during the week for lunch and dinner, lunch only on Saturdays. English speaking staff, non-smoking.

⓫ Nihonbashi Saruya 日本橋さるや

In operation since 1704, this is the only shop in Japan specializing in traditional handcrafted kuromoji, somewhat confusingly translated as "toothpicks." Kuromoji are not to be confused with simple thin store-bought toothpicks. While these can be used to pick your teeth, they are mainly intended for slicing and eating traditional tea sweets. Saruya's kuromoji are handcrafted and sold in boxes made of kiri wood with attractive designs on them. You can even place advanced orders for boxes with personalized calligraphy on the labels, useful as a special gift.

🌐 *http://www.nihonbashi-saruya.co.jp*

🌐 *http://www.norenkai.net/en/portfolio-item/saruya/*

⓬ **Bunmeidō** 文明堂

A maker of castella cake, baumkuchen, and other baked sweets both European and Japanese. The history of Bunmeidō is one of perseverance through the ups and downs of the 20th century. The company dates from 1900 and was originally in Nagasaki. In 1922 they opened their Tokyo branch, which then burned down in the Great Kantō Earthquake. In 1933 they opened a new store in Shinjuku, then in 1939 in the Ginza. In 1941 they had to cancel production due to a shortage of supplies, and in 1945 the store was destroyed in the firebombings of World War II. In 1950 they were able to resume production and in 1951 opened the Nihonbashi store. Since then the company has greatly expanded, with production facilities and shops in various parts of Japan. You can make purchases to go or enjoy something in the attached cafe.

🌐 *https://www.bunmeido.co.jp*

⓭ **Kiya** 木屋

The Kiya cutlery store shares the same name as an older shop named Kiya. The owner of the first gave permission in 1792 to an apprentice to use the name as long as he did not sell the same products. At one time there were several Kiya stores with this arrangement in the Nihonbashi. While kitchen knives form their major product line, they also sell other kitchen items such as sharpening stones, scissors, pots, and ceramics. They also repair and sharpen blades. The location is on the first floor of the COREDO Muromachi 1 building.

🌐 *http://www.kiya-hamono.co.jp*

⓭ **Nihonbashi Information Center** 日本橋案内所

You may want to make this an early stop when visiting the neighborhood. Information centers will often have notices of special events and can suggest places to see. The center is located in the B1 level of the COREDO Muromachi 1 building and is directly accessible from Mitsukoshimae Station.

🌐 *http://www.nihonbashi-tokyo.jp/en/information_center/*

⓭ **Ninben Nihonbashi** にんべん日本橋

Founded in 1699, this shop now specializes in katsuobushi, either whole or shaved in bags. They also sell katsuobushi kezuriki, a box with an inverted plane for shaving your own flakes at home. Also available are several types of bottled dashi, the traditional cooking stock of Japan, and furikake. The shop is located in the COREDO Muromachi 1 building on the first floor. They also have a restaurant in the same building which is open from 11:00 a.m. to 11:00 p.m.

🌐 *http://www.ninben.jp*

🌐 *http://www.norenkai.net/en/portfolio-item/ninben/*

▲ The adorned shutters of paint supply store Yūbendō can be seen in the early morning.

HDO
VISA
MasterCard
中央区
プレミアム付
商品券
取扱店
JCB
PREMO
SECOM
日本橋
有便堂
株式会社
有便堂

⓮ Fukutoku Jinja 福徳神社

Established in the 9th century, this is a shrine to Uka no Mitama no kami, "the spirit of the rice in storehouses," who is also identified with Inari. Also enshrined here are Ōta Dōkan, Benten, and Tokugawa Ieyasu. It is also known by the nickname Mebuki ("sprouting") Jinja, as one of the fresh gate pillars once sprouted a shoot. In the Edo period this shrine was one of very few allowed to hold fundraising lotteries. Due to this association, people hoping to win lotteries come here to pray. The shrine underwent a complete renovation in 2014.

🌐 *https://mebuki.jp*

⓯ Yakuso Jinja 薬祖神社

Ōnamuji no Mikoto and Sukunahikona no Mikoto are enshrined here as medicinal kami. This neighborhood has been a center for pharmaceutical companies since the Edo Period. In 1929 the first shrine was placed on the pharmaceutical guild office's roof, in 2016 it was moved to the present site. The annual festival is on October 17.

⓰ Ibasen 伊場仙

This shop sells traditional flat and folding fans. The range of styles is very large; the patterns on the fans can vary from simple and elegant designs to reproductions of ukiyo-e prints. The business was founded in 1590. Given their long history it is not surprising that their fans are in the collections of many museums, such as the Van Gogh Museum, The British Museum, and The Metropolitan Museum of Art.

🌐 *http://www.ibasen.co.jp*

🌐 *http://www.norenkai.net/en/portfolio-item/ibasen/*

⓱ Chikusen 竺仙

Operating since 1842, Chikusen sells fabric for yukata and kimono in a large selection of designs. The kimono fabrics are done in the Edo komon style, which involves subdued patterns made up of small hand-stenciled dots on silk. The yukata are cotton with lively broad patterns and are perfect for festivals in the warmer months. Their products are sold in many other stores in Japan.

🌐 *http://www.chikusen.co.jp*

🌐 *http://www.norenkai.net/en/portfolio-item/chikusen/*

DETAIL 2

❶ Bank of Japan Currency Museum / Nippon Ginkō Kin'yū Kenkyūjo Kahei Hakubutsukan 日本銀行金融研究所貨幣博物館

This museum opened in 1985 and is operated by the Institute for Monetary and Economic Studies of the Bank of Japan. The museum is free; as it is in a secure building, metal detectors and x-ray machines are used to inspect visitors' belongings. The displays cover

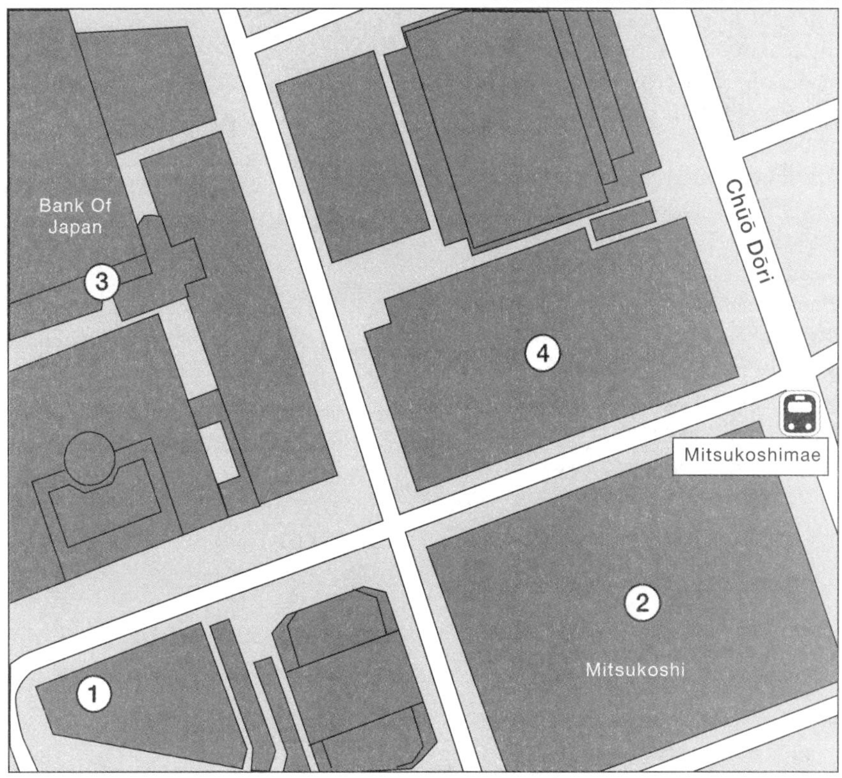

the history of Japanese currency from the early days of the use of coinage to the present. Included are commodities that were used for exchange before coinage entered Japan, up until the development and standardization of paper currency, which started around 1600. World currencies are also displayed to illustrate their development. The exhibits are very well laid out with some English captions. There is a Japanese-English guidebook available.
🌐 *http://www.imes.boj.or.jp/cm/english/*

❷ Mitsukoshi 三越

The main department store of the Mitsukoshi company. Originally called Echigoya, this store was established in 1673 during the Edo period as a kimono fabric shop. The name changed in the Meiji period, as did the stock of the store. The present building was built in 1914 and consists of seven stories plus one basement level. There is also an annex with ten stories plus two basement levels. From the lion sculptures at the entrance—reminiscent of Trafalgar Square—to the rooftop, this store is a delight to the eyes. A centerpiece is the massive hinoki wood sculpture of magokoro, "sincerity," by Satō Gengen that rises for four stories in the middle of the grand stairway. As is typical of such large department stores in Japan, a significant portion of the building is devoted to space rented to specialized businesses selling their own products. There is also an exhibit space that is worth checking out. The rooftop is a good place to rest. It includes a gardening section, as well as a branch of Mimeguri Jinja in Sumida Ward, which has been long associated with the Mitsui family. Given the size of the store, you may want to grab their brochure at the entrance and head to the roof to sit and plan your route. Several restaurants lease space in the building, and you can find places to eat on more than one floor.

🌐 *https://cp.mistore.jp/global/en/nihombashi.html*

Mitsukoshi Lions

Some trivia regarding the lions out front: They are smaller versions of the originals, which were designed and cast for the store by British sculptors Merrifield and Barton and shipped to Japan. During the war the Imperial Navy impounded them to be melted down and made into weaponry. After the war the lions were found in storage and returned.

❸ Bank of Japan / Nippon Ginkō
日本銀行

While the Bank of Japan was founded in 1882, of main interest will be the Neo-Baroque old building, which was completed in 1896 and stands on the location of an old Edo period mint. The architect was Tatsuno Kingo, who also designed Tokyo Station. To the left as you face the structure is the new building, and across the street to the right is the annex. Both of these are rather functional office buildings without the symbolic grandeur of the old building. This being a government office, access to parts of the building is restricted. Tours, with advanced reservation only, are possible for groups of between five and twenty.

Tours of the Bank's Head Office:

🌐 *https://www.boj.or.jp/en/about/services/kengaku.htm/*

❹ Mitsui Memorial Museum / Mitsui Kinen Bijutsukan
三井記念美術館

A fine collection of Japanese art collected over 300 years by the Mitsui family. The predecessor to the museum was the Mitsui Library in Nakano Ward. The present museum opened on the seventh floor of the Mitsui Main Building in 2005. It is relatively small, just six galleries and a lecture hall. However the quality of the works displayed is very high. The museum includes a detailed replica of the interior of the famous Joan tea ceremony room, a cafe,

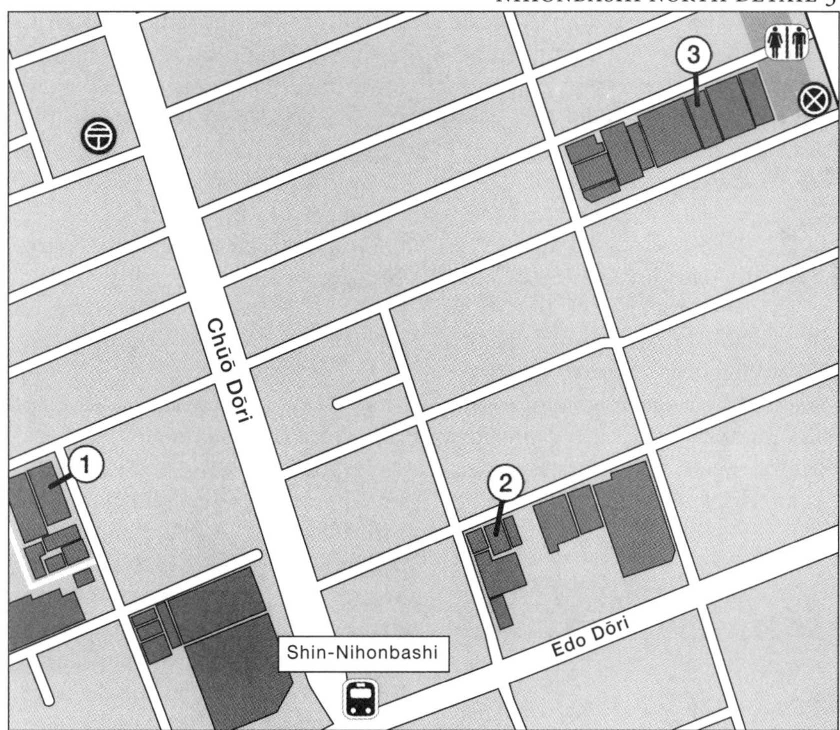

and a museum shop. They also publish catalogs for their special exhibits and other works. Thematic special exhibits are common.

🌐 *http://mitsui-museum.jp/english/english.html*

DETAIL 3

❶ Muromachi Sunaba 室町 砂場

Founded in 1869, this restaurant serves two types of cold soba: zarusoba and morisoba. You can also order tempura to go along with your soba—just order tenzaru or tenmori soba. They have rooms on the second floor that can be reserved for parties. Seating is both tatami and Western style.

🌐 *http://norenkai.net/en/portfolio-item/muromachi-sunaba-2/*

❷ Tenmo てん茂

Originally, in 1885, this was a stall on the street. In 1907 the owner settled into a restaurant, and the current building dates from 1947. Their tempura is made in the Edo style using

sesame oil and is served in set meals. The ingredients change throughout the year along with the seasons. Seating is both traditional on tatami and Western style in chairs. Nonsmoking.
🌐 *http://tenmo.jp/e-index.html*

❸ **Fukuda Inari Jinja** 福田稲荷神社
An excellent example of the many small Shintō shrines that dot the city. The location is on a narrow side street surrounded by taller buildings. This one is unusual in that it is completely enclosed in a tiny structure to protect it from the elements.

DETAIL 4

❶ **Ozu Washi** 小津和紙
This shop has been in the same location since 1653. The original name was Ozu Seizaemon-ten. This large three-story store specializes in traditional washi paper and various products made from it. Picture framing and scroll mounting are also provided. The location includes an exhibit space and a museum on the history of the store. They also offer workshops on papermaking, calligraphy, and ink painting.
🌐 *http://www.ozuwashi.net/en/*

❷ **Hanashō** 華硝
Founded in 1946, this company specializes in high-quality Edo kiriko cut glass. Originally a subcontractor for a major glass company, the founder's son decided to break away from that model and go into direct sales. This is their second store, which opened in Nihonbashi in 2016. The company holds several patents for their designs.
🌐 *http://www.edokiriko.co.jp*
🌐 *http://www.hanashyo.com/index.html*

❸ **Takarada Ebisu Jinja**
宝田恵比寿神社
Ebisu, one of the Shichifukujin, is enshrined here. The statue of Ebisu in the shrine was given to the locals by Tokugawa Ieyasu in 1606. While the statue is usually not displayed, it is shown from January 1–7, and during the Bettara Ichi Fair held on the October 19 and 20. The Bettara Ichi Fair is famous for the sale of a type of pickled daikon called bettarazuke. There is also a variety of other foods available. At night the festival is lit up by some 1,500 lanterns, so you may want to visit then. People often pray here for business, family prosperity, and fire protection.

❹ **Kawashima Kami Ten** 川島紙店
A shop established in 1673 specializing in paper elements for the home: shoji screens, fusuma partitions, sliding doors, wallpaper, decorative items, and a variety of paper accessories. They also sell some ceramics. All are handmade.

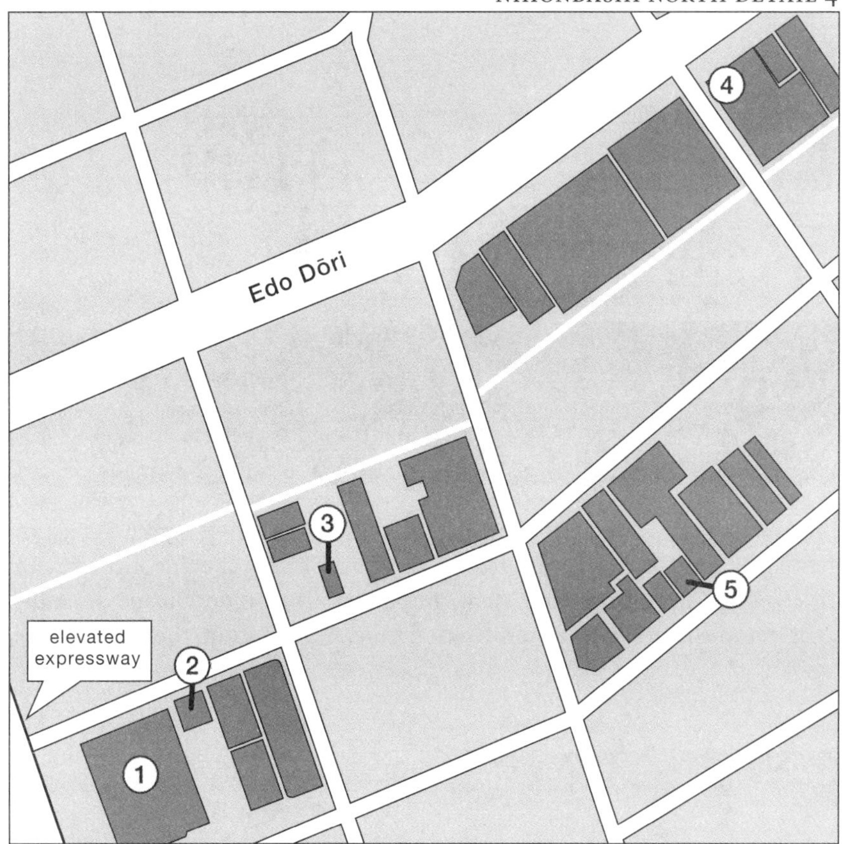

🌐 *http://www.3k-kawashima.co.jp*

❺ **Edoya** 江戸屋

The founder of Edoya was trained in Kyoto and became the maker of cleaning brushes for the shōgun's household. In 1718 he was able to obtain permission to open a shop selling his products. The store is still operating in the original location and sells all sorts of brushes. In the Meiji period the product line was expanded to include brushes that reflected social changes, such as brushes for cleaning Western-style clothing. This is a good place to go if you are looking for a finely made boar bristle brush designed to be used with wool, or a cleaning brush made from horsehair. The brushes are all handmade with natural products.

🌐 *http://www.nihonbashi-edoya.co.jp*

🌐 *http://www.norenkai.net/en/portfolio-item/edoya/*

日本橋地区 南部・京橋・八重洲

NIHONBASHI SOUTH, KYŌBASHI, AND YAESU

The area south of the Nihonbashigawa is often spoken of as if it is part of the Ginza; to be precise, it is just north of the Ginza. Like the other side of the river and the Ginza, it has many high-end shops, older businesses, museums, and shrines, plus a significant financial institution, the Tokyo stock exchange.

DETAIL 1

❶ Yaesu Book Center
八重洲ブックセンター

Designed by Kajima Design and built in 1978 to house the main store of what would become a bookshop chain, the building is influenced by early modernist buildings in Europe. All told there are nine stories to the bookshop if you count the basement. The seventh floor holds the section for non-Japanese language books and magazines: English, French, and Italian are all represented here. Before the store was built, the location was that of the headquarters of Kajima Corporation, a construction company that decided to establish a bookshop. Kajima Morinosuke came up with the idea for the store when he realized that many scholarly books were not easily available in bookshops. His solution was to build the largest bookstore in Japan.

🌐 *http://www.yaesu-book.co.jp*

NIHONBASHI SOUTH, KYŌBASHI, AND YAESU

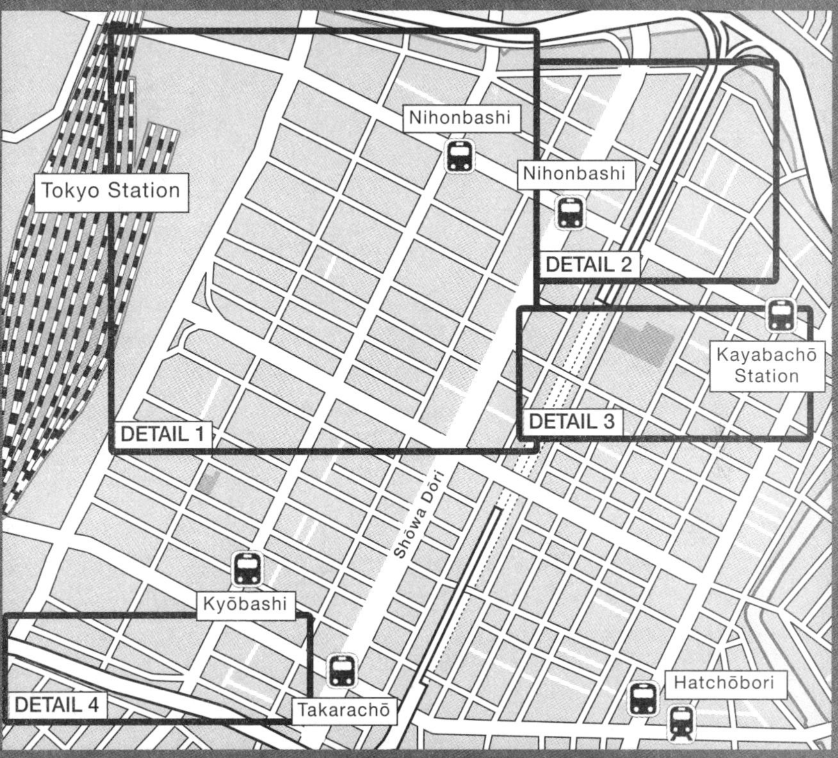

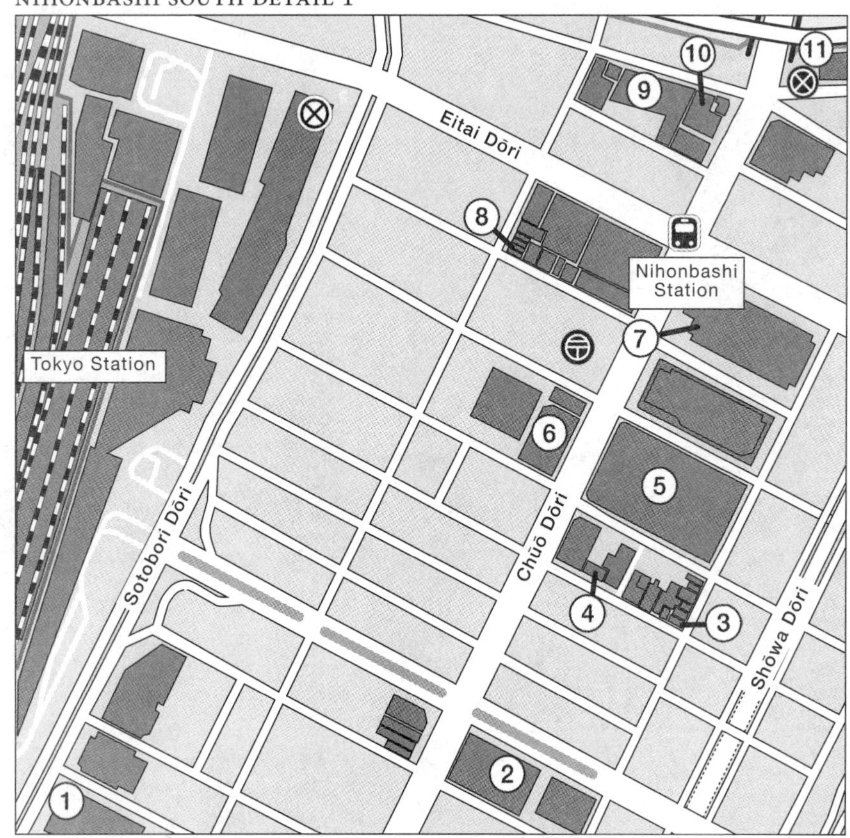

❷ Artizon Museum / Ātizon Bijutsukan アーティゾン美術館

This is a major collection of art in the Bridgestone building. The core collection is mainly by Western and Japanese artists who work in a Western style. Art from earlier periods is also part of the collection. The museum was founded in 1952 as the Bridgestone Museum of Art. The early collection was composed of items owned by Ishibashi Shōjirō, founder of Bridgestone. Over time the space devoted to the museum in the building grew, as did the collection. In 2015 the museum temporarily closed, the nine-story building was demolished, and a new twenty-three-story building built. The museum re-opened in early 2020 under the new name, which was created by combining the words Art and Horizon to signify its rebirth.

🌐 *https://www.artizon.museum/*

❸ Yoshino Sushi 吉野鮨

One of the more famous sushi restaurants in Tokyo, founded in 1879. In 1918 they introduced toro nigirizushi to their customers, and from there it spread throughout Japan. The third owner also has penned several books on sushi. The sushi served are large, an old style of Edo sushi. Lunch is reasonably priced; dinner will set you back more.

❹ Buyodō ぶよお堂

This basement shop sells atlases, maps, topographic maps, globes of all kinds, reproductions of old Japanese maps, even maps of the course of major rivers, as well as map-themed items such as tote bags and coffee mugs. Most of the stock is in Japanese, however they have many unique items such as volumes from the large series of specialized reference atlases put out by Zenrin. The store was opened in 2007 as a subsidiary of the map publisher Buyodō, which was founded in 1897. Buyodō started publishing books early in their history; it was not long before they also started releasing maps, eventually making that the major part of the business after World War II.

🌐 *http://www.buyodoshop.com*

❺ Takashimaya 髙島屋

The first Tokyo store of this chain, founded in Kyoto in 1831, opened here in 1933. This building was the first department store to be registered as an Important Cultural Property by the Japanese government. Even if you are not interested in shopping, the store, with its mix of Japanese and Western design, is a delight to the eyes and worth a stroll inside. If you count the two basement levels and the open rooftop, there are eleven stories to enjoy. There is also a six-story annex. The elevators still have operators who have a set routine to ensure the best possible service—take the elevator to experience this up close. The rooftop includes a large garden with seating areas. If you are ready for lunch you can explore the basement levels, pick up some food to go, and then take the elevator up to the rooftop to sit, relax, and eat outdoors. From 1950 to 1954, the rooftop was also the home of a popular baby elephant named Takako before she moved to the Ueno Zoo.

🌐 *https://www.takashimaya.co.jp/nihombashi/index.html*

❻ Maruzen Nihonbashi 丸善日本橋店

The Nihonbashi branch of the famous bookstore. While the selection is not as large as in the nearby Marunouchi store, it is still extensive. There is an English language section devoted to books, both fiction and non-fiction, related to Japan. One bit of history to note is that this was the original Tokyo location for Maruzen.

❼ Haibara はいばら or 榛原

A shop devoted to traditional paper and products made from it, in business since 1806. The main papers here are washi, gambi, and chiyogami. While washi is made from a variety of plants, gambi paper uses the gambi plant and has a different smooth and glossy texture. Chiyogami is paper with repeating patterns printed on it. The shop stocks a sizeable variety of each, brought in from all over Japan. Besides selling the paper itself, there are boxes, fans, envelopes, and letter paper. The store facade is a pleasant gray with a motif of repeating diamonds, some of which are windows allowing light to shine out.

🌐 *http://www.haibara.co.jp/en/*
🌐 *http://www.norenkai.net/en/portfolio-item/haibara/*

❽ Yabukyu やぶ久

The present three-story building dates from 1960 and is in the original 1902 location. The menu includes a large variety of dishes, with a unique curry called Nanban as their signature dish. It comes with your choice of noodles. Seating is mainly Western style, with traditional seating on the third floor.

🌐 *http://www.yabukyu.com*

❾ Eitarō Sōhonpo 榮太樓總本舗

This shop is especially known for its traditional Japanese sweets. Founded in 1857, it was originally a concession in the Nihonbashi fish market. Today the main store and a tea room are in the Eitarō Building. They produce a large variety of products, some that should be consumed with a couple of days of purchase, others that are dry and will easily last a trip home. They also have a branch in Takashimaya, the Nihonbashi Mitsukoshi, and numerous other locations in Tokyo.

🌐 *https://www.eitaro.com/en/*
🌐 *http://www.norenkai.net/en/portfolio-item/eitaro-confectionery-co-ltd/*

❿ Kuroeya 黒江屋

Japanese lacquer is wonderful stuff. You can paint it on anything, it is water resistant, flexible, and long lasting, and it can be processed to be in several different colors. This long-established shop, in business since 1689, has many examples, ranging from traditional items like serving bowls, trays, cups, and chopsticks to modern products including clocks, mouse pads, LCD magnifying glasses, picture frames, jewelry, and more.

The store is housed on the second floor of the Kuroeya Kokubu Building, which appears to be just an office building at first glance, and so the store is not obvious from the street.

🌐 *http://www.kuroeya.com*
🌐 *http://www.norenkai.net/en/portfolio-item/kuroeya/*

⓫ Nihonbashi Tourist Pier / Nihonbashi Kankō Sanbashi
日本橋観光桟橋

Located just east of the Nihonbashi is a pier from which several cruise and tour companies depart. These currently are the Limousine Boat, which is an enclosed and fast but not cheap form of transportation that also goes to Haneda Airport; Edoventure Cruise for private parties; and (my favorite) Riverboat Mizuha, which does both private charter and scheduled tours with a guide who also speaks English.

Limousine Boat:
🌐 *https://www.limousineboat.com*
Edoventure Cruise:
🌐 *http://www.edoventure-cruise.com*
Riverboat Mizuha:
🌐 *https://www.funaasobi-mizuha.jp/english/*

DETAIL 2

❶ Kabuto Jinja 兜神社

Built in 1878 next to the old stock

▲ The traditional paper goods shop Haibara, with its distinctive facade, is hard to miss.

▼ Along the old stonework is the Nihonbashi Tourist Pier from which tour boats depart.

exchange, the shrine remained when the exchange moved to a nearby location. Uka no Mitama no Mikoto, who is associated with agriculture, is the kami enshrined here. Since many securities firms and the Tokyo Stock Exchange are nearby, it is no surprise that many who come here to pray are involved in finance. The shrine is maintained by employees of the stock exchange.

❷ Tokyo Stock Exchange / Tōkyō Shōken Torihikijo 東京証券取引所
The first stock exchange in Japan was established nearby in 1878 but closed during World War II. The present institution dates from 1949. The present building dates from 1985. The building is open to visitors during trading hours after signing in at the reception desk at a separate entrance.

❸ Meitoku Inari Jinja
明徳稲荷神社
Established in the early Edo period, this shrine is hidden away from the bustle of the street, as it is surrounded by buildings and nestled in a tree-filled lot. The famous writer Junichirō Tanizaki lived near here and wrote about how amateur theater troupes would use the kagura stage for performances.

❹ Hie Jinja Nihonbashi Sessha
日枝神社日本橋摂社
This shrine is away from the busy nearby streets and is surrounded by trees, providing a peaceful spot in the neighborhood. This Hie shrine is a subsidiary of the Akasaka Hie Jinja that is covered in the Marunouchi to Nagatachō chapter. During the Sannō Matsuri, held every two years in June, the procession of mikoshi enters these grounds, a ritual is performed, and then they continue on their way.

DETAIL 3

❶ Yabuizu 薮伊豆
A soba restaurant that first opened in 1882. While the building is modern, the entrance has a traditional feel to it with a tile roof on the gate, old-style walls, and vegetation. The restaurant has three floors with both traditional and Western seating. They also occasionally schedule rakugo performances on the third floor for a reasonable fee.
🌐 *http://www.yabuizu-souhonten.com*

❷ Kabutochō Kayabachō Machikado Museum / Kabutochō Kayabachō Machi Kado Tenjikan
兜町・茅場町まちかど展示館
Located in a park, this is a display of local mikoshi, leather haori that local fire brigades would use, photographs, lanterns, and various other items. These are housed in a building with one side

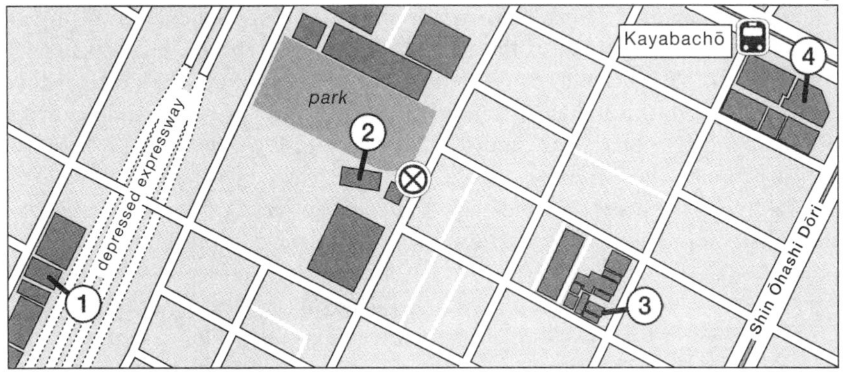

consisting of three large windows, so the items are easily visible.

🌐 *http://chuoku-machikadotenjikan.jp/tenjikan/kabutocho_kayabacho/*

❸ Toritoku 鳥徳

Established in 1897, this restaurant specializes in chicken and eel. Their yakitori and sukiyaki are both popular. All ingredients are delivered fresh every day. The seating is both traditional and Western with the traditional seating in rooms that can have partitions removed to combine them for larger groups.

🌐 *http://www.toritoku.com*

❹ Kayabachō Chōjuan 茅場町長寿庵

Established in 1907, this restaurant specializes in soba made from freshly ground buckwheat as well as tempura made from fresh seasonal vegetables and seafood. The noodles are handmade daily. Besides soba, they have a variety of seafood and reasonably priced set meals.

DETAIL 4

❶ Yokohama Kimijimaya 横浜君嶋屋

A long-established liquor store, founded in 1892 and headquartered in Yokohama. They established the Ginza store in 2008 by moving their Marunouchi store to the present location under the expressway. The store has a very large selection of nihonshu (what Westerners commonly call sake), shōchū, wine, and other alcoholic beverages.

🌐 *https://kimijimaya.co.jp*

❷ Fushimi Inari Jinja 伏見稲荷神社

This small wooden Inari shrine is nestled in the kind of side street that abuts backside of buildings. Once you find the street one block north of the expressway, the shrine is easy to locate, as the bright red torii and fence stands out surrounded by black, gray, and silver structures. This shrine is raised several feet off the street level and has a set of stairs with enough room for one person to get close to it.

❸ Police Museum / Keisatsu Hakubutsukan 警察博物館

Few cities have a police museum, however Tokyo is a city with many small specialized museums. You can spot the building by the large statue of Pipo-kun, the mascot of the Metropolitan Police Department, and a motorcycle on display out front. Those interested in the history of Tokyo's police since the Meiji period will find plenty of interest. There are exhibits on investigative techniques, police equipment, and traffic safety simulation games. Some exhibits have English labeling. Photographs are only allowed on certain floors. Kids can even dress up in uniforms for those photos parents love to take.

🌐 *https://www.keishicho.metro.tokyo.jp/multilingual/english/about_us/Police_Museum.html*

❹ National Film Archive of Japan / Kokuritsu Eiga Ākaibu
国立映画アーカイブ

Originally, in 1952, this was the film library of The National Museum of Modern Art. The museum opened in 1970 as the National Film Center in this location. The present building dates from 1995. In April 2018, the National Film Archive of Japan became an independent entity. The museum houses two cinemas, an exhibit hall, and a library, which are open to the public. The archive collects documents and film prints related to Japanese cinema. They currently have over 80,000 films in their collection, as well as an extensive collection of documents, books, posters, equipment, photos, and more. They are famous for their restoration work on various movies over the years. As film is perishable, reels are stored off-site in temperature- and humidity-controlled facilities.

🌐 *http://www.nfaj.go.jp/english/*

❺ Shirakiya Denbei 白木屋傳兵衛

This shop sells just brooms, cleaning brushes, and some accessories to use with them. But what wonderfully made brooms—all crafted by hand from natural materials, all in designs that have existed since the Edo period when the shop first opened in 1830. Originally this shop made tatami mats; however, you need good brooms for cleaning mats, and later the shop changed their product. If you have any appreciation for fine handcrafted everyday tools that are reasonably priced, this is a shop for you. Even if you don't plan to buy anything, the stock is a delight

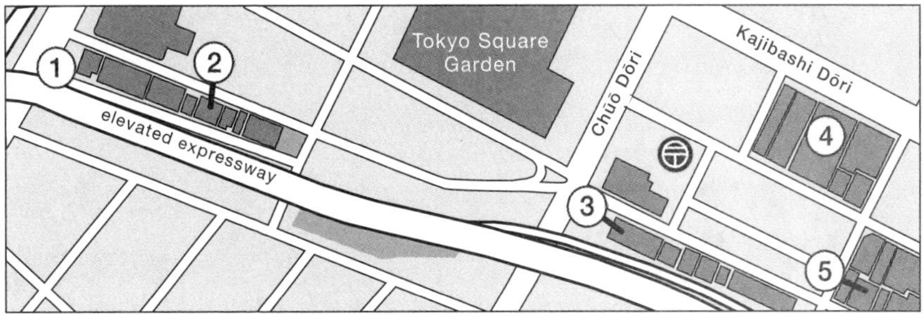

to view, and who knows, you may find a gift for someone or something for yourself.

🌐 *http://edohouki.com.*

🌐 *http://www.norenkai.net/en/portfolio-item/shirakiya-denbei/*

人形町

NINGYŌCHŌ

The name of this neighborhood means "doll town." This was originally a nickname given to the area in the Edo period, when there were many shops making and repairing puppets for the nearby puppet theaters as well as producing items for the nearby kabuki theaters. The name became official in the early 20th century. At one time the Yoshiwara red light district was located in this part of Edo. That ended with the Meireki Fire in 1657, after which the Yoshiwara was relocated to north of Sensōji. Today this area is still rich with artisans and maintains its links to the puppet and kabuki theater, in addition to the geisha community that developed here. Given that Ningyōchō's history goes back to the 17th century, many older businesses are here, just as they are in the neighboring Nihonbashi area. While Nihonbashi tends to upscale and fancy, Ningyōchō tends to have more of a neighborhood feel with its mix of residences and businesses. Ningyōchō is also well known for confectioneries, particularly along Amazake Yokochō. Even so, the area has many high-end restaurants, known as ryōtei, serving some of the best—and most expensive—food in Tokyo.

🌐 *http://ningyocho.or.jp/english/feature/index.html*
🌐 *http://ningyocho.or.jp/english/*

NINGYŌCHŌ

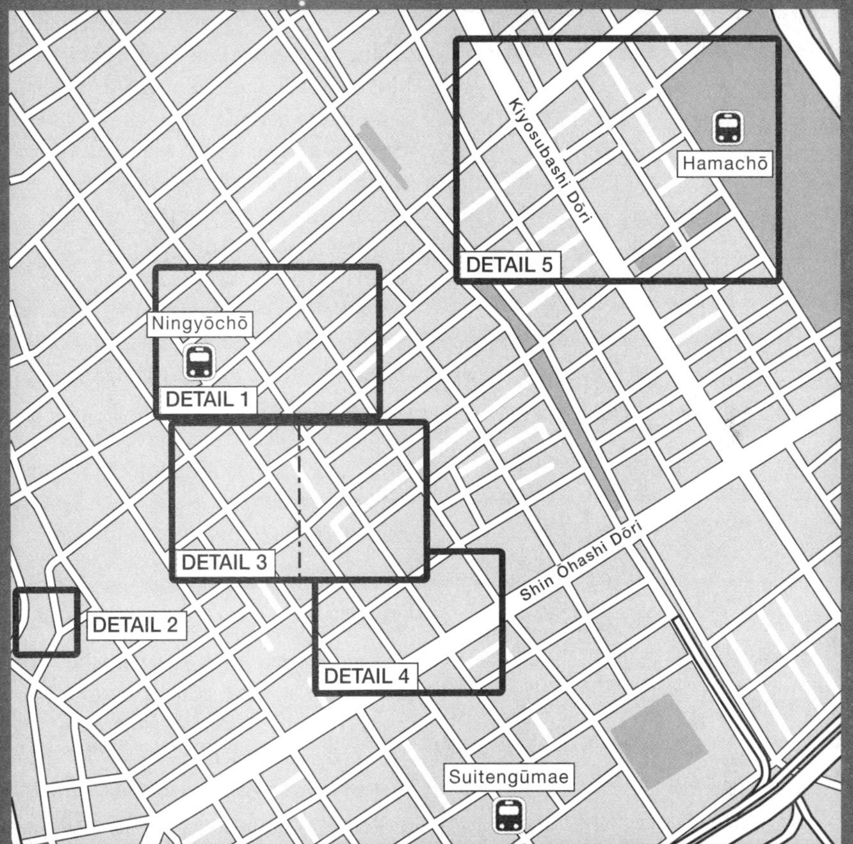
Kiyosubashi Dōri
Hamachō
DETAIL 5
Ningyōchō
DETAIL 1
DETAIL 3
Shin Ōhashi Dōri
DETAIL 2
DETAIL 4
Suitengūmae

DETAIL 1

❶ Kizushi 喜寿司

Kizushi was established in 1924. The current building was built in 1952 and has an old-fashioned look to it, with a tile roof and plants out front. This restaurant serves traditional Edo-style sushi in a relaxed atmosphere. There is an English menu and some English-speaking staff. Seating is both Western and traditional.

NOTE: *Dinner can be expensive, so perhaps not for strollers on a budget. Lunch is more affordable but still not cheap.*

❷ Suehiro Jinja 末廣神社

Founded some time before the beginning of the 17th century, Suehiro Jinja is an Inari shrine. Bishamon is also worshipped here, making this one of the shrines on the Shichifukujin tour for Ningyōchō. In 1675 the main hall of the shrine was being renovated and a suehiro, a type of folding fan, was found by the workers, which gave the shrine its present name.

❸ Hamadaya 濱田家

Established in 1912 and sometimes referred to as Genyadana Hamadaya, this is a high-end restaurant for traditional multicourse meals. Expect prices to range from ¥15,000 to ¥50,000, with lunch being less expensive than dinner. Reservations are required—this is not a place you just drop into. All seating is traditional, all rooms are private, and most have a view of the garden. It is possible to request geisha entertainment for an extra fee.

The name has a dual origin. The Genyadana part is the neighborhood's old name and is a reference to Okamoto Genya and his descendants, who practiced medicine here. The Hamadaya part comes from a famous okiya (residence for geisha) that once was in the area, and the restaurant took that name on its founding.

🌐 *http://www.hamadaya.info/english/*

❹ Tachibana Inari 橘稲荷神社

A small streetcorner Inari shrine. It is a simple structure consisting of a tiny copper-roofed wooden shrine, a torii on the approach, two guardian fox statues, and two red lanterns, all surrounded by a concrete wall. This is a good example of a surviving small shrine in the modern city.

❺ Ubukeya うぶけや

Originally founded in Osaka in 1783, the business relocated to Edo in the mid-19th century. The word ubuke in their name is a term that refers to the softness of a baby's hair, and ya means store. It was once said that their blades were so sharp that they had no trouble cutting a baby's hair, so they took it as

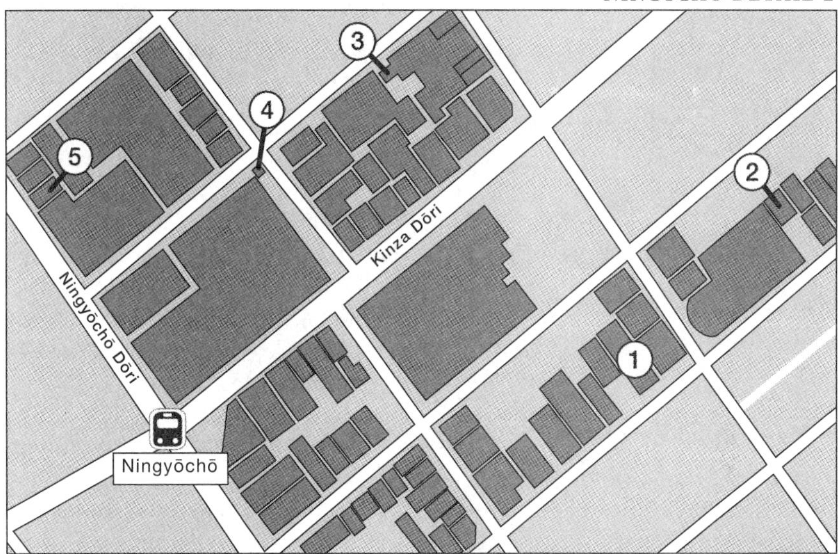

part of the store name. Ubukeya sells some 300 different cutting tools such as straight razors, knives, and scissors. In the Meiji period, Western-style scissors entered Japan and the company added them to their existing list of products. They purchase unsharpened blades from craftsmen and then handle the final finishing and polishing of the edges in the store. They also sharpen and repair knives brought to them by customers. The business sign has an interesting history: the top students of the famous calligrapher Kusakabe Meikaku each wrote one of the characters on the sign. Oh yes, they do sell one item that is not sharp—very high-quality tweezers.

🌐*https://www.ubukeya.com*

🌐 *http://www.norenkai.net/en/portfolio-item/ubukeya/*

DETAIL 2

❶ Koami Jinja 小網神社

This shrine has a long history. Founded in 1466, its present buildings date from the 1920s, having survived the war. Koami Jinja is an Inari shrine where Benzaiten and Fukurokuju are also worshiped. There is a pair of dragon statues, one ascending and the other descending, under the porch roof. There is also a statue of Benzaiten that was originally at Manpukuji. It was transferred to this location after that temple was destroyed. Every November 28 is the Doburoku Matsuri. Sato kagura dances are performed and doburoku, a simple unfiltered sake that can only be made with special government permission, is served. The

NINGYCHŌ DETAIL 2

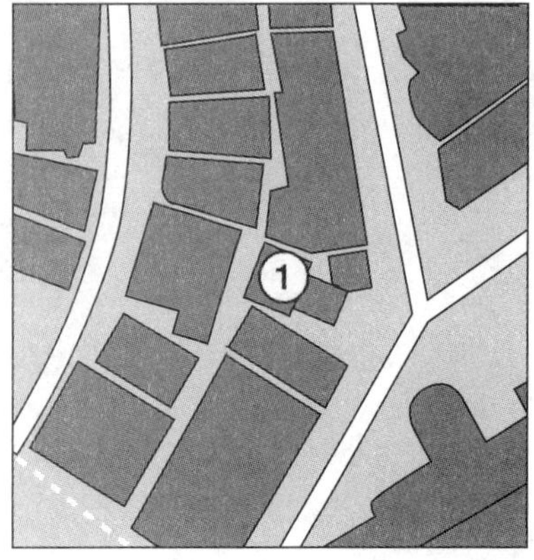

doburoku is served in a cup and must be consumed on site. The festival is modest, mainly consisting of people praying, buying charms, and having a cup of doburoku. If November 28 falls on a weekend, the date will be shifted to the nearest Friday or Monday. Every March 28 there is the annual festival, and every five years on that date a grand procession takes place.

🌐 *https://www.koamijinja.or.jp*

NOTE: *Depending on the time of day there may be more than one line approaching the shrine during the Doburoku Matsuri. One is for people buying charms, such as owls made of pampas grass, and another for praying. I have even seen a third. Check out which line is which so you get in the right one.*

DETAIL 3

❶ Koharuken 小春軒

Operating since 1912, Koharuken is a restaurant serving yōshoku, Western-influenced Japanese dishes, such as curry rice, hamburger steak, and katsudon. The prices are reasonable and an English menu is available. Seating is all Western style at either tables or the counter.

❷ Tamahide 玉ひで

The founder of this restaurant established in 1790 was a falconer who supplied the shōgun's household with meat. Tamahide is known for its oyakodon, a popular dish of chicken and egg on rice that originated here. It is also one of a handful of restaurants that serve chicken sukiyaki, the original version of that dish before beef replaced chicken meat. Their sukiyaki is seasoned with dark soy sauce and mirin, and made with a level of skill hard to duplicate at home. It is served in the evening. Long lines are common. The seating is all Japanese style with horigotatsu, a recessed table. Full-course meals are served in the evening.

🌐 *http://www.tamahide.co.jp*

❸ Kaneman かねまん

Kaneman specializes in seafood, especially wild torafugu, usually translated as "tiger blowfish." Established in 1880, they were the first Tokyo restaurant to obtain a license to serve fugu. The fugu is seasonal, so dishes are pretty much limited to September to April; during the off season they serve kaiseki ryōri dishes. All seating is traditional on tatami. Reservations are required.

❹ Kissako Kaiseiken
喫茶去 快生軒

A simple traditional neighborhood coffee shop with a relaxing atmosphere, located here since 1919. The decor looks like it has not changed in decades, giving the place a cozy retro vibe. In 2010 the popular detective TV series Shinzanmono ("Newcomer") had scenes set in this shop, making it a destination for fans of that show. The novel "Newcomer" by Higashino Keigo, the basis for the series, is available in English. The kanji used for Kissako (喫茶去) is discussed in Chapter Seven of the novel.

❺ Ningyōchō Karakuri Yagura
人形町からくり櫓

These two clock towers on Ningyōchō Dōri were built in 2009 as reminders of the neighborhood's history. The tops of towers are done in the style of a yagura, a type of tower one would see at theaters in the Edo period. Every day on the hour from 11:00 a.m. to 7:00 p.m., mechanical dolls come out of the towers for a short performance. The Edo Rakugo Karakuri Yagura, on the east side of the street, presents a rakugo story set in Ningyōchō, and the dolls come out of both sides of the tower. The Machibikeshi Karakuri Yagura is on the west side further north past Amazake Yokochō Dōri. The performance here is about Edo period firemen, and a fireman doll comes out near the top.

❻ Itakuraya 板倉屋

This shop was founded in 1907 and is also called Ningyōyaki Honpo Itakuraya. It specializes in, and originated, ningyōyaki in the form of the seven lucky gods. There are actually six lucky god designs made by the shop, the seventh being the smiling face of the customer. Itakuraya also makes a few other items such as their senjōyaki, which lacks the sweet bean paste filling. Senjōyaki originated during the food shortages after the Russo-Japanese War, when sugar was hard to get. Their senjōyaki are made with molds from that period and have military-themed shapes including a bugle, cannon, backpack, and tank. Many years ago my friend Ono-san gave some of us a tour of the neighborhood. The fellow behind the counter was delighted when he spotted my T-shirt from Moe's Books in Berkeley, as that was a bookshop he knew well from a visit to the United States.

🌐 *http://www.itakuraya.com/*

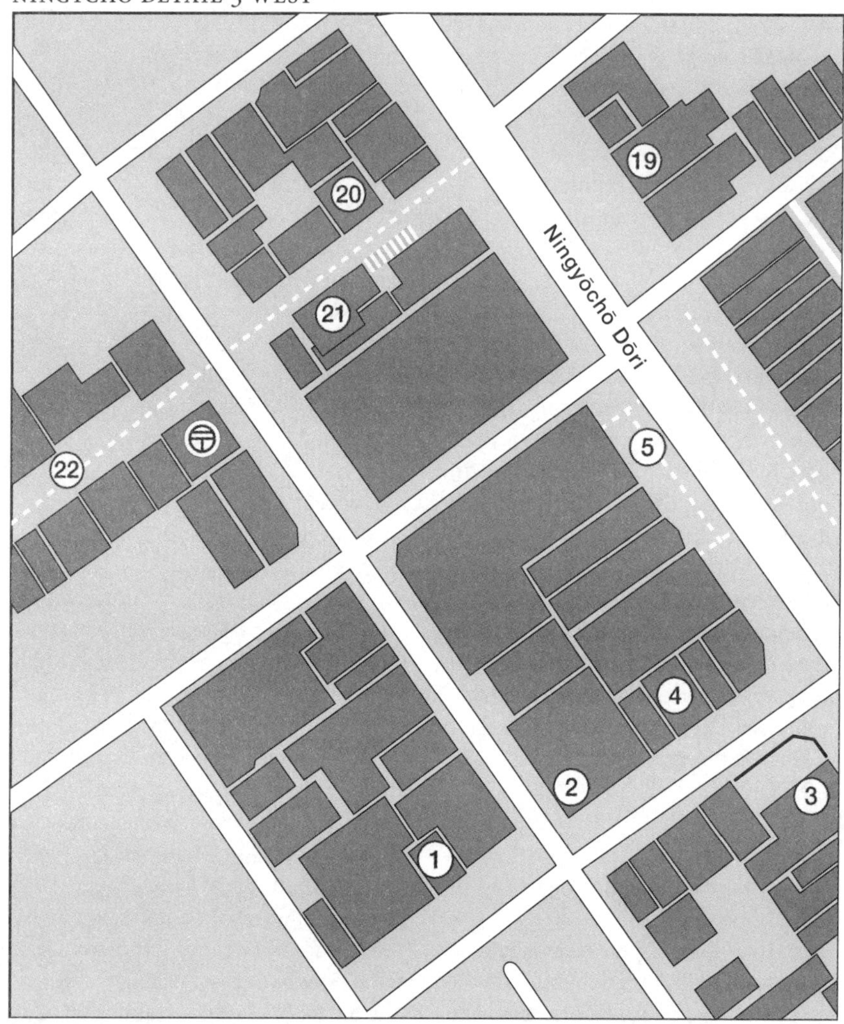

❼ Gyokueidō 玉英堂
Founded in 1576 in Kyoto, Gyokueidō moved to Tokyo after World War II. There are over thirty different pastries sold in the shop, the designs of which vary by season. The two most popular items are the torayaki, a kind of sandwich of two small pancakes filled with sweet bean paste (an), and gyokuman, a large manjū of many layers around a filling with a chestnut in the center. The torayaki (虎家喜) is a variant on

dorayaki (どら焼き) with the shop's own spin on the design.
🌐 *https://www.gyokueidou.com*

❽ Morinoen 森乃園

A tea shop established in 1914. While they sell a large variety of Japanese teas, their specialty is hōjicha, a lightly roasted green tea. They roast the tea on site, so the aroma will help you find

▲ On a small, pedestrian back street of Ningyōchō a restaurant extends beyond its walls.

Fish
Stat
仕度中
祭り
YAYOI

▲ The art on the Edo Rakugo Karakuri Yagura on Ningyōchō Dōri.

▼ The ryōtei of Kogiku Dōri, aka Geisha Alley, are pictured here.

the store. Also available are packaged pastries with tea incorporated into the recipes. The store has a small cafe on the second floor where you can rest, drink tea, eat various sweets, and also enjoy hōjicha ice cream.

🌐 *http://morinoen.jp*

❾ Tōfu no Futaba とうふの双葉

Originally founded in another part of Tokyo in 1907, the Ningyōchō location of this business opened after World War II. The shop specializes in a large variety of tōfu and tōfu products such as ganmo, deep-fried tōfu cakes mixed with several ingredients, and aburaage, deep-fried tōfu slices. There are even doughnuts made from soybean lees and amazake flavored ice cream. Amazake, made fresh daily, has also been sold here since the local shop that specialized in it closed several years ago. They have a bench and chairs on the sidewalk if you wish to sit and enjoy your purchase then and there.

🌐 *http://www.tofunofutaba.com*

❿ Soba Tōshimaya そば東嶋屋

A neighborhood soba restaurant with a relaxed atmosphere. The building has a traditional front with barred windows and potted plants on either side of the entrance. The old-style kanji in the circle on their noren indicates that this restaurant makes its own soba. Seating is Western style and they have an English menu.

⓫ Amazake Yokochō 甘酒横丁

This street of shops, with many selling traditional Japanese confections and crafts, is worthy of repeated strolls to see all that is there. In March a cherry blossom festival is held when the trees blossom. A large portion of the entries in this chapter are on this street.

🌐 *http://amazakeyokocho.jp*

⓬ Yanagiya 柳屋

Considered one of the big three shops for taiyaki, Yanagiya has been operating since 1916. Taiyaki is a type of ningyōyaki in the shape of a tai, a variety of fish sometimes served during special celebrations. As the store is very popular, you can expect to find a line here, but you can pass the time watching them make taiyaki as you wait. Taiyaki is all they make, however given that people line up for it, they don't need to make anything else.

⓭ Iwai Tsuzuraya 岩井つづら屋

This is the last shop in Tokyo that still makes tsuzura. There are only three or four such shops left in Japan. Tsuzura are a type of box that is woven from bamboo, coated in washi paper, then lacquered. They are traditionally used for storing items such as kimono. These days people use tsuzura to store a variety of items and the shop produces them in several sizes. Iwai Tsuzuraya also takes orders for boxes with custom crests. Expect filling such an order to

take six months, as lacquer work is a slow process. While they have been around since the late Edo period, there is a chance the business may end when the current owner retires, so be aware of that if you are thinking of making a purchase. The shop also refers to itself as Iwai Tsuzuraten (岩井つづら店).
🌐 *https://tsudura.com*

⓮ Toritada 鳥忠

Toritada was established in 1911. In the early days it was a wholesaler of eggs, a luxury product at the time. When boxes of eggs arrived, they were inspected to see if any had cracked in shipping. The cracked eggs were still good, so the owner would cook them up as an omelet and take them to the dressing rooms of the nearby Meijiza theater. In time the family quit the wholesale business and went into retail. They sell eggs and fresh chicken, and among their cooked items the grilled omelets are well known. They also sell grilled half chickens and several types of yakitori.
🌐 *http://www.toritada.co.jp*

⓯ Ningyōchō Shinodazushi 人形町志乃多寿司總本店

Handmade inarizushi is the specialty of this takeout sushi shop that opened in 1877. The building is modern with a white stone facade and large windows. They have a variety of boxed sets of sushi for purchase. There are no dining facilities on site. Going to the Meijiza theater for a performance? One of their boxes would be a good thing to enjoy during the intermission. They also sell to various department stores and supermarkets in Tokyo.
🌐 *http://www.shinodazushi.co.jp*
🌐 *http://www.norenkai.net/en/portfolio-item/shinodazushi-sohonten/*

⓰ Sasaki Saketen 佐々木酒店

A liquor store with a very wide selection, in business since 1915. They are especially noted for their broad selection of sake and shōchū from all over Japan, including many items not available elsewhere in Tokyo. They also stock awamori from Okinawa, wine, umeshu, and other alcoholic beverages.
🌐 *http://www.sasas.jp*

⓱ Torihada 鳥波多

Torihada specializes in yakitori, grilled chicken on skewers. They emphasize the freshness of the meat, using only birds processed that day. The menu includes as much of the chicken as possible so there is a large variety of meat and unusual organs. It also includes onigiri, hot pot dishes, and vegetables. Sake, beer, or wine are also available.
Seating is either at the counter or at a table. English speaking staff, non-smoking.
🌐 *http://tori-hada.com*

⓲ Ningyōchō Imahan 人形町今半

This is the main branch of a Tokyo area chain of restaurants specializing in hot pot dishes such as sukiyaki and shabu shabu. The Ningyōchō restaurant is in a traditional two-story brick-red building. Seating is Western, traditional on tatami, or at horigotatsu. They also have other shops where you can buy just the meat or boxes filled with all the ingredients you need to do your own dishes at home.

🌐 *https://www.imahan.com*

⓳ Hiyama 日山

Hiyama was founded in 1912 and specializes in meals centered around beef. Here you can get steak, sukiyaki, and shabu shabu as part of a larger meal. Seating is both Western and traditional. Reservations are required. They also have many branches and operate butcher shops where one can purchase their high-quality meat.

🌐 *https://hiyama-gr.com*

⓴ Yoshiume よし梅

Yoshiume has been in business since 1928 and is located in an old building in a former geisha neighborhood that survived the bombings of World War II. Their specialty is nabe done in an old-fashioned Edo style. The meals are either a la carte or full course. There is an English menu and some of the staff speak English. Seating is Western, but groups may be directed to private rooms with traditional seating on tatami and with horigotatsu.

🌐 *http://www.yoshiume.jp/honten.html*

㉑ Ōkannonji 大観音寺

This temple has an interesting history. During the Kamakura period in the city of Kamakura, there was a temple to Kannon with a statue that was over 26 feet (8 meters) tall. In 1258 the temple was destroyed by a fire; quick-thinking monks were able to save the statue's head by tossing it into a well. In 1699 the head was recovered and a new temple was built. During the Meiji period the government gave orders for the head to be destroyed as part of their suppression of certain Buddhist practices. The head was smuggled out of Kamakura, and in 1877 this temple was built to house it. In the fires after the Great Kantō Earthquake, the temple burned, but the head was again saved. Later both the temple and the head survived the firebombings of World War II.

Access to the temple is up a set of stairs to the east of the buildings.

Monthly fair days are the eleventh and seventeenth; the Kannon head is open for viewing on those days. At 11:00 a.m. on the eleventh, a fire ceremony is performed. The temple is on the Tokyo 33 Kannon Pilgrimage and is sometimes referred to as Daikannonji, since the kanji 大 can be read as ō or as dai.

㉒ Kogiku Dōri 小菊通り
Sometimes called Geisha Alley, this short and narrow pedestrian street is lined with houses and restaurants dating from the days when it was an area where many geisha lived. The number of geisha in Tokyo has declined; after World War II there were some 400 working in Ningyōchō, with some 150 high-end restaurants called ryōtei providing places for them to entertain. Today only a handful of both remain and the ryōtei are mainly near the Meijiza kabuki theater. This area also survived both the Great Kantō Earthquake and the firebombings of World War II so it is lined with many older buildings, often with plants in front.

DETAIL 4

❶ Chanoki Jinja 茶ノ木神社
An Inari shrine that used to be on a larger plot of land planted with tea (cha) plants as part of the Hotta clan residence. In the Edo period there were few fires in this area, so people came to pray at this shrine for protection from fire. Hotei is also enshrined here, so it is a spot on the Shichifukujin tour of Ningyōchō.

❷ Kanmidokoro Hatsune 甘味処初音
Kanmidokoro is a tea shop that serves traditional Japanese sweets such as several types of anmitsu and mochi. Founded in 1837, they pride themselves on using the best ingredients including agar and syrup acquired from domestic sources. All of their deserts are made by hand in the shop. The first episode of the Japanese TV series "Kantarō: The Sweet Tooth Salaryman" has the main character enjoying their anmitsu, a desert made of fruit and other sweets in a bowl.

❸ Kotobukidō 壽堂
A bakery of various pastries. The shop is small, with room for about six to stand. The most well-known product is *kogane imo,* a cinnamon covered cake with a sweet filling that is shaped like a sweet potato. Just follow your nose—the cinnamon smell will guide you.

❹ Tsukushi つくし
Founded in 1877, this combination shop and restaurant specializes in handmade traditional Japanese sweets. Included are several varieties of anmitsu, zenzai (a sweet red bean soup with mochi), and more. A popular item is purin, a caramel-topped custard developed by the founder. Some items are available packaged to take out; others would not do well in that format and are served in the restaurant. The restaurant also serves simple food such as oden.
🌐 *https://tsukushi.tokyo*

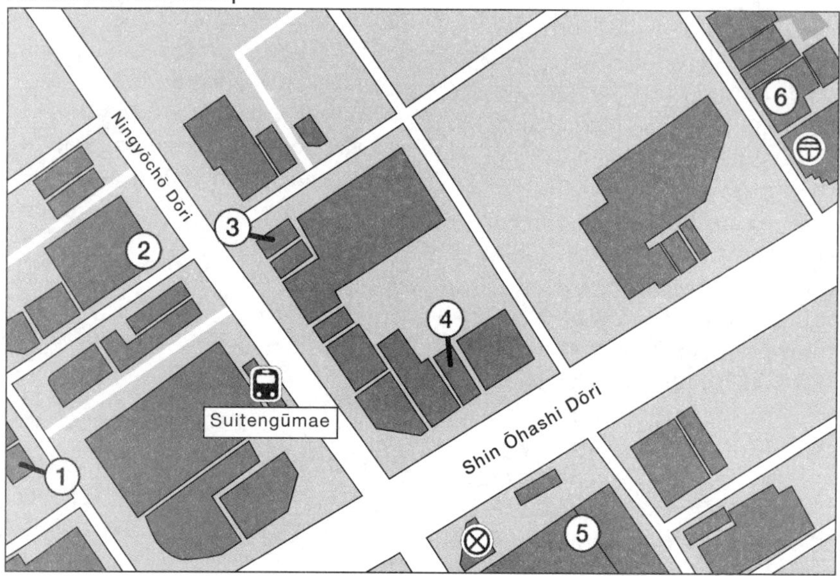

❺ **Suitengū** 水天宮

The child emperor Antoku and his mother Kenreimonin, who died at the Battle of Dannoura, are enshrined here. This shrine is famous as a place to pray for safe childbirth, so it is common to see pregnant women, babies, and couples here. On the grounds, which are actually one story above the street, you will also see interesting sculptures with a maternal connection. One is a mother kappa with children, and another is a statue of a dog and a puppy surrounded by twelve spheres with kanji carved on them that symbolize the Chinese zodiac. Dogs are associated with easy childbirth in Japan, so for this reason the shrine sells items with a dog motif. The shrine was moved to this location in 1672 from the Arima estate in Shiba. Benten is also enshrined here, so it is on the Shichifukujin tour and there is a statue of her by the famous sculptor Unkei (c. 1150–1223).

The fair day is the fifth of every month. On May 5 and 6 there is a festival with mikoshi processions and kagura performances.

🌐 *http://www.suitengu.or.jp*

NOTE: *The entire structure is supported on an underground system to allow it to move during a major earthquake. The planted areas at street level around the site are expansion joints for this system, so avoid them in earthquakes.*

❻ **Matsushima Jinja** 松島神社

The founding date of this shrine is not known. Many of the shrine documents were destroyed in the Great Kantō Earthquake and most of the remainder in the firebombings of World War II. There are some documents indicating that it was rebuilt in the early 14th century. Legends indicate that the location was originally a forested island—Matsushima means "pine island"—and that a fire was kept by the priest to aid boats in navigation. This is an Ōtori Shrine, and the god of harvest, Daikoku, is also enshrined here, so it is on the Shichifukujin tour. As this is a neighborhood shrine, people pray for a variety of benefits, including business prosperity, musical skill, academic achievement, and protection from danger. The shrine sells Ryōmufuda: you write something you desire on it and put it under your pillow, and if you dream about it, the dream is a sign that your wish will come true. You may also go to the shrine and inform the priest so he can pray for your success.

DETAIL 5

❶ Kasama Inari Jinja 笠間稲荷神社

This branch of Ibaraki's Kasama Inari Jinja was founded in 1859 by Makino Sadanao, lord of the Kasama han, on the grounds of his Edo residence. The kami enshrined here are Uga no Mitama, who is identified with Inari, and Jurōjin. This is one of the stops on the Shichifukujin tour of Ningyōchō.

❷ Meijiza 明治座

This theater opened in 1873 under the name of Kishōza in Hisamatsuchō. After fire and other problems the name changed to Hisamatsuza and then to Chitoseza. In 1890 it burned down and was rebuilt in 1893 with the present name. The theater burned down again after the Great Kanto Earthquake and was rebuilt in the present location. It was firebombed during World War II, with thousands dying in the area including those who had taken refuge in the theatre. It suffered from another fire in 1957. Theaters do not do well in the face of fire. From 1990 to 1992 the theater underwent extensive renovation. Performances here have a wide range; one can see kabuki, rakugo, modern dramas, musical acts, comedy, and pretty much anything that will fit on a stage. For meals, there is a cafe and a cafeteria, and you can buy bentō to eat in your seat during intermission. Nearby, about two blocks to the southwest, there is a small park with a statue of Benkei from the famous kabuki play *Kanjinchō*.

🌐 *http://www.meijiza.co.jp*

❸ Meiji Kannondō 明治観音堂

This is a very small Kannon temple, more of a roadside shrine, in the corner of the park next to the Meijiza Theater. It was placed there in 1950 as a memorial to the thousands who died locally in the firebombings of World War II.

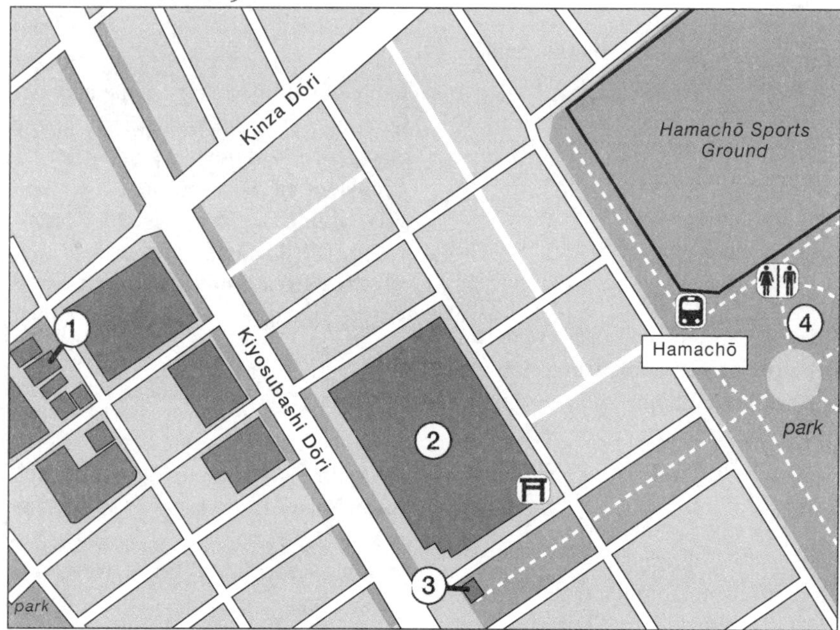

❹ Hamachō Park / Hamachō Kōen
浜町公園

Designed as part of the Tokyo reconstruction after the Great Kantō Earthquake, this park along the Sumidagawa is the largest in Chūō Ward. The land was once occupied by many ryōtei where geisha performed traditional dances and songs for wealthy patrons. It took some negotiation to move these businesses to the west and today a few still exist in the newer location. The park was established not only for recreation but to also function as an evacuation point in disasters. Hamachō Park consists mainly of large open spaces, some benches, trees, and a sports center with a heated swimming pool. If you have been walking for a while, this is a good place to rest. There are cherry trees for springtime flower viewing and gingko trees for fall colors. From here you can access the riverside pathway and stroll along the river.

墨田区北西部

NORTHWESTERN SUMIDA WARD

On the opposite side of the Sumidagawa from the Asakusa neighborhood in Taitō Ward is Sumida Ward. This chapter covers the area on the east side of the Sumidagawa, from Azumabashi and Yokokawa in the south to the northern part of Sumida. The highlights of this area include a Shichifukujin pilgrimage at shrines and temples near the river as well as the Mukōjima hanamachi, one of the last geisha districts in Tokyo. You will notice that this area has many sweets shops that date from the Edo and Meiji periods. If you stroll over the entire area, you may want to stop here and there for green tea and a sweet for a pick-me-up. However, much of this area is of relatively recent construction. Even with all the long-established businesses, old temples, and shrines, much of what you see here was constructed after World War II. Sumida Ward suffered some of the greatest devastation of any part of Tokyo in the war. On March 10, 1945, Sumida Ward incurred one of the highest civilian death tolls of World War II. Even so, the survivors carried on, rebuilding their shops and returning to places of worship and leisure. This history will explain some of what you see here. Those with an interest in literature may be interested to know that Nagai Kafu's famous story "Strange Tale from East of the River" is set about midway in this area.

For many the easiest route to stroll the area would be to start near the river and walk north in the order of the detail maps. Then take a train to Tokyo Sky Tree Station to explore southward from there.

NORTHWESTERN SUMIDA WARD

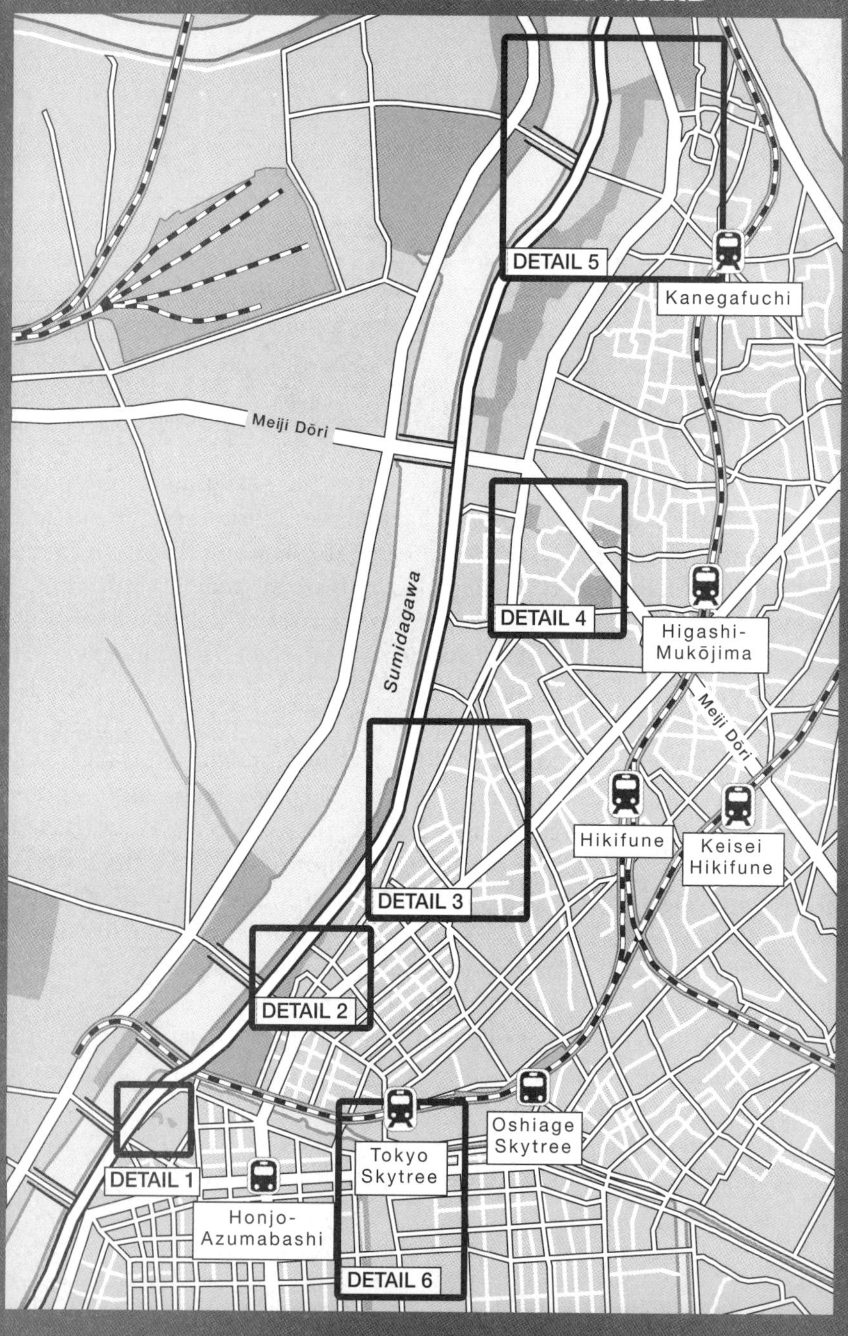

DETAIL 1

❶ Ebiya 海老屋

An Edo-style tsukudani shop dating from 1869 that started using sugar as an ingredient with the second-generation owner. They still use traditional recipes while working on developing new styles such as those with less salt. Their line of tsukudani includes some non-seafood items, such as sweet potatoes, mushrooms, and tōfu. Their products are sold in many department stores in the Tokyo area and they have a branch on block two of the Sensōji Nakamise.

🌐 *https://www.ebiyasouhonpo.jp*
🌐 *http://www.norenkai.net/en/portfolio-item/ebiya-main-store/*

❷ Asahi Group Head Office Building アサヒグループ本社ビル

For most travelers the easiest station to start from when strolling this area is one of the four Asakusa Stations, just across the Sumidagawa. The closest bridge is Azumabashi, which takes you to the headquarters of Asahi Breweries, one of the largest beverage companies in Japan. Founded in 1889, they produce not only beer but also distilled alcohol, wine, and soft drinks. There are two buildings on this site.

The most striking part of this complex is the shorter shiny black building, the Super Dry Hall, completed in 1989 and designed by Philippe Starck and Makoto Nozawa. This building contains a restaurant and a beer hall. The building is most famous for the huge golden sculpture on the roof. It has been nicknamed O Gon No Unko, which can be translated as "Golden Poo."

The taller office building is the Asahi Beer Azumabashi Building, designed by the Nikken Seikei company and completed in 1990. The building is designed to resemble a glass of beer with foam on top. There is a bar on the twenty-second floor, open from 10:00 a.m. to 10:00 p.m., that is known for great views of the area. At night the glass on these buildings reflects the surrounding lights, including that of traffic on Azumabashi, adding to the view from the other side of the Sumidagawa.

🌐 *http://www.asahibeer.co.jp*

❸ Sumida Ward Office / Sumida Ku Yakusho 墨田区役所

At nineteen stories above ground, this building towers over most of the area. There are good views to be found from the elevator area on the fourteenth floor. The building was designed by the Kume Sekkei Company and completed in 1990. In the plaza between the building and the elevated expressway, you will see a statue of Katsu Kaishū, who was born in the Ryōgoku neighborhood of Sumida Ward. In the chapter on Ryōgoku you will find other locations related to him.

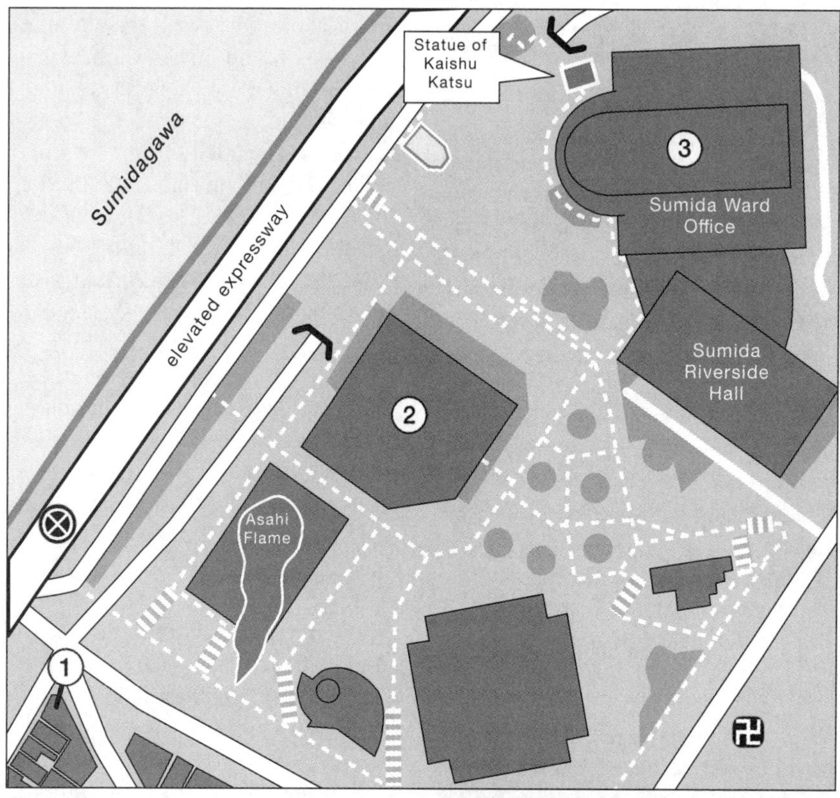

❸ Azumabashi Tourist Information Center 吾妻橋観光案内所

Here you will find the local Sumida Ward tourist information center. I always visit tourist information centers when I am in their vicinity. At such centers you may be able to find information about local sights you may not otherwise have known about. Additionally they are a good source of information on events that are currently taking place.

DETAIL 2

❶ Ushijima Jinja 牛嶋神社

This shrine was built in 860 and dedicated to three kami: Susanoo no Mikoto, Amenohohi, and Sadatoki Shinō. One of the distinctive features of this shrine is an unusual wooden torii in front of the building; this style is known as a Miwa torii. There is also a large statue of an ox that was donated in 1824. Traditionally it said that stroking the same part of the ox statue as the part of your body that is ailing and then offering a prayer will help with healing. There is no clear border between the shrine grounds and Sumida Park, creating a pleasant merging of the two.

The annual festival is held in mid-September, and the grand festival is held every five years.

❷ Sumida Park / Sumida Kōen 隅田公園

This entry covers Sumida Park on the east bank of the Sumidagawa. For information on the west bank side and the origin of this park, see the entry in the chapter for Asakusa. The park begins near the railway bridge for the Tōbu Skytree Line, before going north a short distance beyond the Kototoibashi. This east-bank portion of Sumida Park was the former suburban estate of the Mito Tokugawa daimyō. The Great Kantō Earthquake destroyed the original garden, and in 1931 the area was made a public park. The east side of the park is interesting in that the grounds of the nearby temple and shrine are not clearly demarcated, giving the park a feeling of being more expansive than it actually is. On a Saturday each Spring, the Asakusa Yabusame Festival for horseback archery is held here, with the exact date depending on when the cherry blossoms are out.

❸ Sumida Heritage Museum / Sumida Kyōdo Bunka Shiryōkan すみだ郷土文化資料館

A museum devoted to Sumida Ward history. As you enter you will be facing the information counter and a small gift shop. The museum has three floors with exhibits on the history of the area, including the devastation of the World War II firebombings. There are also exhibits on the Forty-Seven Rōnin, the Sumidagawa, and more. The gift shop has a selection of books related to the area and its history.

❹ Entsūji 圓通寺

Included here for those interested in architecture, this building, sometimes referred to as the Compact Cosmic Temple, is a most unusual structure for a Zen temple. The old temple needed repair. However, the building required so much work as many aspects were no longer up to code that it was decided to rebuild it. The new design by Hara Hisashi with its flat planes and Greco-Roman pillar motifs is vastly different from what one expects from a Buddhist temple. The current building dates from 1990.

❺ Mimeguri Jinja 三囲神社

This is an Inari shrine, also dedicated to Daikoku and Ebisu, making it a site on the Shichifukujin tour twice over. While the shrine was founded in the early 9th century, the name dates

NORTHWESTERN SUMIDA WARD DETAIL 2

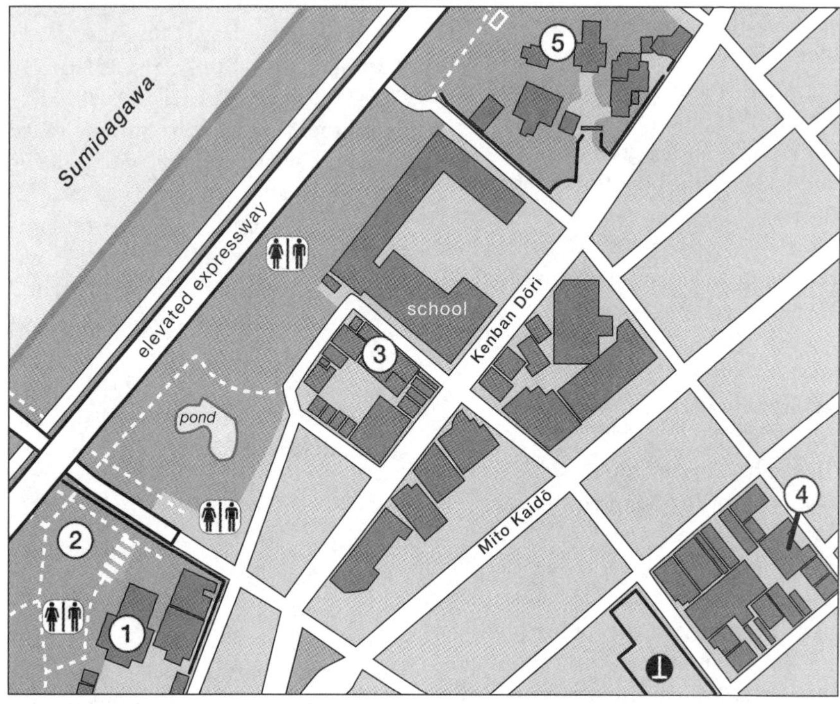

from the 14th century when a priest was working on repairs and unearthed a statue of a fox. Then a white fox appeared and ran around the statue three times—"three circuits" is a translation of mimeguri. The original name had been Tanaka Inari. A later story from the 17th century tells of an old woman who worked along with her husband at the shrine. She would clap her hands to summon a white fox. There is a pair of statues depicting her and her husband behind the main building. Most shrines have guardian dogs, but Inari shrines often have guardian foxes. This shrine has both. You can also view one of the Mitsukoshi lions from their department stores, as this is the shrine for that company. There is a large stone with a poem inscribed on it, found on the right side between the torii and main hall. The poem was Takari Kikaku's contribution to the prayers of the local farmers during a drought; the next day it rained. The grounds also contain many other stones, some sixty of them, with literary inscriptions.

DETAIL 3

❶ Aoyagi Seike 青柳正家

A famous confectioner continuing to make and sell traditional sweets. One of their most noted items is their kiku monaka, chrysanthemum-shaped wafers filled with bean jam. Also well known is their kuri yokan made of azuki bean jelly and containing chestnuts. Their products are also available at a branch in the Ekimise building in Asakusa.

🌐 *http://www.aoyagiseike.jp*

❷ Kado カド

While I tend to only list long-established businesses, that is, those that have existed for more than two generations, this is one of the exceptions to my self-imposed limitation. Kado was opened in 1958 and as a cafe located near several ryōtei where geisha often perform dances and music for parties. Before the days of cell phones, many ryōtei customers would meet here before heading on to their dinner. Today, tourists visiting the nearby Tokyo Sky Tree and art students are more common as customers. The decor at this cafe is Victorian, the cash register dates from the 1930s, paintings displayed are changed periodically, the phone is rotary, and the radios at each end of the counter date from the opening. All in all, a nice place to take a break and grab a sandwich with a glass of juice.

❸ Kōfukuji 弘福寺

An Ōbaku Zen temple founded in 1673, with the main hall and two-story sanmon gate done in a Chinese style. Both were constructed in 1933 after the temple was destroyed in the Great Kantō Earthquake. This temple also has a small attractive garden on one side—you pass under a short bridge to reach it. The grounds contain a shrine to Hotei and this temple is on the Shichifukujin tour. There is another shrine with statues of an elderly couple, the Jiji Baba. Praying here is said to be effective for treating coughing and asthma. These two statues were carved by a recluse priest named Fugai in the form of his parents. No one knows when the curative powers came to be ascribed to the statues. The area nearby is a hanamachi district, with geisha residences and high-end exclusive ryōtei.

🌐 *https://ko-fukuji.wixsite.com/kofukuji/home*

❹ Chōmeiji 長命寺

This Tendai sect temple dedicated to Benten was founded in 1615 and is a stop on the local Shichifukujin tour. There is a story about a time when shōgun Tokugawa Iemitsu stopped by the temple Jōsenji while hunting. He had a stomachache, and when the priest gave him some of the temple spring's water, he quickly recovered. Not long after that, the name of the temple was changed to Chōmeiji, "Temple of Long Life." It is also known for having

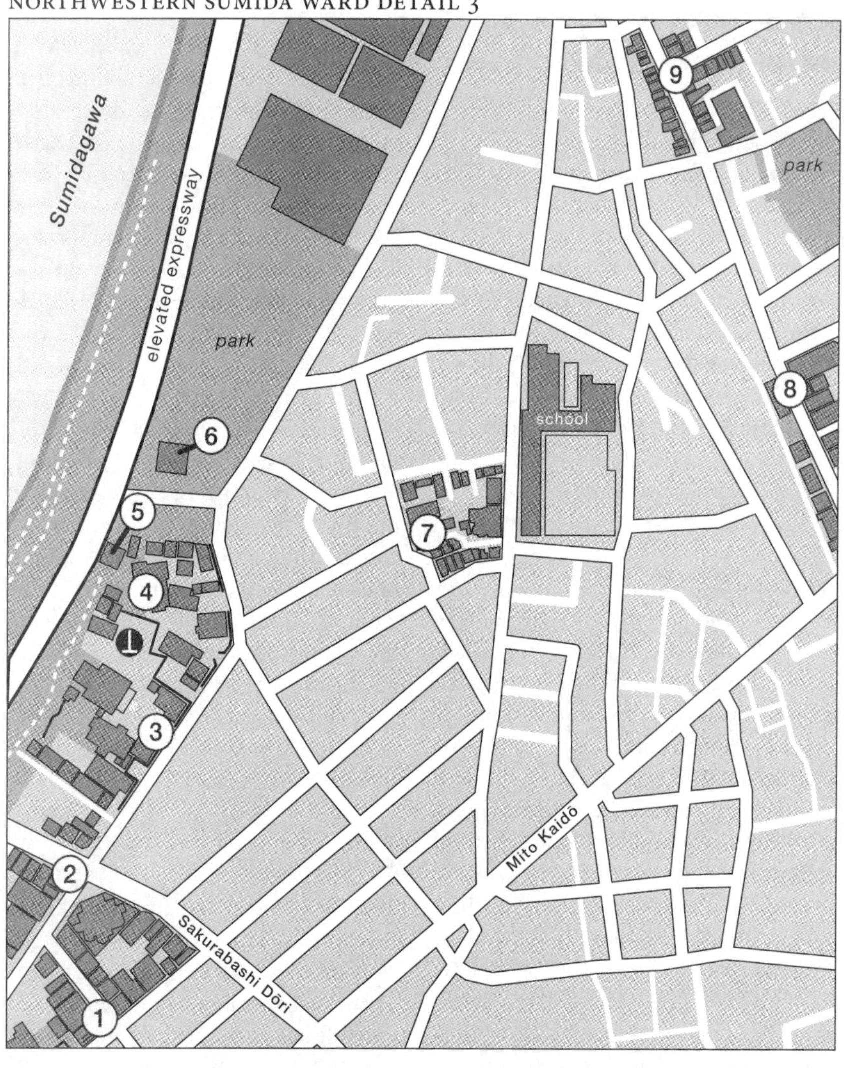

memorial stones to many well-known Edo-period authors. There are also stones with poems inscribed on them, such as one with a haiku by Bashō about snow viewing. Some stones are whimsical, such as one shaped like a wine cup for kōshuin, "lovers of wine," and a phallic one for kōshokuin, "lovers of sex."

❺ Chōmeiji Sakuramochi 長命寺桜もち

A confectionery founded in 1717 and specializing in sakuramochi, a treat of mochi filled with sweet bean paste and wrapped in salt-pickled cherry leaves. They use a method for preserving the leaves that was developed by their founder. You can buy packages of sakuramochi to take with you as gifts or for yourself. It is also possible to enjoy them on site with green tea. They recommend that you peel off the leaves, but some people do eat it with the leaf.

🌐 *http://www.sakura-mochi.com*

🌐 *http://www.norenkai.net/en/portfolio-item/chomeiji-sakuramochi/*

❻ Kototoi Dango 言問団子

Kototoi Dango was established in the late Edo period by a local gardener. His visitors would be treated to his homemade dango, and it was not long before he went into the dango business full time. The current building is a modern concrete structure; the interior is very nice, with traditional motifs. Seating is Western and traditional. The first time I dropped by was on a sunny afternoon when there were only a few customers. I held up one finger, they seated me, and then they brought one order of three dango on a plate and a cup of green tea. There are only three types of dango: one made with miso, which is yellow, white ones made with white sweet bean paste, and red ones made with red sweet bean paste. Their dango are also sold in many shops in the Kantō area. You can buy them to go. The large box holding twenty dango is made of cedar. They should be eaten on the same day that they are purchased. The shop may close early if they sell out.

🌐 *http://www.kototoidango.co.jp*

🌐 *http://www.norenkai.net/en/portfolio-item/kototoi-dango/*

❼ Mukōjima kagai, aka Mukōjima hanamachi 向島花街

One of the few remaining geisha districts of Tokyo, located mainly in Mukōjima 5-chōme across the street from the entrance to Kōfukuji. The borders of this area are roughly Sakurabashi Dōri on the south, national highway 6 (the former Mito Kaidō) on the southeast, and Hatonomachi Dōri on the northeast and north. Don't expect anything fancy, but do keep an eye out for buildings that are different in design from the rest of the area. The high-end restaurants here where the geisha perform dances, play music, pour drinks, and chat with customers are simple on the outside. They are understated structures and can be identified by traditional elements at the doors and windows, and by a few ornaments. Inside they tend to the traditional and a few larger ones may have a garden. But then, dinner with traditional geisha entertainments is not the

▲ A roadside Jizō is found at the east end of the Azumabashi.

▲ Tokyo Sky Tree can be seen from a distance.

▲ Kado's windows may look dark, though, it is indeed open.

サンドイッチ
カド
季節の生ジュース
くるみパン

kind of event your average tourist can book, and charges can be more than $800. Some tour companies do organize large group dinners with geisha. There are also occasional music and dance performances at theaters in nearby Asakusa.

❽ Hatonomachi Market Street / Hatonomachi Dōri Shōtengai 鳩の街通り商店街

An old-fashioned shopping street, where many of the buildings date from not long after the war. The street is narrow and has a variety of shops that a neighborhood would need. If you wander off the main street, you may see some other interesting structures. Hatonomachi translates as "Pigeon Town" and Nagai Kafū wrote about his visit to the area in 1947. At that time, many businesses had off-limits signs stenciled on their fronts to warn occupation forces not to enter. This was once a red-light district—the brothels shut down in January 1958, a couple of months before the new laws required. Few of those buildings still exist. Several had small tiles covering their storefronts, and for many years some still had faded stencils on them. Developers have an eye on the area, so over time we should expect the remaining buildings will be replaced with newer and safer structures. One hopes they will keep a bit of the old style in the designs.

🌐 *http://hatonomachi-doori.com*

❾ Koguma こぐま

This streetcorner cafe has both a typical menu for Japanese cafes and some unique items. They serve curry rice, omelet rice, baked omelet, the spaghetti dish called napolitan, cake, and more. Some dishes are seasonal. Koguma means "baby bear" and their sign has a silhouette of one in a circle. While they opened in 2006, the building dates from 1927, having escaped the firestorm of the World War II bombings. This was a pharmacy before it was remodeled into the present restaurant, with minimal changes. The interior is of simple wooden construction with lattice and shoji dividers between some tables. Seating is Western, using old chairs from a middle school, and some of the tables are from the same school.

🌐 *http://www.ko-gu-ma.com*

DETAIL 4

❶ Jiman Kusamochi 志゛満ん草餅

The specialty of this shop, established in 1869, is kusamochi. This is a type of mochi made with yomogi (Japanese mugwort), a plant with medicinal uses, mixed in. The result is a mochi dark green hue. Their kusamochi can also be found sold in many department stores in Tokyo.

The amount they make each day is limited, and they will close early if they sell out of the day's supply. There are

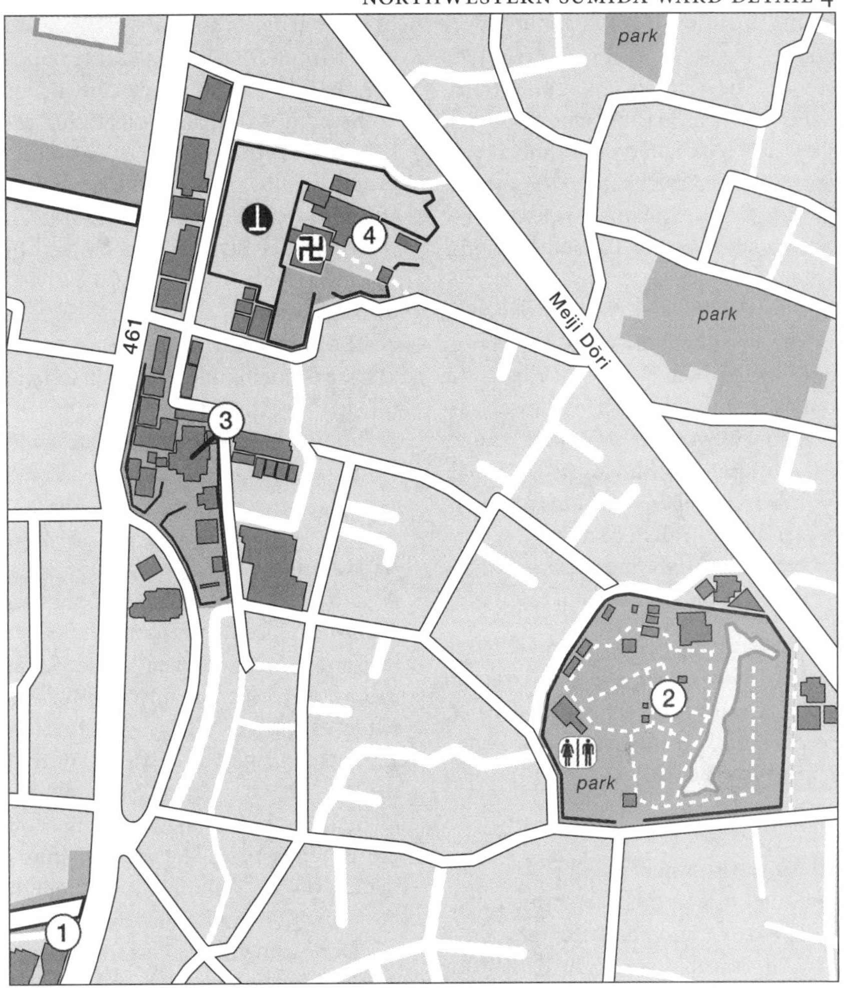

two types: one filled with sweet bean paste (an), and the other plain and served with syrup and roasted soybean powder. They also sell other sweets such as sasamochi and daifuku.
🌐 *http://jimankusamoti.com*

❷ **Mukōjima Hyakkaen** 向島百花園
Mukōjima Hyakkaen was created in 1804 as an informal private garden by Sahara Kikū, a retired antiques dealer. The garden started out with flowering ume trees that he had been given by friends. Over time, various flowering

plants mentioned in literature were added, as were poems inscribed on stones. The name is commonly translated as "Garden of One Hundred Flowers." No matter what time of year you visit, you are likely to see blooms in this garden. The final owner was the businessman Ogura Tsunekichi, whose widow donated it to the city in 1938. The garden was extensively damaged in the firebombings of World War II and repaired after the war. This is the only surviving Edo-period flower garden in Tokyo. It is especially known for a tunnel of bush clover that usually flowers in September, and trellises of wisteria that peak in May.

🌐 *https://www.tokyo-park.or.jp/teien/en/mukojima/index.html*

TRIVIA: *Just outside the entrance is a water storage system and pump called a rojison, which gathers rain runoff from several buildings in the area and stores it for emergency use.*

❸ Shirahige Jinja 白鬚神社

Founded in 951, this is a shrine to Sarutahiko Ōkami and to Shirahige Myōjin, possibly an originally Korean deity, whose name can be translated as "white-bearded god." Also worshiped here is Jurōjin, so the shrine is on the Mukōjima Shichifukujin tour. The shrine is a branch of the one on Lake Biwa near Kyoto. It has a place in labor history, as in 1901 some five thousand attended the first large meeting of labor activists and workers in Japan on its grounds. The 1864 shrine building, which had survived the major 20th-century conflagrations to hit Tokyo, was burned down by arsonists protesting the rituals of the emperor's enthronement ceremony in March 1990. The shrine is also mentioned in "A Strange Tale from East of the River" by Nagai Kafū.

The annual shrine festival is on the first weekend in June. The main festival is held every three years.

🌐 *http://shirahigejinja951.wixsite.com/shirahigejinja*

❹ Hōsenji 法泉寺

A Soto Zen temple which is about 800 years old. Hōsenji was founded by early Kamakura shogunate vassal Kasai Saburo Kiyoshige in memory of his parents. The buildings fell into ruin when the village was destroyed during the Waring States Period. Stone monuments from before the destruction on the grounds provide historical information on the founding. It was rebuilt in 1532 with a land grant given by the local lord in memory of his wife to help support the temple. In the Edo Period the temple was given an annual income by the government. There are two noted Jizō statues on the grounds, a stone statue from 1662 and a bronze standing statue that was cast in 1717.

🌐 *http://www.seikazan-housenji.jp*

DETAIL 5

❶ Shirahige Higashi Apartments 白鬚東アパート

Built in the 1970s, this large complex of eighteen interlocked apartment buildings, each thirteen stories tall, stretches for about a mile (over 1 1/2 kilometers), separating Bokutei Dōri and Higashi Shirahige Park. Part of the function of this string of buildings is to act as a firebreak between the densely populated neighborhoods to the east and the park, an evacuation area, to the west. The buildings include massive fire doors between them to allow evacuation to the park, steel shutters on the entrances and windows, hoses, and balconies with red water cannons.

❷ Higashi Shirahige Park / Higashi Shirahige Kōen 東白鬚公園

A large and very long park parallel to the Sumidagawa and Expressway Route #6. The park is large enough to accommodate a variety of recreational facilities. I once took a break and watched a practice by local baseball teams, possibly from the neighborhood junior high school. The park opened in 1986 and is also an evacuation site for disasters. A large sculpture of a matoi as a tribute to firefighters is located in the plaza between the tennis courts and baseball fields. There are also children's playgrounds, trails among the greenery, over 2,500 trees of fire-resistant species, two ponds, and picnic and barbecue areas. The park has lots of benches; if you started this stroll near Azumabashi, you will probably be ready to rest here for a bit.

🌐 *http://www.kensetsu.metro.tokyo.jp/content/000007544.pdf*

❸ Sumidagawa Jinja 隅田川神社

Established in 1180 by Minamoto no Yoritomo, this shrine was originally called Suijinja. Today it is also known by the name of the enshrined kami, Suijin Sama. The original location was next to the river. When the government decided to build the expressway, they had the shrine relocated inland. An interesting feature is the lack of komainu—instead there are two stone ten-thousand-year turtles, appropriate for a shrine to a water god.

❹ Mokuboji 木母寺

Founded in 976, this temple is best known in the West for its association with the nō play entitled Sumidagawa. In the play a noblewoman, who has already been driven mad, comes to this area searching for her son Umewakamaru, who had been kidnapped. As she is crossing the river, she sees a crowd by the other bank. The ferryman tells her the story of a boy who died a year before after being abandoned by a slave trader because he was ill. The ferryman says the boy's name and the woman realizes it is her son. The ferryman then

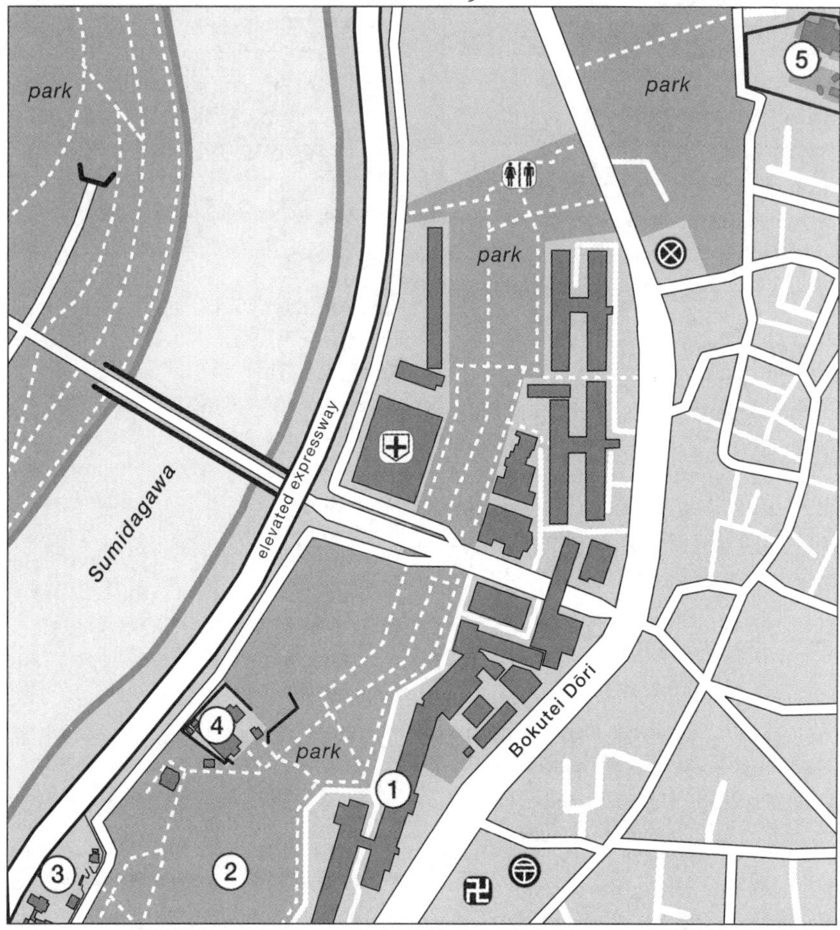

understands what has happened and gives her a bell and urges her to join in with the memorial service the locals are holding. There is a stone mound in the temple grounds dedicated to Umewakamaru's mother, and women often pray there for the health of their children. The temple was heavily damaged in the World War II firebombings and what remains of the old structure is entirely enclosed in a glass building to preserve it.

❺ Tamonji 多聞寺

This Shingon temple was established in the mid-9th century and is dedicated to Bishamon (Tamon is another name for Bishamon). The temple is the northernmost of the local Shichifukujin tour sites. The temple's thatched gate dates from 1718, making it the oldest structure in Sumida Ward and likely the only thatched one in Tokyo. As you enter, look left and you will see a memorial to a pair of tanuki who once lived there. One legend has it that the temple priest left the pine under which they nested standing when he had the ground cleared. The tanuki however caused all sorts of trouble at the temple. The priest's assistant had a dream that Bishamon ordered him to kill them, and the next day the tanuki were found dead. A different legend says that they had always terrified the locals and that while prayers were being offered to Bishamon, a child appeared who killed the tanuki.

🌐 *http://www.sumidasan-tamonji.or.jp/top_eng.html*

DETAIL 6

❶ Tokyo Sky Tree 東京スカイツリー

At a height of 2080 feet (634 meters), Tokyo Sky Tree is the tallest freestanding broadcast tower in the world. The structure completed in 2012 was needed to facilitate digital broadcasting in the region around Tokyo. The previous major broadcast tower in the Kantō region was Tokyo Tower, built in 1958. At a height of 1089 feet (332 meters), it was considered too short for the present when more skyscrapers are blocking broadcasts. Like Tokyo Tower, the Sky Tree has two observation decks, which can be visited after buying a ticket. The highest point in the second observation deck is 1,480 feet (451.2 meters) up, putting you over a quarter mile from the ground. At the base is Tokyo Sky Tree Station, formerly Narihirabashi Station, owned by Tōbu Railway, one of the partners in the tower. There is also the Tokyo Solamachi mall with more than 300 shops and restaurants, the TENKU planetarium, and the Sumida Aquarium. As this is a very popular attraction, you may want to step out of this modern complex with its crowds and stroll through the adjacent neighborhoods.

🌐 *http://www.tokyo-skytree.jp/en/*

❷ Kataoka Byōbu 片岡屏風店 **and the Museum of Byōbu / Byōbu Hakubutsukan** 屏風博物館

Look in any book on traditional Japanese art and you will find pictures and descriptions of byōbu, traditional Japanese folding screens. Byōbu in the past were usually decorated with paintings or calligraphy, as they have a large surface where those arts can be applied. In 1946 this byōbu workshop added a small private museum in the display area of the store. It is even possible to commission a byōbu with personal items incorporated into it. Examples of such have included a deceased

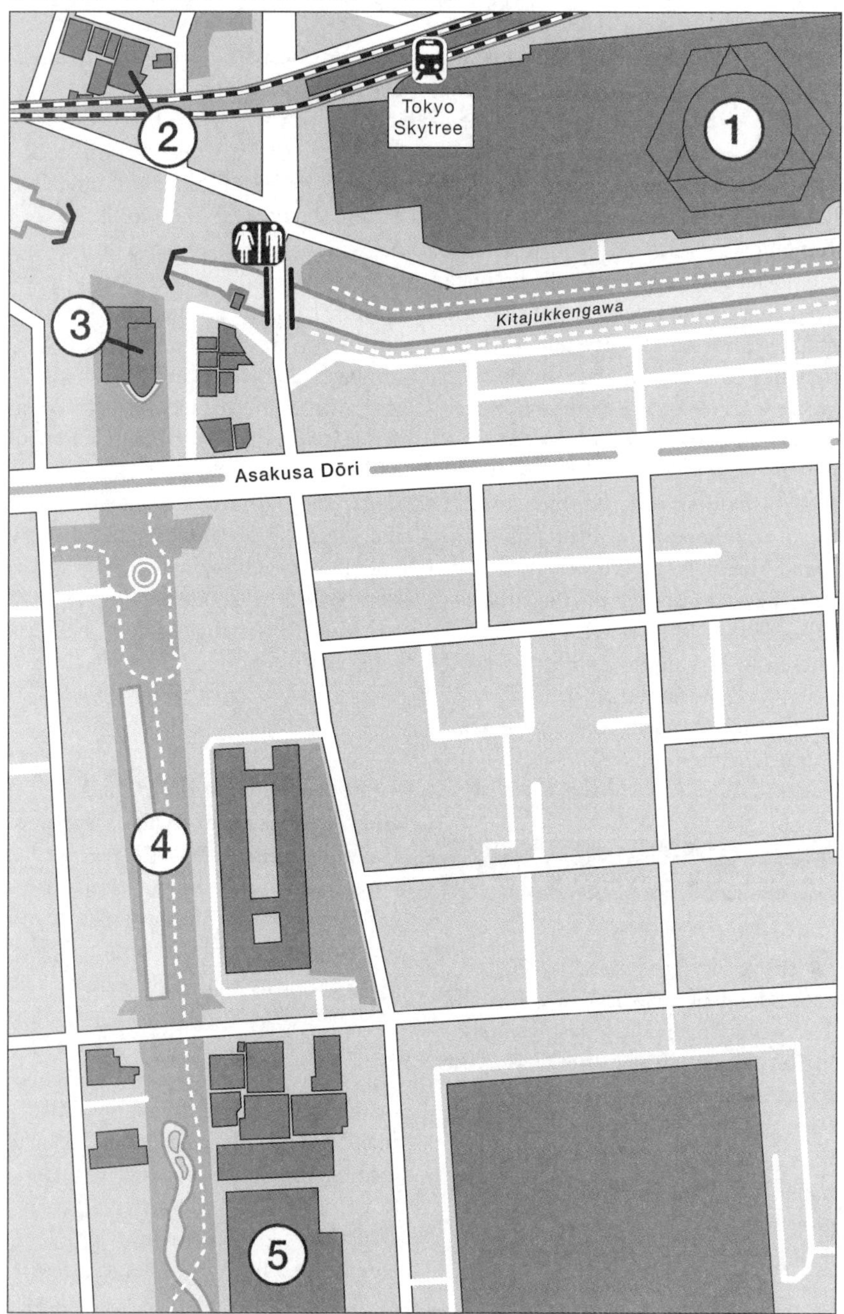
Tokyo
Skytree
1
2
3
Kitajukkengawa
Asakusa Dōri
4
5

husband's favorite neckties, the stole of a nun, parts of kimono, and more. The museum area has displays about tools, screen construction, and the history of the Japanese folding screen.

🌐 *http://www.byoubu.co.jp*

❸ Narihirabashi Information Center 業平橋観光案内所

A local Sumida Ward tourist information center that can be found in a building shaped like a boat. I always check tourist information centers when I am in their vicinity to find local sights I did not know about, as well as information on events.

❹ Ōyokogawa Shinsui Park / Ōyokogawa Shinsui Kōen 大横川親水公園

Established in 1993, this long park along the Ōyokogawa begins at the Kitajūkengawa at the northern end and then runs southward all the way to Kotobashi in southern Sumida Ward. This is a popular spot to walk, jog, picnic, wade, bicycle, or go fishing. The park is divided into five different zones including grassy areas, groves of trees, playgrounds, and even areas to hunt for insects, with lots of benches for resting. The fishing area is near the north end; it is fenced off and opens at 9:00 a.m.

❺ Tobacco and Salt Museum / Tabako to Shio no Hakubutsukan たばこと塩の博物館

This five-story museum has been operated by Japan Tobacco since 1978. The museum was originally located in Shibuya and moved to the present location in 2015. The exhibits on the history of tobacco and of salt are on two separate floors. The collection consists of ukiyo-e prints and various related objects. Items on display illustrate the role of these products around the world. There are also meeting rooms for educational events, a reading room, an AV room, and a special exhibit room. The museum shop has a variety of items for sale including handcrafted traditional pipes, books, and flint and steel fire starting kits.

🌐 *https://www.tabashio.jp/index.html*

表参道・原宿

OMOTESANDŌ/HARAJUKU AREA

If you know Omotesandō, it may not strike you as a strolling neighborhood. This upscale area is best known as an expensive shopping district with many high-end (and high-priced) stores, or for the Ura Harajuku area associated with youth fashion. Being a fashionable area, a large number of the shops don't have Japanese names—instead English, French, Italian, and other European names are common. There are many interesting side streets to explore, as well as one of the highest concentrations of award-winning architecture in the world. In fact, this chapter is mainly about the buildings rather than their contents. If you are interested in photographing buildings, I'd recommend coming early before the streets fill up with pedestrians and returning after dark when the buildings are lit up from inside. I would also recommend approaching the area from Omotesandō Station, located on Aoyama Dōri at one end of Omotesandō, then going uphill past a few blocks of eye-catching buildings before heading back down past the station. The walk will be mainly downhill from Omotesandō Station to the forest around Meiji Jingū. Don't expect many old buildings here; the fifth major firebombing of World War II burned the district down. What was built in the aftermath has been almost completely replaced with much newer buildings.

TIPS: *Skip weekends unless you want to see the brightly dressed kids hanging around Jingūbashi and Takeshita Dōri. I must warn you that these days there are only a few of them left. ALWAYS ask before taking pictures.*

While the variety of award-winning architecture in Omotesandō is a major sight for the stroller, the side streets with their charming smaller shops and restaurants are also worth a look. They are also a good alternative for those who are interested in shopping but do not want expensive brands that you can get in any major city in the world.

DETAIL 1

❶ Comme des Garçons

コム・デ・ギャルソン

This boutique for Kawakubo Rei's famous fashion line is most recognizable for its curved display windows of blue-tinted glass, which form a corridor to the entrance. The shop occupies part of the first floor of an existing building and opened in 1999. It was designed by Future Systems with some work by Kawakubo Rei and Kawasaki Takao handing the interior.

❷ Prada Boutique Aoyama

プラダブティック 青山

This shop was designed by the Swiss firm Herzog & de Meuron and opened in 2003. The six-story building is entirely encased in diamond-shaped glass windows, some of which bulge outward and others that bulge inward. Most of the windows are clear, with only a few being opaque. At night, light illuminates the glass exterior. Photographers will appreciate that part of the lot has been left as a plaza, making the sides of the building even more visible.

❸ Corner building at 5 Chome-3-2 Minamiaoyama

This three-story building was designed by Bruno Moinard and opened in 2009 as a store for the international fashion brand Cartier. Later it housed the Tokyo flagship store of La Perla. As this book was being written La Perla shuttered and the building was occupied by Balenciaga, then Audi House of Progress as a temporary location, now closed. Tenants usually do not change this quickly in Tokyo. The building is often described as being like a diamond, as the intersecting glass-paneled sides resemble the facets of gemstone.

❹ From 1st Building

フロム・ファーストビル

Designed by Yamashita Kazumasa and opened in 1976, this five-story building is occupied by apartments, offices, and fashion boutiques. Covered in red brick, the building extends and recedes to give the appearnce of many intersecting planes. The inside of the building is organized around an inner courtyard and the design makes it a little complicated to navigate.

OMOTESANDŌ/HARAJUKU AREA

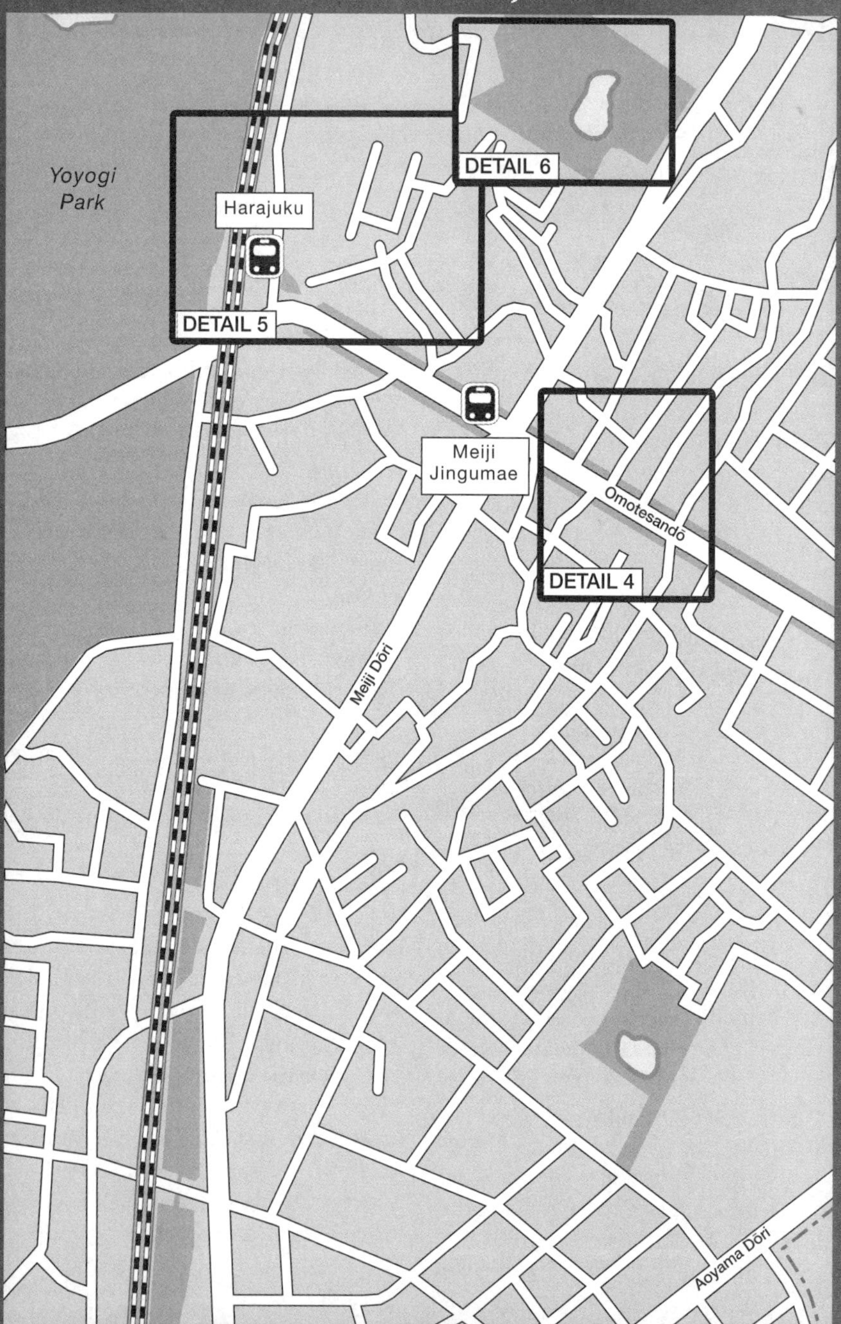

OMOTESANDŌ/HARAJUKU AREA

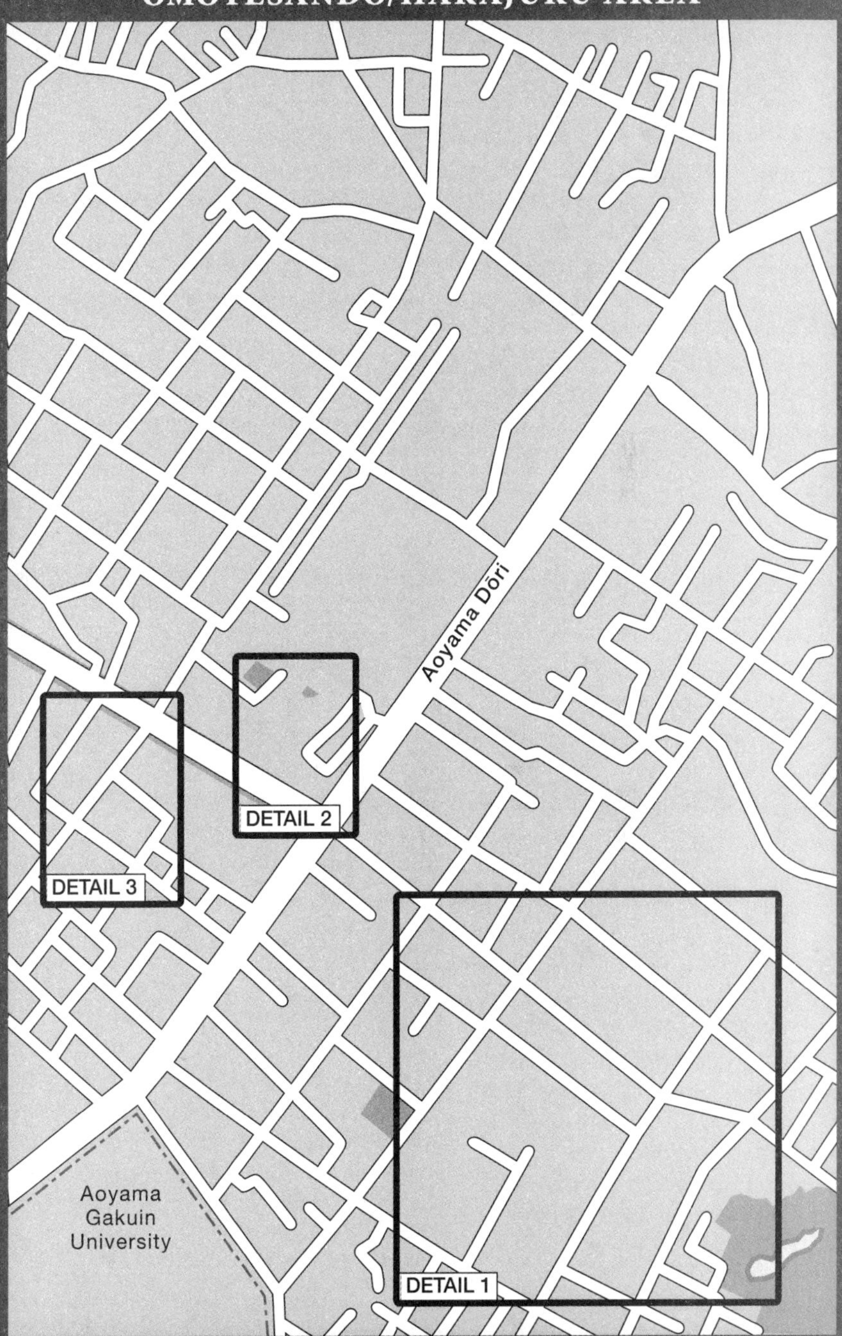

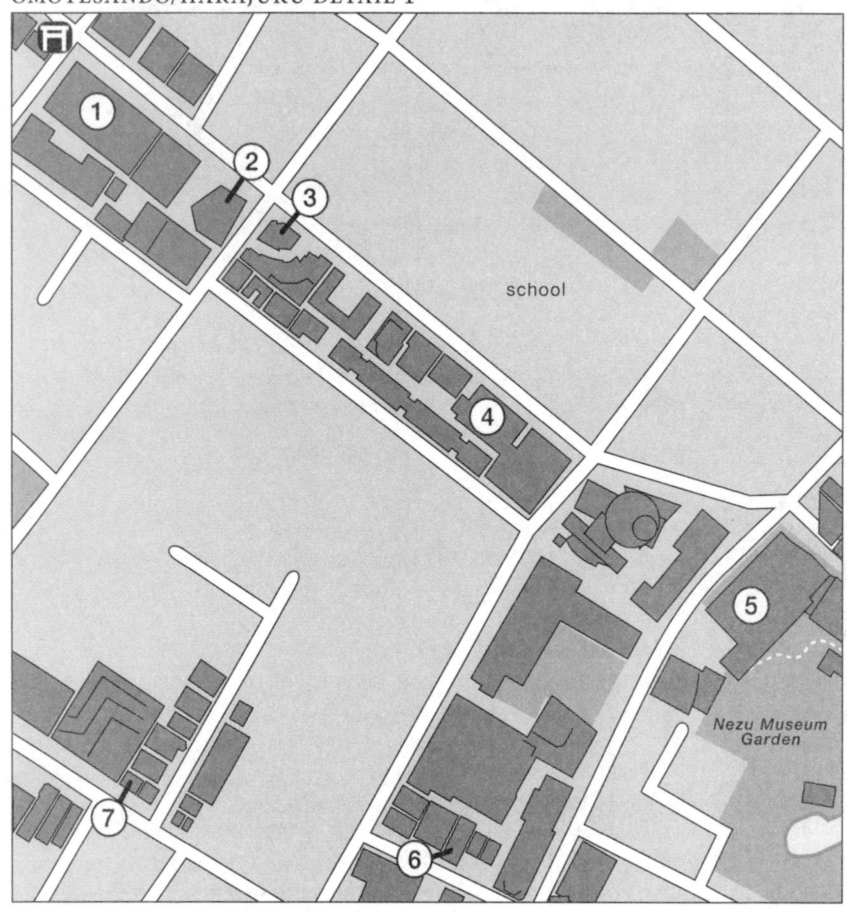

❺ Nezu Museum / Nezu Bijutsukan
根津美術館

The Nezu Museum is based on Nezu Kaichirō's private collection of pre-modern Asian and Japanese art. It is located on the site of the old Nezu family residence and was established in 1941. Most of the building was destroyed in the World War II firebombing of this area. However much of the collection had been relocated to preserve it and exhibitions resumed in 1946. The museum has undergone restoration and various additional construction projects over time, the most recent being in 2009 with a design by Kuma Kengo. One of the most famous paintings in the collection is Ogata Kōrin's screen of kakitsubata, a type of iris. The screen is often displayed around Golden Week, April 29 through May 5.

There is a cafe that serves light meals, and the very attractive garden is a good place to visit in the fall to enjoy the changing colors of the trees.

🌐 *http://www.nezu-muse.or.jp/en/*

❻ Tarō Okamoto Memorial Museum / Okamoto Tarō Kinenkan
岡本太郎記念館

Even if you don't recognize the name Okamoto Tarō, you will likely know his work if you know Japanese art. His most famous saying is "Art is an explosion!" and it shows in much of his work. His best known piece is the Tower of the Sun for Expo '70 in Osaka. Okamoto studied in Paris in the 1930s, where he associated with many surrealists. He returned to Japan in 1940 to be drafted and was sent to China. Upon his return to Tokyo, he found that the family home had burned and all of his previous work was destroyed. The museum is located on the site of the old family home and is a work of art itself, having been designed by noted architect Sakakura Junzō. The building was Okamoto's home from 1954 until his death in 1996. The collection includes drawings, sculptures, paintings, and other works. There is a garden with many sculptures, a cafe, and a museum store with books by and about Okamoto. They even have capsule toys based on his works. Plan to remove your shoes, and plan to have fun.

🌐 *http://www.taro-okamoto.or.jp/en/*

❼ Wing Club ウイング・クラブ

This internationally famous model shop is not the place to buy a regular plastic kit. They sell works made from scratch. Many of their products are sold in museum shops around the world. Wing Club will even do custom builds for fictional items, such as Porco Rosso's plane from the Studio Ghibli animated feature. One of their works can easily range from $300 to over $1,000.

🌐 *http://wing-club.co.jp*

TIP: *Hand your wallet to a friend before you enter, with a pledge to not return it to you until you are several blocks away, and do the same for your friend.*

DETAIL 2

❶ Stone Lanterns on Omotesandō at Aoyama Dōri 表参道の石灯籠

These stone lanterns near Aoyama Dōri mark the beginning of Omotesandō as it continues downhill to Meiji Jingū. Look closely and you will see these are charred from the fires of the firebombing of World War II. Nearby, on the left side of the street as you face down Omotesandō, is a memorial to the civilian dead inscribed with a prayer for peace.

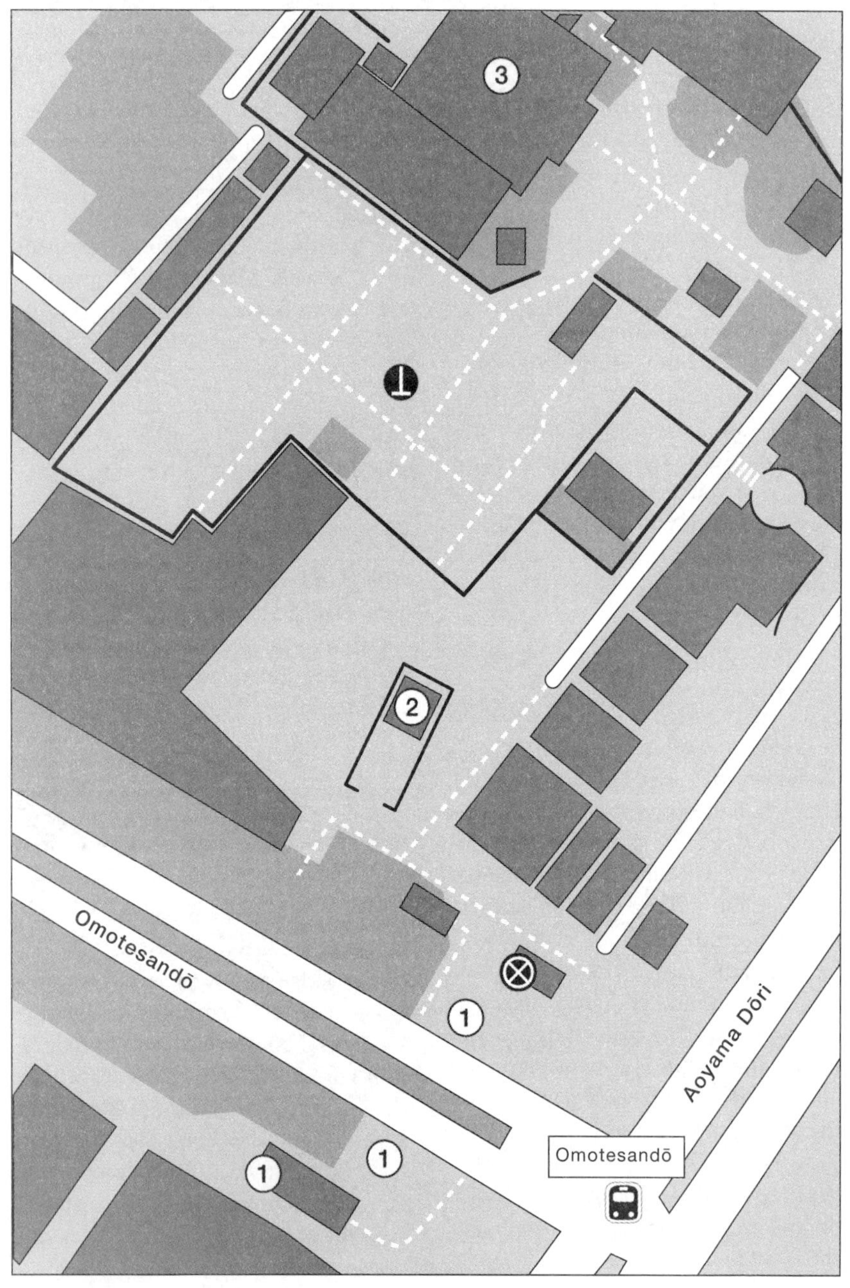
3
2
1
1
1
Omotesandō
Aoyama Dōri
Omotesandō

❷ **Akiba Jinja** 秋葉神社

I can't find much information about this shrine as no guidebook, tourism office, or book on Tokyo that I own contains anything about it. A claim that is repeated on some websites states that it was moved to this location in 1824 by request of Kinokuniya Bunzaemon. However that seems dubious, as the famous Kinokuniya Bunzaemon died in 1734. In any case, it's on a major route and is a good place to hit during your stroll of Omotesandō. It provides quite a contrast to the rest of the neighborhood.

❸ **Zenkōji** 善光寺

This sizeable Jōdo sect Buddhist temple has its entrance on a side street off Aoyama Dōri. As the temple is a short distance from the local street, you have to pay attention when walking by, since the entrance to the temple is narrow and dwarfed by the tall buildings of the main street. Just look for the temple gate with its red pillars. Originally this temple was built in Yanaka in 1601. That temple burned in 1703 and was rebuilt on this site in 1705. The present building dates from 1921, replacing an older structure that burned in 1862.

DETAIL 3

❶ **Aoyama St. Grace Cathedral**
青山セントグレース大聖堂

When I first saw this location on a map I thought, "Oh, a major church, perhaps I'll check it out." When a friend and I approached the location we had our cameras ready to take lots of pictures. Major church? Nope: instead we found a lavish gothic-style chapel for wedding ceremonies with an attached hall for banquets. In fact we ran into several wedding halls in the Omotesandō area, so it must be a popular location for them. In any case, all were interesting structures, so we were pleased to see them and take photos. I must admit I have no idea how most of them look inside.

🌐 *http://www.bestbridal.co.jp/tokyo/stgrace_aoyama/*

❷ **Coach** コーチ

Designed by the firm OMA and opened in 2013, the Coach building looks as if it is made of huge glass bricks arranged in a parquet pattern. There are only two stories, but inside there are several levels accessed by short stairways. The inside of the building repeats the rectangular motif of the exterior in simple white and clear shelving. At night the building is a bright cube, contrasting strongly with its darker neighbors.

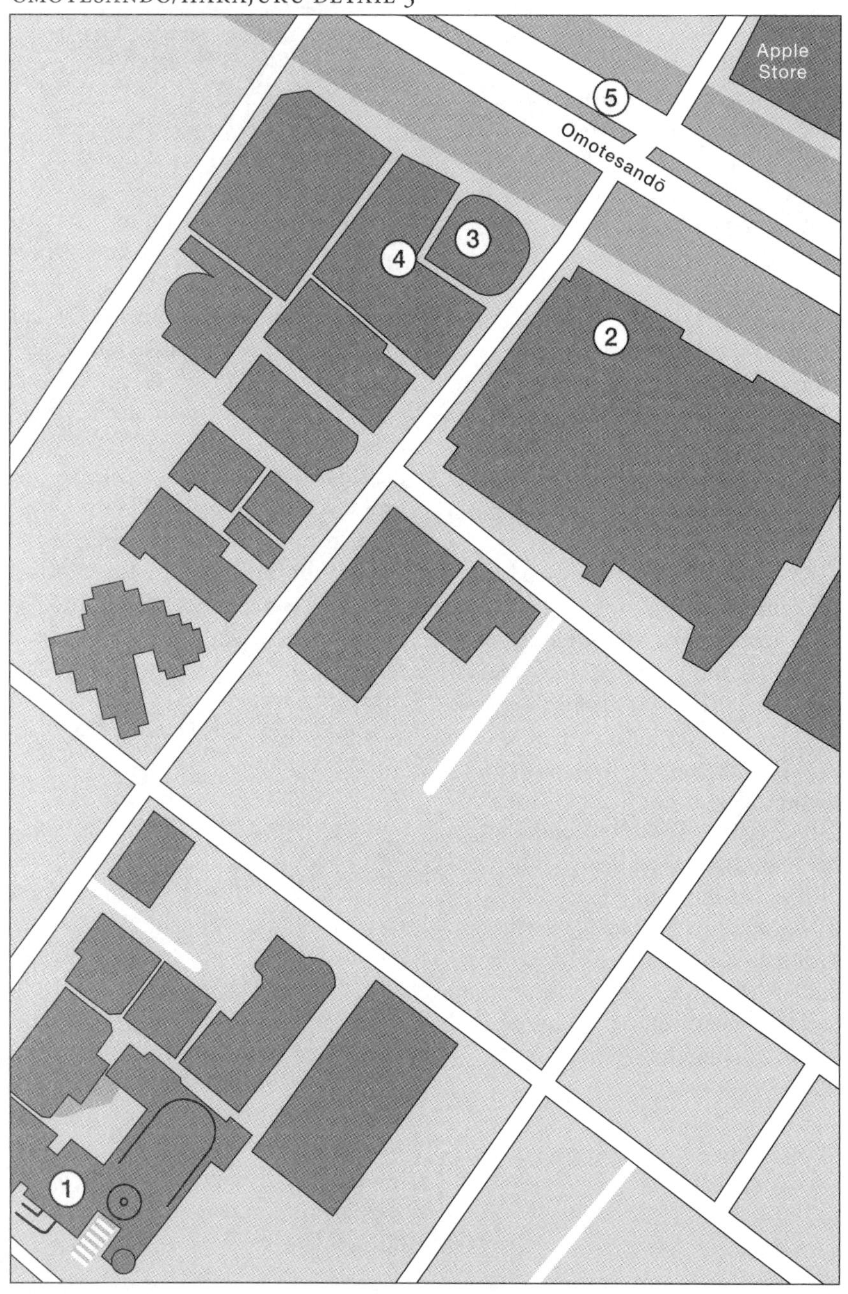
Apple
Store
5
Omotesandō
3
4
2
1

❸ Omotesandō Keyaki Building
表参道 けやきビル

This building was designed by Dan Norihiko for the German fashion brand Hugo Boss and completed in 2013. It's an impressive building: The structure curves inward as it rises to level off a few stories off the ground, curving outward again toward the top.

❹ Kering

There are no identical windows in this seven-story building designed by Toyo Itō and Associates and completed in 2004 for the Italian luxury brand TOD's. Instead the windows form between broad lines of concrete that crisscross on the outside of the structure. Itō Toyoo has explained that these lines are actually based on an abstracted pattern of overlapping tree limbs and are intended to mirror the zelkova trees that line Omotesandō. In March 2020 TOD's sold the building to Kering. The lower portion of the building is devoted to retail space, the upper part is used as office space, including Kering's Japan headquarters. The rooftop includes a terraced garden

❺ Omotesandō 表参道

The broad boulevard Omotesandō was proposed in 1916 and completed in 1921 as the main approach to Meiji Jinja. Originally this area had been mainly forest; the opening of Omotesandō encouraged commercial and middle-class residential construction in what earlier had been a sparsely developed part of Tokyo. Today the street is known for its density of expensive stores and international high fashion. Besides the shops there are temples, shrines, and museums near each end of this zelkova-lined boulevard. Only a handful of the large trees on Omotesandō predate the war. The rest were planted a few years after it ended.

DETAIL 4

❶ Cat Street キャットストリート

This gently curving, gently sloping street of smaller shops is a nice break from the high fashion bustle of Omotesandō. This is perhaps most apparent as you enter it from that busy boulevard by walking through a small park-like area alongside the Gyre building. You will quickly leave shiny steel and glass behind and enter the domain of humbler shops, many of which include the owner's residence on the second or third floor. Further down the street this changes as slicker buildings again predominate. At this point you may want to take a side street to return to Omotesandō. Go ahead and do so, but be aware you will be entering a maze to explore on your way back. Or you may just want to stop for coffee or browse through a vintage clothing shop for bargains.

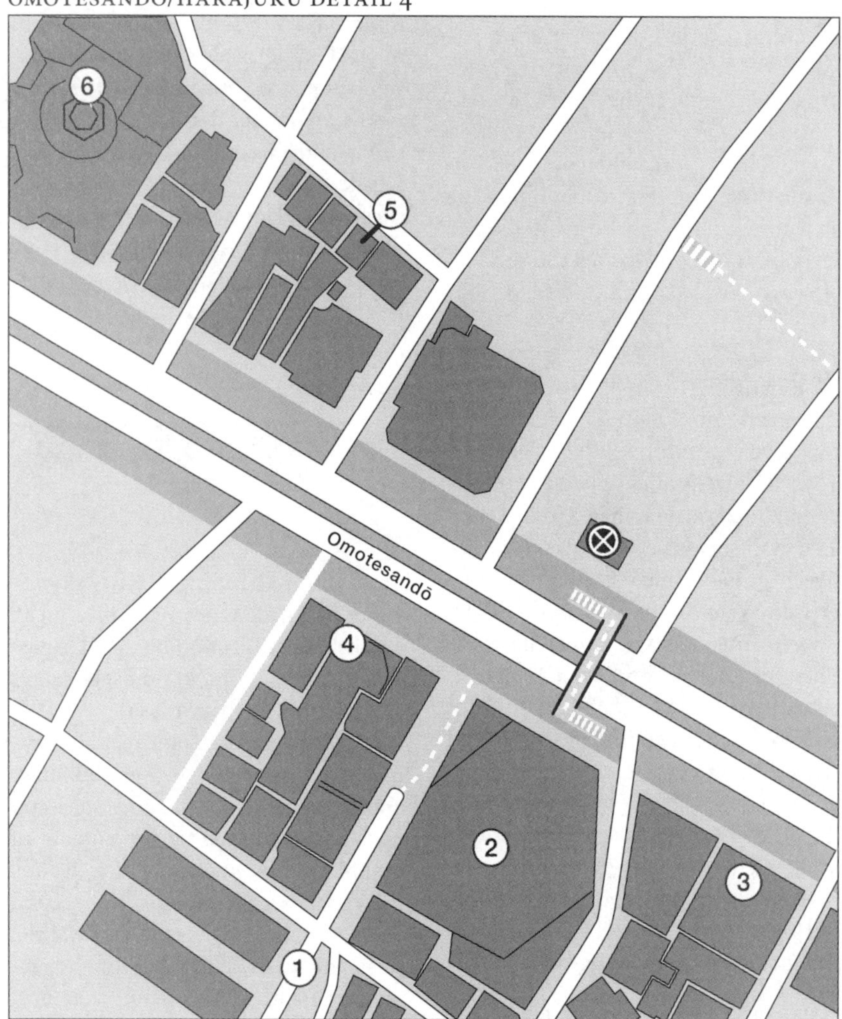

❷ Gyre ジャイル

A mall designed by the Dutch firm MVRDV, opened in 2007. The structure gives the impression of each floor having been stacked on the other in a loose manner and then shifted slightly. Floors recess and overhang, creating a pleasant variety of shapes. Access is from the front or from stairways on the side streets. A photo gallery is centrally located as part of the design.

🌐 *https://gyre-omotesando.com*

❸ Oriental Bazaar
オリエンタルバザー

Originally an antique store founded in 1916, Oriental Bazaar relocated to the present location in 1951 with the aim of developing a market with the US military families who lived in Washington Heights near the end of Omotesandō. It has long been a popular shop for tourists. The cost and quality of the merchandise varies, from cheap goods to fine antiques, the range is broad. In 2021, amidst reports of major international brands wanting to take over the building, Oriental Bazaar announced it was remodeling. This included removing the red and green facade that had made it stand out since 1979. In 2022 it reopened as a compact version of the store. They have English-speaking staff, will ship, and accept payments in yen, US dollars, and euros.

🌐 *http://www.orientalbazaar.co.jp*

❹ Kiddy Land Harajuku
キディランド 原宿店

This is the five-story flagship store of the most famous toy store chain in Japan. Founded in 1950, Kiddy Land is a great place for kids and adults. I especially enjoy their selection of Studio Ghibli merchandise. A friend was pleased to find Japan-only Disney character goods to bring home as gifts. The inventory varies greatly, with many items sold for a few weeks and then replaced by fresh ones.

🌐 *https://www.kiddyland.co.jp*

❺ Onden オンデン

A small, twenty-seat neighborhood curry restaurant serving reasonably priced meals since 1960. The decor is dark wood with diner-style Western seating at the counter or tables. This is a great low-key place to relax with a cup of coffee or lunch. However expect lines, as it is rather popular.

❻ Tōkyū Plaza Omotesandō Harajuku 東急プラザ 表参道原宿

Designed by Nakamura Hiroshi and completed in 2012, this is the local branch of the various Tōkyū Plaza buildings in Tokyo. There are two extremes to be viewed in this building. The first is the entrance, which is lined with a series of polygonal mirrors reflecting the stairs and escalators like an asymmetrical kaleidoscope. The other extreme is the sixth-floor roof garden with its views of the neighborhood. This tree-shaded garden is a good place to give your legs a rest; there is also a coffee shop and restaurant. Both of these extremes are accessible at 8:30 in the morning, but the five stories of shops in between do not open until 11:00 a.m.

🌐 *http://omohara.tokyu-plaza.com/en/*

▲ The polygonal mirrors in Tōkyū Plaza Omotesandō Harajuku reflect the surroundings.

TAX FREE

▲ Light plays on the glass of the Prada store.

▲ Okamoto Tarō's workshop is preserved in his memorial museum.

▼ Dancing to rockabilly at Yoyogi Park takes more than music; you gotta have style.

DETAIL 5

❶ Ōta Memorial Museum of Art / Ōta Kinen Bijutsukan 太田記念美術館

This museum's extensive ukiyo-e collection was based on that of Ōta Seizō, who was president of Tōgō Insurance. Ōta had begun buying ukiyo-e as a young man, amassing a sizeable collection. A portion of his collection was destroyed in the firebombings of World War II. When he passed away in 1977, he owned some 12,000 works. The family then carried out his request to exhibit the works and opened the museum in 1980. Currently the number of prints is about 14,000. The museum also has a scholarship program for those wishing to do research in the field of ukiyo-e.

🌐 *http://www.ukiyoe-ota-muse.jp*

❷ Harajuku 原宿

The Harajuku neighborhood is internationally famous for youth fashion. However the shopping area commonly referred to as Harajuku is mainly north of Omotesandō, spreading out for several blocks with a heavy focus on the stores on Takeshita Dōri. If you don't mind crowds, this can be an interesting neighborhood to wander in. Harajuku is known in the West as a major youth hangout. This is true in the sense of those youth who are into fashion trends and shopping. The heyday of Harajuku being a general youth hangout was actually from the late 1970s to the late 1990s, when part of Omotesandō would become a pedestrian zone on Sundays and holidays. Young people took over when pop culture movements, such as Takenokozoku, moved in with their bright costumes inspired by the Heian period, followed by other styles. When the pedestrian paradise ended, the youth hangout for many of these kids shifted south near Shibuya Station, leaving the rockabilly fans and famous fashion movements behind.

***TIP:** If you are interested in unusually dressed Japanese youth, be aware that many young folks dressed in bright fashions are likely to be non-Japanese tourists checking out the area.*

❸ Jingū Bashi 神宮橋

This bridge at the end of the Omotesandō, just before the entrance to Meiji Jingū crosses, the Yamanote Line train tracks. Originally it was just a pedestrian bridge, however, starting in 1995 the center portion was opened for vehicles. The current bridge dates from 1982 and incorporates some of the design elements of the original 1920 bridge. While no longer as popular of a hangout for the kids visiting Harajuku—the vehicle traffic is to blamed for that—it is still a gathering point. If you are interested in photographing the local kids, this is a good spot on weekends. Be sure to always ask for permission.

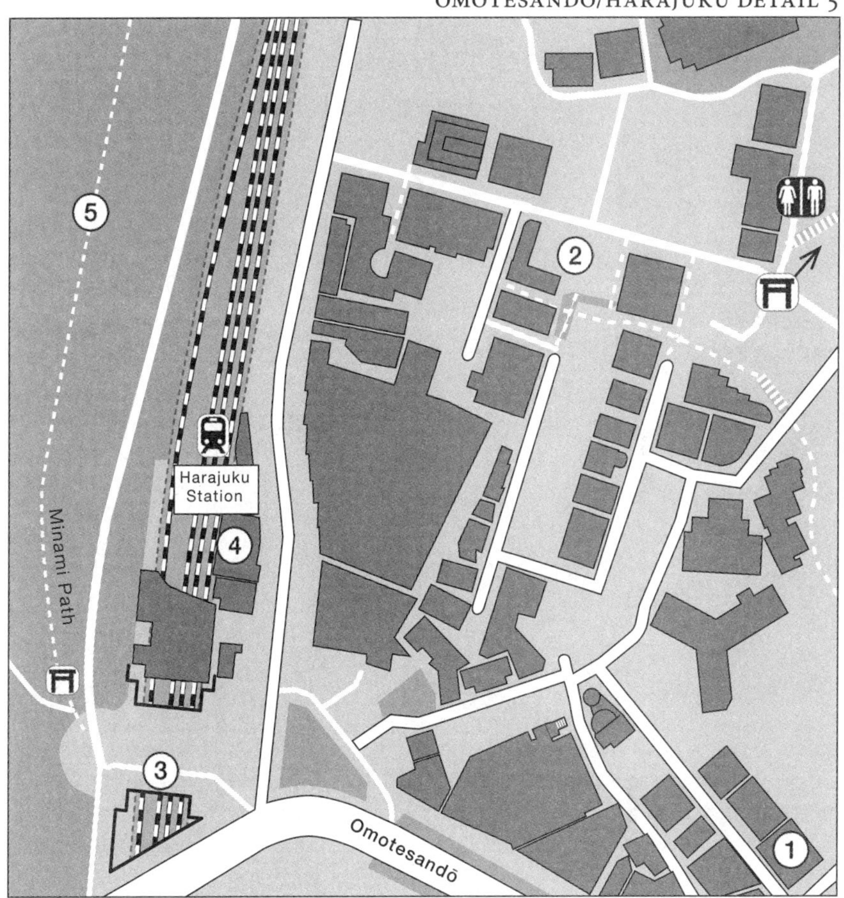

On Sundays, just beyond the bridge in the park, you can see the Rollers dancing to rock and roll from the 1950s.

❹ Harajuku Station / Harajuku Eki 原宿駅

The original wooden train station built in 1924 on the JR Yamanote Line was two stories tall, with a gable roof covered in green copper. The station managed to avoid destruction in the firebombing of the area in World War II. In 2020 a new and larger station opened next to the original. The old station was quite small for handling some 70,000 passengers each day, and not up to current fire codes so it was decided to demolish it. The dismantling and construction were estimated

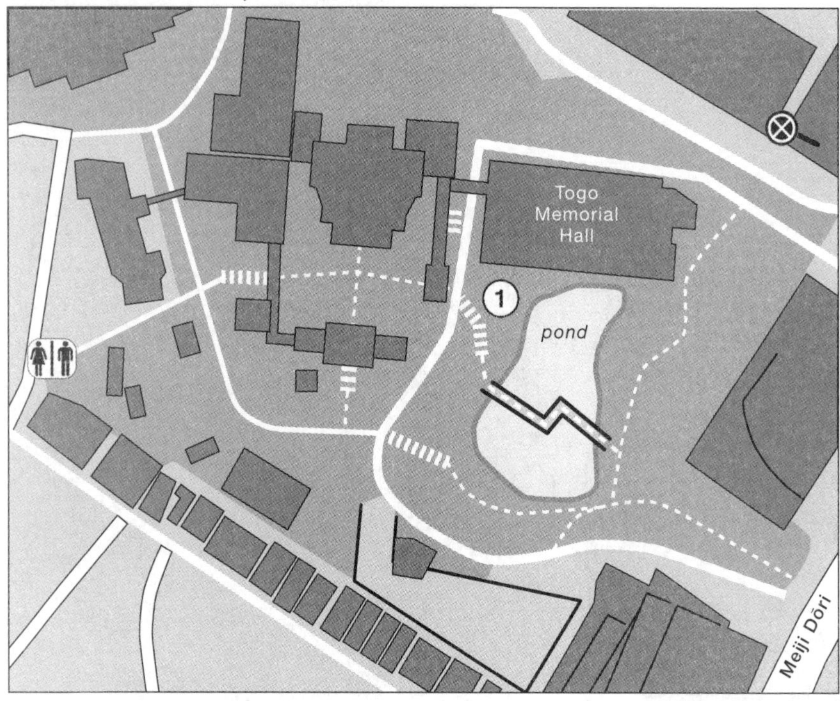

to take over a year as portions of the original structure would be saved and incorporated into a new building on the site preserving the half-timber style of the original.

❺ Meiji Jingū 明治神宮

Meiji Jingū was founded in 1920 to enshrine Emperor Meiji and Empress Shōken. As you pass under the giant torii and walk to the shrine buildings, it no longer feels like you are in the middle of urban Tokyo. You are surrounded by a 173-acre forest of trees donated from across Japan and other nations. This is a good place to appreciate the changing colors in the fall and for bird watching. The shrine area is open for free; the Meiji Jingū Imperial Garden is accessible for a small fee. Flower lovers will enjoy the variety of irises in the garden that bloom in late May and early June. The current shrine buildings date from 1958, as the originals had been destroyed when Tokyo was bombed in World War II. Destroyed by lightning in 1966, the two large torii were rebuilt in 1975. Closing hours vary depending on when the sun goes down.

There are several festivals celebrated

here. Hatsumōde, January 1–3, gets about three million visitors coming and going throughout the three day. The Autumn Grand Festival is held November 1–3. The Chrysanthemum Exhibition takes place late October through most of November.
🌐 *http://www.meijijingu.or.jp/*

DETAIL 6

❶ Tōgō Jinja 東郷神社
The Marquis Tōgō Heihachirō (1848–1934) was enshrined here in 1940. As Marshal-Admiral of the combined Japanese fleets in the Russo-Japanese War, he commanded the fleet in its victory against the Russian navy, defeating the third largest naval power in the world at that time and surprising the world with his success. The complex was destroyed in World War II and rebuilt in a traditional style from concrete after the war. The grounds include an attractive garden and a small museum with a bookshop. The main entrance on Meiji Dōri is identifiable by the torii and the large lantern that accompanies it. From there you can walk over the bridge spanning the pond or walk through the garden. Both routes will take you to the shrine. There is also an entrance to the shrine from the west.

両国

RYŌGOKU

Ryōgoku is a major center for sumō. Host to three fifteen-day tournaments a year, the area is well known as home to many training stables. As you wander through the neighborhood, you may spot restaurants serving chankonabe, a dish traditionally eaten by wrestlers, and statues and monuments related to sumō, as well as rather large guys going about their daily business. The area is also known for the summer fireworks festival dating back to 1733, which is held on the last Saturday of July upstream from the bridge. If you need a break, there are many excellent restaurants in the vicinity of the arena and station. With its parks and museums, this area is a joy to stroll through.

DETAIL 1

❶ Ryōgokubashi 両国橋

The original Ryōgokubashi, built in 1657, was the first bridge to span the Sumidagawa. Now that it was no longer necessary to rely on ferries, development greatly increased east of the river. Originally called simply Ōhashi, "Great Bridge," it was the largest bridge in Japan, with a length of 574 feet (175 meters) and width of 23 feet (7 meters). The name Ryōgokubashi, "two provinces bridge," came later, referring to the fact that it connected two provinces, Musashi on the west bank and Shimōsa on the east. The bridge was rebuilt of steel in 1904, destroyed in the Great Kantō Earthquake in 1923, and rebuilt in 1932, with further renovation in 2008. Interesting design elements include the small decks that extend over the water from the pedestrian walkways, art deco globes at each end of the bridge, and a design motif on the rails in the shape of the fans used by sumō referees. If you cross the bridge to the west, you will find where the Kandagawa meets the Sumidagawa, an inviting stroll along the Kandagawa will take you to Akihabara. In the animated feature *Hokusai's Daughter*, the bridge is crossed several times by various characters.

❷ Momonjiya ももんじや

This restaurant founded in 1718 specializes in boar, bear, and deer meat. If you have a taste for wild game, you may want to visit. The name simply means a place that sells this kind of meat. Despite Buddhist prohibitions on meat consumption, such restaurants existed in several cities in the Edo period. The rationalization was that the meat was eaten for medicinal purposes. On the outside of the building is a simple sign with a sculpture of a boar above the name. They have English-speaking staff on hand.

❸ Ryōgoku Fireworks Museum / Ryōgoku Hanabi Shiryōkan 両国花火資料館

Japanese fireworks are world famous for their spectacular beauty and variety. Fireworks were introduced into Japan by English merchant John Saris in 1613 and soon became popular. The famous annual Sumidagawa fireworks display began in 1733 as part of memorial activities for those who had died in a plague. Open since 1991, the museum has displays on how fireworks are made and on the devices used to launch them, as well as artwork and photographs relating to festivals.

❹ Ekōin 回向院

This Jōdoshū Buddhist temple was established in 1657 as a memorial to the dead from the Great Meireki Fire who were unidentified or had no family to claim their bodies. There is a monument to them called the Banninzuka, or "Mound of a Million Souls." Ekōin has also long been associated with memorials for animals. Shōgun Tokugawa Ietsuna's horse was memorialized here, and Ōta Nampo's *Ichiwa Ichigen* makes reference to six hundred cats buried here after an epidemic in Tokyo. One building, both unusual and controversial, is the three-story Ekōdō, a memorial hall for the remains of dead pets. Such memorial halls and sculptures are not the norm in Japan. There are memorial sculptures with animal themes including one for cats and one for fish. Another sad monument on the temple grounds is the Mizukozuka, "Mound of the Stillborn," for infants who died in birth, miscarriage, or by abortion.

Ekōin was the location for many sumō tournaments from 1833 until the first Ryōgoku Kokugikan opened in

RYŌGOKU WEST

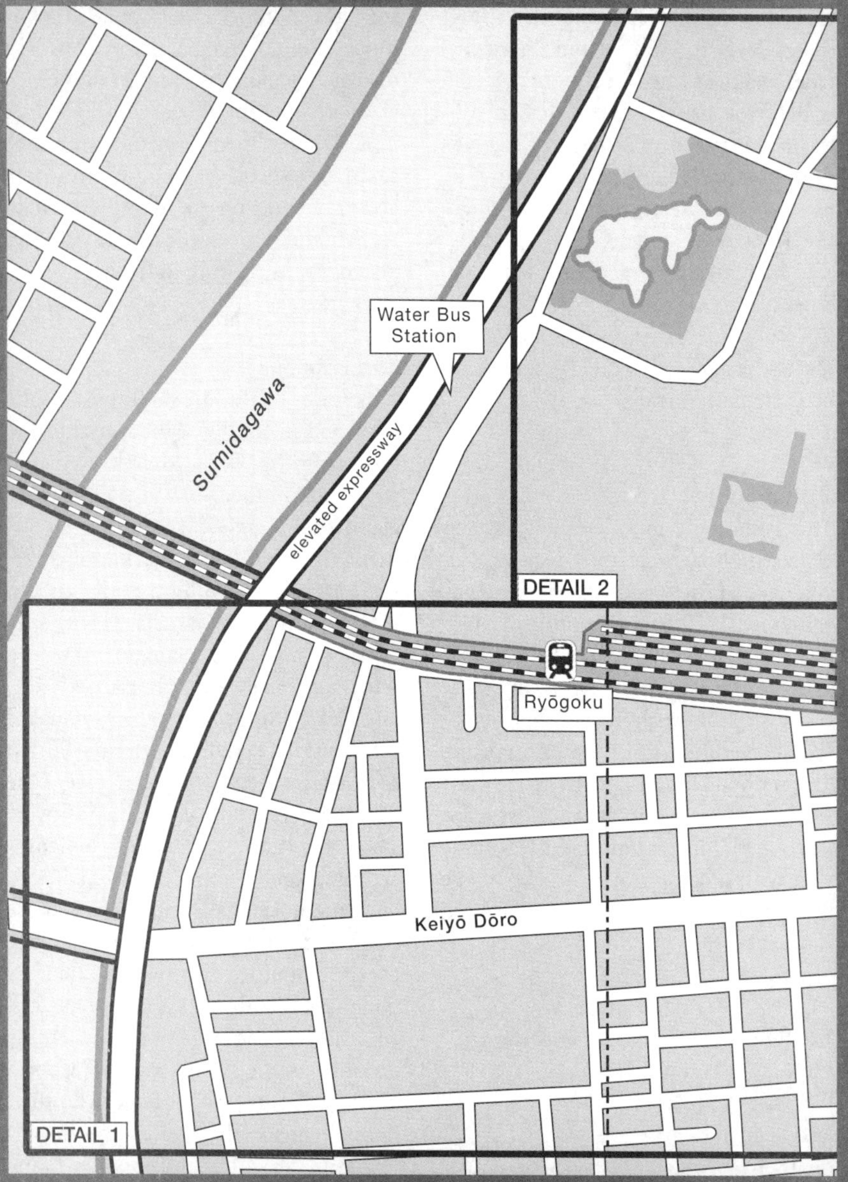

RYŌGOKU EAST

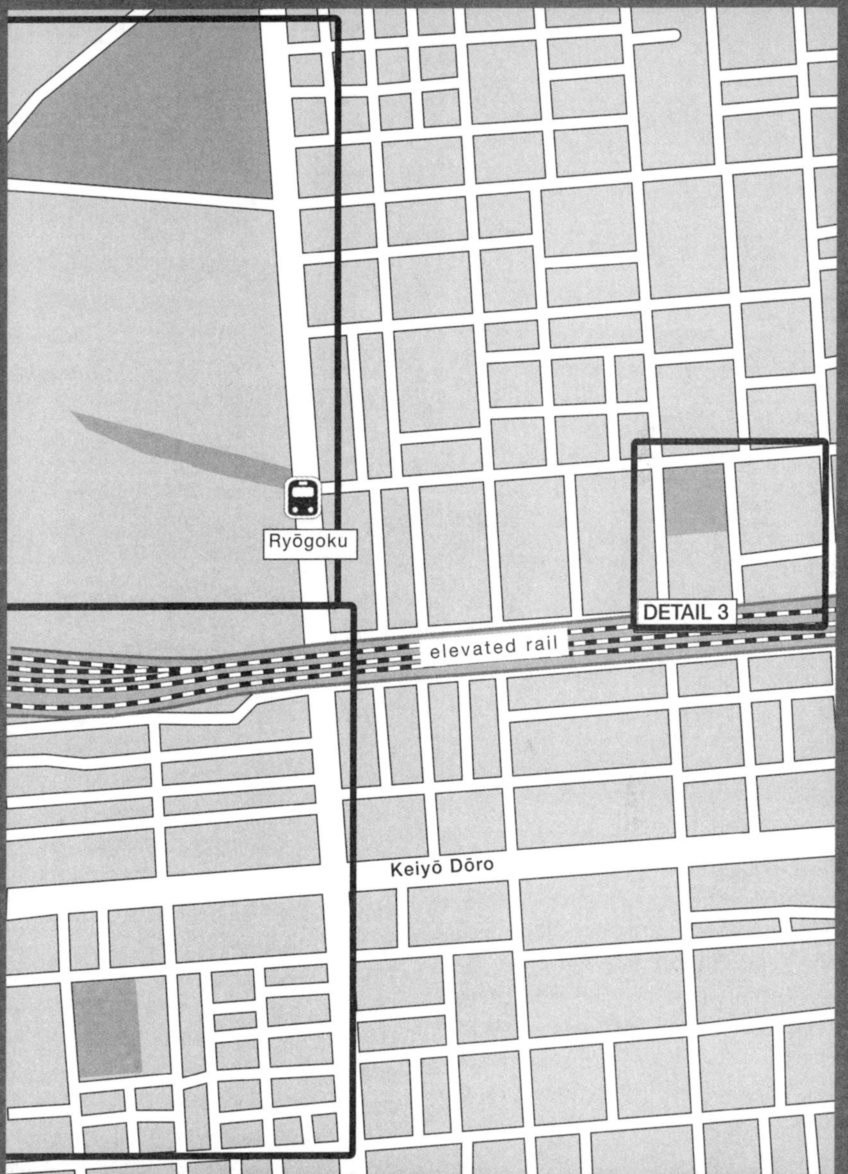

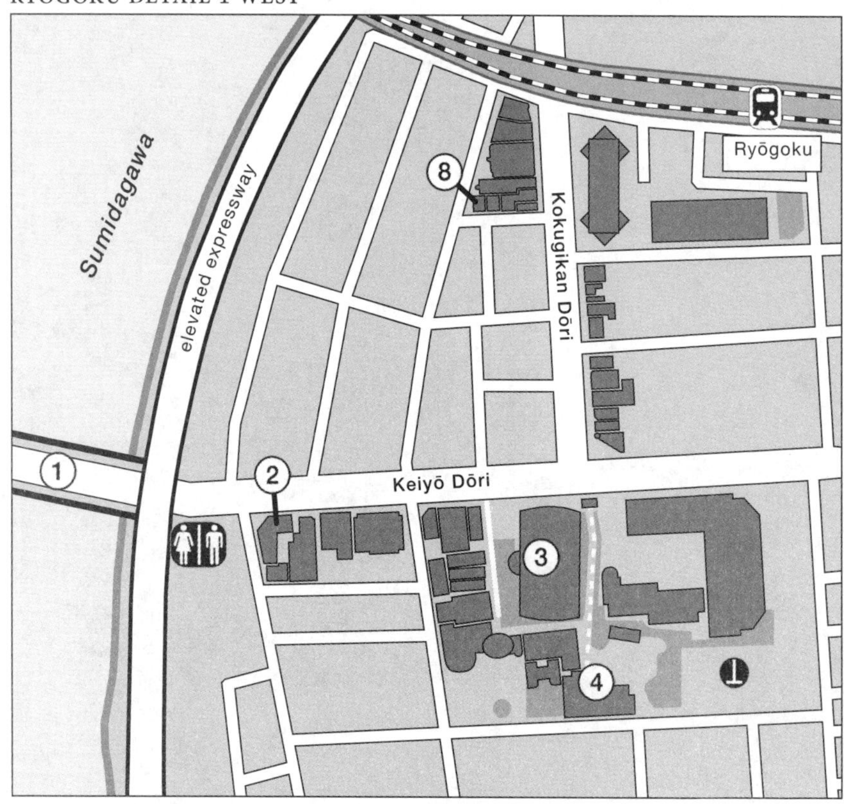

1909. The Chikarazuka, or "Mound of Strength," is a large stone monument where part of the hair cut when famous sumō wrestlers retire is buried. Enter the grounds from the main street, Keiyo Dōri. Look for the red pillared gate with an unusual curved roof. While there is a back gate on the south side, it is often locked. This temple is on the Tokyo 33 Kannon Pilgrimage route.
🌐 *http://ekoin.or.jp*

❺ Honjo Matsuzakachō Park [Kira Residence Remains] / Honjo Matsuzakachō Kōen [Kira Tei Ato] 本所松坂町公園 [吉良邸跡]

This small city park is the site of the famous revenge attack in the story of the Forty-Seven Rōnin, dramatized in puppet theater, kabuki, ukiyo-e prints, and over seventy live action movies. When the property was being subdivided and sold in 1934, a small corner of the extensive grounds was obtained by the neighborhood. It was donated to

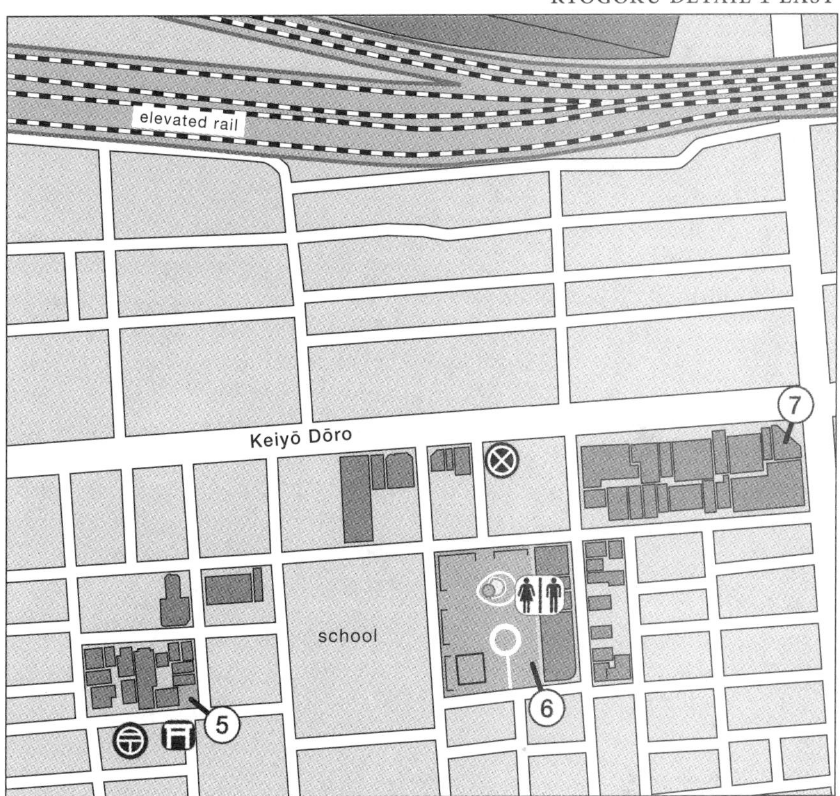

the city and opened as a park in 1935. While the rōnin are portrayed as heroes in the highly fictionalized dramas of the Forty-Seven Rōnin, their victim Kira was quite respected in this area. The grounds contain a small shrine and the well where Kira's head was washed. A plaque lists those who died defending Kira in the attack, and each year on December 14 a ceremony is held in their memory.

❻ Memorial to the Birthplace of Katsu Kaishū / Katsu Kaishū Seitanchihi 勝海舟生誕の地 記念碑
This monument in a corner of Ryōgoku Park marks the birthplace of Katsu Kaishū, who played a major role in the Meiji Restoration and the opening up of Japan. Everything is in Japanese, but much of the exhibit consists of photographs and images, so those interested in mid-19th-century Japan will recognize a good deal of what they see.

The "Rat Boy" of Ekōin

One interesting monument at Ekōin is dedicated to Nakamura Jirokichi, more commonly known as Nezumi Kozō, "Rat Boy." He was a bit of a Robin Hood character who robbed over one hundred wealthy samurai estates before being caught and executed in 1831. The memorial is easy to find as there are two stones; the second one is provided for people to chip off a piece as a good luck charm. This helps to prevent damage to the main stone, which has been replaced several times. There is a plaque with the outline of a thief sneaking away. There is also a memorial to another thief: a cat that would steal money and bring it to its impoverished invalid owner. The cat was caught and killed by staff at a store it had been stealing from. The store's owner heard the story and helped pay for this memorial.

❼ Lion-dō ライオン堂

Lion-dō is a family business established in 1907, patronized mainly by the local professional sumō wrestlers. The store sells what would elsewhere be a very ordinary commodity, men's everyday clothes. Nothing fancy, but they have an unusual specialty: the shop is filled with clothing for very, very large men. If you are looking to buy something for an unusually large person, be sure to have metric measurements handy.

🌐 *http://www.liondo.co.jp*

❽ Chanko Kawasaki ちゃんこ川崎

In a neighborhood filled with chankonabe restaurants, this is considered one of the best and is likely the oldest as it was founded in 1937. Chanko Kawasaki serves proper chankonabe made with free-range chicken and lots of fresh vegetables. Founded by a former sumō practitioner, it is carried on as a family business. This is not a place to dash in for a bite as it takes a little time, so sit back and relax. The cooking is done in front of you and the owners will let you know when it is ready. The restaurant was rebuilt in 1949 and stands out from the newer buildings in the neighborhood by its age and one-story height, but also by the vegetation out front.

DETAIL 2

❶ Sumō Museum / Sumō Hakubutsukan 相撲博物館

This is a small, free museum of professional sumō. The museum opened originally at the Kuramae Kokugikan in 1954. It was transferred to the present location when the Ryōgoku Kokugikan opened. On dispay are photos, woodblock prints, documents, books, referee's lacquered fans, aprons worn by rikishi (sumō wrestlers) at tournament ceremonies, memorabilia, and more.

During the grand sumō tournaments and some other events, the museum is only open to ticket holders.

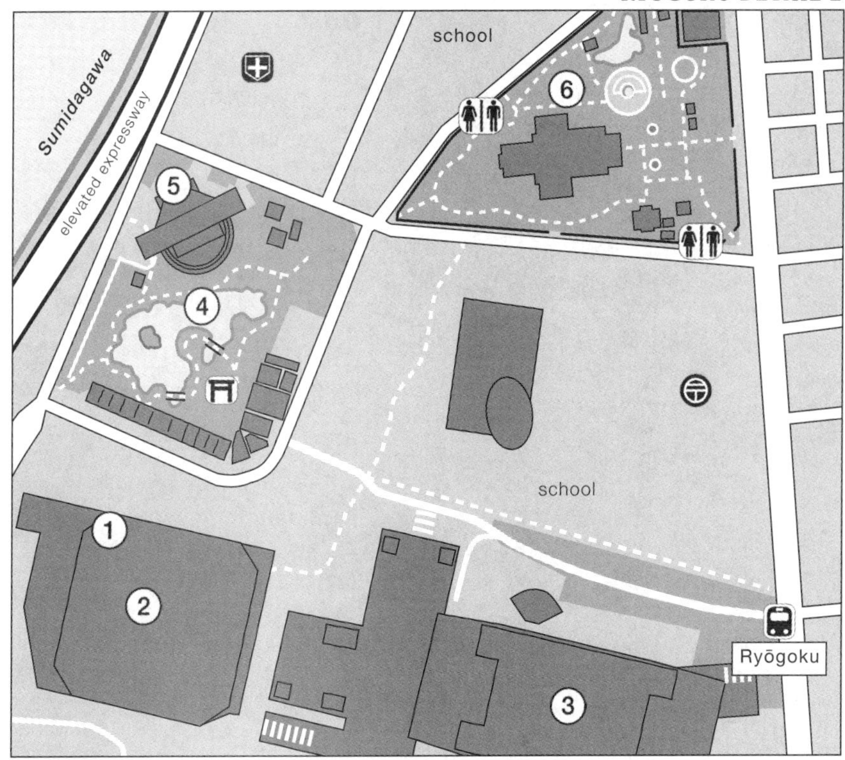

🌐 *http://sumo.or.jp/EnSumoMuseum*

❷ Ryōgoku Sumō Hall / Ryōgoku Kokugikan 両国国技館

This facility is used for sumō tournaments, and at other times for other sports and events. Three major tournaments, called honbasho in Japanese, are held here each year: around the New Year, in the summer, and in the fall. The building seats over 11,000 spectators. In the Edo and early Meiji periods, sumō bouts were held mainly at Fukagawa Hachimangū and later Ekōin. This is the third location for the Kokugikan, the first having been built next to Ekōin in 1909. After World War II the Kokugikan was requisitioned by the occupying forces and sumō returned temporarily to being held at shrines. In 1954 a new Kokugikan was built in Kuramae on the other side of the Sumidagawa. Finally after several decades, the sport returned to the Ryōgoku neighborhood in 1985. The building also stores food and water for use in case of major emergencies.

▲ The dioramas of the Edo-Tokyo Museum lay out the city as it once was.

▲ The modern Sumida Hokusai Museum honors one of the area's most famous artists.

❸ Edo-Tokyo Museum / Edo Tokyo Hakubutsukan 江戸東京博物館

I generally recommend a visit to this museum early on your trip to Tokyo to learn, or refresh your memory, about the city. Designed by Kikutake Architects and opened in 1993, the museum is laid out so you start at the founding of the city called Edo, then travel into the era when the city was renamed Tokyo and down to the present day. The exhibits will help you have a better conceptual framework to understand Tokyo and the transformations it went through over the centuries. You access the main display areas by taking the elevator to the entrance on the sixth floor, then cross a full-scale replica of the original Nihonbashi to a display of very large dioramas of the early days of the city. From there you go down to the next level, which has reproductions of shops, homes, and more from the Edo period. And more? Yep. Test your strength at hefting a pair of sewage collector's buckets on a carrying pole, lift a fireman's matoi, or perhaps enjoy a performance of shamisen, kabuki, or rakugo on the stage. Continue under the bridge and take the path on the left to see the history from 1868 to the present. The first floor is usually the site of special exhibits. The gift shop sells an attractive catalogue of the permanent exhibits.

There is a branch museum, the Edo-Tokyo Open-Air Architectural Museum, listed in the Day Trippin' section of this book.

🌐 *https://www.edo-tokyo-museum.or.jp/en/*

❹ Former Yasuda Gardens / Kyū Yasuda Teien 旧安田庭園

This former daimyō garden was given to the city by the family of financier Yasuda Zenjirō after he was assassinated in 1921. The park was almost completely destroyed by the Great Kantō Earthquake in 1923 but was restored by 1927. It burned again in the firebombings of World War II. The heavy pollution of the postwar period did additional damage. It was again restored in 1971. A large portion of the center of the garden is devoted to a large pond. Originally the pond was connected to the river, so it rose and fell according to the tides. These days that connection no longer exists, but the pond still rises and falls via the action of pumps. This small garden has several benches and houses an old shrine.

❺ Japanese Sword Museum / Tōken Hakubutsukan 刀剣博物館

Designed by Maki Fumihiko, the museum is operated by the Society for Preservation of Japanese Art Swords. Originally opened in Shinjuku in 1978, the museum was moved to this larger three-story location in 2018. Admission is free except for the third floor exhibition space. There is also a rooftop garden with a view overlooking the Kyū Yasuda Teien.

🌐 *https://www.touken.or.jp/english/*

❻ Yokoamichō Park / Yokoamichō Kōen 横網町公園

This park includes the Cenotaph Hall in memory of victims of the Great Kantō Earthquake, which later came to also memorialize the dead from the World War II firebombings of Tokyo. During the fires from the 1923 quake, tens of thousands fled to this location, which at the time was a large open area. The flames from the surrounding area were so hot that some 38,000 are estimated to have perished here. Starting at midnight of March 9, 1945, Sumida Ward was again subjected to fires from planes dropping incendiary bombs, killing large numbers of civilians in one night. In the park you can see warped and melted steel from the burned buildings. Each March 10 a memorial service is held for the dead. The unidentified remains for an estimated 58,000 who died in the earthquake and 105,000 from the firebombings are interned here. The Memorial Museum has exhibits about the horrors of the fires. There is also a peace monument with the names of some 100,000 civilians who died in the war, a monument to Koreans who died in the quake, a garden, and a memorial to children.

🌐 *http://www.tokyo-park.or.jp/park/format/index087.html*

🌐 *https://tokyoireikyoukai.or.jp/multilingual/en.html*

DETAIL 3

❶ Nomi no Sukune Jinja
野見宿禰神社

Nomi no Sukune is venerated as the legendary founder of sumō, so it is no surprise there is a shrine to him in Ryōgoku. In the *Nihon Shoki* there is the story of how, upon request of Emperor Suinin, he defeated and killed the boastful Taima no Kehaya in one-on-one combat. The *Nihon Shoki* also recounts how he convinced the emperor to substitute clay figures for actual human sacrifices in imperial graves. The story may have been influenced by Chinese lore; while clay figures have been found at many high-ranking gravesites, archaeologists have yet to find signs of human sacrifice at any such sites. The shrine is managed by the Japan Sumō Association.

❷ Sumida Hokusai Museum / Sumida Hokusai Bijutsukan
すみだ北斎美術館

Designed by Sejima Kazuyo and opened in 2016, this entire museum is devoted to the life and work of Katsushika Hokusai. The famous ukiyo-e artist was born and spent almost all of his life in this area. The museum incorporates modern technology to enhance viewing of the prints. Select prints are displayed on touch screens that allow you to zoom in to details on the images. This helps the viewer

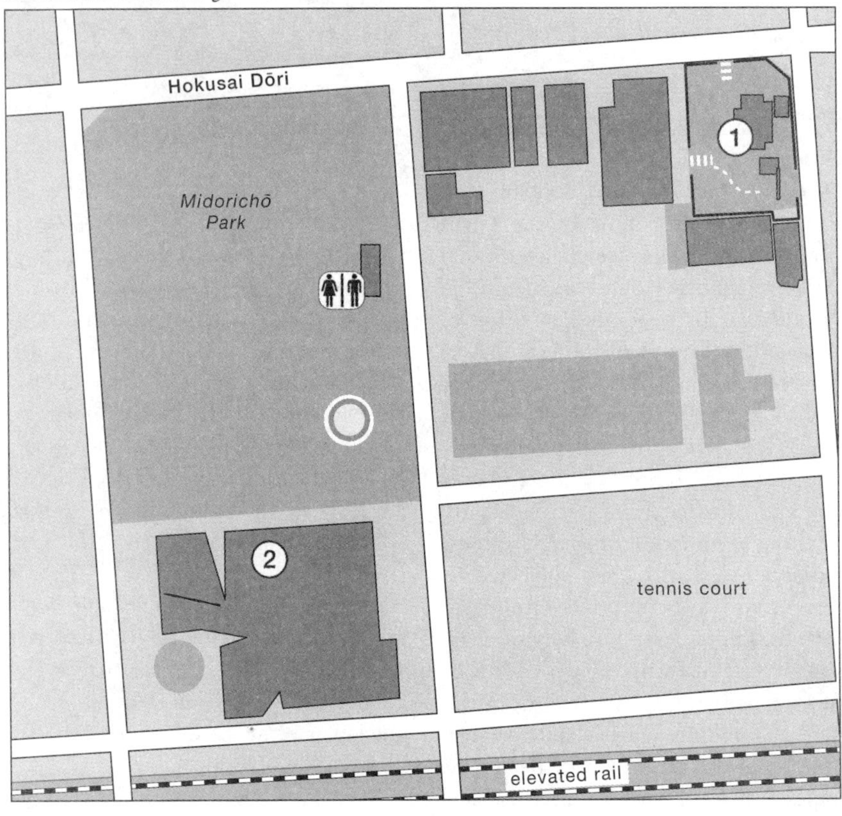

to appreciate both the original designs and the craftsmanship that the carvers employed in transferring the drawings to woodblocks. There are four floors: on two of them the museum hosts several temporary special exhibits a year; so depending on the dates of your stay, you may be able to see more than one. The special exhibits require an additional fee. The museum also has a library and gift shop.

🌐 *http://hokusai-museum.jp*

NOTE: *This area is reached either by following Hokusai Dōri or by going eastward along the north side of the train tracks, away from the Edo-Tokyo Museum.*

柴又

SHIBAMATA

This area preserves some of the look and feel of the Shōwa period, as it was spared from destruction in World War II. There are also some buildings that are even older—much older. If you want to see some of the older Tokyo, this is the place to go. The area is known to many fans of Japanese cinema as the hometown of the main character in the Tora-san movies. Statues of him and his sister grace the plaza next to the train station. The temple and street leading up to it, Taishakuten Sandō, have changed very little since that first movie came out. There are other sights in the neighborhood, including museums, temples, and shrines. The people you see on the streets are mainly Japanese, as few foreign tourists go to this area. In January 2018 a Japanese friend who teaches at a university in Tokyo, my American travel companion, and I were on the train to Shibamata. A couple asked my professor friend if she was going to give us a tour of the neighborhood. She laughed and explained that actually we were the ones giving her a tour, as she had never been there and we had.

You likely will have to transfer at least once to get here. Shibamata is on the very edge of Tokyo; across the Edogawa is Chiba Prefecture. I'll explain an interesting way to get over the river in this chapter.

NOTE: *This chapter is shorter than others and thus contains only one section and a single map.*

SHIBAMATA AREA WEST

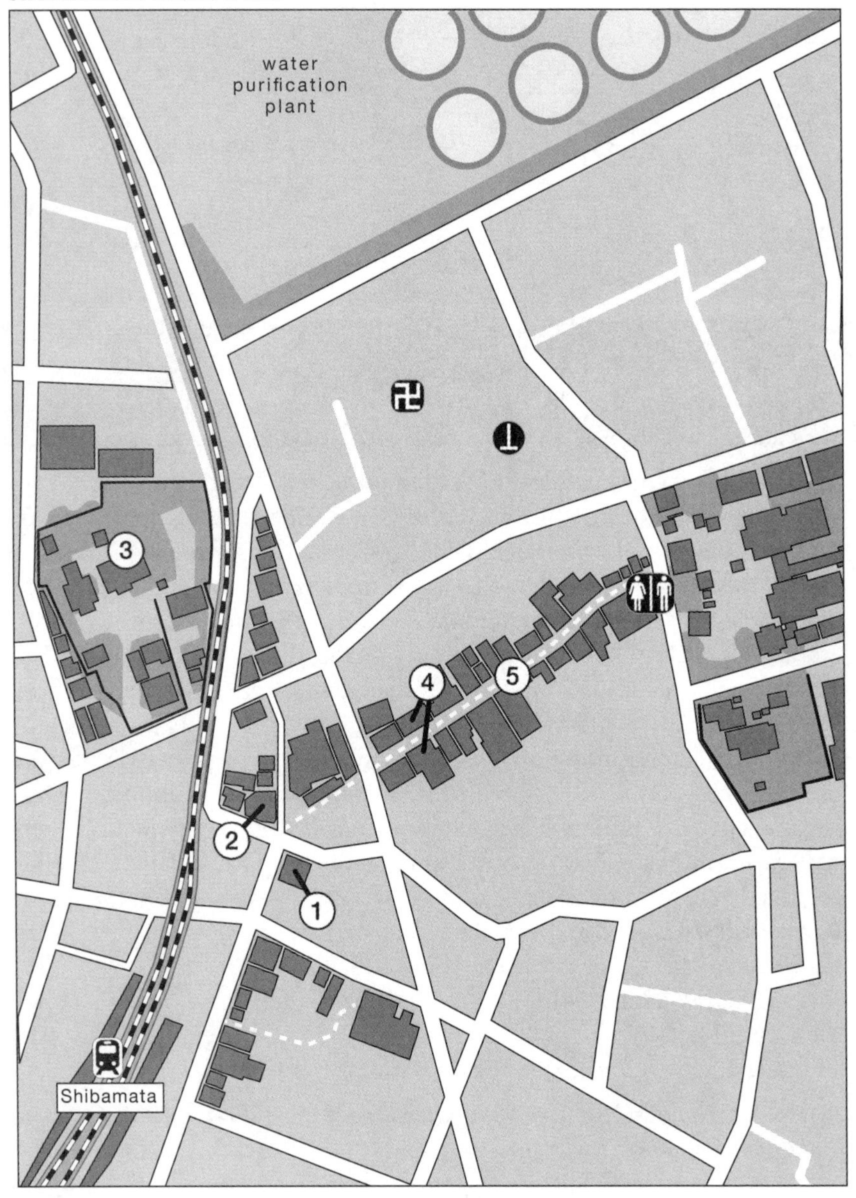

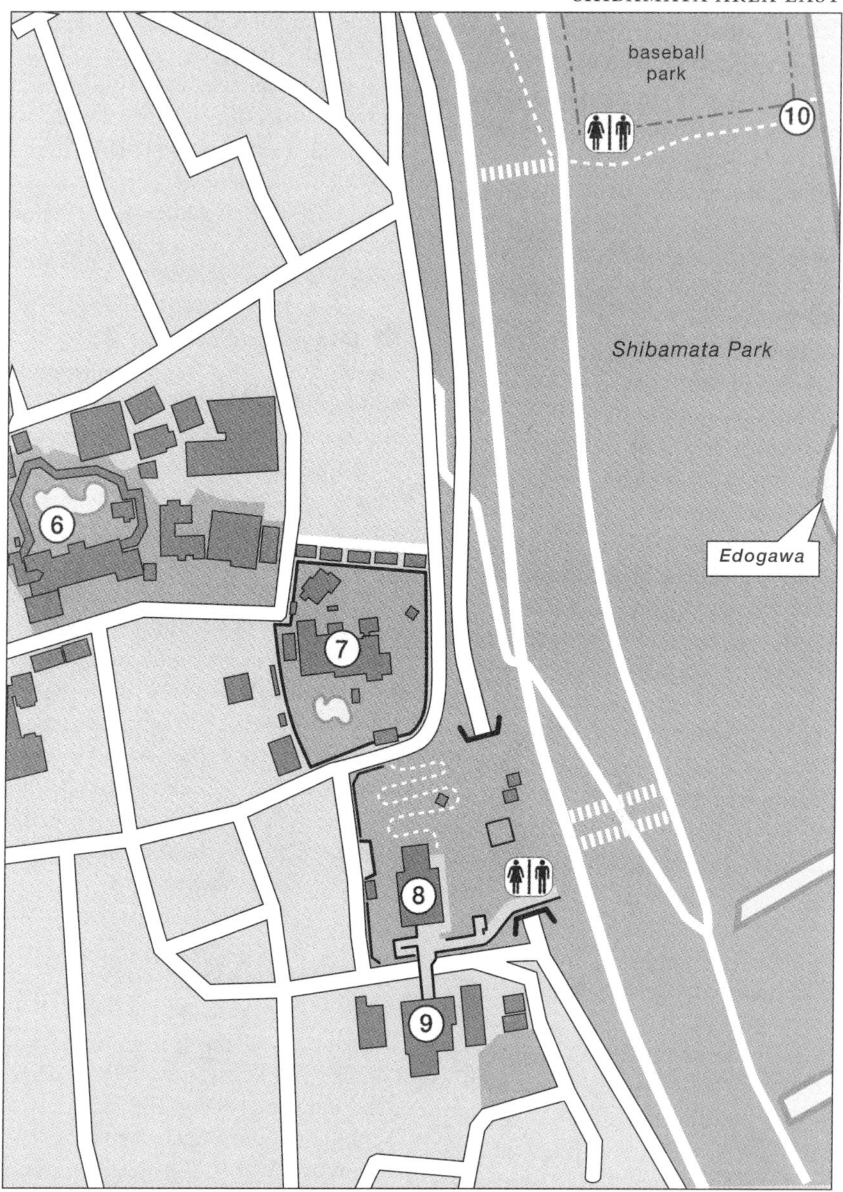
baseball
park
10
Shibamata Park
6
Edogawa
7
8
9

❶ Shibamata Tourist Information Center 柴又観光案内所

A small tourist information center operating since 2007. Like most such centers it is usually worth checking to see if they have information on local sights and events.

❷ Shibamata Toy Museum / Shibamata no Omocha Hakubutsukan
柴又のおもちゃ博物館

When you first walk into this building you think, "This isn't a museum, it's a candy and toy shop." Nope, the museum is upstairs, just buy a ticket at the counter and head on up. There you will find old toys, games, magazines, and perhaps a few other items. After looking at the museum, check out the store, where you can get photo cards of old stars or play on old pinball machines. The interior of the store is divided into several sections and has a Shōwa period vibe. I bet they get lots of adults nostalgic for their youth buying toys and candy here.

❸ Shibamata Hachiman Jinja
柴又八幡神社

This shrine was founded sometime before 721; the earliest mention of it is from that date. The shrine was restored in 1633, and the present building dates from 1943. The building is far enough from the road to make it a quiet area to enjoy as you explore the grounds. It is painted an attractive red with a green roof framed by a group of trees. On the grounds is the remains of an ancient grave mound, the location of which is marked with a four-sided platform and a black hemisphere. Partial excavations recovered human remains, a Haniwa tomb sculpture, swords, and more.

❹ Takagiya Rōho 髙木屋老舗

Established in the early Meiji period and located on the Taishakuten Sandō, this is the inspiration for the shop run by Tora-san's relatives in the famous movie series. The business is successful enough to span both sides of Taishakuten Sandō. Inside you will see photographs taken while the movies were made and of the actors. You can buy some of the sweets seen in the movies, or some oden if you are hungrier. They have some packaged products, including a few designed for ceremonial events including shichigosan, weddings, funerals, and memorial occasions. Some products are seasonal.
🌐 *http://www.takagiya.co.jp*

❺ Taishakuten Sandō 帝釈天参道

A pedestrian-only street leading to Taishakuten Daikyōji from Shibamata Station. The street is 656 feet (200 meters) long and is lined with a variety of shops, many of which date from before World War II. The area was spared from the fires of the war, so many of the buildings predate that conflict. The most famous of the shops to visit is Takagiya Rōho, where you can stop for a snack or a light meal. The street also has shops selling food, toys, souvenirs, ceramics, religious supplies, and clothing, and several restaurants.

❻ Shibamata Taishakuten Daikyōji 柴又帝釈天題経寺

This Nichiren Buddhist temple was founded in 1629. Its formal name is Kyōeizan Daikyōji, and it is famous for an image of Taishakuten that has an inscription on its back by Nichiren (1222–1282). The carving had long been thought to have been lost, until 1779 when it was found in storage at the temple. The discovery happened to be on a Kōshin day. Over time, Taishakuten became associated with the practices associated with Kōshin, and many would make pilgrimages to the temple on those nights. Exterior portions of the main hall are covered with a series of carvings on very large panels depicting scenes from Buddhist tradition. If you visit the temple, you can pay a small fee to view the carvings and see other parts of the building, as well as the garden. At times English-speaking guides are available. The main gate to the temple dates from 1896 and is also richly carved. If you like to take pictures, expect to spend some time here. This is also a temple on the local Shichifukujin tour, as Bishamonten is enshrined here.

🌐 *http://www.taishakuten.or.jp*

❼ Yamamoto Tei 山本亭

The former home of Tokyo businessman Yamamoto Einosuke, who owned the camera part maker Yamamoto Plant, which was also in this area. Einosuke Yamamoto decided to have his new home built in this location after the Great Kantō Earthquake. This had been a family residence for four generations when Katsushika ward obtained the house in 1988 and opened it to the public in 1991. The building is a mix of Japanese and Western styles and has a Japanese garden. There is an old-style dozō (storehouse) on the grounds and a nagayamon, a combination gate, gatekeeper's residence, and waiting room for the attendants of guests. You can also enjoy tea and sweets and occasional music performances here.

🌐 *http://www.katsushika-kanko.com/yamamoto/eng/*

❽ Tora-san Museum / Tora-san Kinenkan 寅さん記念館

This museum was opened in 1997 and is devoted to a series of delightful movies known in Japanese as *Otoko Wa Tsurai Yo* "*It's Tough Being a Man*" and commonly referred to in English as the Tora-san movies. This is the longest running series of films in the world: from 1969 to 1995, forty-eight were made. They only stopped production of the original series due to the death of Atsumi Kiyoshi, who played the title character. Each film involved Tora-san staying with his family in the

▲▼ The detailed woodwork outside of Taishakuten is more than worth the small fee.

▲ The robot vending machine in front of the Shibamata Toy Museum welcomes you.

▲ Stop by Takagiya Rōho to enjoy some dango and tea, or get a takeout order for later.

▼ Tora-san, the neighborhoods favorite fictional son, installing the sign at his museum.

Shibamata neighborhood, losing his temper, and then going out on a journey, but always returning. Tora-san is loud mouthed, uncouth, a bit of a con man, generous to a fault, and prone to fall in love time and again; he actually does so in almost every film. Since then, two other films have been made: *Tora-san's Tropical Fever Special Version* in 1997 and *Tora-san, Welcome Back* in 2019, bringing the total to fifty.

At the entrance there is a statue of Tora-san mounting the last kanji in museum's name on its sign. Inside is the reproduction made for the studio of part of his family's business, called Kurumaya in the movies and based on the nearby Takagiya Rōho. There are also dioramas of the old neighborhood, displays about the films, a photo booth, and, before the exit, murals of all the "Madonnas" that Tora-san fell in love with in the movies. After you exit, there is a plaza with a gift shop and a map of Japan on the ground that notes the movie locations.

🌐 *http://www.katsushika-kanko.com/tora/*

❾ Yoji Yamada Museum
山田洋次ミュージアム

Established in 2012, this museum covers the career of one of Japan's most noted directors, starting with his 1961 film *Nikai no Tanin* "*Strangers Upstairs*" and continuing to the present. While Yamada is best known for the long-running Tora-san series, he also directed a trilogy of samurai films: *The Twilight Samurai, The Hidden Blade,* and *Love and Honor.* These are some of the most acclaimed Japanese films made after the year 2000. The exhibits are well laid out, with an excellent use of images, video clips, and artifacts mixed together in attractive displays. It is quite appropriate that this museum is across the street from the Tora-san Memorial Hall, and that you can buy a discounted ticket for both.

🌐 *http://www.katsushika-kanko.com/yamada-yoji-museum/*

❿ Yagiri no Watashi 矢切の渡し

The last traditional hand-rowed ferry in Tokyo. It operates, weather permitting, for much of the year across the Edogawa between Katsushika ward in Tokyo and Matsudo City in Chiba prefecture. To find it, walk north along the levee from the area near the Tora-san Museum and look for a stand of bushes and small trees with a path leading to it. You may be able to spot either a handwritten sign or the ferry itself. The boat is large enough to handle up to thirty people and takes about ten minutes to cross the river. The first Tora-san movie opens with Tora-san taking this ferry across the river to his old hometown. It also figures significantly in Keisuke Kinoshita's 1955 film *Nogiku no gotoki kimi nariki*, "*She Was Like a Wild Chrysanthemum*."

渋谷駅

SHIBUYA STATION AREA

The area near Shibuya Station is a major commercial center, mainly known for the businesses on the west side. The major intersection between the shops and station is known as the scramble crossing and is one of the most photographed places in Tokyo. This neighborhood increased in popularity among young people in the 1990s after the Sunday street closures near Harajuku ended and much of the youth scene moved south. The streets here meander or intersect at acute angles, and you will find yourself having to walk up and down hills. Most of the buildings in the area are of recent construction, and the streets are filled with shops both large and small. All of this creates an environment that is flashier than the shitamachi neighborhoods yet not as high class as the Ginza or Omotesandō, making it a unique place to stroll through. Wander a little off the busy main streets, with their bright electronic signs, and you will find a variety of places to eat and drink on quiet lanes. As with much of the city, Shibuya is also a mix of old and new. The old just needs a little more explanation.

TIP: *For a view of the neighborhood, head to the rooftop plaza on the forty-seventh floor of the Shibuya Scramble Square building that connects to Shibuya Station. If the weather is bad, there are observation decks on the forty-fifth and forty-sixth floors.*

SHIBUYA STATION AREA WEST

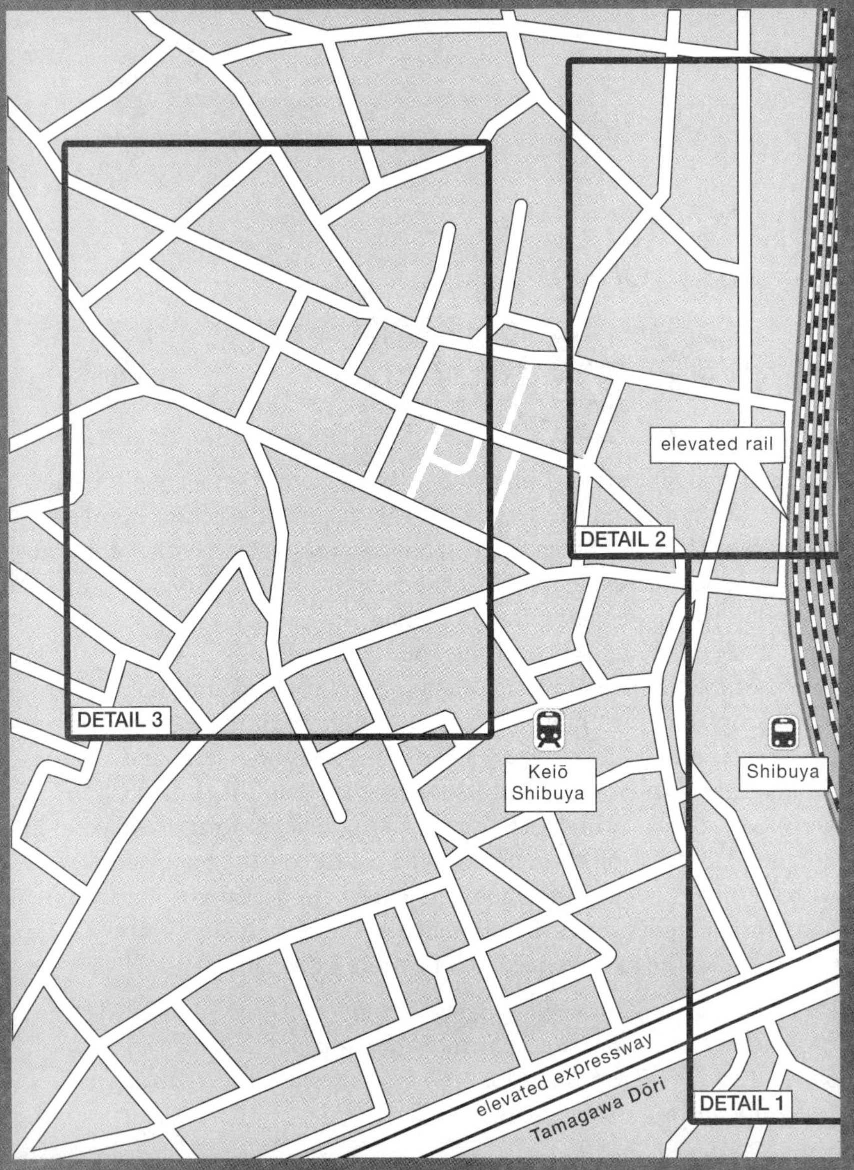

SHIBUYA STATION AREA EAST

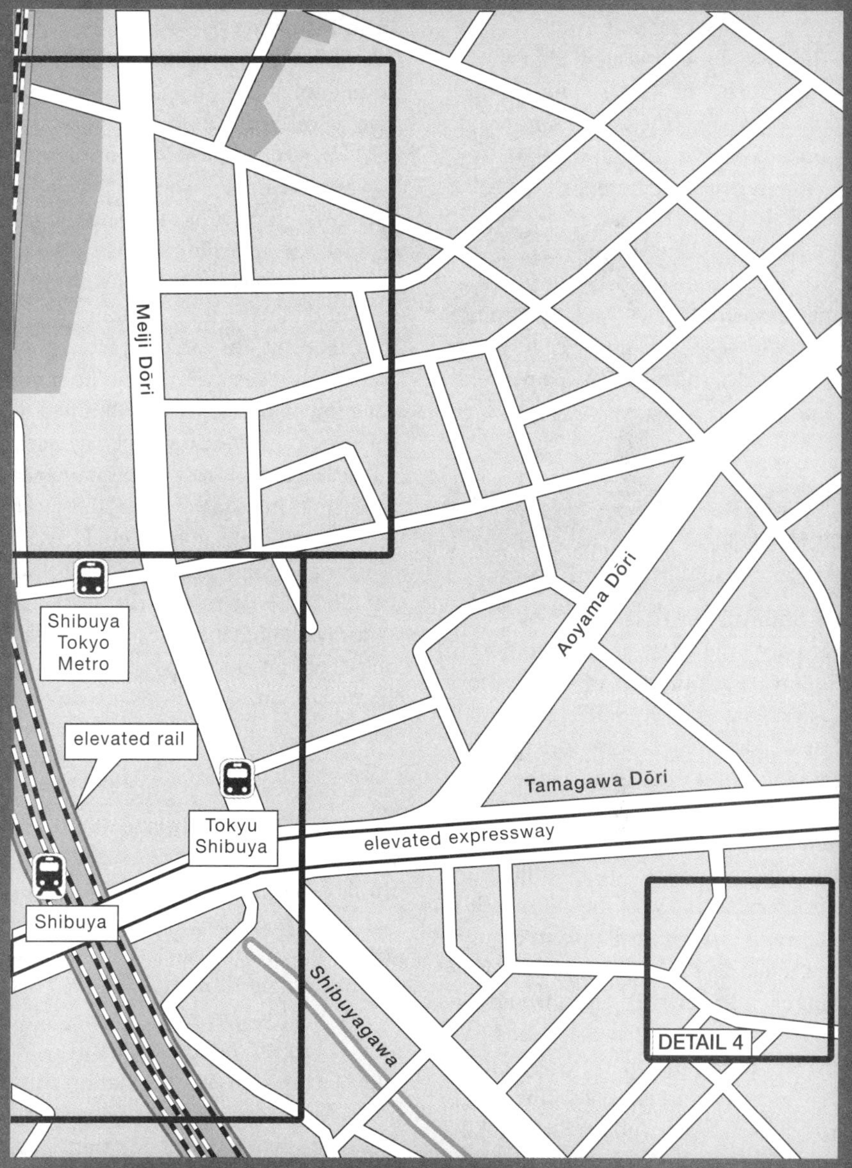

Visting Shibuya

The first time I visited Shibuya it was late in the day, so my friends and I were famished. We found what looked like a small non-smoking sobaya. When we entered, we discovered that they also had a wide range of tempura. We ordered and paid for our food, and then we saw that the place opened up into a large dining area. As we sat, the music came on—pre-Beatles rock heaven. I never did find that place again.

DETAIL 1

❶ Shibuya Sky 渋谷スカイ

One of the newest attractions in Shibuya is at the top of the 47-story (230 meter, 755 feet) Shibuya Scramble Square skyscraper. Shibuya Sky occupies the upper three floors of the building, including a display area, a cafe-bar, and shops. The biggest draw is the rooftop observation deck with a 360° unobstructed view of the city, on clear days you can see Mt Fuji, and at night the lights of the city. There is seating and even hammocks if you would like to lay back and watch the clouds pass by. Shibuya Sky is open from 9 a.m. to 11 p.m. You can also access the building directly from Shibuya Station. Like many high observation areas in Tokyo there is an admission charge.

❷ Shibuyagawa 渋谷川

The Shibuyagawa was quite polluted and smelly by the early 1960s. To cope with this problem, before the 1964 Tokyo Olympics, most of the river was covered up, so the flow now runs through culverts. The Shibuyagawa surfaces just southeast of Shibuya Station. That section is lined with concrete and runs behind buildings, and until recently was largely visible only from the bridges that cross it. Looking at it a few years ago, I was reminded of deep vertical stone canyons I have seen in the Sierra Nevada Mountains of California. Instead of stone, the walls were of concrete and steel. However, here and there bushes grow, just as they do in the Sierras. Today there are walkways along the river so you can look down into its deep concrete-lined channel. Don't worry—it no longer stinks.

❸ Moyai Statue / Moyaizō 渋谷モヤイ像

This is a large statue of a head with two faces. It is made from the pumice-like koga stone that is quarried on Niijima, one of the Izu Islands, which are part of Tokyo. This statue was given by Niijima village to Shibuya Ward in 1980. Like Hachikō, this is a popular meeting point. Moyai is a word not often heard these days that means tying things together, sharing something, or to help each other out.

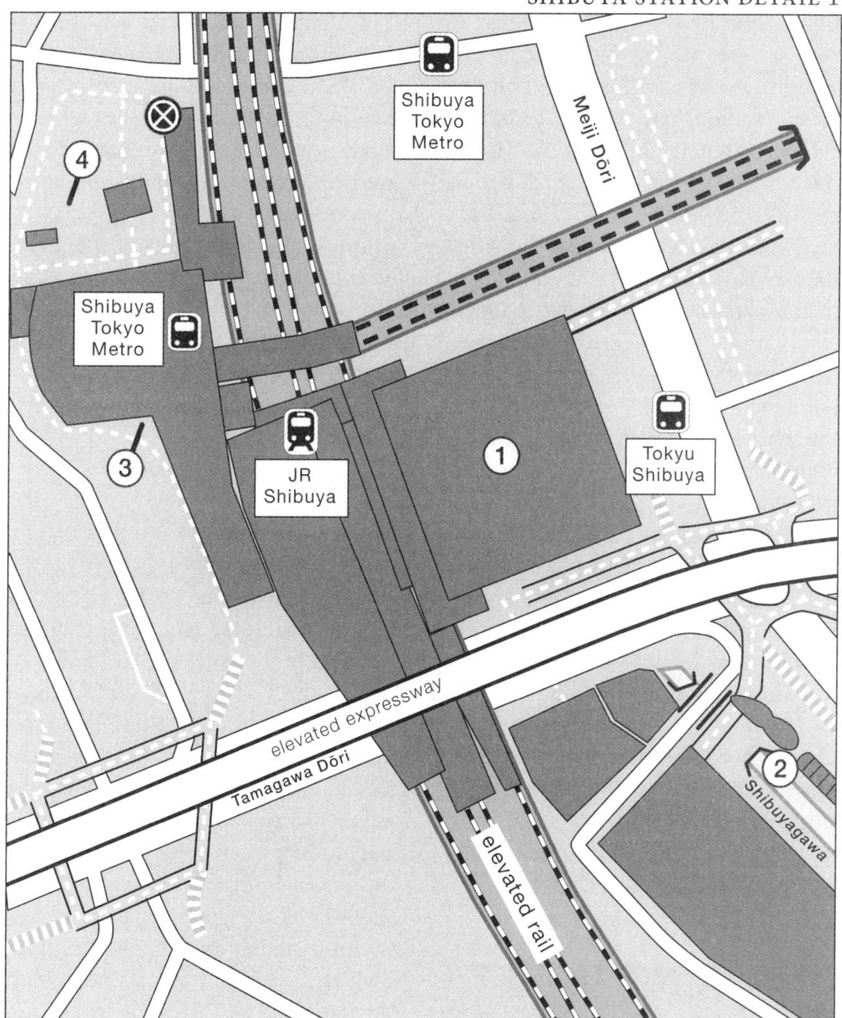

❹ Hachikō Memorial Statue

ハチ公像

Japan's most famous dog, Hachikō, was an Akita who would accompany his owner, Ueno Hidesaburō, to Shibuya Station every day and then wait for him to return. One day in 1925 Professor Ueno passed away while lecturing at Tokyo Imperial University. Hachikō then was taken in by Ueno's relatives in Asakusa, but he continued to head toward Shibuya every day. A family friend who lived in Yoyogi offered to take in the loyal dog. Now that he was close by, it was easy for Hachikō to go to the station, and he did regularly, even spending the nights there. He did this for ten years, during which people got to know him. His story made the loyal Akita a celebrity whose fame further spread when he was written about in the papers. In 1934 a statue of the loyal dog by Andō Teru was cast and placed at the station. Hachikō would pass away the next year. Before long the statue was taken by the government and melted down to produce armaments. In 1948 a new casting of the statue was made by Andō Takeshi, the son of Andō Teru, and placed where it now stands. Professor Ueno is buried in Aoyama Cemetery in a fenced-off plot that he shares with Hachikō. The story was adapted to film not only in Japan in *Hachikō Monogatari* but also in the United States with *Hachi: A Dog's Tale*. The statue has long been a place for people to meet up, and on any given day it can be seen surrounded by those who join Hachikō in waiting.

DETAIL 2

❶ Miyamasu Mitake Jinja 宮益御嶽神社

This is a neighborhood shrine that was founded in the 14th century and can be located at the top of a long stairway. This shrine is known for its unusual guardian statues: Instead of the standard lion-dog komainu statue, this shrine has statues of wolves. I have found people confuse this shrine with another, Mitake Jinja, that is not far to the south.

The annual festival is in September, but they also celebrate the Tori no Ichi festival in November. The entrance is on Miyamasuzaka, part of the major road to the south.

🌐 *http://www.shibuyamiyamasu.jp/mitake/main.html*

❷ Drunkard's Alley / Nonbei Yokochō のんべい横丁

In the late 1940s and early 1950s this alley of small bars and cheap eateries grew out of the ashes of World War II. Don't expect fancy and don't expect large—most places seat less than half a dozen, one even has an upstairs accessible only by ladder. Don't expect to find many open during the day either; most places open only at night. Do expect informal and inexpensive. Nonbei Yokochō has been gaining recognition among tourists over the past few years, but still holds its own as an old-fashioned yokochō for locals and office workers. A rule of thumb is, don't spend more than two hours in a place—make room for someone else by moving on.

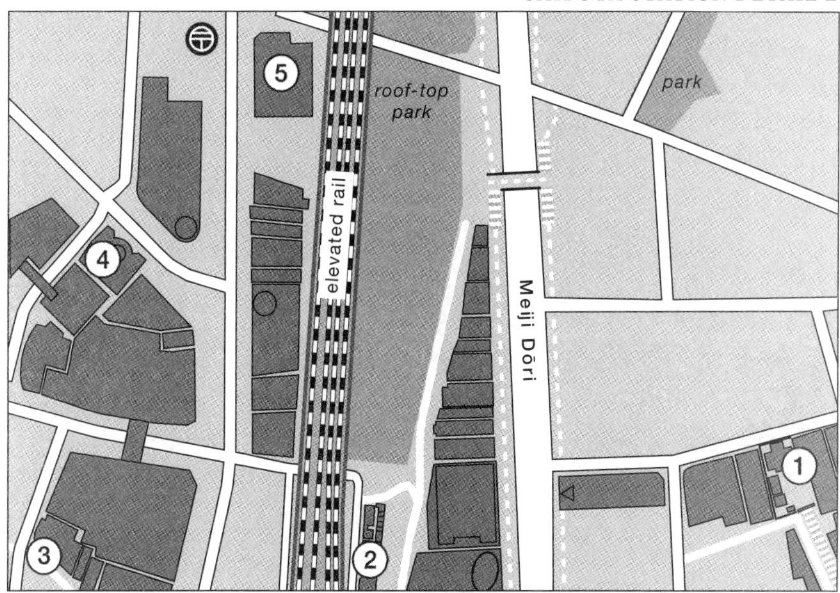

❸ Center Gai センター街

A vibrant pedestrian-only street lined with shops that is very popular with young people. In an attempt to improve the—in their eyes—seedy image of the area, the street was strangely rebranded as Basketball Street (バスケットボールストリート) by the local government in 2011. But who really calls it that? The new name was considered very silly by many; at least Shibuya has a basketball connection with the local professional team the Sun Rockers Shibuya. Today the sign says Center Gai, showing that tradition, even in an area as modern as Shibuya, can persevere.

🌐 *http://center-gai.jp*

❹ Humax Pavilion ヒューマックスパビリオン

Designed by Wakabayashi Hiroyuki and completed in 1992, Shibuya's Humax Pavilion is a ten-story multi-use structure with restaurants, shops, clubs, and a movie theater. With its curving front and distinctive design elements, including flying buttresses on the upper floors, the building stands out in this neighborhood of fairly conventional buildings.

🌐 *https://www.humax.co.jp/english/*

❺ Tower Records Shibuya タワーレコード渋谷

The Tower Records of my college years is long gone in the United States, but

▲ The Humax Pavilion looks like a building out of a science fiction manga.

▲ The sculpted entrance to this Mandarake branch is hard to miss.

▲ One of a series of murals from the reconstruction of the Parco shopping mall, 2017–19.

▲ Okamoto Tarō's famous mural the Myth of Tomorrow.

▼ With all the new construction in Shibuya, somehow Drunkard's Alley has survived.

▲ The stairway of Spainzaka has shops lining either side.

not in Japan. In 2002 the management of the Japanese branch bought out their stores, becoming independent from the parent company. When the main company folded, the Japanese stores continued to operate, and there are now over eighty. The Shibuya store, moved to the present location in 1995, is one of the largest record shops in the world. If you are looking for music, and not just Japanese music, this is a place to check.

Tip on buying records in Japan: If you are looking for a specific album, have a copy of the cover to show staff.
Tower Records Shibuya:
🌐 *https://tower.jp/store/Shibuya*
Shibuya Blog:
🌐 *http://towershibuya.jp/blog*

DETAIL 3

❶ Dōgenzaka 道玄坂
A slope and district that share the same name. They are either named after Ōwada Dōgen, a highwayman whose clan rebelled against the Kamakura shōguns and who preyed upon travelers in this area, or else after Dōgenan, a Buddhist temple in the area. In any case, Ōwada Dōgen is said to have given up crime and become a monk. The Ōwada name also continued in the Ōwadachō district found here until recently when the name was changed.

Today there are still a few businesses with Ōwada in their name. Endō Shūsaku's novel *The Girl I Left Behind* has a scene set in Ōwadachō. For some time the area was known for izakaya, karaoke joints, sex-trade shops, and a section called Love Hotel Hill. Recently nightclubs and live music houses have moved in, changing the mood slightly.

❷ Love Hotel Hill / Rabu Hoteru Zaka ラブホテル坂
This is one of the largest concentrations of love hotels in Tokyo, with lots of interesting architecture. Expect them to be mixed in with other kinds of businesses and apartment blocks. One clue that you're looking at a love hotel is the name—often they have non-Japanese names such as Hotel Amore or Hotel Claire. Some are lit up at night with eye-catching colors. Want to try one out? Rooms are usually rented to couples in blocks of two or three hours under the category of "Rest." It is also possible to get a room for "Stay," that is, overnight. Prices go up on Friday and Saturday nights. Be aware that few will allow same-sex couples and some will turn away non-Japanese.

❸ Love Letter Alley Site / Koibumi Yokochō Ato 恋文横丁跡
After World War II, occupying troops were billeted in Washington Heights, not far from Shibuya Station. Where you have troops, you have relationships with local women. When soldiers were

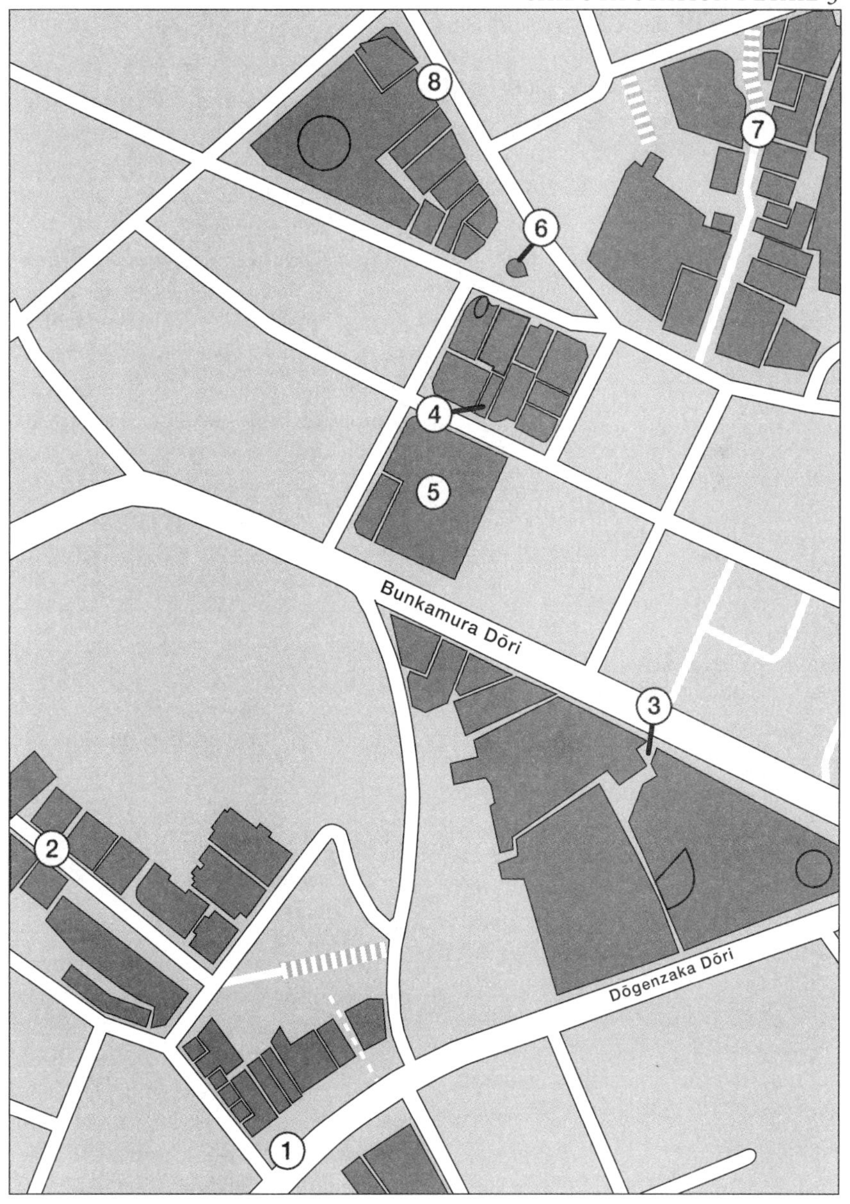
8
7
6
4
5
Bunkamura Dōri
3
2
Dōgenzaka Dōri
1

assigned elsewhere, their sweethearts wanted to stay in touch, but could not read or write anything but Japanese. In 1947 Sugaya Tokuji, who could compose letters in English and French, set up Koibumi no Mise "Love Letter Shop" on a small lane not far from the station. There he provided services translating letters to and from Japanese. The lane soon earned the nickname Koibumi Yokochō. The lane was demolished in 1977, and Sugaya would pass away in 1985 with the knowledge that he had played a role in about 300 marriages. The lane is now marked with a sign carved on a narrow upright post next to a wire fence.

❹ The Aldgate ジ・オールゲイト

Got an urge for fish and chips that you cannot repress? This British-style pub, around since 1995, can fulfill it. They have a broad food menu, twenty kinds of beer from around the world, and a variety of other alcoholic and non-alcoholic beverages. Fans of rugby and football (the real thing, with a white ball kicked around) can enjoy matches from all around the world on four screens.

Open evenings, 100% non-smoking, with free wi-fi. Credit cards accepted. Japanese, English, Spanish, Portuguese, Italian and Serbian are spoken.

🌐 *http://www.the-aldgate.com*

❺ MEGA Donki (MEGA ドンキ)

The local store of the Don Quijote chain, aka Donki, the largest in Japan with seven above-ground floors plus two basement levels. While known as a discount chain, the products range from cheap novelties to clothes, food, and pricey watches—yes the Japanese still wear watches. If you like to browse, these stores are packed with all sorts of items. I do mean packed as every square millimeter is jammed with goods. This is a good place to get unusual gifts for friends or pick up snacks in the food section. I have found each store is unique with stock tailored to the customers of that neighborhood. Some even have game arcades and stage theaters; the Ebisu one even has a Ferris wheel.

The Shibuya store is open 365 days a year, 24 hours a day. The floor guide outside near the entrance includes English and there is a tax free counter on the 3rd floor.

🌐 *https://www.donki.com/en/*

❻ Udagawa Kōban 宇田川交番

This koban was designed by Edward Suzuki and completed in 1985. When seen from the front, it gives the impression of a beaked face. The "beak" area contains a space with plants just off the second-story tatami mat room that the officers use to rest in. The design is influenced by the limitations of the lot, a V shape due to an intersection where the road splits.

❼ Spain Slope / Spainzaka
スペイン坂

This steep brick-lined slope is short—only 328 feet (100 meters)—and partly consists of stairs, but it is dense with small shops. The name was given to the slope in 1975 by Café Arabica owner Yasuo Uchida, who was reminded of similar streets in Spain. Café Arabica no longer exists but the name of the slope continues. In keeping with the name, some of the shops have a Mediterranean feel to their designs.

❽ Mandarake まんだらけ

The Shibuya branch of the famous chain of second-hand shops for fans of anime, manga, movies, and video games is located in the B2 level of the Shibuya BEAM building. The entrance is on the east side of the building and is topped with a large metal sculpture consisting of a clock, pipes, and a screen. The stairway going down is plastered with posters and illustrations. There also is an elevator in the building. Everything is in one large room and English-speaking staff may be available to assist. Once I was shopping with a friend who had been looking for a photography book for several years, and there it was.

🌐 *https://www.mandarake.co.jp/dir/sby/*

OFF THE CHARTS:
Myth of Tomorrow / Asu no Shinwa
明日の神話

This is a massive mural by Okamoto Tarō, who also created the Tower of the Sun for Expo '70 in Osaka. It is located in a second floor concourse inside the Shibuya Mark City mall, in the passage leading to the Keio Inokashira Line's Shibuya Station. The Myth of Tomorrow depicts the explosion of an atomic bomb and symbolizes the human ability to hope for a better tomorrow in the worst of circumstances. Okamoto made the work for the Hotel de Mexico in Mexico City; however that project went bankrupt and the mural disappeared. Long thought to have been lost, the mural was discovered in the Fall of 2003 after thirty years. After a long and expensive restoration it was brought back to Japan and exhibited. In November 2008 it was unveiled in the present location to expose the work to as many people as possible. In 2011 the guerilla art group Chim ↑ Pom added a new section, carefully using double sided tape on a section of blank wall to avoid any damage to the original. This depicted the disaster at the Fukushima reactors after the 2011 earthquake.

NOTE: *The Tarō Okamoto Memorial Museum is described in the chapter on the Omotesandō/Harajuku Area.*

DETAIL 4

❶ Konnō Hachimangū 金王八幡宮
A shrine founded in 1092. The present building dates from 1612, making it the oldest building in Shibuya Ward. The main hall is in the gongen-zukuri style of the early Edo period. The grounds contain a cherry tree that is a descendant of a tree planted by Minamoto no Yoritomo around the end of the 12th century. This tree has unusual flowers that are not all identical—there are both single- and double-petaled blossoms on each branch. The ornate shrine gates date back to at least 1769. The shrine grounds were once part of the residence of the Shibuya clan. Ceremonies are held at 9:00 a.m. each day.

The annual festival is held on September 15.

🌐 *https://www.konno-hachimangu.jp*

SHIBUYA STATION DETAIL 4

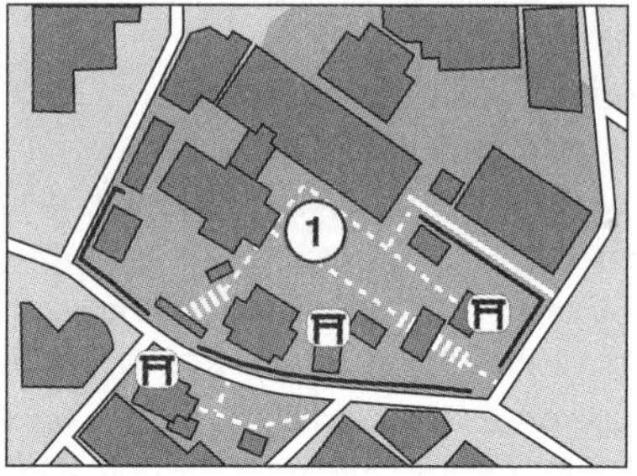

新宿駅

SHINJUKU STATION AREA

The Shinjuku Station area has two sides—literally. Well, also metaphorically, as you will come to see as you wander in the area. The massive Shinjuku Station complex, which gets about 3.5 million travelers a day, divides east and west. The tracks of the JR Yamanote Line run through the neighborhood from north to south, adding to the division. Both sides have modern buildings, interspersed with temples and shrines. One colorful aspect of the neighborhood is the Shinjuku Tiger, who has been dressing up and wearing a tiger mask for more than forty-five years. Perhaps you will see him delivering newspapers on his bike in the morning or evening. He is the subject of a documentary by Satō Yoshinori entitled *Shinjuku Tiger*.

All in all there is lots here, so pick your focus and perhaps divide this chapter into more than one visit.

Shinjuku West Side / Shinjuku Nishi 新宿西

The west side of Shinjuku Station has far fewer of the old temples, shrines, and businesses found in the east. Much of the area had been large a marshland until the Meiji period, until the Yodobashi Water Purification Plant, Japan's first modern water plant, was built in 1898. The plant continued operation until 1968, at which time the land was marked for development and the building boom began. The west side of the station is filled mainly with department stores, modern hotels, skyscraper office towers, and the massive Tokyo Metropolitan Government complex. Don't discount the area as not very good for strolling, as there are interesting sights scattered about.

SHINJUKU STATION AREA WEST

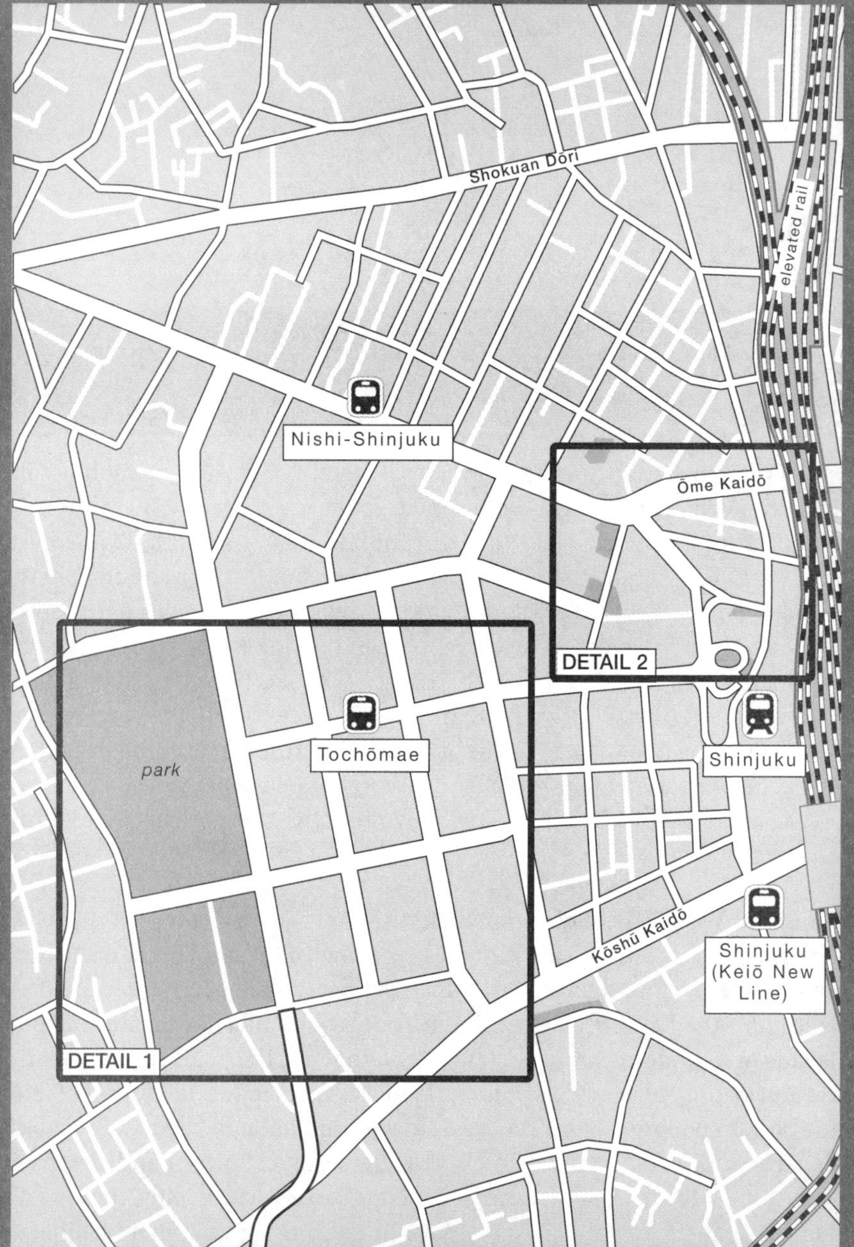

SHINJUKU STATION AREA EAST

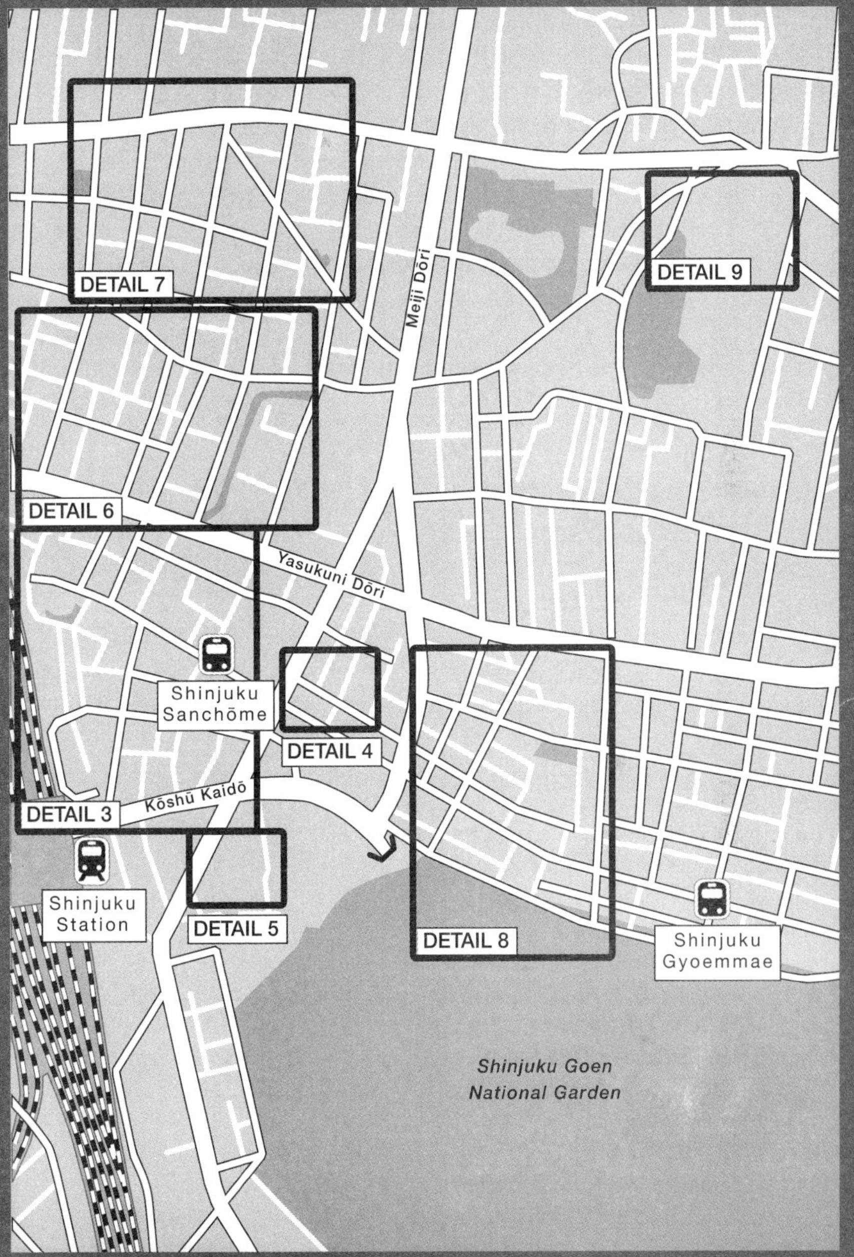

Shinjuku East Side / Shinjuku Higashi 新宿東

There are so many entries for the east side that the latter portion of this chapter—detail maps 3 through 9—is devoted to it. This is the part of the Shinjuku Station area with the richest history. In the 17th century, a new rest station with inns and other businesses for travelers was established here on Kōshū Kaidō, one of the five major roadways of the Edo period. In time other businesses moved in. Eventually, the train station was built, and other train lines converged here, bringing a steady stream of passengers. More businesses followed, and the area developed into what it is today. The east side is where you will find many major department stores, numerous smaller businesses, restaurants, and a varied (but seedy at times) bar district.

DETAIL 1

❶ Bunka Gakuen Costume Museum / Bunka Gakuen Fukushoku Hakubutsukan 文化学園服飾博物館

You won't find cosplay on exhibit here: This is a museum focusing on normal apparel. The museum was established in 1979 and moved to the present location in 2003. The initial collection was composed of garments from the West, Japanese Western-style clothes, and kimono, which the school had started collected before the war. After World War II they began expanding by adding a collection gathered by an organization connected with the Japanese military. There are four thematic exhibits each year and the museum is closed when they are preparing them.

🌐 *https://museum.bunka.ac.jp/english/*

❷ Shinjuku NS Building 新宿NSビル

This thirty-story building was designed by Nikken Sekkei and completed in 1982. The first through third floors house various commercial businesses. The top two floors are home to restaurants, with a sky bridge on the twenty-ninth floor. The remaining floors consist of offices. The roof is glass with lights for nighttime illumination. The most stunning aspect of the building is the atrium, which extends the full height of the structure. There is a huge water-powered clock in the atrium that spans several floors.

🌐 *http://www.shinjuku-ns.co.jp*

❸ Tokyo Metropolitan Government Building / Tōkyō To Chōsha 東京都庁舎

The Tokyo Metropolitan Government Offices are in three buildings. Security

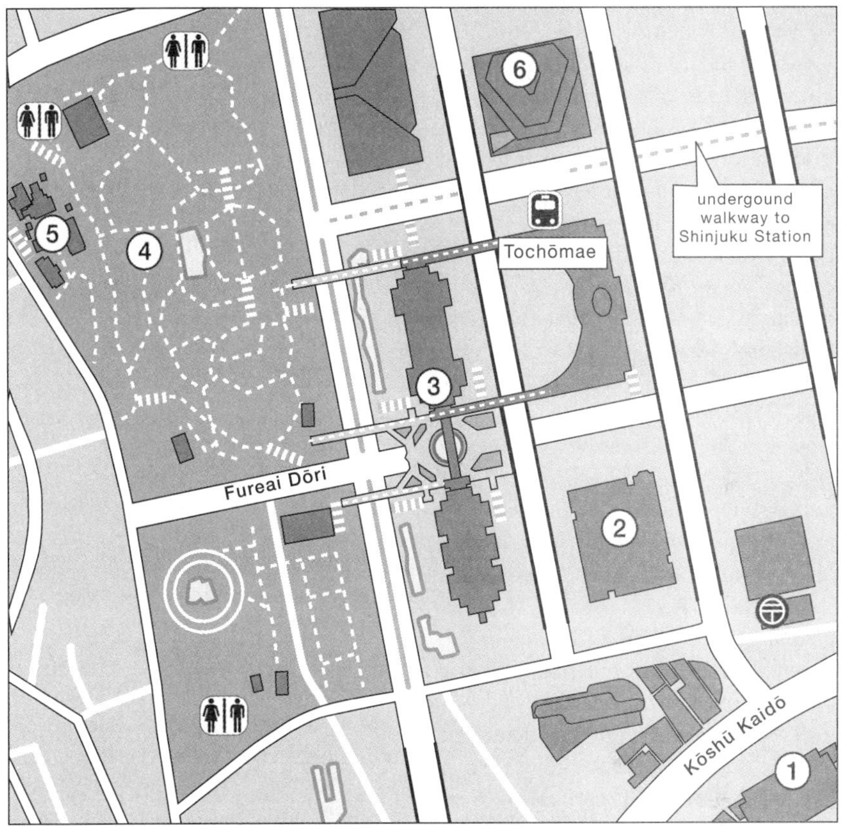

is tight in all three and many areas are not open to the public. The most famous of the three is the tallest, the twin-towered Office Building Number One, designed by Tange Kenzō and completed in 1991. The building also has two tourism information centers, one for Japan on the second floor and one for Tokyo on the first. You may want to visit them to pick up some useful fliers. The two towers are popular destinations for their views of the city as each have observation decks on the forty-fifth floor. Both also have souvenir shops and restaurants. Building Number Two is pretty much just offices. The Tokyo Metropolitan Assembly Building has a large plaza with statuary, which is a good place to take photographs of Building Number One.

🌐 *http://www.yokoso.metro.tokyo.jp/en/*

❹ Shinjuku Central Park / Shinjuku Chūō Kōen 新宿中央公園

This park was established in 1960 on a portion of the old Tokyo Yodobashi Purification Plant. The park includes hills, playgrounds, ponds, waterfalls, and fountains, and contains 80,000 trees. A portion of the land was once part of Jūnisō Kumano Jinja, so many of the trees are older than the park. This is a pleasant place to stroll and take a break. When I first visited the park many years ago, there was a small cluster of shelters built by local homeless in the corner closest to the local police station. Given the Japanese government's ongoing efforts to reduce homelessness, such shelters are rarely seen today. An excellent view of the park from above can be had from the observation floors of the Tokyo Metropolitan Government Building.

The homeless main characters in Satoshi Kon's excellent movie *Tokyo Godfathers* live in this park.

❺ Jūnisō Kumano Jinja 十二社熊野神社

Kumano shrines are devoted to the three sacred mountains Hongū, Shingū, and Nachi. This Kumano shrine was established sometime in the Muromachi period. The buildings and grounds are impressive. One can also find interesting small sub-shrines and some large painted ema, with at least one dating from the 18th century. The local ponds and waterfalls were a popular viewing spot before they were eliminated in the Meiji period to create the modern waterworks. In his series *Hundred Views of Edo* Hiroshige included a print of a large pond with part of this shrine visible near the bottom.

You can get to the shrine from the road on the west side near the pedestrian overpass or through Shinjuku Central Park.

🌐 *http://12so-kumanojinja.jp*

❻ Memorial Museum for Soldiers, Detainees in Siberia, and Postwar Repatriates / Heiwa Kinen Tenji Shiryōkan 平和祈念展示資料館

This museum opened in 2000 and is sometimes referred to as the Peace Memorial Museum. It is devoted to the experiences at the end of World War II of those Japanese who were sent overseas as soldiers or settlers. Many were not able to evacuate as the war ended and were either imprisoned as POWs or stranded as foreign civilians. Many ended up in camps in Siberia where they suffered hardships. Others were separated from their families in the confusion at the end of the war. The voyage back to Japan is included in the exhibits, showing items people brought back with them and documents involved in the process of repatriation. The museum is located on the thirty-third floor of the Shinjuku Sumitomo Building.

🌐 *https://www.heiwakinen.go.jp/english-index/*

DETAIL 2

❶ MODE GAKUEN Cocoon Tower モード学園コクーンタワー

Designed by Tange Associates and completed in 2008, this fifty-story building houses three schools, with a student body of roughly 10,000. The main school is MODE GAKUEN, which focuses on design, arts, and fashion. There are two other MODE GAKUEN campuses in Osaka and Nagoya, which also have very interesting buildings. The other two schools in this building are: HAL Tokyo, focusing on IT, music, computer graphics, and game design; and Shuto Ikō, a school devoted to training medical care staff. One interesting feature of this structure: Buildings beyond a certain height are required by law to have a helipad for emergencies. Here, the lack of a flat roof is dealt with by having the helipad folded up when not needed.

🌐 *https://www.mode.ac.jp/tokyo*

NOTE: *The school prefers people not sightsee in the building. Please enjoy the exterior.*

❷ Sompo Museum of Art 美術館

A museum devoted to the paintings of Tōgō Seiji (1897–1978) and his contemporaries. Tōgō received many awards in his lifetime, including the Western Art Promotion Award in 1928 and the Japan Art Academy Award in 1957. He was made an Officier d'Ordre des Arts et des Lettres by the French government in 1969, and was awarded the Order of the Rising Sun, Second Class, with Rays in 1976. After his death, the Japanese government named him a Person of Cultural Merit of the fourth court rank. The museum was established in 1976 and is located on the forty-second floor of the Sompo Japan Nipponkoa headquarters building.

🌐 *https://www.sompo-museum.org/en/*

❸ Jōenji 常圓寺

The date of the origin of this Nichiren Buddhist temple is unknown, however it is known that the temple was moved to this location in 1585. The temple was damaged in the firebombings of World War II and the current main hall dates from 1964. One unusual feature of the temple is that the stone with the temple name is both in kanji and Roman letters. This temple has an extensive graveyard and a cherry tree that is one of the "Edo sanboku," the three famous trees of Edo.

Access can be found on the south side.

🌐 *https://joenji.jp*

❹ Shinjuku Omoide Yokochō 思い出横丁

The official name of this small group of shops translates as "Shinjuku Memory Lane." This is the remains of a black market established around 1946. The

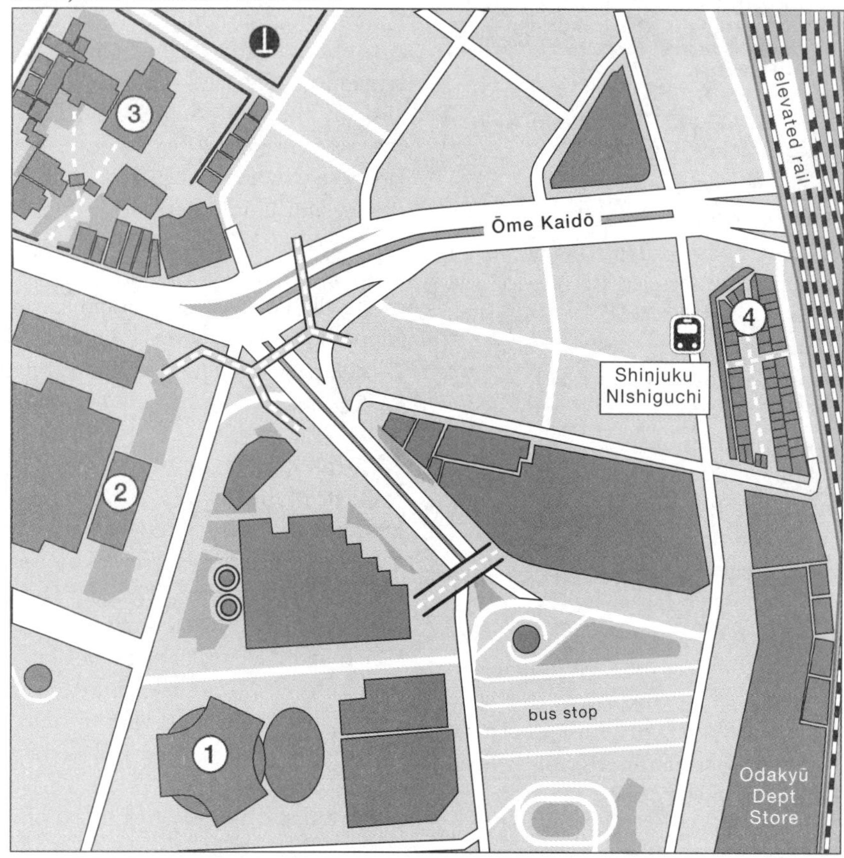

area grew from a series of stalls selling all sorts of things including roasted meats—mainly offal, which was not rationed—obtained from US forces during the early postwar years. Several were owned by squatters who were forced to leave in the 1960s and their shops torn down. The present shops remained, preserving some of the old flavor of the neighborhood. Today some of the shops still serve a variety of motsu, as offal is known in Japanese. The clientele is varied, even international, so dive in and enjoy. Don't be picky—try as many different things as you can. Most of the shops open around 4:00 p.m. Some have English menus. By the way, this area is commonly referred to by its old nickname, shōben yokochō "Piss Alley." In the old days it lacked toilets, so any place that was convenient was used to empty full bladders. Today there are toilets.

🌐 *http://shinjuku-omoide.com/english/*

DETAIL 3

❶ Studio ALTA スタジオアルタ
A landmark and major meeting point near the east exit of the JR Shinjuku Station. Designed by Toda Corporation and completed in 1980, the Studio ALTA building contains mainly shops catering to young women. There is a TV studio with a huge screen on the street that displays the current broadcast, making this an easy location to find. You can get a good view of it from the plaza across the street, which is a common meeting place for people in the area. The first time I met up with a friend in Shinjuku we chose the nearby plaza as an easy place to meet. While we waited, we hung out and watched the scouts that recruit talent for local clubs repeatedly approaching, and getting rebuffed by, the young women walking through the area.

❷ Kinokuniya Shinjuku
紀伊國屋書店 新宿
This is not just another branch of this international bookstore chain; the original store occupied a two-story building on this lot in 1927. In those days Kinokuniya was a charcoal dealer that started selling books on the side. The present nine-story building dates from 1964 and has several stories devoted to the bookstore. There is also an art gallery, a theater, and a tea shop. The shop has a very good section devoted to books in English and is worth checking out for items published in Japan that are hard to obtain overseas. There is another store in the Takashimaya Times Square Annex, near the Yamanote Line tracks southeast of the station.
🌐 *https://store.kinokuniya.co.jp/store/shinjuku-main-store/*

❸ Horse Trough / Basuisō 馬水槽
This is a British water trough as would have been found in London in the late 19th century. It was donated by a London association during Dr. Nakajima Eiji's tour of Europe and the United States in 1901. Such water sources provided not only clean water for animals but also water that was fit for human consumption. The front has a trough for horses, below that is a tray for dogs and cats, and the back has a drinking fountain for people. Dr. Nakajima played a key role in modernizing the water system of Tokyo, so this item was an appropriate gift. Originally located in front of the old Tokyo government offices, it was moved several times. In 1964 it was finally placed in this location, where it has remained.

❹ Nakamuraya 中村屋
Originally a branch of a restaurant in Hongō founded in 1901, the Shinjuku restaurant opened in the 1920s and enjoyed success with their curry dishes and Chinese dumplings. Today the

SHINJUKU STATION DETAIL 3

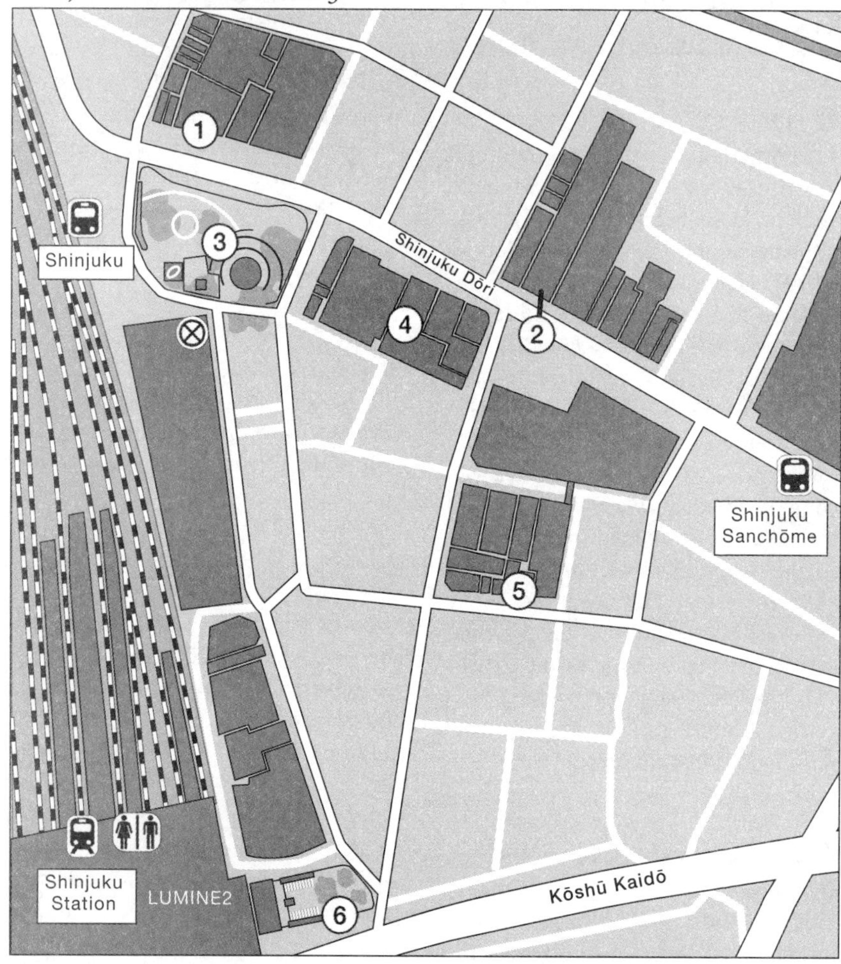

building houses several restaurants and confection shops. The Nakamuraya has a long history of association with artists, writers, and the theater. This is reflected in the Nakamuraya Salon, an excellent small art museum on the third floor of the building. Sōma Aizō, the founder of the Nakamuraya, was a Christian philanthropist and social activist who aided many struggling artists and fought for social betterment. He also solicited advice for his business from non-Japanese and hired foreign residents. During World War I he helped the Indian revolutionary Rash Behari Bose, who later became

Sōma's son-in-law and played a role in their starting to sell curry.
🌐 *https://www.nakamuraya.co.jp*

❺ Disk Union Shōwa Kayō Kan ディスクユニオン昭和歌謡館

The Disk Union store I have marked here is only one branch of the music store chain. This one specializes in music from the Shōwa period. Disk Union shops handle new and used recordings on all types of media, as well as books and other materials related to music. There are roughly forty stores in Tokyo, several with a very specific genre focus. Nineteen of them are in Shinjuku. In many cases you will find several specialty stores in the same building. Given how busy retail stores in major shopping areas like Shinjuku are, you may want to check their English store list on the website before visiting.
🌐 *http://diskunion.net*

❻ Shinjuku Tourist Information Center 新宿観光案内所

Here you will find the usual tourist information, such as brochures and maps. There are also multilingual touchscreen information panels, an ATM, free wi-fi, and a currency exchange. Staff are available who speak a large range of languages.
🌐 *http://www.kanko-shinjuku.jp/office/-/index.html*

NOTE: *There are information counters in stations and some large stores, so you can also keep your eyes out for those.*

DETAIL 4

❶ Suehirotei 末廣亭

This is a yose, a theater specializing in rakugo and iromono (variety shows). Suehirotei is the oldest yose in Tokyo, and the current building was built in 1946. Given the age of the building, this is a good place to experience traditional entertainments. Seating is either in chairs or on cushions on tatami. This is the last yose in Tokyo to offer traditional seating. Programming is done in ten-day blocks starting on the first of the month, with a special performance called a yoichikai that is held each month on the on thirty-first and on Dec 29. There are two rakugo associations that alternate programming on each ten-day block. Saturday also has late night shows for young talents. Each program's performance includes rakugo and various other entertainments. The rakugo presentation follows a hierarchy, with the lesser talents performing first, building up to the most noted performers for each day. A full program lasts about four hours. It is permissible to arrive late. Feel free to have something to drink, however alcohol is not permitted. Advance tickets are sold only at least a week in advance for groups of ten or more. Souvenirs

SHINJUKU STATION DETAIL 4

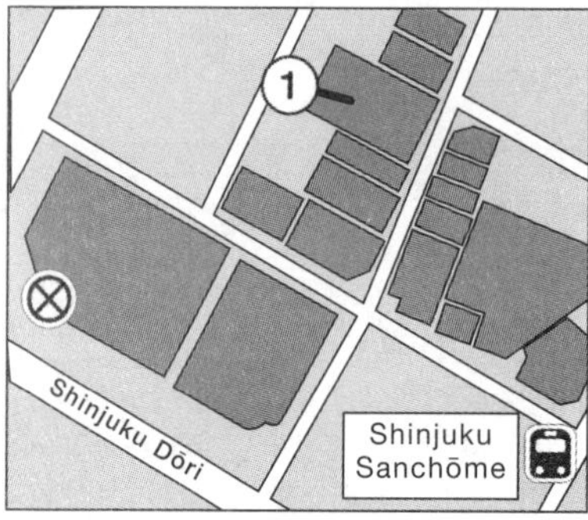

SHINJUKU STATION DETAIL 5

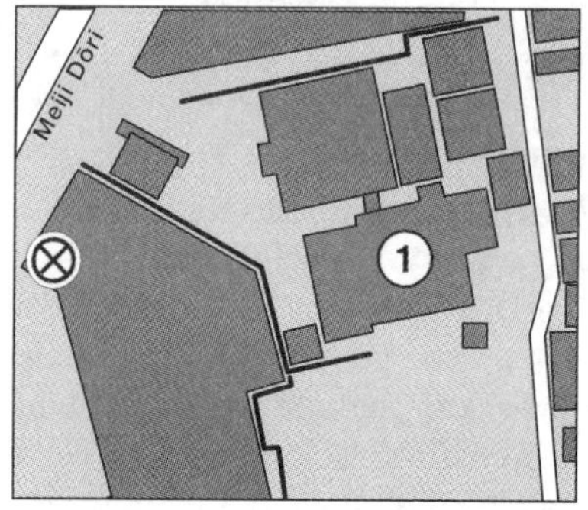

are sold at the theater. The first time I visited, I bought a cellphone strap from the capsule toy machine out front.
🌐 *http://www.suehirotei.com*

DETAIL 5

❶ Tenryūji 天龍寺

This temple was founded in 1591. The entrance is on Meiji Dōri through an impressive wooden gate on the temple's west side. The temple bell is one of the three famous bells of Edo that were used to ring the hours (the other two are in Ueno's Kaneiji and Ichigaya Hachiman). These bells are each referred to as a "toki no kane," a bell of time. This bell would also be rung a half hour before the Naitō Shinjuku brothel district gates were closing to alert customers that it was time to head home. This got the bell the nickname of oidashi kane, "chasing out bell."

DETAIL 6

❶ Kabukichō 歌舞伎町

No, you won't find a kabuki theater in Kabukichō. There were attempts to build a kabuki theater here after World War II, so the area's name changed in 1947. The theater never came, but the name stayed. Before 1958, when the anti-prostitution law came into effect, this was also one of Shinjuku's brothel districts. As a result of that law Kabukichō became more of an entertainment district, with bars, movie theaters, restaurants, and the legal sex trade, including strip joints and soaplands. In the 1960s the neighborhood became popular with intellectuals and artists for its coffee shops and movie theaters that played foreign films. While Kabukichō has a reputation for having a high crime rate, it is currently safer than entertainment areas in many American or European cities. Most of

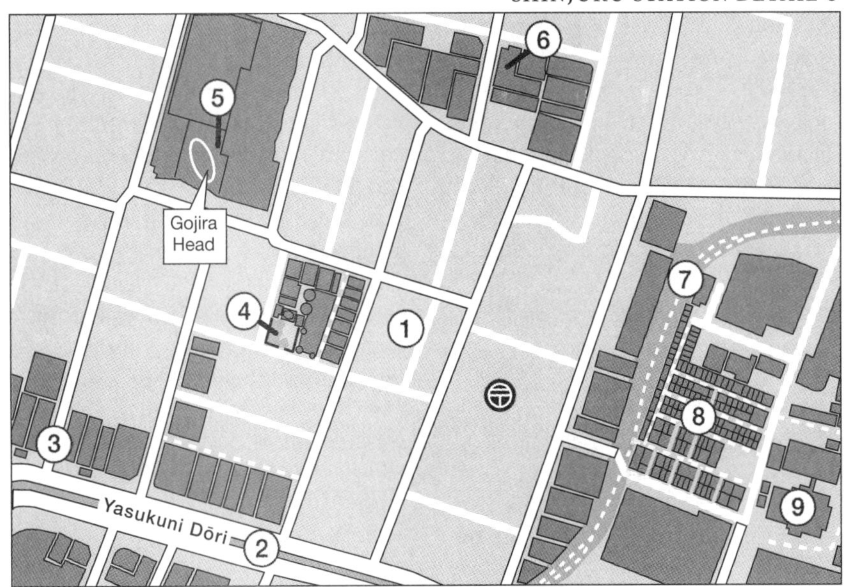

the crime consists of things like immigration law violations, prostitution, and the occasional tourist having their drink spiked and bank account cleared out. The government, in fit of puritanism, shut down many legal sex trade businesses in 2004. The result: Many women became unemployed and turned to street prostitution, which reportedly produced a spike in STD rates. Keep an eye out and you will see certain businesses that continue to survive in spite of government attempts to clean up the district.

🌐 *http://www.kabukicho.or.jp/index.php?lang=en*

TIP: *Want to read some good information on Kabukichō? Check out the book* Tokyo Vice *by former Yomiuri Shimbun police reporter Jake Adelstein, whose beat was the neighborhood.*

❷ Shinjuku Subnade
新宿サブナード

As one strolls Tokyo, one becomes increasingly aware of the verticality of the city, and not just the many-storied buildings. There is another realm below. In addition to the long pedestrian tunnels that shelter you in bad weather and help you avoid street crossings and crowds, there are also underground shopping streets. One of the big ones is here in Shinjuku, boasting over 100 stores. Located below Yasukuni Dōri, and stretching from Shinjuku Dōri near the tracks to Kuyakusho Dōri near the Shinjuku Ward offices, is the

Shinjuku Subnade. A very large percentage of the stores are clothing and accessory shops. However, a quick look at their website turns up other interesting shops and restaurants as well. There is direct access from the JR Shinjuku Station, Tokyo Metro Shinjuku Station, and the Seibu Shinjuku Station.

🌐 *http://www.subnade.co.jp*

❸ Kabukichō Ichibangai
歌舞伎町一番街

The famous sign off Yasukuni Dōri marking one of the entrances Kabukichō is a landmark seen time and again in movies, anime, and manga. This is not the biggest street going into Kabukichō; it just happened to be graced by this iconic sign. The sign is a major landmark that strollers should be aware of. So wander in and scope out the variety of businesses, which range from ordinary to quite sketchy.

❹ Kabukichō Benzaiten
歌舞伎町弁財天

After this Bentendō burned down in 1945 during the firebombings, Suzuki Kihei, the head of the local neighborhood association, built a temporary replacement even before the area was restored. Benten is worshiped here as the neighborhood guardian. The lanterns on the left side and the wood plaques on the right of the red gate indicate donors. This is an interesting, if a bit rundown, site, as you can access it from the park in the front. The red gate is high off the ground, limiting access to the shrine proper. A stairway on the right leads to what could be an office. There is a statue of Benten on the right and a black and white mural with a tiger and dragon. As Benten is associated with music, dance, and business, this location is appropriate for a temple to her. Bentendō is said to date from the Edo period when this area was marshland.

OFF THE CHARTS

NTT Docomo Yoyogi Building

NTTドコモ代々木ビル

This building is not on the maps as it is quite a distance to the south, but it towers over the neighborhood, tall enough to be a major local landmark. It was designed by the architectural firm Kajima Design for the major mobile telecommunications company NTT and completed in 2000. The bottom-three stories are devoted to commercial space, and there are twenty-four stories of offices. The rest—almost half the building—is for telecommunications equipment. The top sections step inward, providing room for communications antennas, and there is a communications tower at the apex. The height of this tower, 790 feet (240 meters), makes it one of the tallest buildings in Tokyo.

❺ Shinjuku Tōhō Building
新宿東宝ビル

This multi-use complex built in 2015 replaced other buildings that were on the site, including the Koma Theater. The most obvious tenant is the Tōhō Cinemas Shinjuku, with twelve screens and over 2,300 seats. On the roof is a full-sized head of Gojira (Godzilla), however I'm not sure which version of Gojira this is, as the character changed and got larger over time. There is also a hotel, a pachinko parlor, restaurants, and shops.

🌐 *https://www.toho.co.jp/shinjukutoho/*

🌐 *https://hlo.tohotheater.jp/net/schedule/076/TNPI2000J01.do*

Kabukichō in Media

Kabukichō shows up in several gangster movies, and not only Japanese ones; there are Chinese films set here, as in the 1990s it was the site of gang wars involving immigrant gangs. Perhaps the most famous depiction of the area is the montage at the beginning of *Dead or Alive* that weaves in and out of strip clubs, ramen joints, restrooms, and street scenes. It is also the setting, under the name of Kamurochō, for Sega's series of *Ryū ga Gotoku* video games, which are known in the West as *Yakuza*.

❻ Samurai Museum
サムライミュージアム

A small private museum opened in 2015 with an attached shop for fans of all things samurai. The museum is on two floors and has an interesting collection of armor and weapons. "Small" means it does not go into great detail on samurai history. However, it covers the high points, and for most folks that is plenty. For free you can enjoy sword drawing demonstrations or don armor for a photo. With reservations and for a fee, there are calligraphy lessons and lectures on Japanese swords. Signage is in Japanese, English, Chinese, and Korean. The gift shop has a variety of items for sale. They sell swords, from cheap replicas for less than $100 to actual swords for over $14,000. Swords, of course, are shipped. Though, depending on where they are sent, they may not make it past your country's customs inspectors. The T-shirts are a safer bet, and cheaper too.

🌐 *https://www.samuraimuseum.jp/en/*

❼ Four Seasons Pathway / Shiki No Michi 四季の路

The twenty-three wards of Tokyo used to have many streetcar lines. At that time this park was a section of one of them. The streetcar line was eliminated in 1970 and the park took its place in 1974. The area is attractive, with the walkway curving along the old track line. The trees are relatively young but have enough growth to provide

▲ Kabukichō Ichibangai the iconic symbol of the most (in)famous bar district in Japan.

▼ The small and cozy bars of Golden Gai; old, worn, and lovely in their own ways.

▲ An alley used as a pedestrian walkway with access to small shops.

▲ Surrounded by shady businesses, the Kabukichō Benzaiten still is a place of prayer.

▼ Suehirotei, a classic yose (variety theater) providing entertainment for generations.

good shade. I remember the first time I walked through the park many years ago with friends on a rainy night after dinner. It was quite the contrast to the hustle and lights of Kabukichō.

The 1968 yakuza film *Outlaw: Gangster VIP* has some scenes that take place along the streetcar line, so you can get an idea of what it looked like before the park was built.

❽ Shinjuku Golden Gai 新宿ゴールデン街

Some 170 tiny bars are packed into a small area here, many with unique themes. Each is on a tiny separate plot, preventing developers from getting their hands on the land as every owner would have to agree to sell. The buildings are two or three stories. In the past the upper stories were residences, and some still are. Many bars have a clearly posted seating charge or are private clubs (a way to make sure regulars have a spot to sit). This area was originally called Hanazono Gai until the new name came into use in 1965. During the day things are very quiet, but it is still worth exploring for the unique exterior decorations. At night things liven up as the bars open, many around 9 p.m. Some of the bars are long established; some are new enterprises with young proprietors who took over from retiring owners. The area has long had a reputation for being popular with artists, writers, journalists, movie directors, and other artistic types. Each spring and fall there is a flea market. The dates float, but you may stumble on it when you visit.

The original *Old Boy* manga has many scenes that take place in a bar here—alas, the bar Moon Dog was fictional. The Wim Wenders documentary *Tokyo-Ga*, which is included on the Criterion release of *Late Spring*, has some scenes shot in the bar La Jetée.

🌐 *http://www.goldengai.net*

❾ Hanazono Jinja 花園神社

This is one of the older shrines in this area. The present buildings date from 1965, as the shrine burned down in World War II. The origin of the shrine goes back to well before the Edo period—it is said that Yamato Takeru founded it in the 1st century. In the 17th century the shrine was moved from where the Isetan department store is now to a garden belonging to a branch of the Tokugawa family. This explains the name, as hanazono means "flower garden."

To the right on the way to the main hall is a row of small red torii. These mark the path to Itoku Inari Daimyōjin. If you choose to walk down that row, be sure to duck if you are tall. Toward the end of the path look up and you will see a large wooden penis mounted on the last torii behind the carved sign. Couples pray at this small shrine for marital happiness and children.

In the northeast corner of the

grounds you will find Geinō Asama Jinja. Since the Edo period, performers have prayed here for success in the arts and in hopes of improving their talents. The writing on the wall is the names of entertainers who have prayed here.

Close to the right of the main shrine building is Osame Daimyōjin. This is where old talismans and charms are gotten rid of. This small shrine is also popular for people praying to get rid of anything that angers them.

While the main entrance is on the east side, you can also approach the shrine from the west or south.

On Sundays a flea market is held here. The shrine festival is held on the Saturday, Sunday, and Monday closest to May 28.

Even though Inari shrines are not usually associated with Tori no Ichi, Hanazono Jinja is known for its celebration of this particular festival each November, complete with a sideshow.

DETAIL 7

❶ Kabukichō Kōban 新宿警察署歌舞伎町交番

A four-story kōban is rare—they usually are two stories or fewer. Given that Kabukichō does occasionally get out of hand, it makes sense to have a larger facility here, and the kōban is a busy one. The building is rather nice and distinct enough to stand out from the rest of the neighborhood, a good feature in a kōban.

There are usually English-speaking staff available here; it was one of the first kōban in Tokyo to provide this on a regular basis.

❷ Love Hotel district 歌舞伎町のラブホテル街

Located in the north end of Kabukichō, this area has a mix of commercial hotels and love hotels. I have known people who booked hotel rooms in this area and were shocked (or delighted) at the "other" hotels in the vicinity and at having to walk through Tokyo's most (in)famous bar district to get to their accommodations. There are also bars, host clubs, and restaurants mixed in with the hotels. The architecture is rather creative and varied. If you like unusual architecture, this is an area for a stroll with your camera.

❸ Ichibankan 一番館

This is what is called a zakkyobiru, an often-narrow building with multiple shops housed in a single vertical structure. These are seen all over Tokyo, and in this neighborhood most have little to distinguish them other than their brightly lit signage at night. Even during the day, the Ichibankan stands out in its mixed-use neighborhood on the edge of the love hotel district with its unique shape and striped exterior.

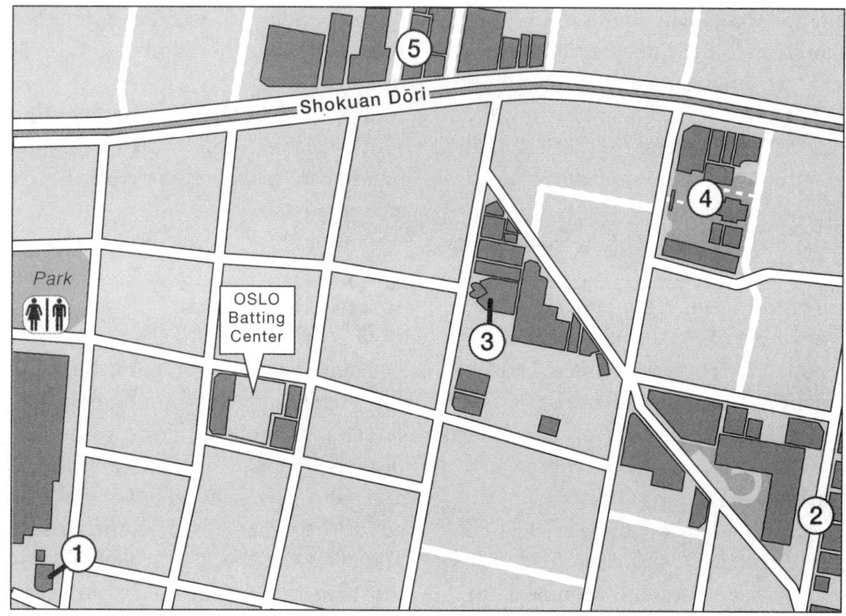

It was built in 1969 and designed by Takeyama Minoru.

❹ Inari Kiō Jinja 稲荷鬼王神社

A local Inari shrine with a history going back to 1653. There is a small shrine to Ebisu on the grounds that is on the local Shichifukujin tour—it is to the left of the office building. To the right of the office building is an Asama shrine on a small fujizuka. The fujizuka used to be larger but was reduced when the shrine was renovated.

At the entrance, to the right of the torii, is a statue of a demon with a large stone water basin called a mizubachi on its head. The story goes that at night the basin made a sound as if water was pouring on it. The owner was disturbed by this and tried to break the basin but failed. After that he had a streak of bad luck and so gave the basin to the shrine. By the way, Kiō (鬼王) in the name of the shrine means oni king, "demon king," unsual for a shrine name.

People pray at this shrine for relief from skin diseases and other health problems.

The annual festival is on September 18.

❺ Korea Museum / Kōrai Hakubutsukan 高麗博物館

Established in 2001 and located on the seventh floor of this building, the museum is devoted to the history of

Korean-Japanese relations and ethnic Koreans in Japan. The neighborhood is one of the largest ethnic Korean neighborhoods in Tokyo. Exhibits cover a variety of related topics: the history of diplomacy, art, ethnic discrimination, music, and more. Visitors can also try on traditional Korean clothing for photographs.

🌐 *https://kouraihakubutsukan.org*

Encounter at Inari Kiō Jinja

The first time I visited this shrine was on a January 2. As I waited outside the shrine grounds for my friend to finish taking pictures, I spotted an elderly man in kimono walking down the street accompanied by three tough-looking men in suits. One can never tell when one will spot a yakuza boss making a New Year visit in this part of Tokyo.

DETAIL 8

❶ Jōkakuji 成覚寺

A Jōdoshū Buddhist temple with an entrance on the broad Yasukuni Dōri. Jōkakuji looks pretty ordinary; however, as you walk between the temple gate and main hall you will see three interesting items on the left. The first is the Asahi Jizō, a memorial to nine couples who committed love suicide. Next is a monument marked Shiraitozuka, which is related to a kabuki play about the romance between the prostitute Shiraito and her customer Suzuki Mondo. The largest is a mass grave that was established in 1860 for prostitutes who had no one to claim their bodies. Over 2,000 are buried here. There is a similar mass grave in Tokyo, at Jōkanji, which is mentioned in the Yoshiwara and Sanya chapter. Elsewhere on the grounds there is the grave of Harumachi Koikawa, who played a crucial role in creating the highly popular Kibyōshi genre of satirical illustrated literature in the Edo period. When he got into trouble with the authorities during a moralistic crackdown, he passed away before they could question him.

❷ Shōjuin 正受院

A Jōdoshū Buddhist temple founded in 1594. Here you can see a statue of the Datsueba, the old hag who strips the dead of their clothes before they cross the river into the afterlife. People have traditionally prayed to Datsueba here to stop a cough; the statue has the nickname of wata no obaba "cotton grandmother." Since 1957, each February 8 a hari kuyō "memorial service for broken needles" has been held. There is a harizuka "needle mound" where they are buried.

❸ Shinjuku Nichōme 新宿二丁目

Tokyo's most famous (but not only) gay bar district. During the day this

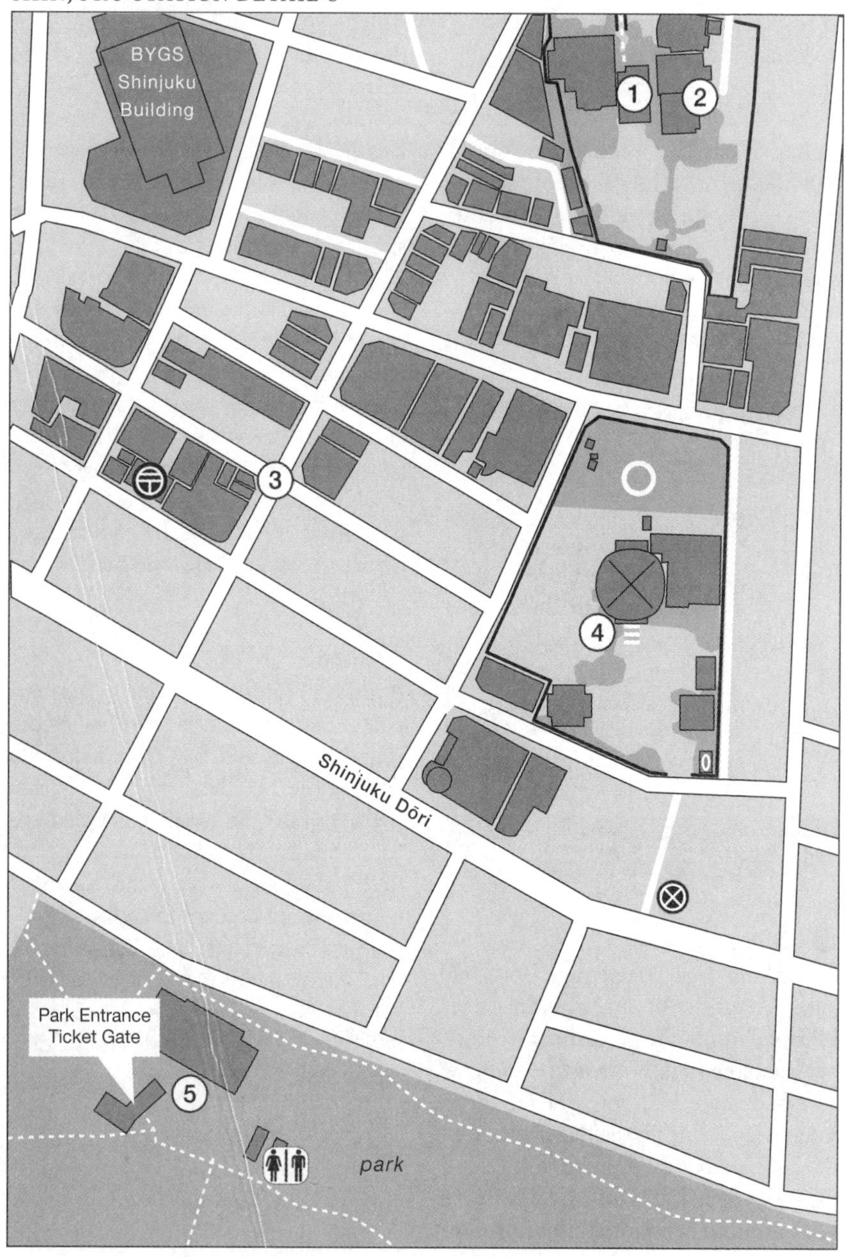
BYGS
Shinjuku
Building
1
2
3
4
Shinjuku Dōri
Park Entrance
Ticket Gate
5
park

area looks rather sedate, until the bars open at night. The compact neighborhood consists mainly of small bars, cafes, and other businesses. Most bars in the area have a specialty depending the taste of the clientele: bars for those who like older guys, chubby guys, and so on. There are also many places for lesbians, and bars where straight and gay patrons can mix. Before the anti-prostitution law came into effect in 1958, this area had been a brothel district. Like Kabukichō, this neighborhood became a bar district. The history of gay hangouts in East Shinjuku goes back to the immediate postwar period with places like Yakyoku, one of Mishima Yukio's hangouts. By the way, the term "gay bar" was apparently introduced into Japan by American soldiers in the 1950s.

❹ Taisōji 太宗寺

Originally this was a thatched hut residence established in 1596 by the monk Taisō. Later it became a temple for the Naito daimyō family. There are interesting statues here. The statue of Enma, the judge of the dead, dates from 1814; however, the body was severely damaged in the Great Kantō Earthquake and replaced in 1933. The other main statue is of Datsueba, the old hag mentioned in the entry for Shōjuin above. There is a button you can push to turn on a light to get a better view of the statues. There is also a statue of Hotei that is on the Shichifukujin tour in one of the buildings. The grounds have a famous bronze seated Jizō, one of the Edo Roku Jizō from the 18th century. The architecture here is a mix of new and old, with the statues mentioned above in a traditional building.

The entrance is on the south side.

❺ Shinjuku Gyoen National Garden / Shinjuku Gyoen 新宿御苑

This very large garden covers 58 hectares (143 acres) and contains wooded areas, ponds, and numerous structures. Originally this was the location of the daimyō mansion of the Naitō clan. In 1872 it was turned over to the imperial household and used for agricultural experiments. In 1906 the garden was done over in the style of a European park. In 1949 it became a public park with sections devoted to English, French, and Japanese styles. The garden is known for its roses, cherry blossoms in the spring, and chrysanthemums and autumn foliage in the fall. Each November from the first to the fifteenth, there is an exhibit of chrysanthemums grown by the gardeners. A small admission fee is required for entry and is very much worth it.

The 2013 film *Garden of Words*, directed by Shinkai Makoto, is largely set here.

🌐 *https://www.env.go.jp/garden/shinjukugyoen/english/index.html*

DETAIL 9

❶ Nishimuki Tenjinsha 西向天神社
Built in 1228, this was the guardian shrine of Higashi Okubo village. Sugawara no Michizane is the main kami enshrined here. The name of the shrine comes from the direction the main hall faces: Nishimuki means "facing west." The buildings are older wooden structures approached by a stairway leading up to the crest of the slope. There is a fujizuka on the grounds.

❷ Senpukuji 専福寺
Senpukuji was founded in 1631. The current temple is a plain-white modern concrete structure. Even the gate is modern, being made of wrought iron. Those interested in Japanese art may want to pay respect at the grave of the famous late Edo and Meiji period ukiyo-e print designer Yoshitoshi.

SHINJUKU STATION DETAIL 9

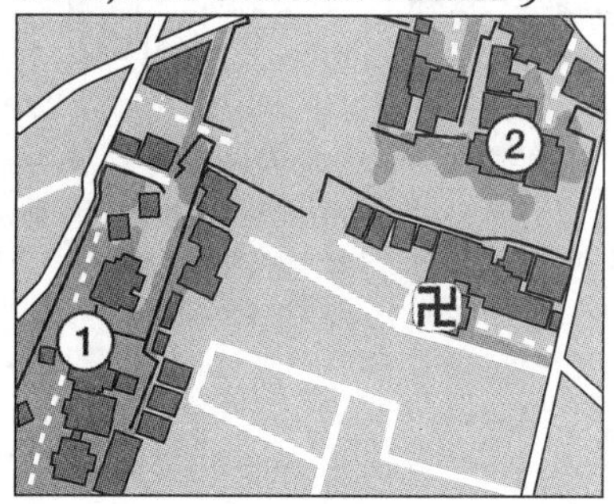

築地

TSUKIJI

The name of this area on the west side of the Sumidagawa means "constructed land." In the early Edo period, the area was part of Tokyo Bay. Over time, waste items that could not be reused or composted were used to fill in marshy areas. The bay receded, creating this part of town. In 1869 the Japanese government planned that this area would become a settlement for foreigners. The Western businesses ended up staying in Yokohama; however, missionaries, educators, and medical workers came to Tsukiji. Several significant private universities in Tokyo had their start in this area, and a hospital founded in those days remains, as do some churches. Most of Tsukiji burned down in the fires after the Great Kantō Earthquake, which also damaged the Nihonbashi fish market. In 1935 the new fish market opened up in Tsukiji and recently the market became a popular tourist destination. The days of the Tsukiji fish market ended in October 2018 when the market moved to Toyosu in Kōtō Ward. However the narrow streets and old shops of the outer market still remain.

NOTE: *This chapter is shorter than others and thus contains only one section and a single map.*

❶ Kachidokibashi 勝鬨橋

This double drawbridge with a split central span was opened to traffic in 1940. It was constructed to allow large ships to continue upstream from this location. The name of the bridge commemorates a victorious sea battle during the Russo-Japanese War:

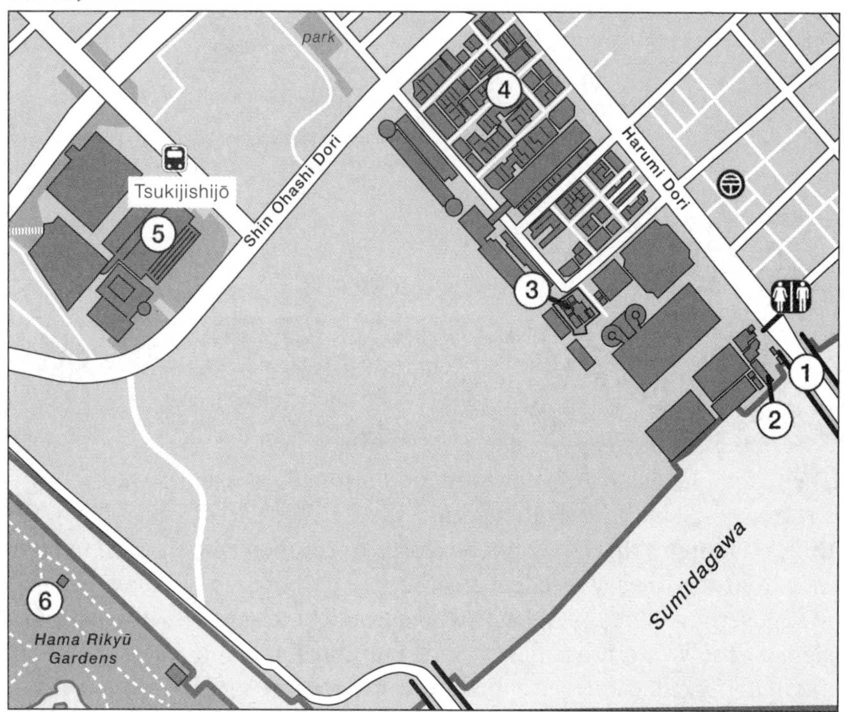

kachidoki means "a shout of victory." Over time the large ships using the river declined as trucks came into heavier use for moving goods. The drawbridge was last opened on November 29, 1970.

❷ Kachidoki Bridge Museum / Kachidokibashi no Shiryōkan 勝鬨橋の資料館

A small two-story museum next to the bridge in Tsukiji. The building was originally a power substation for the bridge and was converted into a museum in 2005. Included are historical exhibits, logbooks, the control panels, and equipment such as large electric engines. Every Thursday there is a tour of the piers. There is also a large stone monument to the Kachidoki no watashi "Kachidoki ferry" in front of the museum. The ferry service ended with the opening of the bridge.

🌐 *http://www.kensetsu.metro.tokyo.jp/jigyo/road/kanri/gaiyo/kachidoki/kannai.html*

❸ Namiyoke Inari Jinja 波除稲荷神社

The name of this neighborhood shrine means "protection from waves." The original shrine was founded in 1659; the present buildings date from 1937 and survived World War II. The grounds also include several kuyōzuka, "memorial mounds," for various animals sold at the Tsukiji fish market. These were erected by business organizations within the Tsukiji area and groups in the broader Tokyo region. These mounds are mainly along the wall to the left of the shrine. They include memorials for shrimp, ankō (anglerfish, monkfish), clams, eggs, one for anything killed for sushi toppings, and one for any living fish killed at the local market. The very lively shrine festival is in June, during which the Senkangu Mikoshi and the two lion heads, the male Tenjō Ōjishi and the female Benzaiten Ohaguro Ōjishi, are carried through the streets. The two lion heads are usually in their own small shrines on either side as you pass under the torii. The Tsukiji Shishi Matsuri grand festival is held every three years.

🌐 *http://www.namiyoke.or.jp/index.html*

❹ Tsukiji Outer Market / Tsukiji Jōgai Ichiba 築地場外市場

Some 500 businesses are located in this small maze of streets and walkways between shops. Many of the buildings in this area go back to well before World War II. It is not unusual for the owners of these businesses to live on the second story and operate their shop below. The businesses range from shops selling seafood, cutlery, or kitchenware to very small restaurants serving prepared food. My favorite has just five stools at a counter separated from the sidewalk and covered with a shutter when it is closed. Some are even smaller. Note that a few of the businesses are wholesale only, so are not set up for individuals making small purchases. The outer market remained in this location when the inner market relocated to Toyosu in October 2018.

🌐 *http://www.tsukiji.or.jp/english/*

❺ Asahi Shimbun Head Office 朝日新聞

One of the major newspapers of Japan, the Asahi Shimbun was founded in 1879. With over six and a half million subscribers, it is the second largest newspaper in the world. There are tours of the facility, which are given in Japanese and usually require a reservation. The building includes a gift shop that is open only on weekdays during business hours.

❻ Hamarikyū Gardens / Hamarikyū Onshi Teien 浜離宮恩賜庭園

Originally this was a marshy area that became popular with the Tokugawa clan for falconry. In the 1650s the Lord of Kōfu, Matsudaira Tsunashige, who was a great-grandson of Tokugawa Ieyasu, had a villa and garden built here. As the fifth Tokugawa shōgun had no heir, Tsunashige's son Ienobu

▲ The outer market remains after the internationally famous fish market moved in 2018.

料理　道具
常陸屋
TOKYO
2F
東京都中央区築地 4-14-18
妙泉寺ビル 2F
03-5565-5521
2F
TAX
FREE
大
年末

was made shōgun. It was Ienobu who had the garden renovated and the villa transformed into a rest house. The villa and gardens, which contained six teahouses, were referred to as Hama Goten, "seaside palace." In the Meiji period it came under the control of the Imperial Household as a detached palace and was used for diplomatic receptions. This is where former US President Ulysses S. Grant stayed and met the Emperor Meiji in 1879. The garden was damaged during the Great Kantō Earthquake and bombed in World War II, as the military had stationed anti-aircraft guns there. In 1945 it was given to Tokyo, repaired, and opened to the public in 1946. The Nakajima teahouse, situated over the largest tidal pond, is the only building that remains from the Edo period. Part of the garden is fenced off as a bird refuge, and in another area you can still see the two 18th-century duck blinds that staff would use when hunting. The garden website lists various flowers which can be seen all year round, especially cherry in March, rape in mid-March to early April, and peony in late November to mid-February. The autumn foliage is best in late November to early December.

There is a water bus stop near the garden that can take you to Asakusa or a short distance south to Hinode Pier.

The entrance is at the northern tip of the garden. You can get there by waterbus from Asakusa; the ticket price includes admission.

Members of the Suwa Falconry Institute do falconry demonstrations here, and early in January a larger demonstration is held.

🌐 *https://www.tokyo-park.or.jp/teien/en/hama-rikyu/index.html*

上野

UENO

This area manages to pack a certain density into a small space. There is the famous park, which contains many of Japan's major museums, the zoo, various temples, shrines, long-established shops, and interesting history from the early Edo period to the present. The park is also a relaxing place to visit. The shopping areas south of the park bustle to a degree I never anticipated before I went there. Fans of Akira Kurosawa's films may recognize this neighborhood as the place where the gun dealer in *Stray Dog* lived.

Each summer from mid-July to around mid-August, the Ueno Natsu Matsuri (Summer Festival) takes place.

DETAIL 1

❶ **Marishiten Tokudaiji** 徳大寺
This Nichiren sect Buddhist temple has an interesting location above some Ameya Yokochō shops. Due to the elevated location, I walked past the temple on several trips before I knew it was there. In fact I did not find out about this temple until I was back in the US and read about it in the Kajima Institute's book *Made in Tokyo*. The entrance is on a side street. If you follow the road on the west side of the tracks southward and look down the streets to your right, you will see a set of wide stairs. These lead up to Marishiten Tokudaiji. The sacred and secular are often in very close proximity in Tokyo. Marishiten is enshrined here and there is also a Jizō, which is said to help preserve your health if you wash it. People come here to pray for success in business, family safety, and health.
🌐 *http://www.marishiten-tokudaiji.com*

UENO

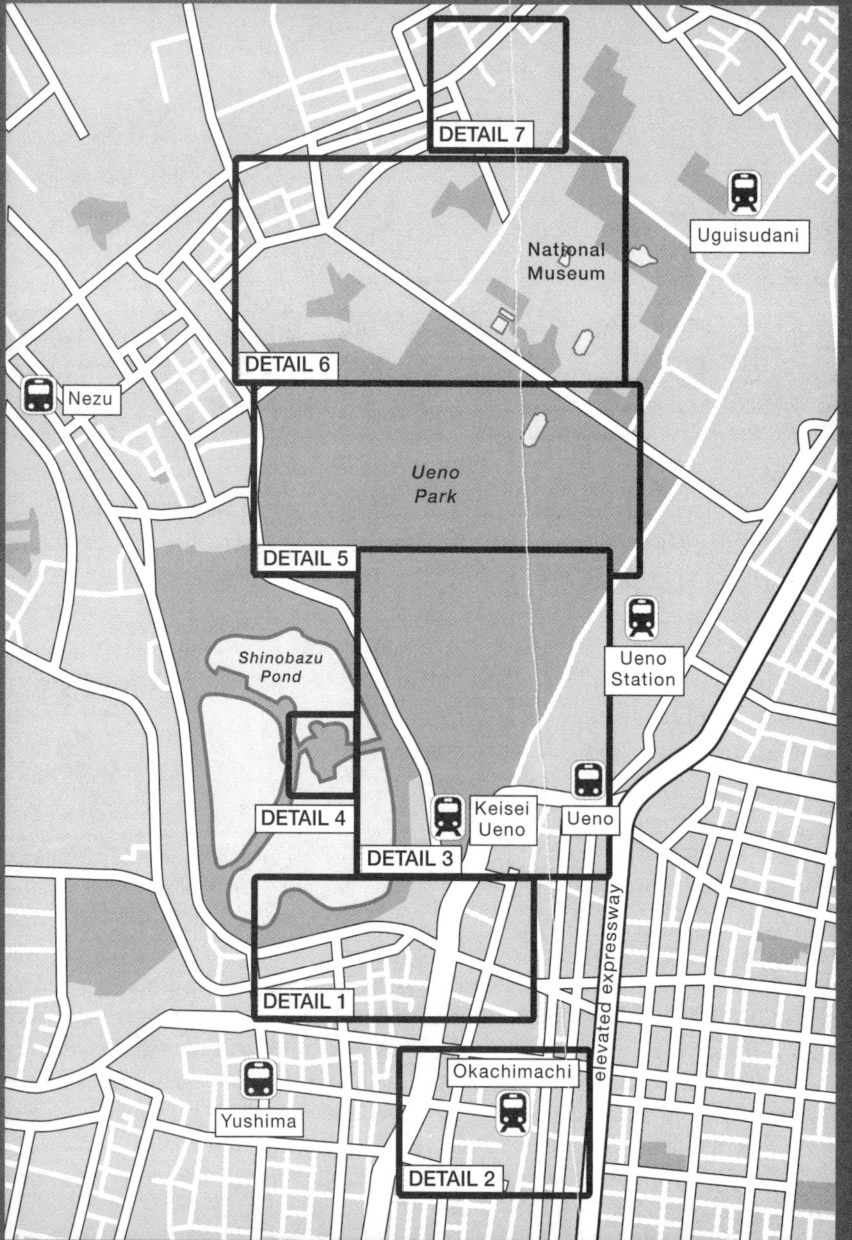

DETAIL 7
DETAIL 6
DETAIL 5
DETAIL 4
DETAIL 3
DETAIL 2
DETAIL 1
National Museum
Uguisudani
Nezu
Ueno Park
Shinobazu Pond
Ueno Station
Keisei Ueno
Ueno
elevated expressway
Okachimachi
Yushima

❷ Iseoto Shōten 伊勢音商店
Founded in 1875, Iseoto Shōten was originally an offshoot of a wholesale shop founded in the early 1860s. This branch of Iseoto Shōten will appeal to serious cooks, and specializes in high-quality ingredients for making the Japanese stock dashi, including katsuobushi, various small dried fish, kelp, and shiitake mushrooms. Also found are some other dried food products such as wakame, scallops, shrimp, and squid. For many of their products they have several varieties so you can choose the one you prefer. They even sell katsuobushi kezuriki so you can freshly shave your own rather than rely on packages of pre-shaved katsuobushi.
🌐 *http://www.iseoto.com*

❸ Ueno Kameido 上野亀井堂
Operating since 1890, this shop specializes in senbei and other small confections, such as ningyōyaki in the shape of bunraku puppet heads. Like many other places, this store burned down in the fires after the Great Kantō Earthquake. They also had to stop confectionaery sales during the war due to food shortages and were only able to reopen in 1949. The present building dates from 1988 and includes a tea room.
🌐 *http://www.kamei-do.co.jp*

❹ Ameya Yokochō アメヤ横丁 aka Ameyoko アメ横
A lively and very, very busy shopping district with hundreds of shops along and under the Yamanote Line tracks just south of Ueno Station. This area is famous for a variety of inexpensive goods sold in shops of a variety of sizes. I once bought a belt buckle in a shop the size of your average closet. The neighborhood gets very crowded on the weekends, so I highly recommend a weekday visit. This commercial area is a remnant of one of the largest Tokyo black markets of the postwar period. The black market stretched along the tracks from here all the way to Akihabara Station. Do keep your eyes out for the unusual, and be aware that some shops are in basements.
🌐 *https://www.ameyoko.net*

❺ Suzumoto 鈴本演芸場
The oldest yose in Tokyo, operating since 1857. Here one can enjoy a variety of entertainments, the most well known of which is rakugo. Other performances presented here include magic tricks, paper cutting, folk songs, comedy—in short, entertainment for the masses. Shows change every ten days. Feeling hungry? Go ahead and grab a bentō and a beer, perhaps some sweets, at the kiosk in the theater before the show starts. The seats have folding tables so you can enjoy the show and your food in comfort.
🌐 *http://www.rakugo.or.jp/index.html*

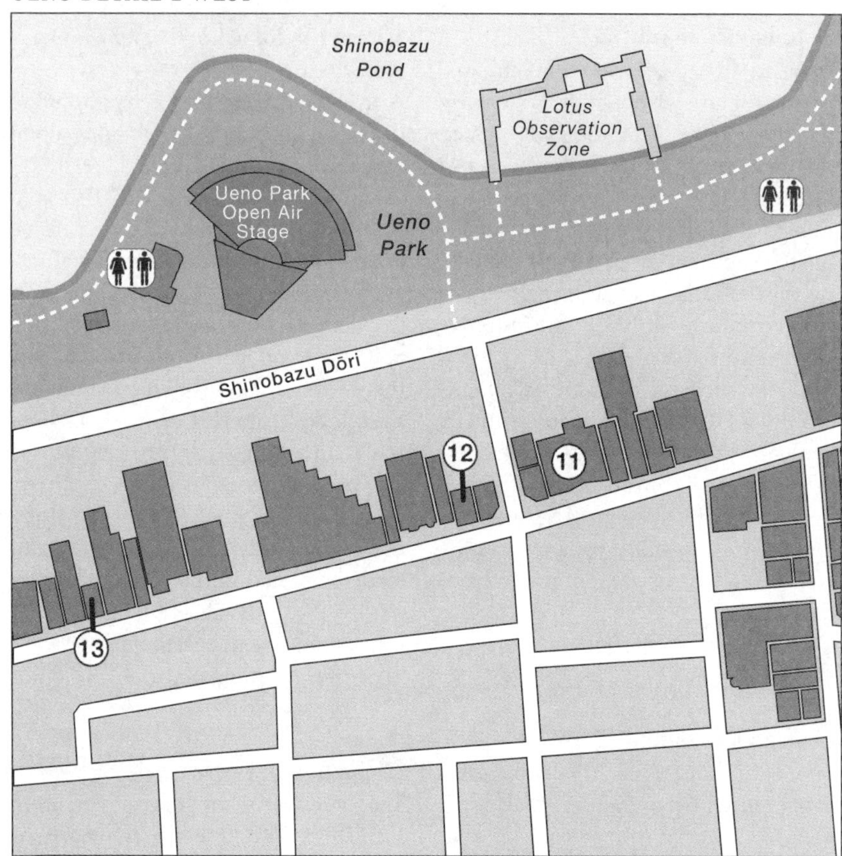

❻ Shuetsu 酒悦

Shuetsu has been selling Japanese pickles since 1675. The store is right on Chūō Dōri, with its distinctive logo of a bag tied with a cord. You can't have Japanese cuisine without the pickles. The range they stock here is impressive: jar after jar, package after package. So many different things are pickled in Japan, and this is probably the place where you will see this more clearly than anywhere else on your trip. As their products are usually well packaged, you can pick up something to take home with you.

🌐 *https://www.shuetsu.co.jp*

❼ Izuei 伊豆榮

Originally this unagi restaurant was a roadside shack that was established sometime when Tokugawa Yoshimune

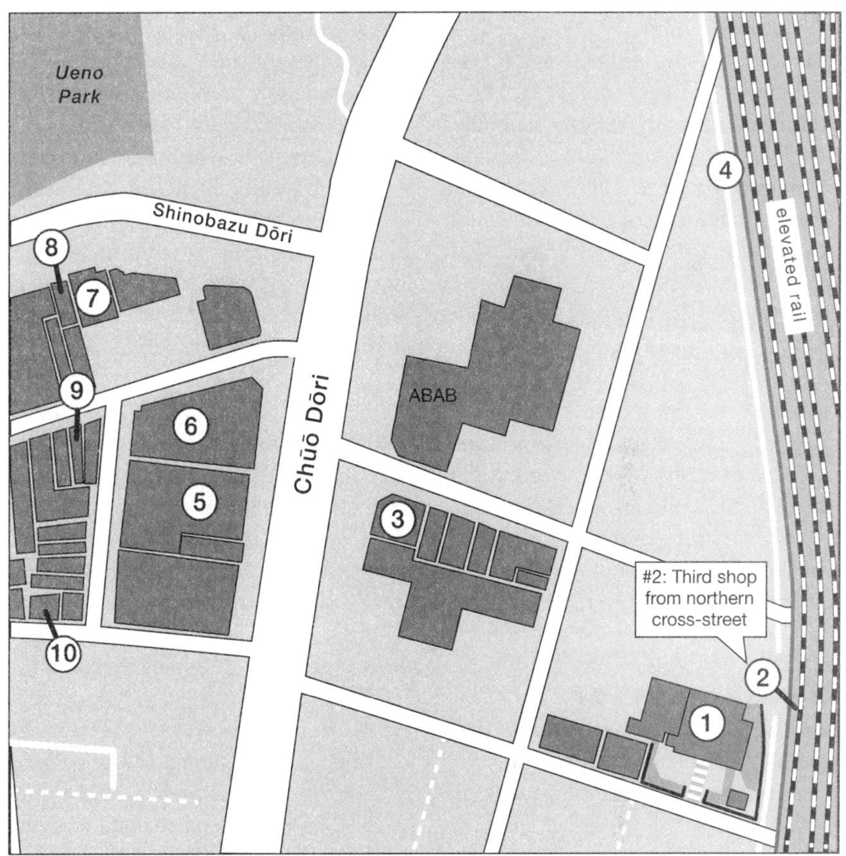

was shōgun, which means between 1716 and 1745. While there are branches in other parts of Japan, this is the main restaurant, which was remodeled in 1984. I first discovered this place when my friend Ono-san asked if I would like unagi for dinner. Now, we were in Asakusa when he asked, so I assumed he meant one of the many local places. A short subway ride and walk later, we were at Izuei. The staff graciously showed us to our table, one well-dressed Japanese gentleman and three very casually dressed Americans. You will find the food delicious. If you are on a budget I recommend the eel box, which is soup, unagi over rice, and Japanese pickles. It comes in three sizes depending on how much eel is included.

🌐 *http://www.izuei.co.jp/en/*

❽ Jūsanya 十三や

This shop has specialized in traditional handcrafted wooden combs since 1736. Making good combs is a task that takes great skill and requires wood that has been aged for years. There are various types of combs here, many of which are traditional designs developed when Japanese hairstyles were quite different than today's. The combs may be plain wood or lacquered with patterns. The shop name is a pun, as jū san means "thirteen" and the numbers nine "ku" and four "shi" together can be pronounced as kushi, which means comb. The shop is small and you may actually see the crafting of a comb while you are there. A good comb well treated will last for decades, even generations.

❾ Rengyokuan 蓮玉庵

Rengyokuan has been serving soba noodle dishes since 1859. The present location is the second one, as the restaurant moved from next to Shinobazu Pond after World War II. The building is the oldest one on the block, with an attractive wood and plaster front. This restaurant was popular with the intellectual and literary crowd in the Meiji period. Higuchi Ichiyō was one of the famous writers who ate here, and it is mentioned in Mori Ōgai's *The Wild Geese*.

🌐 *http://www.norenkai.net/en/portfolio-item/rengyokuan/*

❿ Musashino 武蔵野

This restaurant in business since 1948 bases much of its menu around variants of tonkatsu, a deep-fried cutlet usually made with pork. They also have some seafood and seasonal items. The restaurant is on the second floor of the building. Seating is Western style, servings are generous and inexpensive, and the place is 100% non-smoking.

🌐 *https://tonkatsu-musashino.tokyo*

⓫ Morita Jihei Shōten 守田治兵衛商店

The oldest patent medicine shop in Tokyo, operating since 1680. They were successful in incorporating Western medicine into their formulas from early on. In the Meiji period the company was exporting to China and the United States and became a pioneer in advertising both in newspapers and with posters throughout Japan. The company even published a magazine, *Hōtan Zasshi*, in the Meiji period, and the narrator in Kafū's *A Strange Tale from East of the River* buys some old issues at a used bookshop. The company was well enough known that their intestinal medicine Hōtan is mentioned in Natsume Sōseki's *I Am a Cat* and Mori Ōgai's *Wild Geese*. Hōtan is still one of their major products, so famous that the shop is sometimes called Morita Hōtan (守田宝丹).

🌐 *http://moritahoutan.jp*

⓬ Dōmyō 道明
This company founded in 1652 produces products using the kumihimo style of braiding. Kumihimo has a long history and is used in a variety of ways. It involves interlacing several colors of threads to produce items such as cords of varying thickness depending on the intended use. The process takes time, but the resulting product is one that will be recognized by anyone who has an interest in traditional Japanese crafts, as such braided cords are often used to make other items. This shop has employed the technique to make many contemporary products including bracelets, broaches, earrings, and various types of ties.
🌐 *http://domyo.co.jp/en/about/*

⓭ Takokyū 多古久
Established in 1904, this is a humble neighborhood haunt famous for their oden and seafood. This place is perfect for night owls, especially when the weather turns chilly. You can't go wrong with warm oden and a cold beer or sake. Just look for the tile and wood facade with the noren out to indicate that they are open.

DETAIL 2

❶ Mataro Dolls / Mataro Ningyō 真多呂人形
Established in 1919, Mataro Dolls makes exquisitely crafted kimekomi dolls for occasions such as Girl's Day and Boy's Day, and for general display on various themes. Some of the design themes include Heian period costumes, warriors, geisha, miniature armor sets, nō performers, and kabuki actors. They also sell tiered displays for Hina Matsuri doll sets. The company has a staff who can handle each of the stages of crafting such dolls, from the making of molds to the paint and textiles. The owner is certified by Kamigamo Shrine in Kyoto, where kimekomi doll making began.
🌐 *https://www.mataro-doll.com/en/*
🌐 *http://www.mataro.co.jp*

❷ Ponta Honke ぽん多本家
This restaurant has been operating since 1905 and claims to have invented tonkatsu, which is possible since that dish did originate in this area. The founder was a chef for the imperial household who specialized in Western cooking. There is both tatami and chair seating. They have an English menu, are 100% non-smoking, and accept credit cards. The restaurant is very accessible; it is barrier free and has an elevator. The menu is limited to only a few items, and the food is more

expensive than most other tonkatsu restaurants in the area.

❸ Hōraiya 蓬莱屋

Established in 1912, this was the first restaurant to use pork filets in making the popular dish tonkatsu. The famous director Ozu Yasujirō was a regular customer—the restaurant would even make deliveries to the film studio for him. Their menu is small, only four items, perhaps the ultimate of which is called Tokyo Monogatari Zen. It is named after Ozu's famous movie known in English as *Tokyo Story*. The building is postwar but old-fashioned, with chair seating at a counter and traditional seating in a tatami room.

🌐 *http://www.ueno-horaiya.com/egindex.html*

DETAIL 3

❶ Shitamachi Museum / Shitamachi Fūzoku Shiryōkan 下町風俗資料館

This museum opened in 1980 and is devoted to the commoner's "low city" as it was found in the Taitō Ward of the 19th- to mid-20th-century. The first floor has life-sized reproductions of the tenement houses, small shops, and businesses common in that period. This museum was the first in Japan to have such reproductions. You can even take your shoes off and enter several of them. The second floor contains photo displays and artifacts from daily life. One display of special note is a table of traditional toys that you can play with. Many of these toys I played with as a child growing up in California, as they were readily available in corner stores at that time. The exhibits and toys are changed seasonally. The gift shop sells books, some in English, published by the museum.

🌐 *http://www.taitocity.net/zaidan/shitamachi/*

❷ Ueno Yabu Soba 上野藪そば

A simple, long-respected soba restaurant in operation since 1892. This is a good choice for refueling with soba or tempura. The building has a traditional brick facade with a large lantern suspended at the corner.

❸ Saigō Takamori Bronze Statue / Saigō Takamori Dōzō 西郷隆盛銅像

Saigō was the commander of the Imperial Army when it marched on and took control of the city of Edo in 1868, causing the former shōgun Tokugawa Yoshinobu agreed to leave. He was also in charge of the troops during the Battle of Ueno. After serving for some time in the new government, he resigned in protest over policies and returned to his native Satsuma. In 1877 he found himself at the head of a rebellion: the leader of some 40,000 young men dissatisfied with the current regime. After nine months he was wounded in battle and chose to commit seppuku rather than be captured. Even so, he was still a hero to many for his struggles against the shōgun, and in 1898 the government had this statue by Takamura Kōun placed in the park. After the Great Kantō Earthquake the statue was covered in messages from those attempting to contact loved ones they had been separated from.

❹ Tomb of Shōgitai Warriors / Shōgitai no Haka 彰義隊の墓

While Edo was surrendered peacefully to the Imperial Army in 1868, not everything went smoothly. The Shōgitai, a group of about 2,000 samurai loyal to the Tokugawa, acted as a volunteer police force during the transition of power. In March 1868 Kaneiji became the headquarters for the Shōgitai. They came into conflict with the Imperial Army, which resulted in the Battle of Ueno. The bodies of the dead were left to rot in the ruins of the temple grounds. The priests gathered up the corpses and cremated them, sending most of the ashes to a temple north of Ueno. The rest of the ashes were buried where the bodies were burned. One of the surviving members of the Shōgitai,

UENO DETAIL 3

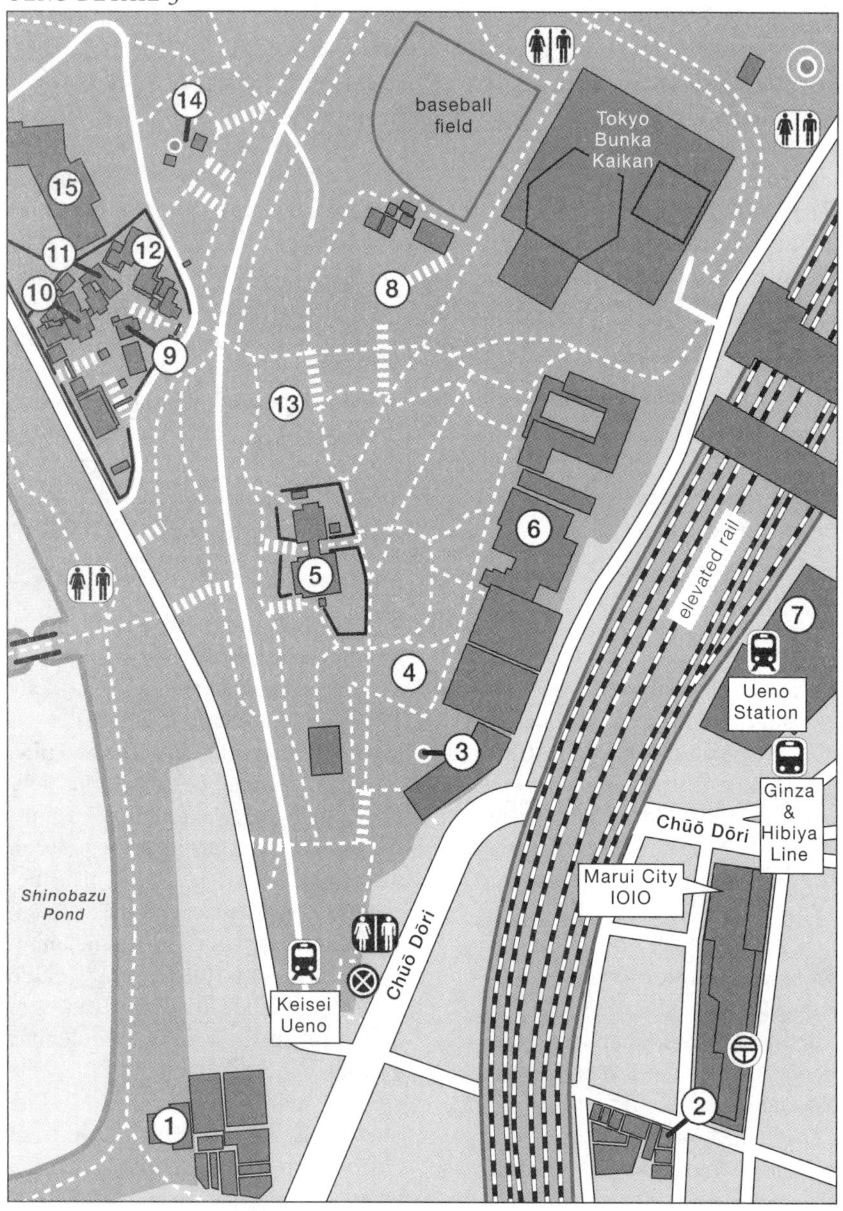

with support of other survivors, petitioned to be allowed to place a memorial marker on the site. This request was granted six years later. His family tended the plot until 2003 when the Tokyo government took over the task.

❺ Kiyomizu Kannondō 清水観音堂

This is a Tendai Buddhist temple built in 1631 under the supervision of the priest Tenkai. Originally built on Suribachiyama, it was moved to the present location in 1694. The building survived the Battle of Ueno, the Great Kantō Earthquake, and the firebombings of World War II, making it one of the oldest temple buildings in Tokyo. A multiyear restoration of the building was completed in 1996. Kiyomizu houses a Senju Kannon statue donated by the famous Otowasan Kiyomizudera of Kyoto. The statue is a hidden image and is only shown to the public on the first horse day of February. This temple mirrors the Kyoto Kiyomizudera in several ways, particularly its stage over the steep slope overlooking Shinobazu Pond. There is also an image of the Kosodate Kannon to the side of the altar, which people pray to for children. If the prayers are successful, they then offer dolls in thanks. This temple is part of the 33 Kannon Pilgrimage of Tokyo. Each September 25 the Ningyō Kuyō, a memorial service in which the offered dolls are burned, is held. On the seventeenth of each month there is a recitation of the Kannon Sutra at 10:00 a.m.

While the entrance is on the south side, you can approach from the west and southeast.

🌐 *http://kiyomizu.kaneiji.jp/english*

❻ Ueno Royal Museum / Ueno no Mori Bijutsukan 上野の森美術館

This is a private museum that has been run by the Japan Art Association since 1972. There are no permanent exhibits—instead the museum hosts a variety of shows each year. For this reason, there are often times when the museum is closed between exhibits.

🌐 *http://ueno-mori.org*

❼ Ueno Station / Ueno Eki 上野駅

Ueno Station was the terminus for trains to and from the north until the tracks were extended southward. Today it is still a major station on the Yamanote Line as well as the JR Akita Shinkansen, Hokkaido Shinkansen, Hokuriku Shinkansen, Joban Line, Jōetsu Shinkansen, Keihin-Tōhoku Line, Takasaki Line, Tōhoku Shinkansen, Utsunomiya Line (Tōhoku Main Line), and the Yamagata Shinkansen.

After the destruction of World War II, there were an estimated 5,000 refugees sleeping in the station at night. This situation continued for some time and probably helped shape local attitudes to the homeless. These days you don't see many homeless thanks to aggressive government programs to get them into housing. When you do see them, you may be surprised how tolerant the Japanese are, even often allowing them to set up shelters in parks, something that is rarely seen these days.

❽ Suribachiyama 摺鉢山
An ancient Yayoi period burial mound now covered with trees. The name is used for several such mounds in the Tokyo area and means "Mortar Mountain." This one is believed to date from the 5th century and was one of the earlier locations for Gojō Tenshinsha. It was also the first location for Kiyomizu Kannondō from 1631 to 1694. That was not the end of possible religious uses of the site, as in the Meiji period there was a movement to build a Christian church on the site that did not come to fruition. The top of the mound has benches and is a nice place to take a break.

❾ Ana Inarisha 穴稲荷社
Located next to Hanazono Inari Jinja, this small Inari shrine is easy to overlook. Ana 穴 in this case means a hole or opening. From the base of the stairs to Hanazono Inari, marked by the red torii gate, simply turn and walk in the opposite direction to find this small shrine. Keep an eye out for a gate to a narrow, dark passage to your left, and enter if the gate is unlocked. At the end you will turn left to find a delightful shrine built into the hillside. I first found this shrine out of sheer chance and curiosity.

❿ Gojō Tenjinsha 五條天神社
The present building dates from 1928. This shrine was originally on Ueno hill before the temple complex was built. It was relocated to the nearby Hirokōji neighborhood, then shifted to another location in that neighborhood to make way for the railroad line, and finally moved here. As kami of medicine and learning are enshrined here, Gojō Tenjinsha is associated with medicine and academic success. One can buy charms for health or good exam results. On the tenth of every month special rites are performed. The shrine festival is held every May 25.

⓫ Hanazono Inari Jinja
花園稲荷神社
If you are on the major pathway of the park, with its grand cherry trees, you can identify this shrine by a row of red torii along a set of stairs going down toward the west. Warning: Tall folks may have to duck. When you reach the bottom of the stairs, Hanazono Inari is immediately to your right. This shrine is popular with those praying for matchmaking and fertility. Go ahead and check the ema for prayers in English—you may even spot some with artwork. The date of founding is not known; the present building dates from 1928.

⓬ Inshōtei 韻松亭

Inshōtei is kaiseki ryōri (traditional multicourse meal) restaurant, in operation since 1875. A meal here could easily cost $100 per person, cash only. Even if you are on a budget and don't plan to drop that much on dinner, you can still enjoy the attractive exterior of this restaurant, with its large cherry tree out front and slip bamboo fencing. The building dates from the establishment of Ueno Park, when the government encouraged the creation of a restaurant in this location as part of the facilities. Seating is both traditional and Western style.

🌐 *http://www.innsyoutei.jp*

⓭ Ueno Park / Ueno Kōen 上野公園

The area that is now Ueno Park was once the site of three daimyō residences. The priest Tenkai, who advised the first three Tokugawa shōguns, wanted to build temples in the area. In 1622 the land was turned over to him and he established the shrines and temples, which still exist in the park today. Tenkai also had the famous cherry trees planted that make this a popular flower viewing destination. In the fall the ginkgo and maple leaves change color. The Battle of Ueno between samurai loyal to the Tokugawa family and imperial forces took place here on July 4, 1868. Many of the temples were destroyed in this battle, which involved artillery pieces set up on the other side of Shinobazu pond. After the Meiji Restoration, the 300 acres of temple land were confiscated by the government and in 1873 became a park, which in 1924 was given to the city in celebration of the marriage of Crown Prince Hirohito. Ueno Park today has the highest concentration of major museums in Japan. Another less famous battle was fought between the police and danshō (cross-dressing male prostitutes) on November 22, 1948. This one was well documented by reporters, since it started during a press tour given by the superintendent of police to show off the success they were having in cleaning up the park. While today there are gay bars in the area, the days of the danshō are long gone. However you may see various street entertainers as you wander through the park, especially in the area near the kōban.

🌐 *http://ueno-bunka.jp/en/*

⓮ Ueno Daibutsu 上野大仏

While Nara and Kamakura have famous giant seated Buddha statues, Edo/Tokyo also had its own daibutsu in Ueno Park. During the Great Kantō Earthquake the head of the statue fell off, and during World War II almost all of the statue was confiscated by the military and melted down for munitions. All that now remains is the face, which was mounted on a small hill in 1972 along with a small pagoda.

▲ Formerly a black market, Ameya Yokochō draws crowds seven days a week.

▼ Shinobazu Pond with views of the Bentendō and apartments beyond.

▲ All that is left of the Ueno Daibutsu, the rest used to make weapons in World War II.

▲ The Hyōkeikan at the National Museum seen during a January snowfall.

▲ A kōban designed by Kurokawa Tetsuro's; ask for directions here if you are lost.

▲ Easy to spot from the sakura-lined main road, these torii lead to Hanazono Inari Jinja.

⓯ Ueno Seiyōken 上野精養軒

The original Seiyōken was a hotel catering to non-Japanese that was established in the foreign settlement at Tsukiji in 1872. When the Ueno Seiyōken restaurant opened in 1876, it was one of the first restaurants serving Western cuisine in Japan. It is known for several dishes that combine Western and Japanese elements, including its hayashi rice and beef stew with lotus root. The multistory building itself is of recent construction and not terribly impressive on the outside. The dining areas are spacious, and there are terraces with great views over the park and Shinobazu Pond. There are also special halls for banquets, wedding receptions, and Buddhist memorial services. There are other branches, including one near Ueno Station.

🌐 *http://www.seiyoken.co.jp*

🌐 *http://www.norenkai.net/en/portfolio-item/ueno-seiyoken/*

DETAIL 4

❶ Shinobazu Pond / Shinobazu no Ike 不忍池

A large natural pond famous for the lotus plants that fill part of it and the Bentendō in the middle. During World War II the pond was drained and turned into fields to grow crops. The pond is divided into three parts by walkways. There are lotus plants in the south, boating in the west, and a cormorant rookery, considered a part of Ueno Zoo, in the north. Recently a deck extending into the lotus field was added. This is a good place to take photos of the surrounding area. The lotus are usually in bloom from mid-July to mid-August. The pond is also popular with birders, who set up tripods with cameras outfitted with telephoto lenses.

From mid-July or early August, the Ueno Summer Festival is held at the area on the south edge of the pond.

❷ Shinobazu no Ike Bentendō 不忍池弁天堂

This temple to Benten was built in the early 17th century on the island in Shinobazu Pond. It was designed by the priest Tenkai to be symbolic of the Benzaiten shrine of Chikubushima island on Lake Biwa. Originally one needed to be ferried out to the island; it is now accessible via causeways. The original temple was destroyed in World War II and rebuilt in 1958 preserving the original style. The Bentendō was a common subject for ukiyo-e prints and today is popular with photographers. There are several memorial monuments and sub-shrines. Some of the memorial stones are dedicated to animals killed for restaurants: chickens (the torizuka), turtles, fugu, and fish and shellfish in general. Throughout the island you will see the lotus as a motif on lanterns and other objects.

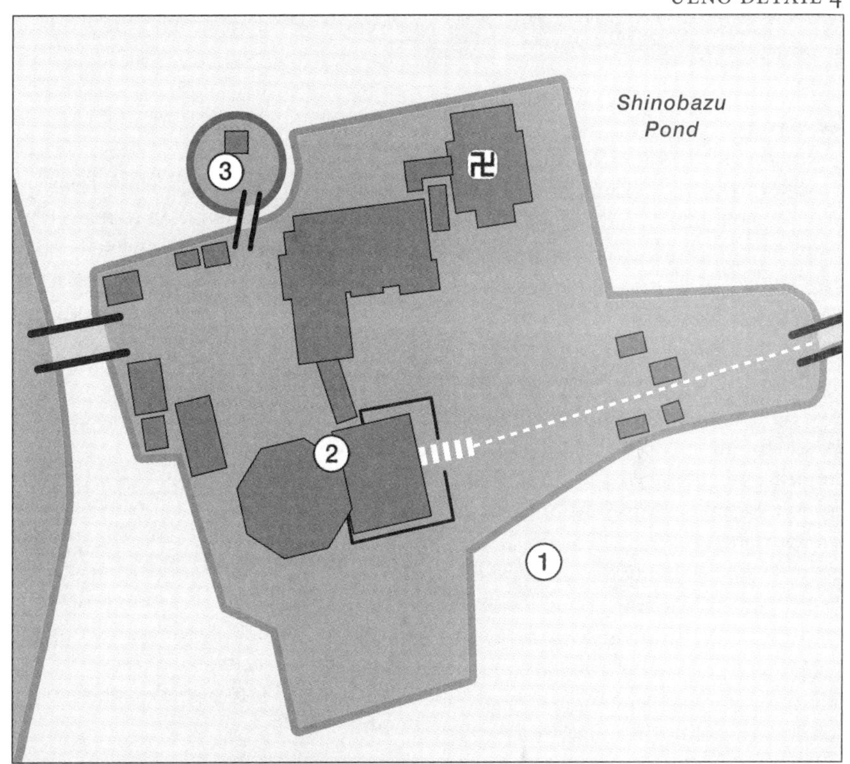

❸ Shōten Isle / Shōtenjima 聖天島
Behind the Shinobazu no Ike Bentendō is Shōten Isle, connected to the island that houses the Bentendō with a bridge. The Shōten Isle has a small Shōten shrine, some sacred carvings, and a phallic stone. One side of this phallus has a figure carved into it; however, it is usually visible only from a distance when standing inside the zoo. While the stone is old, the carving dates from the Meiji period. It was likely an attempt to prevent the phallus from being destroyed in one of the government's crusades of morality when religious depictions of sexual imagery were banned. The carving is commonly referred to as Hige Jizō (Bearded Jizō), but in 1922 Shizume Tōsen identified it as a carving of En no Gyōja and it is similar to other carvings of him. The island is fenced off and the gate is usually locked unless there is a special holiday. Once around the New Year, I was able to get on the island along with a group of women who had come to pray at the shrine.

DETAIL 5

❶ **Eiyo Gongen** 栄誉権現

A tiny shrine inside the Tōshōgū shrine complex. This tanuki guards the area, and prayers are offered for good luck and passing exams. You can purchase ema that depict chrysanthemums and tanuki wearing purple priest robes.

❷ **Ueno Tōshōgū** 上野東照宮

Founded in 1627, this shrine was moved and rebuilt at the present site in 1651. Significant restoration work to these original buildings was finished in 2013. It was originally founded to honor the first Tokugawa shōgun Tokugawa Ieyasu and enshrine him as Tōshō Daigongen. Presently three Tokugawa shōguns are enshrined here: Ieyasu, Iemitsu (the third shōgun), and Yoshinobu (the last shōgun). The shrine is in an ornate one, dense with paintings from the Kano school, carvings, lacquer, and gilding. The grounds contain nearly 200 lanterns donated by various daimyō around Japan, fifty of which are copper. The beautiful Karamon with its famous carvings of two dragons has a legend attached to it that the dragons would leave at night to go drink in Shinobazu Pond. To the left of the entrance is the Obakedōrō, a stone lantern so large that it gained this nickname that means "monster lantern." The shrine is also famous for its peony garden, which is popular with flower lovers. As you look around the grounds of the shrine you will also see peony patterns repeated here and there. This shrine is popular for prayers for family and safety on the road.

Festivals include: Ueno Tōshōgū Taisai, April 17; and Botan Matsuri (Peony Festival), mid-April through mid-May. The garden also has some forty varieties of winter blooming peony.

🌐 *https://www.uenotoshogu.com/en/*

❸ **Gojū no tō** 五重塔

A five-story pagoda built in 1639 as part of the temple complex at Kan'eiji. Given to the city of Tokyo in 1958, it is actually in the grounds of the Ueno Zoo. You can also get a good view of it from Tōshōgū Shrine. The design is unusual as each tier is in a Japanese style; the usual pattern is to have the top tier in a Chinese style.

❹ **Ueno Zoo / Ueno Dōbutsuen** 上野動物園

Ueno Zoo was founded 1882 as Japan's first Western-style zoo. Over time it has grown to cover some thirty-five acres including part of Shinobazu Pond. The zoo is divided into two parts, as a road runs through it. One can take a pedestrian bridge to get between the two sections. Since 1972 the superstars of the zoo, placed near the entrance, have been the giant pandas. The zoo has a wonderful exhibit of nocturnal animals. Once I was standing there when

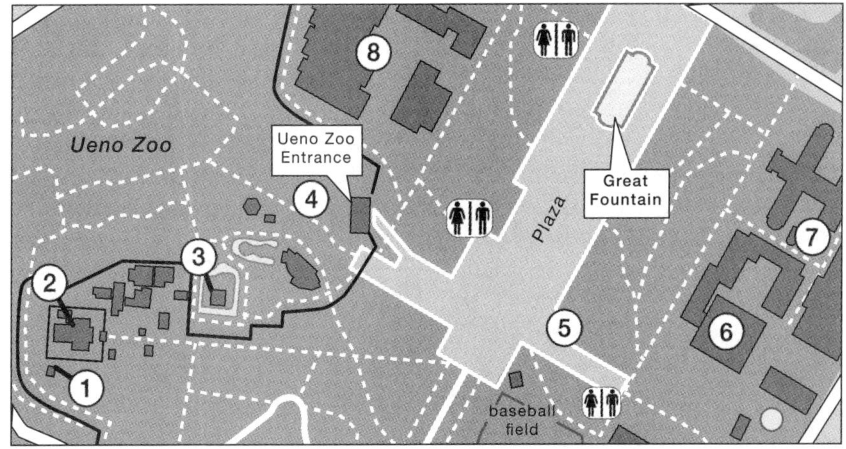

a group of preschoolers in their yellow caps came through, and as they passed the aye-ayes they suddenly began to sing a song about them.

🌐 *https://www.tokyo-zoo.net/english/ueno/index.html*

❺ Ueno Keisatsusho Dōbutsuen mae Kōban 上野警察署動物園前交番

One landmark of Ueno Park is the kōban, not far from the Ueno Zoo entrance, that was designed by Kurokawa Tetsuro and built in 1990. The four inverted and elongated pyramid units above it make this two-story metal structure unusual among kōban. Need directions? Just ask here.

❻ National Museum of Western Art / Kokuritsu Seiyō Bijutsukan 国立西洋美術館

If you are like me, your first thought may have been, "Why would I want to look at Western art on a trip to Japan?" Well, there are certain things one can only see here. The core collection of the museum belonged to Matsukata Kojirō, who bought the works in France. After World War II the French government declared them French property and confiscated them; in 1959 France gave them to Japan. The building that houses the collection was appropriately designed by Le Corbusier, with a new wing in 1979 by Maekawa Kunio. From that core group of some 400 items, the collection has been added to over time. Some of the works are actually outside the museum, such as Rodin's *The Thinker* and *The Gates of Hell*. Labeling is in Japanese and English. The museum often has excellent temporary exhibits loaned from other institutions.

🌐 *https://www.nmwa.go.jp/en/*

❼ National Museum of Nature and Science / Kokuritsu Kagaku Hakubutsukan 国立科学博物館

Originally opened in 1877, the building was damaged in the Great Kantō Earthquake and rebuilt in 1931. Further renovations occurred in 2007. This museum is a major research institution participating in research not only in Japan but all over the world. The original building has six floors, three of which are underground. There are areas on all six floors devoted to different parts of the world, and on three floors exhibits specifically on Japan. Be sure to visit the large modern exhibit space behind the older building—it is all too easy to miss that second structure. The museum shop sells a guidebook to the collections. I highly recommend that you stop here if you have any interest in natural sciences or archaeology, or if you just need to get out of the rain.

🌐 *http://www.kahaku.go.jp/english/*

NOTE: *If you are over 65, show your ID at the ticket counter for free admission.*

❽ Tokyo Metropolitan Art Museum / Tōkyō To Bijutsukan 東京都美術館

Originally founded in 1926 as the Tokyo Prefectural Art Museum, in 1943 the museum was given the present name. The current building dates from 1975 and is designed by Okada Shinichiro. The new building was constructed adjacent to the old building so the museum could still operate during construction. In 2012 the museum reopened after two further years of work on the building. The old site is now a garden. There are four floors with galleries on each, two restaurants plus a cafe, a breastfeeding room, a lounge to relax in, and a library. Exhibits are international in scope and occasionally highlight young upcoming artists.

🌐 *https://www.tobikan.jp/en/*

DETAIL 6

❶ Sōgakudō Concert Hall of the Former Tokyo Music School / Kyū Tōkyō Ongaku Gakkō Sōgakudō 旧東京音楽学校奏楽堂

The oldest concert hall in Japan, in use since 1890. In the early 1970s it was going to be torn down and replaced with a modern building. A movement of locals and Tokyo University of the Arts alumni were able to stop the demolition. It is now maintained by the Taitō Ward government, which had it moved to Ueno Park. There is another modern hall with the same name on the grounds of the Tokyo University of the Arts.

🌐 *http://www.taitocity.net/zaidan/sougakudou/*

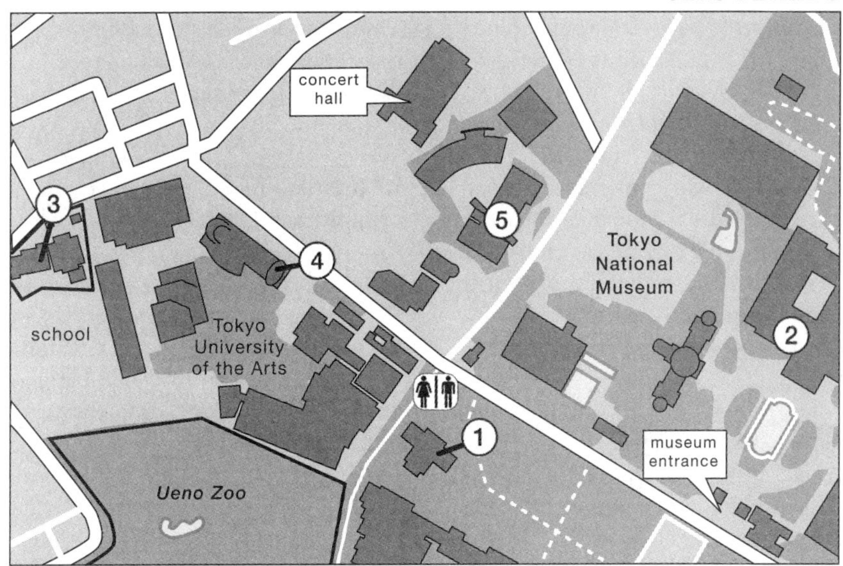

❷ Tokyo National Museum / Tokyo Kokuritsu Hakubutsukan
東京国立博物館

This museum consists of several buildings and includes the largest collection of Japanese art in the world, as well as art from other Asian countries. It also has an extensive collection of Japanese archaeological artifacts. Josiah Condor designed the original main hall, the Honkan (本館), which opened in 1881. The Honkan was damaged in the Great Kantō Earthquake and replaced by the present structure designed by Watanabe Jin, which opened in 1938. The central Honkan houses Japanese art from the Jōmon period to recent times and the museum store. It consists of twenty-four rooms in two stories. To the right of the entrance is the Tōyōkan (東洋館), which has five floors of Asian art. Opened in 1968, its long frontage gives the impression of it being a shorter building than it is. To the left of the entrance to the grounds is the Hyōkeikan (表慶館), which opened in 1908 to commemorate the wedding of the crown prince in 1900. Beyond it, the Hōryūji Hōmotsukan (法隆寺宝物館) houses treasures from Nara's famous temple given to the imperial household in 1878. This 1999 structure designed by Yoshio Taniguchi is one of the most modern and minimalist buildings in Ueno Park, with a simple pond and a square canopy in front of the entrance. Next to it is the Shiryōkan (資料館), the Research and Information Center, which is mainly for scholars researching the document collection. Further on and to left of the Honkan, connected to it by a passageway, is the Heiseikan (平成館), which contains the archaeological gallery plus four special exhibit galleries. It was constructed to commemorate the wedding of the crown prince in 1993. Behind the Honkan are several buildings that are part of the museum and the garden.

🌐 *http://www.tnm.jp/?lang=en*

❸ Gokokuin 護国院

This temple was founded in the 17th century. The main building dates from 1722. The main statue of the Buddha is hidden behind a statue of Daikoku, who is also enshrined here, so Gokokuin is on the Shichifukujin tour for the area. The third day of each month is a special day for prayers with a Tendai goma fire ritual performed around 2:00 p.m.

❹ The University Art Museum, Tokyo University of the Arts / Tokyo Geijutsu Daigaku, Daigaku Bijutsukan 東京藝術大学 大学美術館

Ueno Park is not the only place in this area with art museums. The Tokyo University of the Arts has its own collection housed in a new facility that opened in 1999. Included in the collection are student works dating back to the founding of the school. Besides the main building, there are the Chinretsukan Gallery, Masaki Memorial Gallery, and the Toride Annex.

🌐 *https://www.geidai.ac.jp/museum/*

❺ International Library of Children's Literature / Kokusai Kodomo Toshokan 国際子ども図書館

Built in 1906 as the Imperial Library, in 1949 it became the Ueno Library. Starting in 1998 the present building was reworked by Andō Tadao. The most visible changes seen from the outside are the modern entrance hall encased in glass, a cafeteria of similar design directly opposite the building, and a third-floor extension above the garden that is also encased in glass. In 2000 it reopened under its present name as a branch of the National Diet Library, with a collection of over 500,000 books. As is most appropriate for such a library, there are diaper changing rooms and a nursing room. Adults are welcome in the Children's Library. The fountain at the library has a bas-relief of Koizumi Yakumo, who is better known in the West as Lafcadio Hearn.

🌐 *http://www.kodomo.go.jp/english/*

DETAIL 7

❶ Kaneiji 寛永寺

A Tendai Buddhist temple established in 1625 by the order of the shōgun

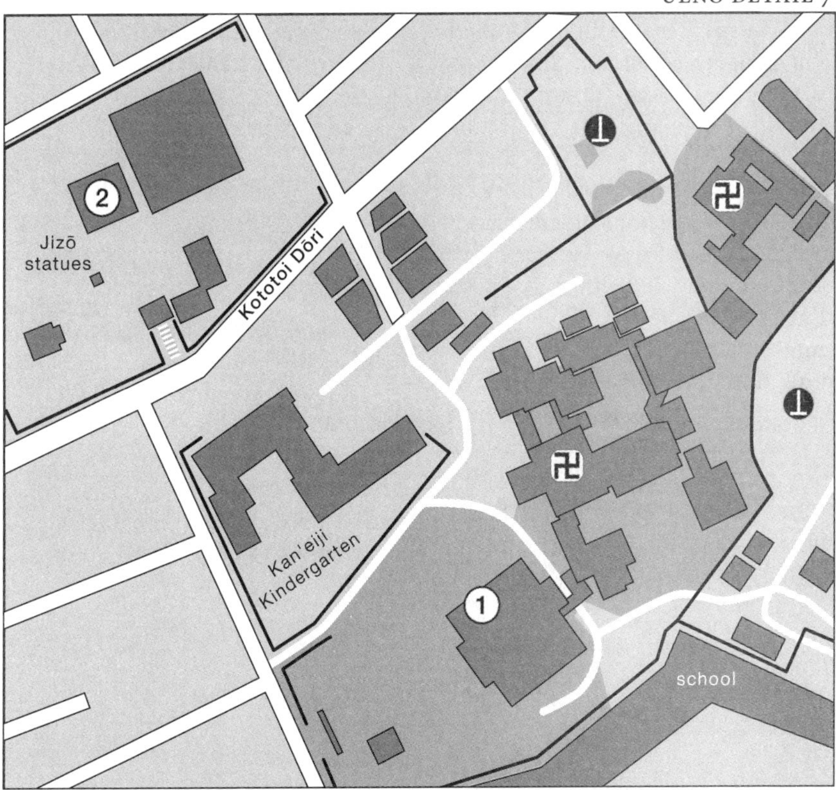

Tokugawa Hidetada. This temple is also officially known as Tōeizan Kaneiji. Kaneiji became one of the official family temples of the Tokugawa shōguns. The original temple was part of one of the largest religious complexes in Edo. The complex was mostly destroyed in the Battle of Ueno. The present Kaneiji, much smaller than the original and once a sub-temple in the original complex, is located in the area north of the National Museum. It houses the original temple's image of Yakushi Buddha. Six of the Tokugawa shōguns are buried here in a private cemetery viewable from the street. In the Edo period the city had nine bells that would toll at six in the morning and six in the evening; one of them was the bell at Kaneiji.

The entrance is to the southwest., but you can also enter from the southeast or northwest.

❷ Jōmyōin 浄名院

This Tendai Buddhist temple was founded in 1666. Sometimes the name is romanized as Jyōmyōin. The grounds contain thousands of stone Jizō statues, part of a project started in 1850. More are added regularly. The temple has set a goal of 84,000 statues, as this is a symbolic number in Buddhism. A tradition speaks of 84,000 different teachings by the Buddha for various people based on their needs. There is a beautifully crafted large bronze Jizō dating from 1906 that is a memorial to the dead from the Russo-Japanese War. Early in Tran Anh Hung's film *Norwegian Wood* there is a scene that was filmed among the stone Jizō here.

Each August there is a hechima memorial service where prayers are offered for relief from coughs and asthma. The sap from hechima, known as loofa in the West, is an old treatment for coughs.

The entrance is to the south.

Kaneji Memorial

One interesting item on the grounds of this temple is the mushizuka, a memorial mound for insects killed in the production of the *Chūchijō*, a famous book of realistic insect illustrations that is in the National Museum. The mound has a large boulder surrounded by plants with the kanji 冢蟲 carved on it above an inscription.

谷根千

YANESEN

Yanesen is a name used to refer to the area consisting of Yanaka (谷中), Nezu (根津), and Sendagi (千駄木). This area is rich with over 110 temples and shrines that flourished during the Edo period. Owing to the difficulty in finding reliable information about these temples, I only cover a few, in some cases with very little detail. Many older structures can be found here, as most of the area managed to avoid burning down in the fires after the 1923 Great Kantō Earthquake and the firebombings of World War II. On the whole Yanesen is a delight, with its quiet streets, small shops, older buildings, shrines, and temples. On one trip I had a conversation with a local resident about the bullet holes, which date back to the Battle of Ueno in 1868, in one of the temple gates—he was surprised I knew what caused them. The area also has a long history of being popular with artists as a place to live, perhaps partly due to the close proximity of the Tokyo Fine Arts School and the Tokyo Music School, which later merged to form Tokyo University of the Arts.

You never know who you will run into here. My Tokyo friend Ono-san once told me about the traditional Japanese painter Allan West, who lives in Tokyo. A few years later Ono-san was showing me around Yanaka when we ran into Mr. West. He gave my friend an autograph using an antique portable ink and brush set called a yatate.

As for shops, I have tended to focus on the older ones, which are likely to still be here years from now. Mixed in with these are newer businesses, which I hope will be around for just as long. So stroll, peek inside stores,

YANESEN

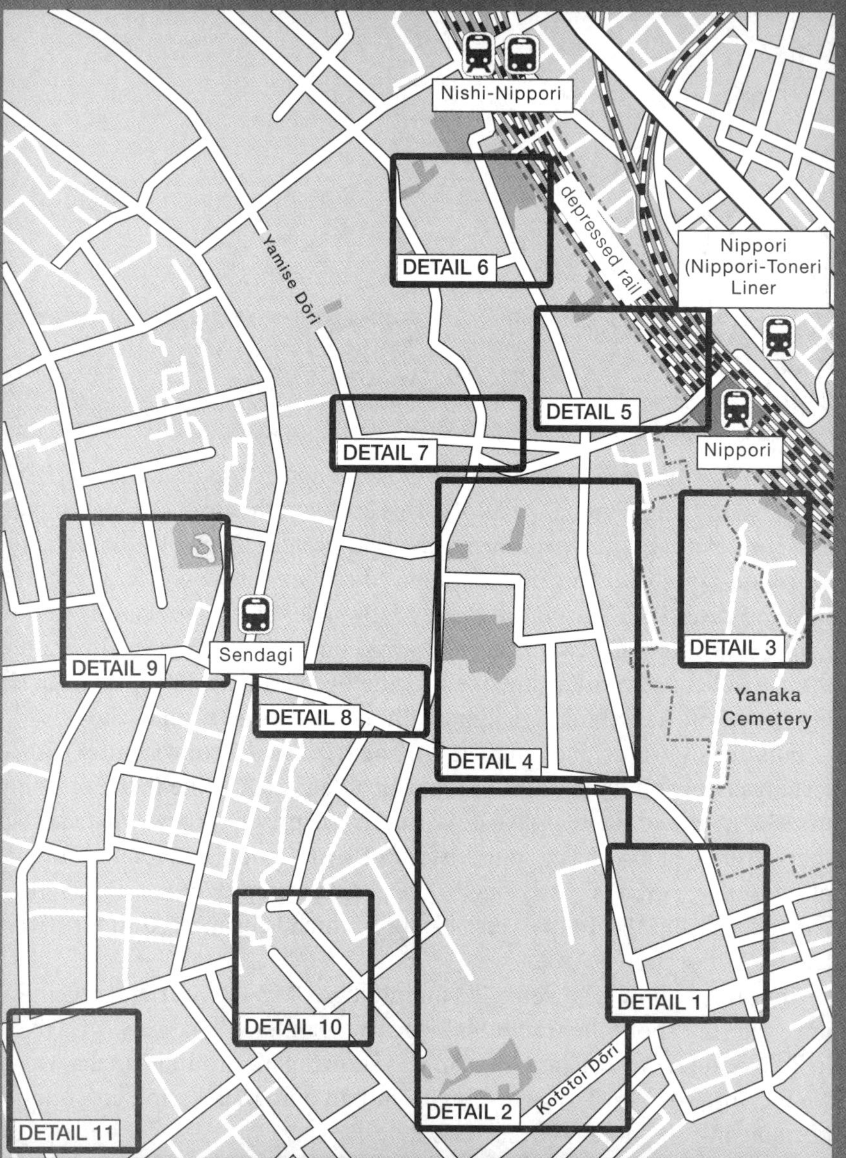

Nishi-Nippori
depressed rail
Nippori
(Nippori-Toneri
Liner
Yamise Dōri
DETAIL 6
DETAIL 5
DETAIL 7
Nippori
DETAIL 3
Yanaka
Cemetery
DETAIL 9
Sendagi
DETAIL 8
DETAIL 4
DETAIL 1
DETAIL 10
DETAIL 11
DETAIL 2
Kototoi Dōri

pet the neighborhood cats, and see what catches your fancy. For those interested in festivities, early each October the Yanaka Matsuri takes place.

DETAIL 1

❶ Kayaba Coffee カヤバ珈琲
This coffee shop is located in a tradesman's house built in 1916. The dashigeta zukuri style of this building is a rare these days. Kayaba Inosuke opened the cafe in 1938. When he passed away in 2008, a local non-profit organization and the SCAI The Bathhouse gallery worked together to refurbish the interior and reopen Kayaba Coffee in 2009, keeping the original name. The second floor is a tatami room. They serve the kind of inexpensive, simple fare, such as sandwiches and desserts, that one would expect to have found here in earlier decades.
🌐 *http://taireki.com/en/kayaba.html*

❷ Yoshidaya Former Liquor Store / Kyū Yoshidaya Saketen 旧吉田屋酒店
A liquor store originally built in 1910 with additional work in 1935. The upper story was employee housing. When the building was scheduled to be demolished in 1986, a local group lobbied to preserve it. It was then obtained by the Taitō Ward government. It was moved to the present location and became the Shitamachi Museum Annex in 1987.

❸ Daiōji 大雄寺
Also called Chō Shiyōzan Daiō, this Nichiren temple is known for its towering 300-year-old camphor tree. The gate, which is on the east side, is rather small and easy to miss. So if you plan to visit, keep an eye out for it.

❹ Daigyōji 大行寺
This is a Nichiren Buddhist temple that was built in 1588. The design of Nichiren temples is often rather simple, even plain. This one has an attractive gate and some nice details in the carving on the temple building. There is a cherry tree near the main building, which adds to the beauty of the grounds in the spring.

❺ Ichijōji 一乗寺
Established in 1617, Ichijōji is a Nichiren temple also referred to as Daihonzan Ichijōji. This temple is easy to spot from the street, with its black tiled roofs visible over the wall and attractive gate. The grave of the famous Confucian scholar Ota Kinjo (1765–1825) is on the grounds.

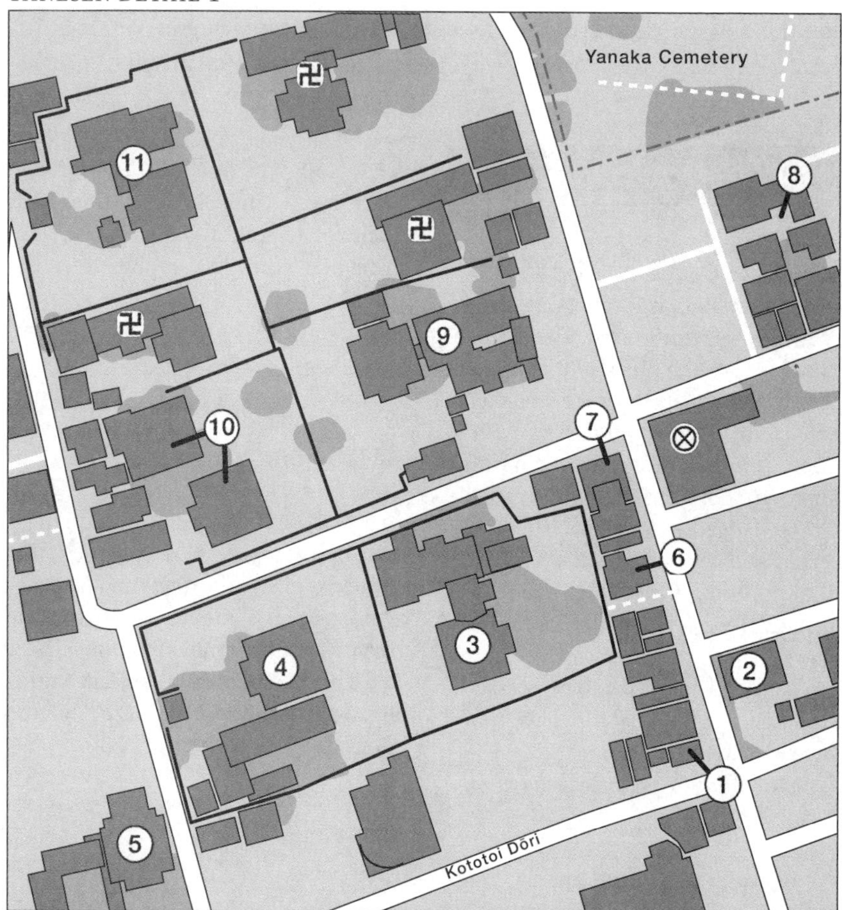

❻ Yanaka Okanoeisen
谷中岡埜栄泉

A sweet shop in business since 1900, located in an old two-story wooden building. Yanaka Okanoeisen is best known for its mame daifuku filled with sweet bean paste (an) and for its ukigusa, a small baked cake with a hint of ginger. All items are handcrafted in the shop. To reduce fire risk during World War II some buildings, such as this one, were dismantled to create firebreaks. The shop had to be rebuilt after the war. The signboard from the original building was stored at a local temple and so survived. They use an interesting wrapping paper printed with a map of Yanaka, an incentive to get a snack if I ever heard one.

🌐 *https://www.yanaka-okanoeisen.jp*

❼ SCAI The Bathhouse
スカイザバスハウス

The building is a former bathhouse, which existed for some 200 years after its founding in 1787. When the Kashiwayu bathhouse closed in 1991, the seventh master consulted a local group and the SCAI The Bathhouse gallery was established in 1993. The simple interior of the bathhouse was easily adapted to a gallery for contemporary art by Japanese and international artists. Besides exhibits here, the organization is involved in events and projects in other locations. One such project noted above is Kayaba Coffee.

🌐 *https://www.scaithebathhouse.com/en/*

❽ Ueno Sakuragi Atari
上野桜木あたり

This is a group of three old two-story houses from 1938 that have been converted into business spaces. It is an interesting place to relax and enjoy the mix of Western and traditional architecture often found in such buildings from the 1930s. The owners had considered converting the location into a parking lot. Instead they agreed to work with a local nonprofit to preserve the site and provide locations for small businesses and an event space. The events that are sometimes held here are quite varied, so you never quite know what you may find when you visit. The family has a long interest in tea ceremony, so events related to tea often take place.

🌐 *http://uenosakuragiatari.jp*

❾ Kanda Kannōji 神田感応寺

Established in 1596, this is a Nichiren temple. It is home to the grave of Shibue Chūsai, a physician and Confucian scholar who became famous through his 1916 biography written by Mori Ōgai.

❿ Jishōin Aizendō 自性院 愛染堂

This Shingon monastery was established in 1611 in Kanda and moved to Yanaka in 1648. It is known for its statue of Aizen Myōō, which is housed in a separate hall. The statue is said to contain inside of it a smaller statue of Aizen Myōō that the priest Kankai obtained during a pilgrimage to Mount Kōya. People pray here for luck in getting married and for household harmony.

⓫ Chōkyūin 長久院

This Shingon Buddhist temple was established in Kanda in 1611. It relocated here in 1658 after the Meireki Fire of 1657 as part of the redesign of the city. The temple is nicknamed Ajisai Dera, "Hydrangea Temple," due to the many hydrangea plants here. There is also a statue of Enma in the garden that dates from 1726; it is unusual for a statue of Enma to be outdoors. Look closely at the gate and you will see bullet holes from the Battle of Ueno.

DETAIL 2

❶ Rinkōji 臨江寺

This Rinzai Zen temple was established in 1630 and moved to this location in 1681. To your left after you enter the gate is a grouping of memorial stores that date from the Edo period. These stones do not mark graves, as commoners were forbidden to have gravestones, so at times memorials like these would be set up. The oldest is from 1673, but most are from the 18th century.

❷ Gyokurinji 玉林寺

This is a Sōtō Zen temple established in 1591. The grounds have plenty of trees including a large Himalayan cedar and a large chinquapin in the back. There is also a statue of Chiyonofuji, the 58th Yokozuna, which was added to the grounds in 2011.

❸ Daimyō Clock Museum / Daimyō Dokei Hakubutsukan 大名時計博物館

This one-room museum housing a private collection of old Japanese clocks opened in 1974. Don't expect something fancy, but if you are interested in timepieces, this humble museum can be very interesting. Traditionally the Japanese day was divided into twelve hours: six equal hours for daylight and six equal hours for night. This meant that as the day or night got longer or shorter, so did the hours. The mechanical clocks in the museum were made so they could be adjusted slightly to accommodate the changing lengths of the hours. If it is during operating hours but the museum is closed, you may need to call out "gomen kudasai!" to get someone to come out and open it for you.

❹ Enjuji Nichikadō 延寿寺日荷堂

This Nichiren Buddhist temple established in 1656 is related to Saint Nichika, a priest who is legendary for the strength of his legs. In 1772 a statue of him was relocated here from the main temple. People come here to pray for healing from leg troubles. You will see many old ema tablets with pictures of sandals, actual sandals, or writing on them left as offerings by worshipers. The tenth of every month is a special prayer day for such healing.

🌐 *http://nichika-do.jp/*

❺ Konreiji 金嶺寺

The grounds of this temple, built in Kanda in 1611 and relocated here in 1648, are rich in plant life. There is a

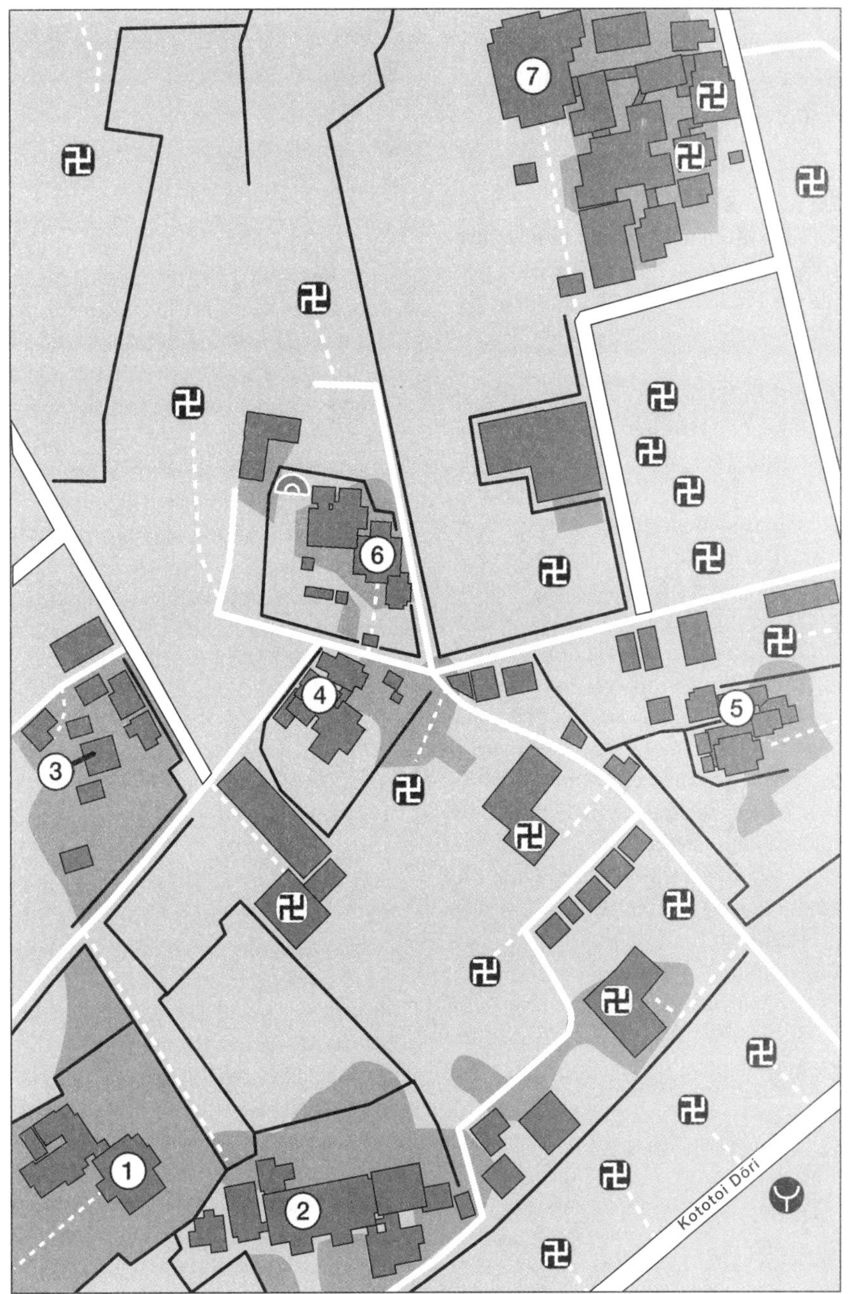
7
6
4
5
3
1
2
Kototoi Dōri

roofed blackboard near the entrance where wise messages are posted.

Access is at the east side.

❻ Rengeji 蓮華寺

This Nichiren temple built in 1630 has a striking red gate. For some reason people pray here for healing from worms.

❼ Zuirinji 瑞輪寺

Zuirinji is a Nichiren temple that was established in 1591. You will see the Tokugawa family crest on the building, as well as some impressive wood carvings. The founding priest was Nisshin, who had been the calligraphy teacher of the young Tokugawa Ieyasu. Ōkubo Monto, who pioneered Edo's sophisticated drinking water system in the 17th century, is buried here. His grave and those of other members of his family are in an enclosure near the rear of the bell tower. At one point Ōkubo gave Ieyasu some sweets that so impressed him Ōkubo's family were made the confectioners for the shōguns for several generations. For more on the water system I recommend visiting the Tokyo Waterworks Historical Museum in Bunkyō Ward, which is listed in the Hongō chapter.

DETAIL 3

❶ Tennōji Chūzaisho 天王寺駐在所

This police box located in Yanaka Cemetery is often referred to as a kōban, but it is actually a chūzaisho, a type of police box with a resident police officer and often a spouse. Chūzaisho in cities are rare—they are usually found in rural areas. When I first visited Yanaka cemetery I noticed a woman hanging laundry out on the second story balcony in the rear, which let me know this was not a typical kōban. There is a private entrance on the side street and a carport for a private vehicle. Given that this is not a populous area, having a chūzaisho rather than a kōban next to such a large cemetery makes sense.

❷ Yanaka Five-Storied Pagoda / Yanaka Gojūnotō 谷中五重塔

Tennōji had a famous pagoda that was the model for Kōda Rohan's famous story "The Five-Storied Pagoda," which is included in an English translation in the book *Pagoda, Skull & Samurai*. The pagoda was destroyed in 1957 when an adulterous couple committed double suicide by setting the pagoda on fire around themselves. Today the foundation stones are still visible in the cemetery near the police chūzaisho. Inside the office at the chūzaisho are photos of the pagoda. Plans for the original pagoda were later found and there is a movement to rebuild the structure.

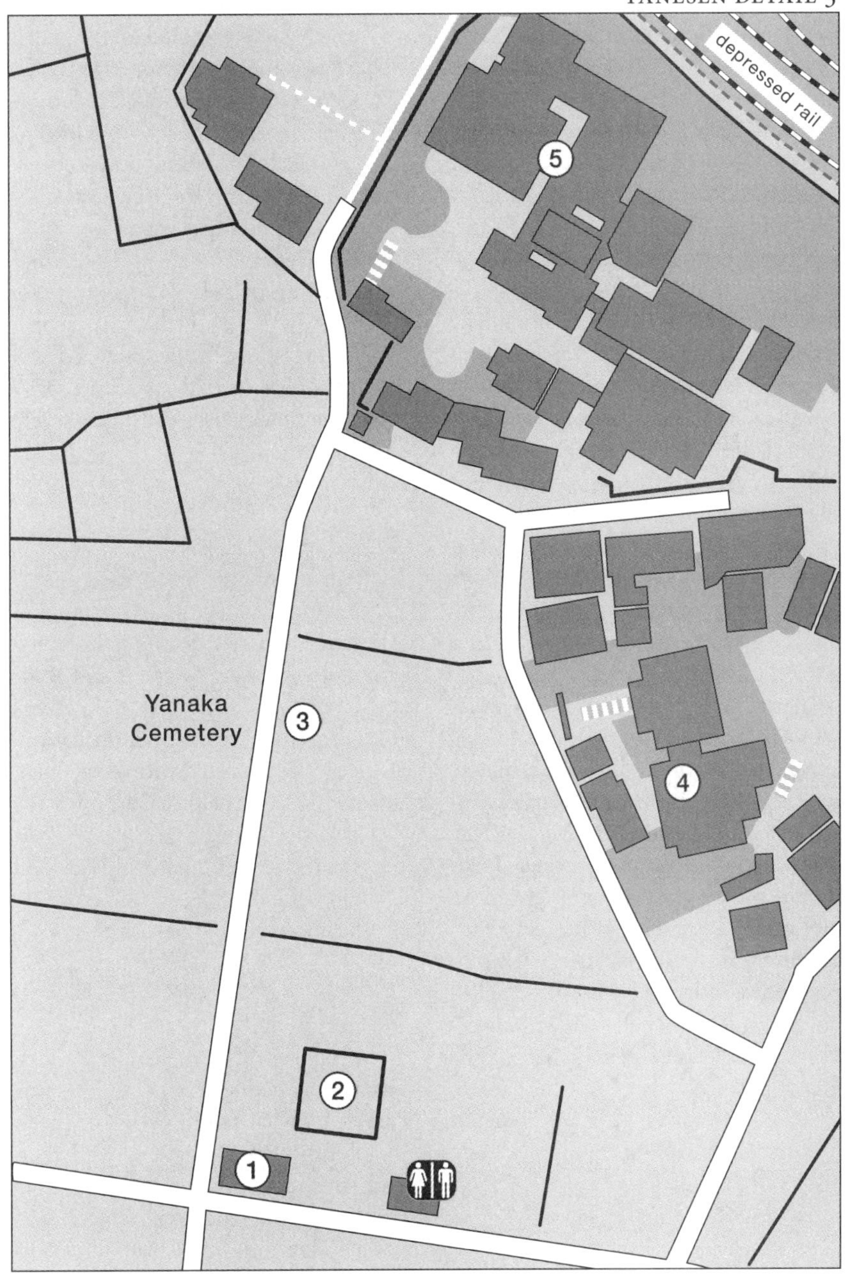
depressed rail
5
Yanaka
Cemetery
3
4
2
1

❸ Yanaka Cemetery / Yanaka Reien 谷中霊園

This is one of the oldest and largest cemeteries in Tokyo. The original name was Yanaka Bochi, "Yanaka Graveyard." In 1935 it was changed to the more pleasant Yanaka Reien "Yanaka Spirits Garden." This was the cemetery for Tennōji until 1874 when it was taken over by the government and made a public cemetery. Yanaka Cemetery is a relaxing place to wander through, with many paths to stroll. The grounds are rich with greenery, including large cherry trees, especially along the major avenue. As it is next door to the cemetery for Kaneiji, it seems a little larger than it is, since you can wander from one to the other without knowing where the border is. Such a pair of old and venerated cemeteries of course have the graves of many famous individuals and families. Among these are Enchi Fumikogai, Higuchi Ichiyō, Kikuchi Yōsai, Hasegawa Kazuo, Nikolai Kasatkin, Mori Ōgai, Natsume Sōseki, and Tokugawa Yoshinobu, whose grave is on a fenced-off plot of land. The chūzaisho has a map of famous graves in Japanese. The officers may not be able to speak English but will still try to help you with directions. In any case, the map makes for a nice souvenir.

🌐 *http://www.tokyo-park.or.jp/reien/park/index073.html*

Takahashi Oden

There is a memorial stone in Yanaka Cemetery to Takahashi Oden, a woman who in 1879 was one of the last people to be executed by decapitation in Japan. Inscribed on the stone is "I no longer wish to be part of this hapless world…." The stone was put up in 1881 with funds collected by writers, which makes sense given the number of fictionalized accounts of her story that became serialized in newspapers in the days after her execution.

❹ Anryūin 安立院

Established in 1826, this Nichiren temple is famous for its wooden statue of Amida Nyorai. The statue is only visible if the building is open, and Buddhist temples usually are not, unless it is a feast day or a special occasion. There is a nice garden with a variety of flowers that can help make up for the fact that the statue is not always visible. The name of translates as "Peaceful Dragon Temple."

The entrance is to the east.

❺ Tennōji 天王寺

The origin of this temple goes back to 1274 when a statue of Nichiren that was carved by Nichiren himself was given to his host Seki Nagateru, who then built the temple to house the statue. Originally the Nichiren temple was named Kannōji, but it was forced to convert to Tendai Buddhism under orders of the government in 1699 as a response to radical sect teachings. As you enter through the modern gate, you will see on the left a Bronze Buddha cast in 1690. The tea house where the famous beauty Kasamori Osen worked was at the entrance to the grounds. Tennōji was one of the three famous locations in Edo that held lotteries. There is a shrine to Bishamon built out of material from the famous five-storied pagoda after it was destroyed in a fire, so this shrine is also on the local Shichifukujin circuit.

DETAIL 4

❶ Manekineko Yanakadō 招き猫谷中堂

Like cats? This is the spot for you. This shop specializes in manekineko figures, those beckoning lucky cats one sees in Japanese businesses. The building is old, and has a manekineko on the sign and in the window. Some of their designs are seasonal. Feline fanciers will be tempted to open their wallets as they also have lots of items related to cats in general.

There is a sister store next door, Café Nekoemon, where you can sit, sip tea or coffee, enjoy a cat-themed pastry, and decorate a small ceramic cat figurine with colored pens. The cafe owner speaks English.

🌐 *http://www.yanakado.com*

❷ Zenshōan 全生庵

This Rinzai Zen temple was established in 1883. It was founded by Yamaoka Tesshū as a place to pray for those who died in the Battle of Ueno. Yamaoka Tesshū was a famous swordsman and calligrapher who served both the last Tokugawa shōgun and Emperor Meiji. Also buried here are the composer Hirota Ryūtarō (1892–1952) and the famous rakugo performer San'yūtei Enchō (1839–1900), who was known for telling scary stories. During the month of August the temple holds the Yanaka Enchō Matsuri, displaying their collection of some fifty famous ghost scroll-paintings, which were left to them by Enchō. Many of the scrolls were painted by Maruyama Ōkyo (1733–1795), who is said to have been frightened by one of his own paintings that came to "life." Why show ghost scrolls in August? The hottest time of the year is the traditional time to tell scary stories in Japan, ideally stories scary enough to give you the chills.

❸ Anryūji 安立寺

This temple was established in 1630. The grounds are rich with greenery. In the graveyard you will find the tomb of the famous Japanese painter Kanzan Shimomura, which includes a statue of him.

YANESEN DETAIL 4

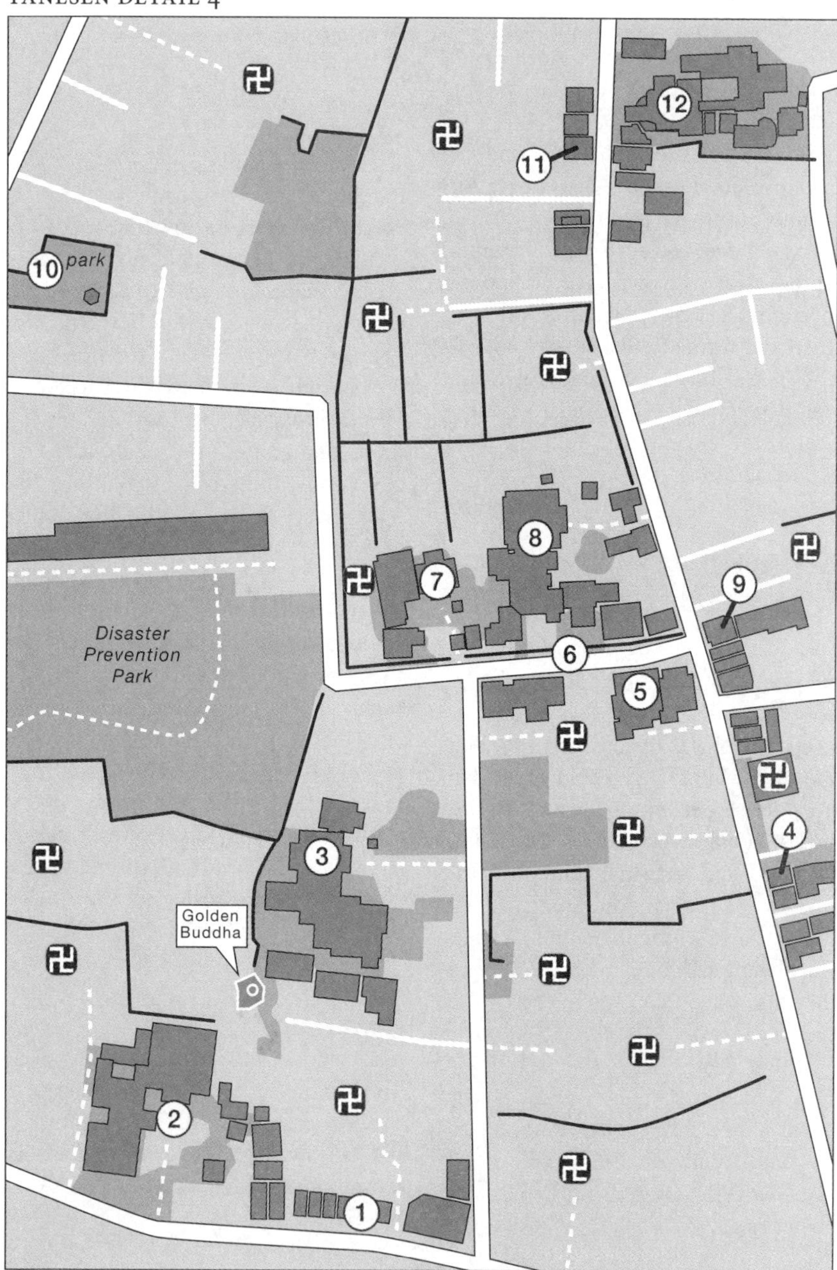

❹ Former Oguraya / Kyū Oguraya 旧倉屋

A former pawn shop that was founded in the early 18th century and closed in 1945. In 1993 the art gallery Space Oguraya opened here and operated until December 2020. As the gallery was in a traditional building visitors would remove their shoes and put on slippers. The main building itself dates from the Taishō period, some of the other structures on the land date from the Edo Period. The tower next to the main building is an old-style fire-resistant storehouse where the pawn shop's goods would have been kept.

🌐 *http://www.oguraya.gr.jp*

❺ Chōanji 長安寺

This humble Rinzai Buddhist temple was established in 1669. Meiji period painter Kanō Hōgai (1828–1888), who was traditionally trained but experimented with Western art styles, is buried here near the center of the graveyard. He worked along with Okakura Tenshin to found the Tōkyō Bijutsu Gakkō (Tokyo Fine Arts School) and passed away shortly before the school began operation. This is also the temple for Jurōjin on the Shichifukujin tour.

❻ Tsuijibei 築地塀

On the street next to Kannōnji there is a traditional tile-roofed mud wall made of alternating layers of flat roof tiles and clay. It is about 200 years old. The wall has become something of a symbol of the neighborhood and is often photographed or included in paintings. This type of wall is rare in Tokyo—you are far more likely to see them in Kyoto. There is another wall of a different design across the street, bordering the grounds of Chōanji.

❼ Kanōin 加納院

This Shingon Buddhist temple was established in Kanda in 1611 and relocated here in 1680. The temple and grounds are small. However, the red and black gate is quite impressive. A statue of Kūkai, the founder of Shingon, is the main object of worship here. The temple is also known for its beautiful flower garden.

The entrance is to the south.

❽ Kannōnji 観音寺

If you have trouble finding this temple, look for the large camphor tree or the tsuijibei, the earthen wall mentioned above. Kannōnji has a connection with the famous Forty-Seven Rōnin immortalized in plays, stories, and cinema. A young man studying here named Bunryō was the brother of two of the rōnin. He would later go on to become head priest under the name of Chōzan. The pagoda to the right of the main hall is a memorial to the Forty-Seven Rōnin.

The entrance to the temple is on the east side.

❾ Gamō Residence / Gamōke

蒲生家

This two-story wooden structure built around 1906 is the former residence of the Gamō family. It is an excellent surviving example of the type of ordinary merchant's home that existed in much of Tokyo in the Meiji period. The projecting eaves are of a type called dashigeta zukuri, which can also be seen on the Yoshidaya Former Liquor Store.

❿ Okakura Tenshin Memorial Park / Okakura Tenshin Kinen Kōen

岡倉天心記念公園

This small park is dedicated to the Meiji era intellectual Okakura Kakuzō (1862–1913), who wrote under the name Okakura Tenshin. He was one of the founders of the Tōkyō Bijutsu Gakkō (Tokyo Fine Arts School). He would later become the first head of the Asian art division of the Museum of Fine Arts in Boston. He is best known in the West for his popular *Book of Tea*, which remains in print. This park is located on the site of his former residence and the Nihon Bijutsuin (Japan Art Institute), which he helped found.

⓫ Yakuzen Curry Jinenjo Yanaka

薬膳カレーじねんじょ 谷中店

A small neighborhood restaurant specializing in Japanese curry made with medicinal herbs. Seating is Western. The decor is simple with lots of wood.

⓬ Asakura Museum of Sculpture / Asakura Chōso Museum

朝倉彫塑館

This complex was the home, workshop, and private art school of Asakura Fumio, until his death in 1964. The modern concrete portion of the building that houses his studio was completed in 1935. The traditional portion of the building existed before the studio was added, and had been Asakura's residence since 1908. The exhibition space in the former studio has many of Asakura's works on display. One feature of the studio was a lift that allowed him to raise or lower a statue he was working on, rather than rely on scaffolding. A section of the museum is devoted to sculptures of cats, a favorite topic for this artist, who kept several. A noted and prolific sculptor, Asakura not only designed the studio but also the garden. The garden is named Goten no Suitei, "Water Garden of Five Precepts," and a series of five large stones symbolizing Confucian virtues are a central motif. The blooming plants were chosen carefully so that a series of colors would follow the year. Actually there are two gardens; the other is on the roof and was originally used to grow vegetables as part of the hands-on training of Asakura's students. The building was designated a National Tangible Cultural Property in 2001, and the garden was designated as a National Place of Scenic Beauty in 2008.

🌐 *http://www.taitocity.net/zaidan/asakura/*

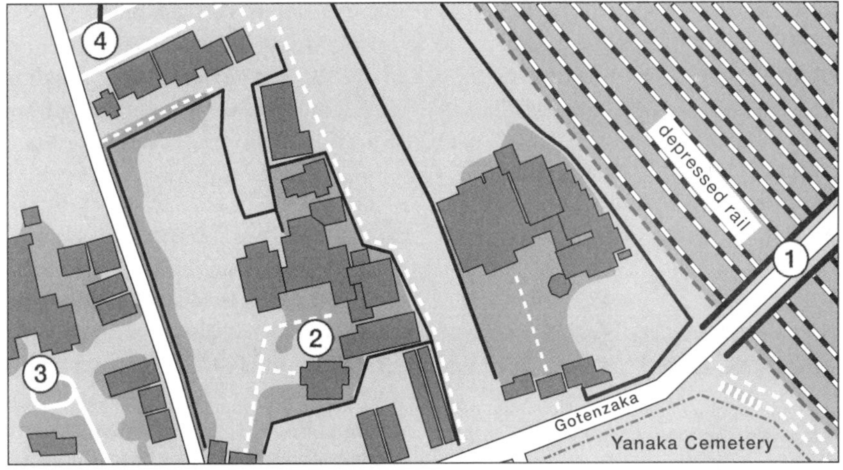

DETAIL 5

❶ Shimogoinden Bashi 下御隠殿橋
This bridge goes over the tracks just north of Nippori Station. The side opposite the station has a good view of the train traffic, and closer to the east side of the bridge there is a small viewing deck. Here you can see over twenty types of trains on the fourteen tracks below. Around 2,500 trains pass under the bridge each day. For this reason the bridge is sometimes referred to as a train museum, and you often see people taking photos here.

❷ Kyōōji 経王寺
This is a small Nichiren temple dating from 1655. It has an especially attractive main building. This is another temple where you will see bullet holes from the Battle of Ueno on the gate doors.

❸ Enmeiin 延命院
This Nichiren sect temple was founded to pray that the birth of Tokugawa Ietsuna would be an easy one. The temple is not hard to locate—just look for the gigantic pasania tree on the grounds. The tree is estimated to be over 600 years old, older than any of the temples in the area. The gate here also has bullet holes from the 1868 Battle of Ueno.

❹ Yōfukuji 養福寺
Yōfukuji is a Shingon-sect Buddhist temple. As you approach the Niōmon you will notice that it is unusually large. The two Niō statues in the gate were carved sometime around

1704–1711 by Unkei, who was famous for his Niō statues. While the main hall of the temple was destroyed during the war, the gate survived. To the right of the main hall is a statue of Kūkai, who brought Shingon to Japan.

Entrance from the west on the main street to the north of map.

DETAIL 6

❶ Fuji Viewing Slope / Fujimizaka 富士見坂

This was long a famous spot to enjoy an unobstructed view of Mount Fuji on clear days. Alas, this is no longer the case: A high-rise apartment building was constructed blocking much of the view, and other buildings are in the works that will obliterate it entirely. There is posted information about the neighborhood's struggle to preserve the view. This includes photographs of what it looked like in the past.

❷ Jōkōji 浄光寺

This Shingon sect Buddhist temple gained the nickname of "Snow Viewing Temple" because it was a popular place to watch snow drifting on the breeze. It is also known for the Sandai Shōgun Okoshikake no Ishi, "Rock where the Third Shōgun Sat," since Tokugawa Iemitsu sat here to enjoy the view during a day of hunting. It's an interesting little bit of preserved history in Tokyo. A more artistic item is the 9.8-foot (3-meter) bronze standing Jizō statue, one of two remaining from Kūmu Shōnin's famous series of six.

❸ Shushōin 修性院

This Nichiren Buddhist temple founded in 1573 is on the local Shichifukujin tour, as Hotei is also enshrined here. The statue of Hotei in the basement is one of my favorites, embodying great humor. The wall along the street has a series of ceramic-tile murals of Hotei and children.

❹ Suwa Jinja 諏方神社

Suwa Jinja was founded in 1322 by the Toshima clan. The kami enshrined here is Takeminakata no Kami, who is worshiped as the protector of Yanaka and Nippori. The shrine is surrounded by ginkgo trees, making it a stunning sight in the fall when the leaves turn gold. If you like trains, this is a good spot to take photographs, as it overlooks Nishi Nippori Station and several different lines run through here. In the Edo period this was a popular spot and many poems were written about the view at that time.

❺ Seiunji 青雲寺

This Rinzai Zen sect Buddhist temple has the nickname of Hanami Dera, "blossom viewing temple," due

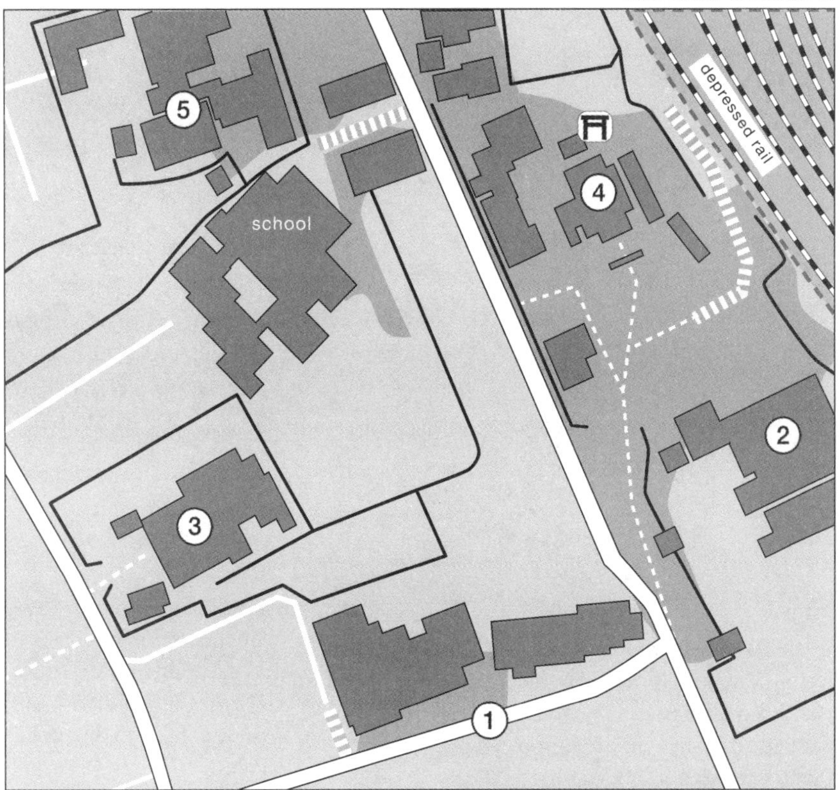

to the cherry trees and azaleas on the grounds. Ebisu in enshrined here, so it is one of the Shichifukujin tour temples for the area. The kanji for this temple's name can also be pronounced as Shōunji, so you will at times see the temple referred to by that name.

DETAIL 7

❶ Yūyake Dandan 夕やけだんだん
This stairway going down to Yanaka Ginza from near Nippori Station was named by a public poll. The name translates as "Sunset Stairs" and this is considered a great place to see the sun go down. No matter what time of day you are there, I recommend stepping off to one side at the top of the stairs and admiring the street view.

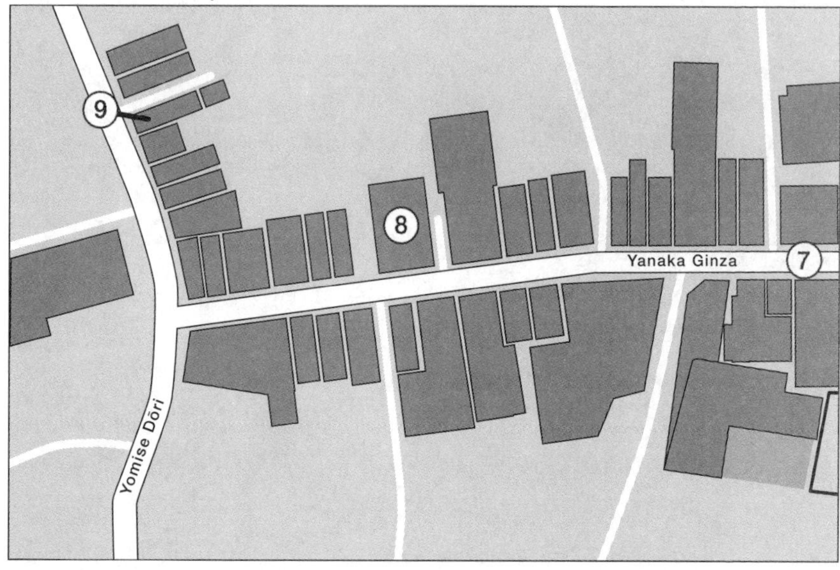

❷ **Ariya** 蟻や

A small family-run restaurant located on Yanaka Ginza near the base of the Yūyake Dandan. They offer simple tasty meals at a good price. You can get items like yakitori and set meals. Seating is Western, and English is spoken here.

❸ **Midoriya** 翠屋

Midoriya has specialized in bamboo crafts since 1908. They sell pretty much anything you can imagine made from bamboo, including flower baskets, boxes, insect cages, and even modern items such as coasters. If you wander toward the back of the store, you may get to see Buseki Suiko, an acclaimed master craftsman and one of the owners, working on a project. Some of the works by this shop are in museum collections such as the Metropolitan Museum of Art in New York and the MOA Museum of Art in Shizuoka.

❹ **Gotō no ame** 後藤の飴

This old-fashioned Japanese candy store has been in business since 1922. The variety is large and some items are seasonal. One of the interesting items made and sold here is a small red candy ball made from tomato. These candies can make a good gift to bring back home. On the side street, the second floor of the building sports a series of black and white images symbolic of Yanaka.

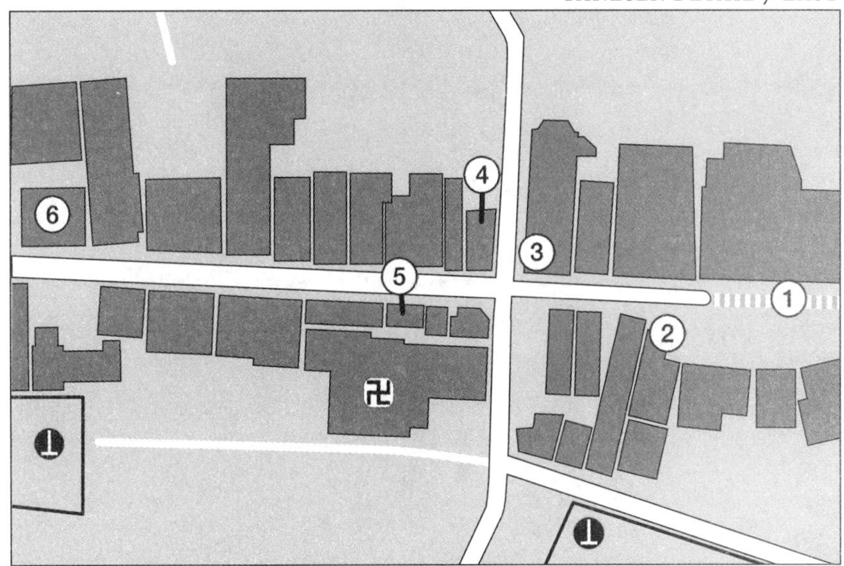

❺ Tamaru 多満留
A tiny shop selling materials related to rakugo and to Yanesen. Why rakugo? Well, Yanesen has long been one of the centers for the traditional performance art. Minobe Mitsuko, the eldest daughter of famous rakugo performer and actor Kokontei Shinshō V, decided to open this shop after his death in 2001. It sells a variety of items relating to Kokontei Shinshō, such as rakugo CDs, figures, and ceramics with his image. Do you need to pick up postcards to send back home? This place has an interesting selection, many of which are handcrafted or only available here.

❻ Niku no Suzuki 肉のすずき
Originally a butcher shop established in 1933, the third generation owner added cooked food to their products. They are known for serving a variety of croquettes, especially their popular menchi katsu, a meat and vegetable croquette. The store has been featured on TV shows and written up in magazines, and sports a selection of photographs of famous celebrities eating their croquettes.

❼ Yanaka Ginza 谷中ぎんざ
The major neighborhood shopping street of Yanaka has about seventy businesses in its vicinity. Yanaka Ginza is mainly composed of older buildings, many of which predate World War II,

▲ Torii at Nezu Jinja are low enough that tall people may have to duck to walk through.

▲ A man sweeping the stairs at Komagome Inari Jinja on an autumn afternoon.

▲ Railing art overlooking the tracks on Shimogoinden Bashi.

▼ Strolling Yanaka Ginza, you may spot Kokontei Shinshō V depicted Tamaru's sign.

some going back much further. At first glance the shops look rather ordinary, and many are. However, a closer look and a little historical knowledge goes a long way. Take your time, glance into the shops, see what you can find, grab a bite to eat, and stroll through the neighborhood. Check out the shops on the side streets. Yanaka as a whole is known for a love of cats, and cat motifs are common on Yanaka Ginza. Keep an eye out for the business signs, many of which are hand carved. Some of the carved shop signs on Yanaka Ginza were made by Fukuzen Sakai Kanban in Asakusa.

🌐 *https://www.yanakaginza.com*

❽ Echigoya 越後屋

An old liquor store in a two-story wooden building. On the eaves there is a statue of a white cat looking down on the street. At times there is informal seating outside on inverted crates for consuming alcohol on site. Many will buy a croquette from the nearby Niku no Satō and sit to enjoy it with a beer.

🌐 *https://www.sake-echigoya.com*

❾ Yanesen Tourist information and Culture Center
ツーリストインフォメーション
YANESEN

This small office has fliers in several languages and other information about the area. I recommend dropping in and getting a flier as you stroll through the neighborhood to supplement what I have in this book. They also offer workshops and presentations related to Yanesen.

🌐 *https://www.ti-yanesen.jp*

DETAIL 8

❶ Daienji 大円寺

The dates of the establishment of this Sōtō sect temple are unsure, but it is mentioned in documents from the late 17th century. Located to the right as you enter the grounds are memorial stones for the 18th-century ukiyo-e artist Suzuki Harunobu and for Kasamori Osen, a local beauty often depicted in his prints. The stones are on either side of a Kannon statue. Note that the cemetery is off limits to the public. The temple grounds are very attractive, and the temple's wooden eaves have beautifully detailed carvings. There is also a very unusual Jizō here, the Hōroku Jizō or "Earthenware Jizō." People with head ailments leave offerings of hōroku, a type of platter. Inside the hall there are some beautiful statues. The temple burned during the war but the seated Buddha was saved, as it had been buried for protection. The temple is unusual as Inari was enshrined here in the Edo period, making it both a Buddhist temple and a Shintō shrine. Traditionally people have prayed here for healing from smallpox and skin

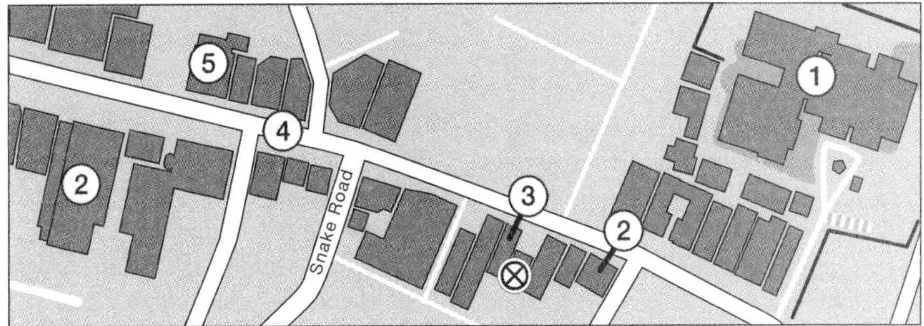

diseases. Daienji is one of the temples on the 33 Kannon Pilgrimage of Tokyo.

On October 14 and 15 the temple holds the Kiku Matsuri, a chrysanthemum festival. The flowers are displayed, some in the form of figures, and potted chrysanthemums are sold.

❷ Isetatsu いせ辰

Isetatsu was founded in 1864 in Iwamotochō, an area south of Akihabara, and relocated here in 1942. There are actually two locations on the same street: the main shop in Yanaka and the other in Sendagi, close to Sendagi Station. The shops specialize in hand printed chiyogami paper made using hand carved woodblocks. Often the patterns were originally designed for fabric and then adapted to paper. The process is similar to that for woodblock prints in that it involves a painter who produces the design, a carver who cuts the block, and a printer who applies it to the paper. All of this means no modern printing techniques are used; everything is done as it was when the shop was founded. As you look around, open drawers and you will find many interesting items within. They also handle a variety of traditional paper products such as prints, fans, papier-mâché items, and more. They also sell a few printed cloth items such as tenugui.

🌐 *https://www.isetatsu.com*

🌐 *https://shinisetsuhan.net/collections/isetatsu*

🌐 *http://www.norenkai.net/en/portfolio-item/isetatsu/*

❸ Hirai Hakimono Ten 平井履物店

This maker and seller of traditional Japanese footwear has been in business since 1926. Everything is made using traditional natural materials such as wood, woven plant fibers, silk, cotton, lacquer, and leather. They mainly do wholesale but operate this one retail shop. Some traditional Japanese footwear is seasonal, so the stock on display may vary.

🌐 *http://hiraitokyo.co.jp*

❹ Sansakizaka 三崎坂

The kanji 坂 in Sansakizaka means "slope." In Tokyo, ordinary streets rarely have names, but slopes may, adding to the complexity of location identification in this city. This slope is also called Misakizaka, as the kanji 三 can be pronounced either as san or as mi. The slope has an interesting nickname, Kubifurizaka, "Head Moving Slope," as traditional etiquette calls for respectfully bowing as one passes a temple or shrine, and there are several on the street. There is also a literary connection here: San'yūtei Enchō's famous rakugo version of the old ghost story *Botan Dōrō* is set on this slope. At the top of the hill is Yanaka cemetery.

❺ Kikumi Senbei 菊見煎餅

This shop has specialized in senbei (rice crackers) since 1875. The senbei here have an unusual square shape. Their four main types of square senbei are shōyu senbei, a common type brushed with soy sauce; spicy tōgarashi senbei; cha senbei, which has a sweet coating containing green tea; and their white sweet ama senbei. The shop is located in an older building with a wood-framed-glass counter display that has globes filled with small crackers on it. The store sign is round, on a tile section of roof.

DETAIL 9

❶ Dangozaka 団子坂

This slope running east to west near Sendagi Station has a name that is said to come from a dango shop that was once at the bottom of the hill. Originally there was a steeper angle to the slope, but it was leveled to make the grade easier. Dangozaka was also known as Shiomizaka, "Tide Viewing Slope," as at one time you could see Tokyo Bay from here. This was also once the location of a famous chrysanthemum festival. There one would pay to view dolls with papier-mâché heads and bodies fashioned from the flowers, as well as recreations of famous scenes from history or plays. Today you can still buy traditional snacks such as dango here. The famous writer Mori Ōgai spent most of his last thirty years in this area.

❷ Amezaiku Yoshihara Sendagi
あめ細工吉原 千駄木

Since 2008 this store has sold a traditional handcrafted candy called amezaiku, which comes in various forms. Today there are only about thirty people in Japan who produce this traditional product, usually at festivals. In the past these sweets were sold on the street, in parks, or at temples and shrines. Wandering peddlers would often craft them in front of their customers, as is done here. Due to modern

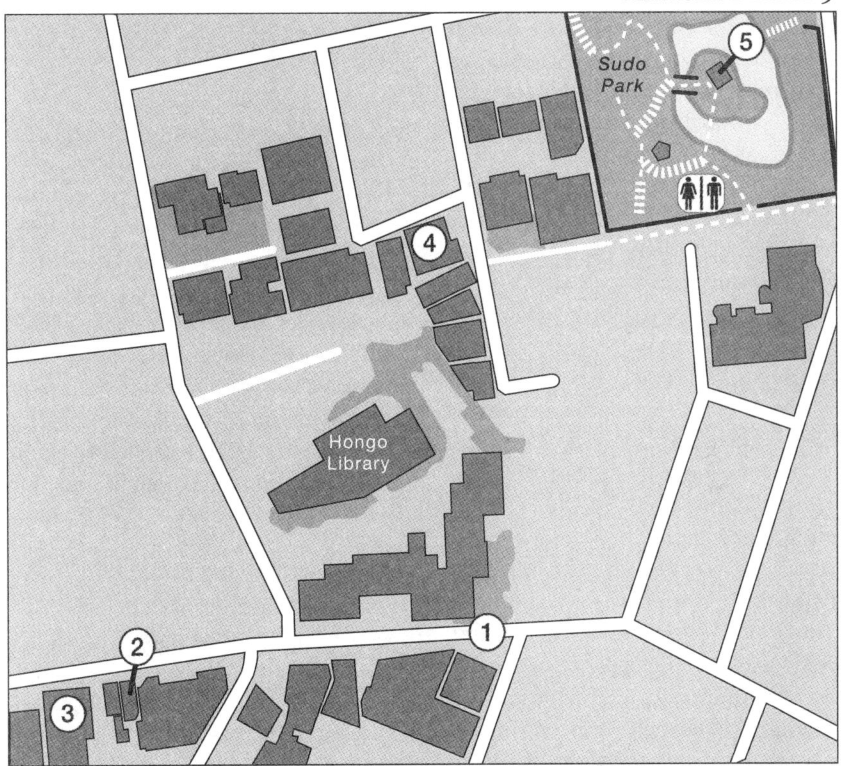

hygiene standards, they are now made in shops like this one. The staff also are available for demonstrations and can be hired to create custom-shaped candies. Amezaiku sometimes show up in movies: For example, when we first see the character Yaji early in the movie *Yajikita Dōchū Teresuko* ("*Three for the Road*"), he is making an amezaiku rabbit for a little girl.

🌐 *http://ame-yoshihara.com*

❸ Mori Ōgai Memorial Museum / Bunkyō Kuritsu Mori Ōgai Kinenkan 文京区立森鷗外記念館

Mori Rintaro (1862–1922) is best known by his pen name Mori Ōgai. He was an acclaimed writer and translator, and was Surgeon General of the Japanese Army until 1917 when he took over the duties of Secretary General of the Imperial Museum and Head of the Imperial Library. Ōgai spent the second half of his life on this site, where his residence was located. In 1950 the empty lot was made into a memorial

park by the Bunkyō Ward government, and in time the museum was constructed here to open in 2012. The museum has three floors including a basement level. There are two exhibition rooms, a lecture room, a library, a garden with a lovely gingko tree, a cafe, and a museum shop.
🌐 *http://moriogai-kinenkan.jp*

❹ Isego 伊勢五
A sakeya (liquor store) that is proud of their knowledgeable staff. They hold regular meetings to educate their employees about their products. Operating since 1706, they have a broad selection of craft sake, shōchū, Japanese wine, Japanese whisky, and more. The front of the store is stone with narrow windows—light damages sake, so small windows are a good thing. The interior is spacious, with bottles displayed on wood shelving. There are two stores, this one and another in the artsy neighborhood of Naka-Meguro. Some of the staff speak English.
🌐 *http://www.isego.net/english/*

❺ Sudō Park / Sudō Kōen 須藤公園
Originally a garden in part of a daimyō residence, the land was later purchased by businessman Sudō Kichizaemon and the family donated the park to the city in 1933. The park is hilly, with plenty of trees, and has a large pond with an island that includes a small temple to Benten accessible by a red bridge.

DETAIL 10

❶ Snake Road / Hebimichi へび道
The name of this street translates as "Snake Road." It was originally the path of a local stream that meandered very much like a snake on the move. In 1921 the stream was culverted and still flows under the street, which is lined with private homes and small businesses. This is a pleasant walk past small shops and cafes in what is mainly a residential neighborhood. Natsume Sōseki mentions the original stream in his 1908 novel *Sanshirō*.

❷ Chōjiya 丁子屋
An old shop specializing in dyed goods that has been in operation since 1895. The street here was once filled with such shops; Chōjiya is the last one. This is a good place to pick up a variety of hand dyed goods such as tenugui, folding fan cases, cell phone cases, and book covers.

DETAIL 11

❶ Nezu Jinja 根津神社
According to tradition this shrine was founded in the 1st century by Yamato Takeru in what is now Sendagi, a little to the north of the present location. Nezu Jinja enshrines Susanoo no

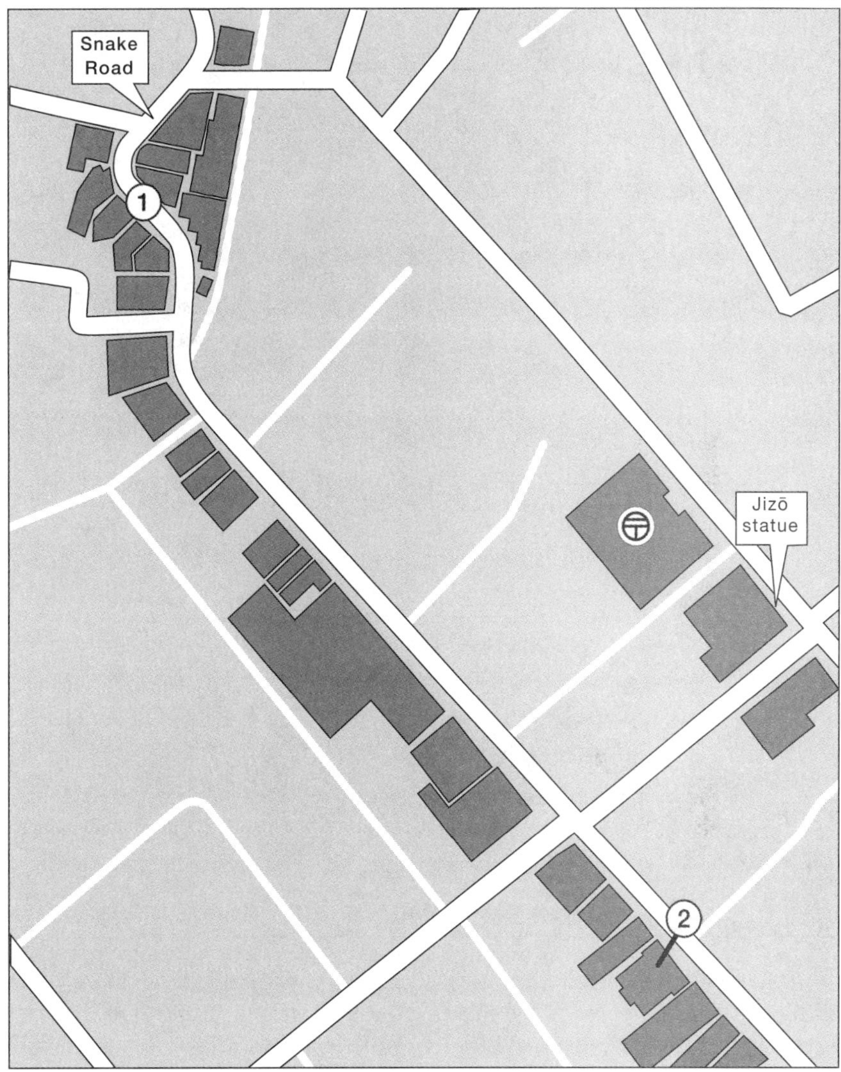

Mikoto, Oyamakui no Mikoto, and Homudawake no Mikoto. The buildings that stand today are from 1706, with repairs from the 1960s for some damage done in World War II. Much of the main shrine is in red and black lacquer done in the Momoyama style. The main gate at the south is a two-story rōmon with two guardians armed with bows and swords.

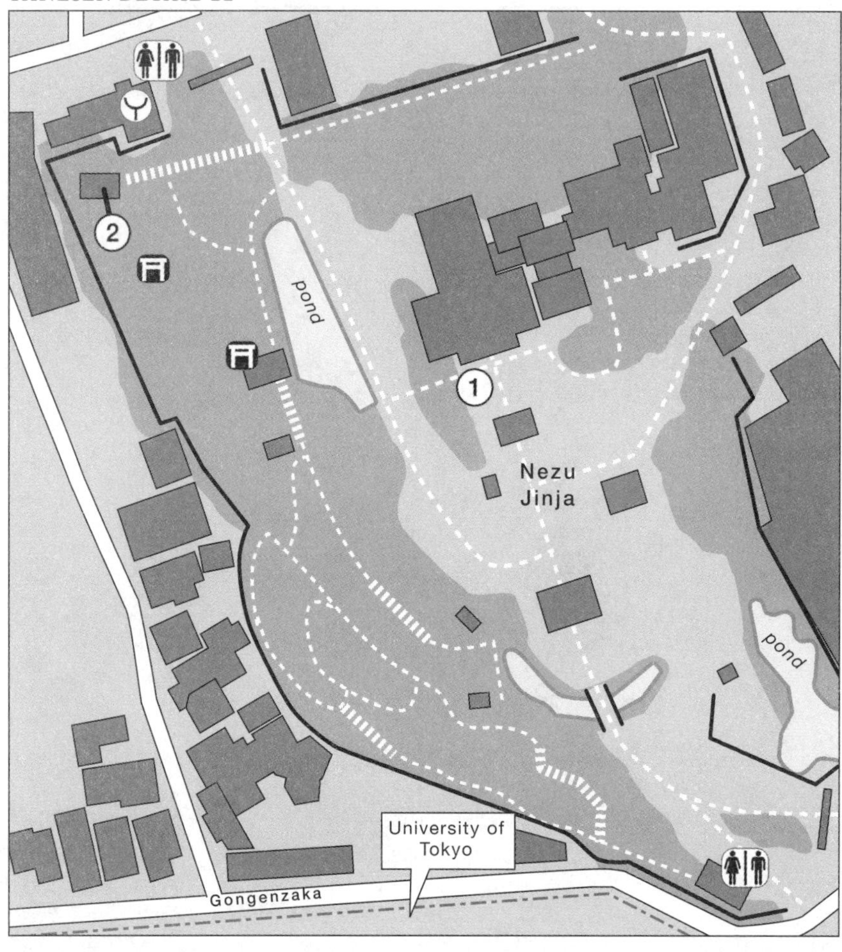

If you follow the path that leads to the left as you approach the main entrance to the shrine, you will find Otome Inari shrine. There is also a pond on the grounds below Otome Inari. You can approach this shrine from the right or the left by walking along a tunnel formed by rows of torii. Do be careful if you are tall or you might bump your head—and more than once. If you look up and to the left, you will see a house higher up on the hill. This is the former location of a house Mori Ōgai lived in for a time; later Natsume Sōseki lived at that location for three years while he taught at Tokyo University.

Between mid-April and early May

the Tsutsuji Matsuri (Azalea Festival) is held, which draws many to view the thousands of azalea bushes on the grounds.

In September the shrine holds its annual Tenka Matsuri.

🌐 *http://www.nedujinja.or.jp*

❷ Komagome Inari Jinja

駒込稲荷神社

A stone stairway leads to Komagome Inari Jinja surrounded by trees on a small hill. I had first approached the shrine after spending part of the day wandering through a very modern neighborhood and walking along a busy street. The quiet and green grounds were a relaxing break and transition point for the rest of the day's stroll. Devotees of Japan's iconic mountain will be pleased to discover there is a fujizuka here.

吉原・山谷

YOSHIWARA AND SANYA

These are two neighborhoods with a colorful history. The Yoshiwara was Edo's first licensed pleasure district, and Sanya became infamous after World War II as a slum with large numbers of day laborers. The Yoshiwara is no more and Sanya's days as a slum are in the past. You won't even find the Yoshiwara and Sanya on contemporary maps due to administrative name changes. Sanya was split up into several neighborhoods during an administrative restructuring in 1966. Reminders of the history of both neighborhoods remain in several locations and make for a good stroll for those interested in history.

DETAIL 1

❶ Yoshiwara Benten 吉原弁財天
This is a Benten shrine near the former Yoshiwara. The shrine has a large, attractive mural depicting Benten seated on a lotus blossom. On the grounds there is an 8-foot (2.5-meter) statue of Kannon as a memorial to the 630 Yoshiwara prostitutes who died in the fire caused by the Great Kantō Earthquake. Many of the women and neighbors had fled into the Benten Pond only to drown or die from the heat of the flames. A photo displayed on a nearby wall shows the pond entirely covered in bodies. The memorial and statue were placed here in 1926 at the edge of the pond. Most of the pond was filled in for construction in the 1950s so only a very small part remains. If you visit this memorial, you will commonly see offerings of drinks and food left at the base. Each

YOSHIWARA AND SANYA

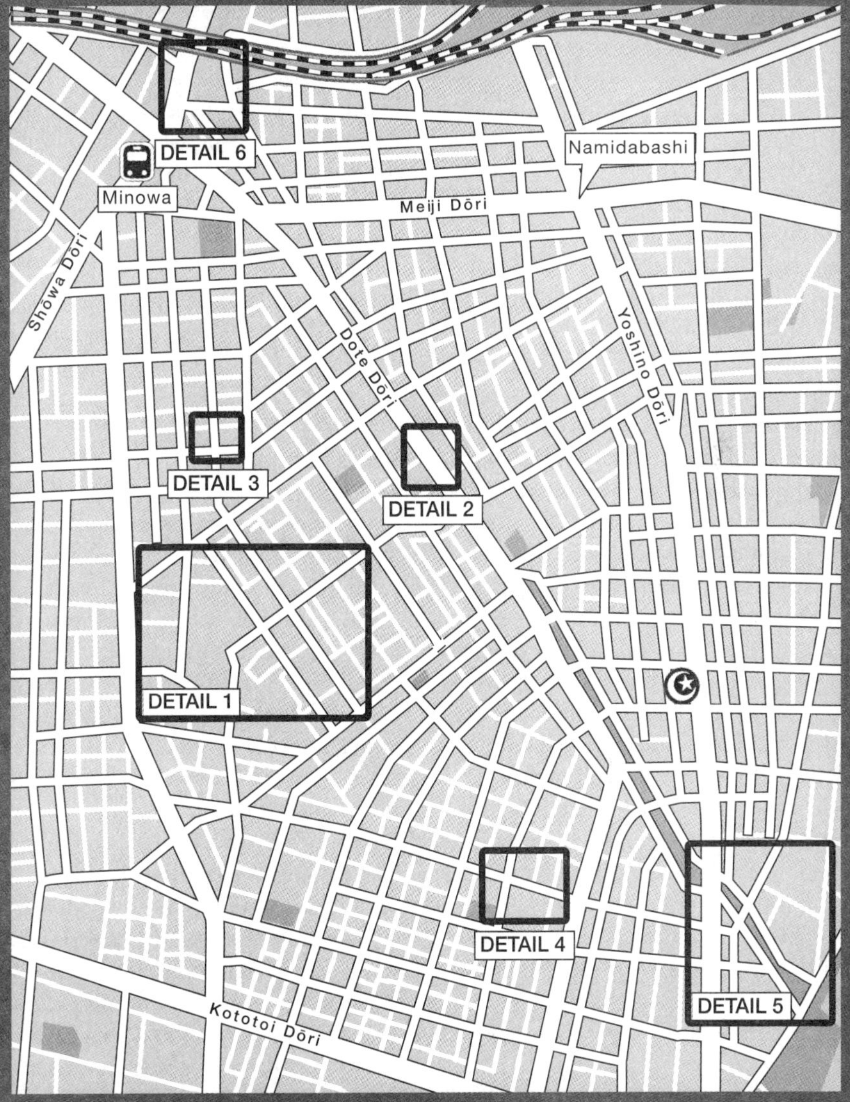

September 1 there is a service in memory of the women.

The entrance to the shrine is on the west side.

❷ Ōtori Jinja 鷲神社

Ōtori "great bird" Jinja is located just west of the former Yoshiwara on Kokusai Dōri. The shrine's official name is Washi "eagle" Jinja, but is almost always referred to as Ōtori Jinja or Ōtorisama. This shrine is most famous for the lively Tori no Ichi festival held two or three times each November. At this festival, traditional decorated lucky rakes are sold at hundreds of stalls. The number of visitors is very large—the line can be eight or so people wide—however it keeps moving at a good pace. As you wait in line you will pass food vendors, so feel free to step out of line, sit and eat a little, then get back in line. The regular monthly festivals are held on the first and fifteenth of each month. This shrine is on the Shichifukujin pilgrimage for Asakusa: Jurōjin is enshrined here. People often pray here for success in business.

The main entrance is on the west side; you can also enter on the north side.

🌐 *http://www.otorisama.or.jp/english.html*

❸ Yoshiwara Jinja 吉原神社

This shrine was formed in the late 19th century by the merging of five local Inari shrines—one from the entrance to the Yoshiwara, the others from the four corners—in one location. The Yoshiwara Jinja burned down in the Great Kantō Earthquake and again in the World War II firebombings. The current restored building was built in 1964.

There are festivals held on the third Friday, Saturday, and Sunday of May.

The entrance to the shrine is on the south side.

❹ Yoshiwara 吉原

This is former location of the official prostitution district of old Edo, which was established in 1617 near Nihonbashi and relocated here in 1657 after the Meireki Fire. It is at times referred to as the Shin Yoshiwara "New Yoshiwara." The Yoshiwara was enclosed with walls and a moat to control access as well as prevent runaway prostitutes. It was so isolated that it had its own dialect; only a few elderly people today can speak it. The Yoshiwara continued to exist as a Tokyo brothel district until the anti-prostitution law took effect in 1958. Today it still has an area with several legal sex shops that operate openly since they do not (officially) allow the services forbidden under the law. Tourists are discouraged from entering these shops.

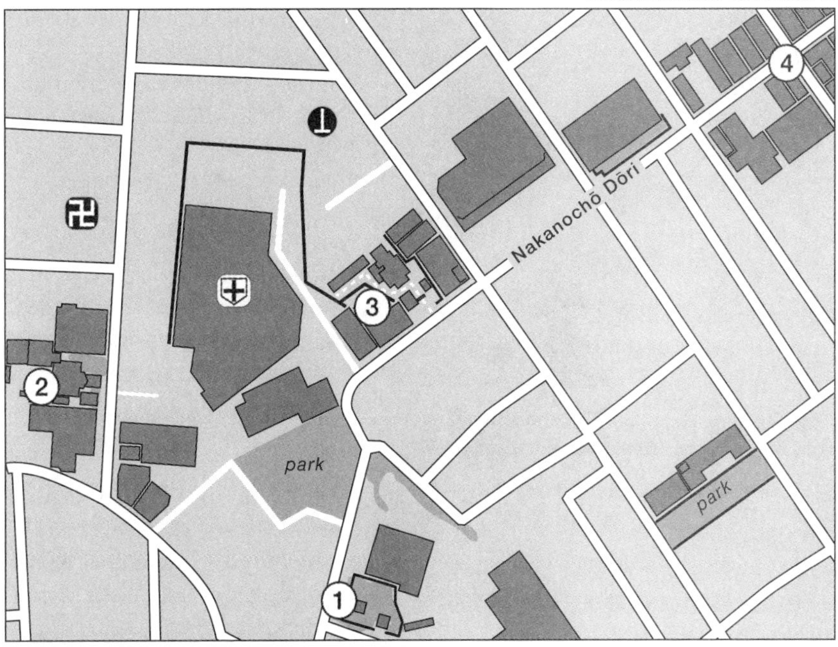

DETAIL 2

❶ Ashita No Joe Statue
あしたのジョー像

A statue of Yabuki Joe, the title character of the hit manga *Ashita no Joe*, which ran in Shonen Magazine from 1968 to 1973. The story concerns Joe, a young drifter who meets a down-on-his-luck, drunk boxing promoter. Long story short, Joe finally agrees to train to be a boxer. *Ashita No Joe* was very successful and when a major secondary character died, the reaction was so strong that the poet and director Terayama Shūji called for there to be a funeral. The publisher held a Buddhist memorial service and hundreds of fans showed up to mourn. The gym Joe trained in was further north under the Namidabashi, "Bridge of Tears," where in the Edo period prisoners about to be executed could take their last look at loved ones. The bridge is now an intersection, the river having been culverted. The statue presently marks the edge of Joe's neighborhood, Sanya. Once a major slum infamous for its day laborer population, today Sanya is increasingly popular as a place for tourists to find inexpensive lodgings.

The first animated feature adapting the manga was released in English with the titles *Champion Joe* and *Tomorrow's Joe*.

YOSHIWARA DETAIL 2

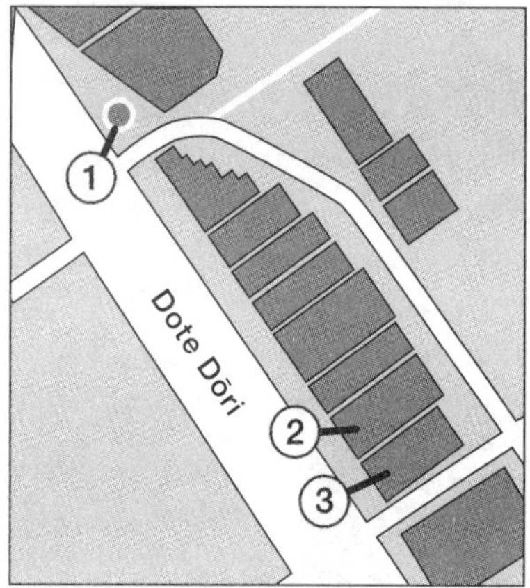

❷ **Nakae** 中江

This restaurant has specialized in dishes made with horsemeat since 1905. In the Edo period there was a folk belief that eating horsemeat protected against syphilis, and the restaurant is conveniently located right outside the old entrance to the former Yoshiwara red light district. Among the dishes made with horsemeat here are nigirizushi, thinly-sliced horse meat sashimi called basashi, and a hot pot called sakura nabe, which is said to have originated in this part of Tokyo in the Meiji period. In 2000 they began selling their own line of cosmetics made with horse oil, which is supposed to be very good for the skin. The original building was destroyed in the Great Kantō Earthquake and rebuilt in 1924. This is the building that stands today, having survived the 1945 firebombings of the area. It is listed as a national cultural property.

Seating is traditional, both on tatami and at horigotatsu, so expect to remove your shoes.

🌐 *http://www.sakuranabe.com/eng/*

❸ **Dote no Iseya** 土手の伊勢屋

Sometimes referred to as just Iseya, this is a popular neighborhood tempura restaurant that has been in business since 1873. Nothing fancy or formal, just large servings of good, solid food loved by the locals. There are only six tables and some are communal, so you may have to share when it is crowded. Seating is both traditional on tatami with cushions and Western style on benches. They do not take reservations, so expect to wait in line on weekends. There is a bench outside to sit on while waiting. The original building was destroyed in the Great Kantō Earthquake and rebuilt in 1924. This is the building that still stands, having survived the 1945 firebombings of the area. The fixtures are old and the shoyu (soy sauce) containers are antiques. The owner likes it that way and so do I.

DETAIL 3

❶ **Ichiyō Memorial Museum / Ichiyō Kinenkan** 一葉記念館

A four-story museum dedicated to the

YOSHIWARA DETAIL 3

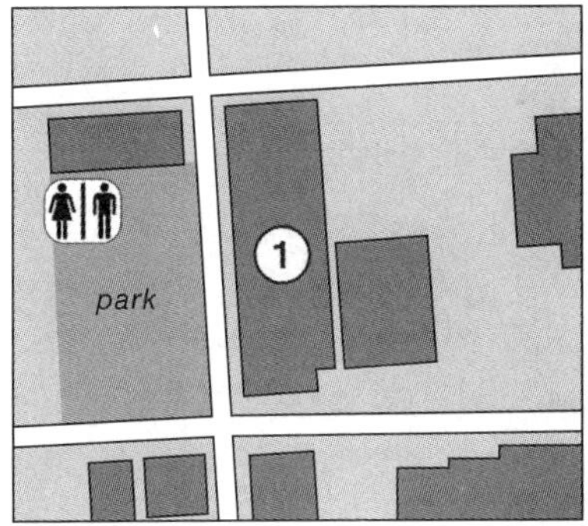

life and work of Higuchi Ichiyō (1872–1896), a major writer of the Meiji period. The collection on display includes a model of the street she lived on, manuscripts, tanka poems, her desk, and more. She turned to writing at the age of eighteen to support her widowed mother and sister, and quickly gained recognition from many notable writers of her time, including Mori Ōgai. There is a gift shop with a variety of items such as handmade paper stationery, book covers, and postcards. The museum was opened by the Taitō Ward government in 1961; the present building was opened in 2006. Her image appeared on the 5,000 yen note in 2004—the Japanese tend to put writers and intellectuals on their bank notes rather than dead politicians.

Not to be confused with another museum to her, which is described in the Hongō chapter.

🌐 *http://www.taitocity.net/zaidan/english/ichiyo/*

DETAIL 4

❶ Asakusa Fuji Asama Jinja
浅草富士浅間神社

This shrine is also known as Asakusa Fuji Sengen Jinja. The Tokyo area has several Sengen Jinja. These are branch shrines of the main one on Mount Fuji and are devoted to the worship of that sacred mountain. This one is the most famous. It is also known for an annual plant festival held on the last Saturday of May and June and on the first of July, where hundreds of stalls sell potted plants on the nearby streets. Potted plants are still very much a part of life in the parts of the city that historically were home to commoners. In the 9th century this tradition resulted in many foreigners expressing surprise at how green Tokyo was in comparison to cities in their home countries. The shrine was founded around 1671, the inner shrine building dates from 1878, and the main building from 1998. There is a fujizuka on the grounds. The entrance is on the south side.

🌐 *https://www.asakusajinja.jp/en/sengenjinja/*

❷ Edo Kiriko Asakusa Ojima
江戸切子浅草おじま

This is the retail shop for a company established in 1930 to produce Edo kiriko, a style of cut glass that originated in the Edo period. The shop is on Denbōin Dōri just west of the

▲ A memorial to the Yoshiwara prostitutes who died in the Great Kantō Earthquake.

▲ Yabuki Joe looking in the direction of Sanya, the neighborhood he lived in.

YOSHIWARA DETAIL 4

Nakamise, and the studio is at the corner, one block west of Umamichi Dōri before the Fuji Elementary School. They offer educational workshops (in Japanese) on the carving techniques for grade six to adult. Reservations are required.

🌐 *http://www.edokiriko.jp*

DETAIL 5

❶ Imado Jinja 今戸神社

There are several kami enshrined here. The principal ones are Hachiman, Izanagi, and Izanami. Izanagi and Izanami are the couple who legend says created the Japanese islands. Many single people come to this shrine to pray for a partner for this reason. Imado Jinja is also a shichifukujin shrine for Asakusa and enshrines Fukurokuju. The shrine has a claim to be the place of origin for the famous manekineko "beckoning cat" statues. A legend says that in the 16th century, a poor woman in the area dreamed of a cat urging her to make and sell statues of cats. In 2007 the shrine erected a stone on the grounds with a pair of the cats to commemorate this story. Founded in 1063, the shrine was originally called Imado Hachiman Jinja; however, in 1937 it was merged with the nearby Hakusan Jinja and renamed. The shrine was destroyed in the Great Kantō Earthquake and the firebombings of World War II. The current buildings date from 1971.

The main entrance is on the east side, but you can also enter on the west.

❷ Sanyabori Park / Sanyabori Kōen 山谷堀公園

This is a long and narrow park stretching from the Sumidagawa to a point near the former location of the Yoshiwara. The detail map for this section only shows a portion of the park. It follows the path of the former Sanyabori canal, which was used as a boat route to and from the Yoshiwara. Today the canal is still carrying water underground in a culvert, and the land above it was transformed into the present-day park. Much of the park is just a trail with plants on one or both sides, and the occasional playground and seating area. The park widens in the blocks closest to the river, where in the spring the cherry trees fill with blossoms. As you walk toward the river, you will be facing in the direction of Tokyo Sky Tree for most of the route.

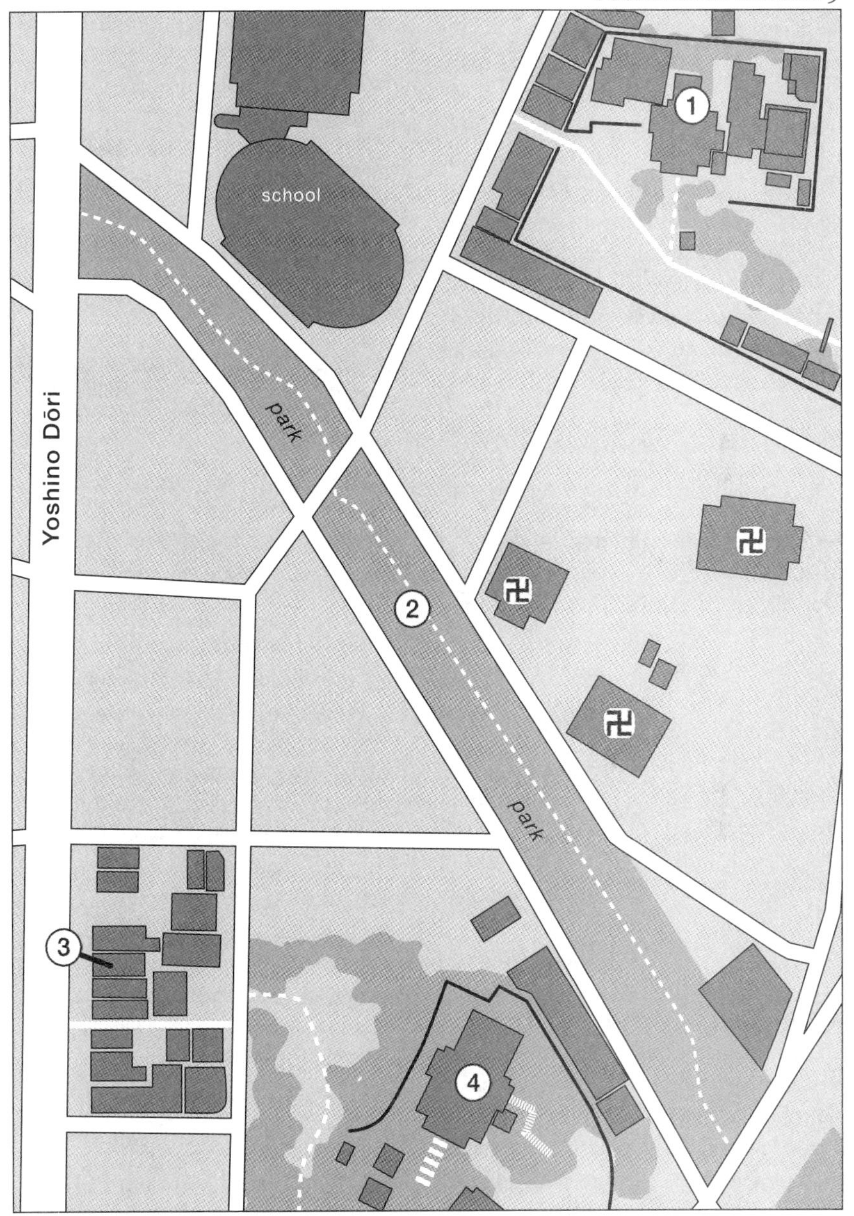
school
park
Yoshino Dōri
park
1
2
3
4

❸ Kissa Akane 喫茶あかね

Sometimes you want to take a break in a good old-fashioned neighborhood cafe. Established in 1976, Kissa Akane's menu offers both Western and Japanese food, including bentō, waffles, burgers, breakfast sets, and omelet rice. Most restaurants in Japan open for lunch, but since Kissa Akane opens early they also serve breakfast. They also host events with board games, whisky nights (!?), magicians, live music, and more.

🌐 *http://cafeakane.favy.jp*

❹ Matsuchiyama Shōden
待乳山聖天

This temple of the Buddhist Shō Kannonshū sect was founded in 601 and is a subordinate temple to Sensōji in Asakusa. The formal name of the temple is Matsuchiyama Honryūin. The temple burned down after the Great Kantō Earthquake and the firebombings of World War II. The present building dates from 1961. The elephant-headed Buddhist deity Daishō Kangiten is enshrined here. Do not expect to view the statue housed here as it is a hibutsu "hidden image," which is not displayed to the public. The temple is located on a small wooded hill near the Sumidagawa between Kototoi Bridge and Sakura Bridge. Images of forked daikon, associated with a happy marriage, and a money pouch, associated with business prosperity, are seen throughout the grounds. The grounds include a kaguraden, a stage for the performance of kagura. Each January 7 they hold the daikon matsuri, "daikon festival."

The entrance is to the south. Disabled access is on the east side at the parking lot.

🌐 *http://www.matsuchiyama.jp/english.html*

DETAIL 6

❶ Jōkanji 浄閑寺

Jōkanji is located a bit north of the sites in the rest of this chapter. It is just east of the Nikkō Kaidō, "Nikkō Highway," not far from Minowa Station and Meiji Dōri, but south of the train tracks. This small Jōdo sect Buddhist temple is nicknamed Nagekomidera, the "Dump or Throw Away Temple." In the old days when a prostitute from the nearby Yoshiwara died and had no one claim the body, it would be taken to this temple. Temple records list the names of over 21,000 women left here between 1743 and 1801. Their average age was twenty-two, and syphilis was the most common cause of death. One of the reasons for the young age is that most prostitutes started their contract in their teens and ended it in their mid-twenties. In the graveyard there is a crypt filled with urns of their ashes, where offerings are often left. The crypt is easy to identify by the statue of the

YOSHIWARA DETAIL 6

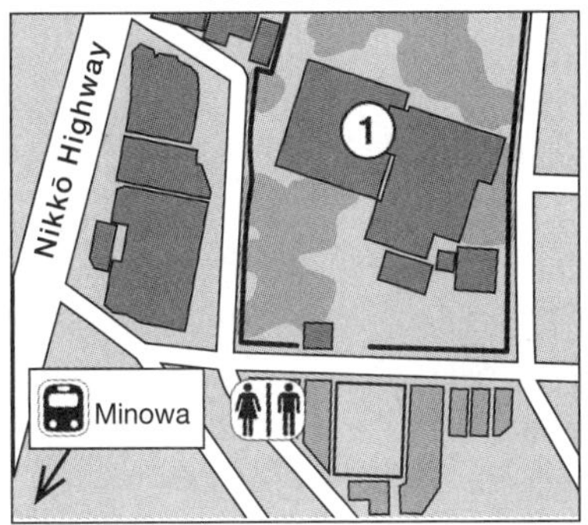

seated Jizō in front of the pillar on top. Across from the crypt is a large stone memorial to the writer Nagai Kafū.

The entrance is on the south side of the grounds.

🌐 *http://www.jyokanji.com*

Day Trippin'

You may tire of the urban landscape and want to head to a place where the population is of a much lower density. If you do so, I strongly recommend you plan to leave very early in the day as you will find the extra time before sundown enjoyable. Consider the following sights, which are just an easy train ride or two from Tokyo. While I note the terminal stations on the lines, you may find it more convenient start at a station closer to you on the same line.

NOTE: *Weekends at these locations will be more crowded than during the week.*

Mount Takao / Takaosan 高尾山

This location is actually still in Tokyo. Mount Takao is in the far Western part of Tokyo where one finds mountains, forests, and wild monkeys, as well as temples and shrines. The local train station is Takaosanguchi Station, which was designed by Kuma Kengo. Once there, you can avoid much of the climb by riding a funicular that takes you to the trail that goes to the Shingon Buddhist temple Yakuōin. You can keep walking past Yakuōin to the top, and if it is a clear day, enjoy the view of Mount Fuji in the distance. Close to the station is the Takao 599 Museum, which has displays about the mountain.

To get there

Start at the Keiō Shinjuku Station and take the Keiō Takao Line to Takaosanguchi Station.

Takao 599 Museum:
🌐 *http://www.takao599museum.jp/?lang=en*

Keio Line, Mount Takao Area:
🌐 *https://www.keio.co.jp/english/sightseeing/takao.html*

Nikkō 日光

Nikkō is such a famous tourist spot among the Japanese that I strongly warn you against going on weekends or holidays. During the slower weekdays the place is still packed with visitors. Just across the river from the town are numerous temples and Shintō shrines. The most famous of these is the large Nikkō Tōshōgū, which includes the grave of Tokugawa Ieyasu. Tōshōgū is well-known for the polychrome carvings that cover the buildings.

To get there

There are several routes from Tokyo with different prices and different schedules that will put you into one of two stations in Nikkō. Nikkō is quite a distance from Tokyo, so keep that in mind when deciding on which train line to take.

- Tōbu Asakusa Station to Tōbu-Nikkō Station, two trains each hour. You can take a local or express train.
- Shinjuku or Ikebukuro to Tōbu-Nikkō Station, a limited express runs four times a day. A JR Pass can be used for part of the cost.
- Utsunomiya Station to JR Nikkō Station. The JR Pass can be used.

Nikkō Tourist Association:
🌐 *https://www.visitnikko.jp/en/*

Shōnan 湘南

A famous historical resort and beach area also known for its surfing. The two main places in the Shōnan area I suggest you consider are Enoshima and Kamakura.

To get there

- JR Yokosuka Line from Tokyo Station to Kamakura Station
- JR Shōnan Shinjuku Line from Shinjuku to Kamakura Station
- Odakyu Railways from Shinjuku Station to Fujisawa Station, take the Limited Express Romancecar. This is a longer trip but cheapest if you

get the reasonably priced Enoshima Kamakura Free Pass, which also allows you to use some local transportation.

Transfer to the Enoshima Electric Railway Enoden train. The Enoden is a trolley that winds through neighborhoods to Enoshima Station, then along the coast to end at Kamakura station.

🌐 *https://www.odakyu.jp/english/passes/enoshima_kamakura/*

Enoshima 江の島

Part of the city of Fujisawa includes a lovely island just off the Shōnan coast. Before the causeway to the island was complete, you would need to take a boat out or walk at low tide. The entire island is dedicated to Benten, who according to legend caused the island to rise from the bay in the 6th century. She did this so she could take up residence there, and to deal with a five-headed dragon that had been terrorizing the locals. The dragon promised to cease its evil, then faced the island and transformed into a nearby hill. The island and its temples have been the subject of many woodblock prints. The island has many restaurants, both as you first step foot on it and later as you reach the upper portion. Expect to use stairs, lots of them—more stairs than it seems at first. If you have trouble with stairs, there is a series of escalators that you can use for a fee.

Enoshima Shrine (in Japanese):
🌐 *http://www.enoshimajinja.or.jp*

Fujisawa City Tourist Association:
🌐 *https://www.discover-fujisawa.jp*

Kamakura 鎌倉

Located in Kanagawa Prefecture, Kamakura is famous as the capital of the Kamakura shōguns from 1185 to 1333. Political power resided here until the revolt of Emperor Go-Daigo resulted in the rise of the Ashikaga shōguns in Kyoto. During the Kamakura period the emperor was reduced to a ceremonial role while the samurai held the real power from this city.

Kamakura is famous for temples, shrines, and the huge statue of the Buddha. Portions of the city are scattered over a series of hills, making a stroll through it much like an easy hike in the country. The landscape stretches from the bay to the hills, with many different walking routes to choose from. Be sure to pick up a map at the train station or tourism office when you arrive.

Official Visitor Guide Visit Kamakura:
🌐 *https://www.city.kamakura.kanagawa.jp/visitkamakura/en/*

Kawagoe 川越

Often referred to as Ko-Edo "Little Edo" due to the number of old buildings in the town. Once you are there, grab a map at the station and plan where you want to start. There is the Ko-Edo Loop Bus that goes to three local stations—you can buy either a ticket for one ride or an all-day pass. From the JR Kawagoe Station you can also take the Koedo Famous Locations Loop Bus. Tickets for this bus are day passes. The area was famous for growing sweet potatoes and there are many foods here that incorporate the tuber as an ingredient. Each October on the third Saturday and Sunday, the Kawagoe Matsuri is held. This is a lively festival where twenty-nine large two-story floats are paraded through town. When they meet at several locations, they have competitions with music.

To get there

- JR Kawagoe Line from Shinjuku, local to Kawagoe Station
- Seibu Shinjuku Line from Seibu Shinjuku, Limited Express to Hon-Kawagoe Station
- Tōbu Tōjō Line from Ikebukuro, Express to Kawagoe Station or Kawagoeshi Station

Koedo Kawagoe Tourist Association:
🌐 *https://koedo.or.jp*

Edo-Tokyo Open Air Architectural Museum / Edo Tokyo Tatemonoen 江戸東京たてもの園

This is a branch of the Edo-Tokyo Museum that I covered in the Ryōgoku chapter. This museum consists of a series of buildings ranging from rural to urban. These are not replicas: rather they are entire buildings that were relocated here to become part of the collection. Several of these structures were used for reference when Studio Ghibli staff were designing the village in *Spirited Away*. The museum's mascot is Edomaru, a green caterpillar that was designed by Miyazaki Hayao.

To get there

Take the JR Chūō line to Musashi-Koganei Station, then take a bus. The bus stops are #2 and #3. Get off at Koganei-Kōen Nishiguchi, which is next to Koganei Park. You can't miss the park as it is heavily forested and very large. Just keep an eye out for the museum once you enter the park. You won't see it for a while, so enjoy the walk.

Edo-Tokyo Open Air Architectural Museum:
🌐 *http://www.tatemonoen.jp/english/*

The Railway Museum / Tetsudō Hakubutsukan 鉄道博物館

A massive four-story museum devoted to rail travel in Japan. The museum is so large that it contains a functioning railway turntable, numerous engines, and passenger carriages. It also has a library, hands-on exhibits, a museum shop, and—my favorite—an ekiben stand. Ekiben are a type of bentō sold at train stations that you can eat on trains.

To get there

From either Tokyo or Ueno Station, take the Ueno-Tokyo Line to Ōmiya Station and transfer to the New Shuttle line to the museum.

Main page (Japanese):
🌐 *http://www.railway-museum.jp*

Museum Guide English:
🌐 *http://www.railway-museum.jp/pdf/flmap_eng.pdf*

Further Reading

These are books you may find informative. Some may be out of print; your public library can borrow books for you if the titles are not in the local collection. Some are available as e-books, making them handy to have on a tablet or smartphone for reference while you are in Tokyo.

History

Naitō, Akira. *Edo: The City That Became Tokyo*. Tokyo: Kodansha International, 2003.

A well-illustrated history of Edo up to 1868. The illustrations in this book provide an excellent visual presentation of the changes that went into the creation of the city and the lives of those who lived and worked within it.

Seidensticker, Edward. *A History of Tokyo 1867-1989*. Tokyo: Tuttle Publishing, 2019.

Two of Seidensticker's works, *Low City, High City* and *Tokyo Rising* in a single volume. This book covers the history of Tokyo from 1867 to 1989, with many details about the changes to many neighborhoods in this period. Tuttle repackaged the book as *Tokyo: From Edo to Showa 1867–1989* in 2010, and then renamed it to the present title in 2019, so don't be confused and buy it twice.

Waley, Paul. *Tokyo: City of Stories*. New York and Tokyo: Weatherhill, 1991.
——. *Tokyo Now and Then: An Explorer's Guide*. New York and Tokyo: Weatherhill, 1984.

These two books cover much of the same material. *Tokyo: City of Stories* is a highly revised version of *Tokyo Now and Then: An Explorer's Guide.* Each book has information not found in the other, so I own and read both.

Food

Hosking, Richard. *A Dictionary of Japanese Food: Ingredients and Culture.* Rutland, VT: Charles E. Tuttle Company, 1996.

The only dictionary of Japanese food in English. Pretty much anything related to food or cooking that you will encounter in Tokyo is found here. The book can be useful if you are shopping or trying to identify an item on the menu.

Ono, Tadashi and Harris Salat. *Japanese Soul Cooking: Ramen, Tonkatsu, Tempura, and More from the Streets and Kitchens of Tokyo and Beyond.* Berkeley: Ten Speed Press, 2013.

I find cookbooks for Japanese food generally lacking in that they rarely have what you commonly see in restaurants in Japan. This one is a major exception. This is the food you will find in Tokyo. Even if you don't plan to cook the recipes, this book is an excellent reference that should be studied before your flight.

Culture

Chavez, Amy. *Amy's Guide to Best Behavior in Japan.* Berkeley: Stone Bridge Press, 2018.

The best book on Japanese etiquette for travelers I have seen. Chavez has put together a guide to daily interaction in Japan. Earlier guides tended to cover far less material or focus on etiquette for businesspeople and their families living in Japan. This one is far more practical for travelers.

Powles, Marcus. *The Tokyo 33-Kannon Pilgrimage.* N.p: Marcus Powles, 2014.

A self-published guide to the temples on the Tokyo Kannon pilgrimage. Many of the temples are in the areas covered in this book. If you wish to do the pilgrimage, offer a prayer, then purchase a goshuinchō

(御朱印帳), "book of seals", at the first temple. At each temple, pray, then head to the office to have the book inscribed and sealed. A small fee is charged for adding the seal at each temple. Powles has also published other guides to the Tokyo area: one on Christian churches, a general guide to Buddhist temples, and one on the Musashino 33 Kannon Pilgrimage.

Web Resources

Tokyo Stroll Supplemental Materials

Additions, corrections, updates, and anything else related to the book:
🌐 *http://www.koyagi.com/TokyoStroll/TSmain.html*

Updates to using bookmarks in Maps.Me and Google Maps will be tracked on my blog:
🌐 *http://www.gillespoitras.blogspot.com.*

Rail and Subway Maps

JR East Tokyo area maps, including some with the subway lines:
🌐 *https://www.jreast.co.jp/e/downloads/index.html*

Tokyo Metro Map for subway lines:
🌐 *https://www.tokyometro.jp/en/subwaymap/*

Event-related Web Sites

Go Tokyo Event Calendar:
🌐 *https://www.gotokyo.org/en/event-calendar/index.html*

Japan Times Events page:
🌐 *https://www.japantimes.co.jp/events/*

NOTE: *You can limit the display by place, type, and dates.*

Tokyo Cheapo Events:
🌐 *https://www.tokyocheapo.com/events/*

Tokyo Weekender Events Calendar:
🌐 *https://www.tokyoweekender.com/events-calendar/*

Festivals in Tokyo Wikipedia page:
🌐 *https://en.wikipedia.org/wiki/Festivals_in_Tokyo*

NOTE: *Several of these websites only cover events in the near future, so check them as the time for your trip approaches. Most of these lists tend to not include specialized events such as Comiket or many shrine and temple festivals. Many lists are often more geared to the local "go out and party" crowd.*

Tourism and Travel-related Sites

Tokyo weather for the next week:
🌐 *https://www.jma.go.jp/en/week/319.html*

Go Tokyo, operated by the Tokyo Convention and Visitors Bureau:
🌐 *https://www.gotokyo.org/en/index.html*

Tokyo Cheapo, devoted to doing things in the Tokyo area on a budget:
🌐 *https://www.tokyocheapo.com*

Japan National Tourism Association (JNTO), Tokyo section:
🌐 *https://www.japan.travel/en/destinations/kanto/tokyo*

Glossary

Most names of Buddhas, bodhisattvas, kami, and individuals are not included.

Amazake (甘酒): A sweet drink made by fermenting rice until most of the starch has been turned into sugar. It is served cold or hot depending on the time of year. While often translated as sweet sake, it has almost no alcohol.

Anime (アニメ): Animation produced by Japanese companies for the Japanese market.

Awamori (泡盛): An Okinawan alcoholic beverage. It is made by brewing rice and then distilling it to a high alcohol content, typically 60–86 proof. The type of rice and brewing process are different than those used for making rice-based shōchū.

Benten (弁天), Benzaiten (弁財天), Bentendō (弁天堂): Benten, also known as Benzaiten, was originally a Hindu goddess, Sarasvatī. She was adopted into Buddhism as many Hindu deities were, and eventually reached Japan. In Japan she is associated with wisdom, eloquence, and music. She is therefore seen as a patron of the arts. She is also associated with financial prosperity and many Bentendō will have a place where you can wash your money to make it multiply. Bentendō are halls of worship for her; while the dō indicates Buddhism, she is also worshiped as a Shintō kami.

Bentō (弁当): Meals served in boxes, often with separate compartments for each item. These are typically portable and can be found served in reusable or disposable containers. Some restaurants specialize in take-out bentō. You can also buy them at convenience stores, and people often make them at home for lunch. Larger train stations sell ekiben, bentō for eating on long distance trains.

Bodhisattva / Bosatsu (菩薩): Those who are about to attain enlightenment but delay entering nirvana in order to assist others. In Japan the most commonly seen Bodhisattva is Jizō.

Buddhism / Bukkyō (仏教): Buddhism entered Japan in the 6th century. Over time new schools of Buddhist thought entered the country and evolved. Today the major forms are Nichiren, Shingon, Tendai, Zen, and Pure Land sects such as Jōdoshū and Jōdo Shinshū. The majority of Japanese practice some form of Buddhism as well as Shintō; neither religion demands sole allegiance.

Bunraku (文楽): The dominant style of commercial puppet theater originating in the 17th century. It involves large puppets, each with more than one puppeteer. Many famous kabuki plays were originally bunraku plays.

Chankonabe (ちゃんこ鍋): A type of one pot stew made of any kind of vegetable with either fish or chicken. It is served in sumō stables to help bulk up the wrestlers. In sumō, the bout is lost if one touches the ground with anything but the feet, so four-legged animals are traditionally not used to make chankonabe.

Daifuku (大福): A confection consisting of mochi with a sweet filling, commonly sweetened red bean paste. There are several varieties depending on the filling. The mochi may also have ingredients mixed in it in order to color it—pink and green are common.

Daikon (大根): The kanji mean "big root." Daikon are a type of winter radish found in many parts of Asia. In Japan it is a common food that is cooked and pickled in a variety of ways. It is also served grated to accompany some dishes, as it helps digestion of oily foods.

Daimyō (大名): Samurai lords. Each controlled his own domain with his own samurai army and administration. During the Edo period they were required to reside in Edo for a year and then in their domain for a year. The wife and children of a daimyō would have to stay in Edo. This required them to maintain an Edo estate with a full staff.

Dango (団子): Basically balls of food. The most common forms are made from grain flour, steamed or boiled, and served with a topping. They can also be dipped in soy sauce and grilled. Dango made of meat are either deep fried or boiled.

Dōjinshi (同人誌) : Self-published works. These are usually sold by their creators at special events, the largest of which is Comiket, which draws over 700,000 buyers twice a year. Non-Japanese often believe dōjinshi are just erotic parodies, but this is not accurate as a large percentage are not.

Edo (江戸): See page 15 in the front.

Edo period / Edo jidai (江戸時代): Also called the Tokugawa period, from 1603 to 1868. This is the period of samurai rule under the Tokugawa shōguns, who controlled political power from their capital in Edo. This was a period of peace when the arts flourished. The Edo period saw the rise of ukiyo-e, kabuki, bunraku, various types of popular literature, music, improvements in urban planning, and more.

Ema (絵馬): Small wood plaques one can purchase at Shintō shrines and Buddhist temples. Worshipers write prayers or wishes on them and hang them on racks provided on the grounds. Some worshipers will also add a drawing. It is permissible to read what is written on them. Ema also make a good souvenir or gift to bring home with you. Some locations may have large, specially commissioned ema hanging under the eaves.

Ennichi (縁日): A feast day for a shrine or temple. These are at least once a month; sometimes there are two or three. Traditional belief is that visiting on such a day carries more merit than visiting on regular days.

Firebombings of Tokyo in World War II: See page 16 in the front.

Forty-Seven Rōnin / Shi jū shichi shi (四十七士): A group of rōnin who conspired against and killed Kira Yoshinaka, a government official who had been instrumental in the death of their daimyō. Their tale was quickly adapted to bunraku and kabuki plays that continue to be popular to this day.

Fudō Myōō (不動明王): One of the thirteen major Buddhas and Bodhisattvas in Shingon Buddhism. He is a ferocious protective deity who removes obstacles to enlightenment and subdues evil.

Fujizuka (富士塚): In the Edo period, religious devotees of Mount Fuji in the Kantō Plain would organize pilgrimages. Not everyone could go on such a trek, so a miniature Mount Fuji would sometimes be constructed using stone brought from the mountain. Some are large enough to actually climb.

Furikake (振り掛け): A dried seasoning sprinkled on top of rice. The variety of ingredients is large; usually they are a mixture of several, seafood being a common type.

Fusuma (襖): A sliding panel that functions as a door, opening into closets or rooms. These are made from several layers of paper and usually have artwork painted on them.

Geisha (芸者): Entertainers who perform traditional music and dance. They also will converse with clients and pour drinks. They are sometimes mistaken for prostitutes, as in the Edo period they could only perform in the red-light districts. At that time, any geisha selling her body would lose her license and could be sentenced to serve for up to seven years in a brothel without compensation.

Geta (下駄): Traditional footwear similar to zōri but made of wood with a base that keeps the foot elevated above ground. The most common design has two blocks of wood raising the geta off the ground. The purpose was to keep the hem of kimono from touching the ground, something that is useful in bad weather.

Great Kantō Earthquake / Kantō Daijishin (関東大地震): See page 16 in the front.

Hanafuda (花札): A type of playing card developed after Western-style cards were outlawed due to gambling. Gamblers still used them but as other games used the deck, they remained legal. In 1889 a small company called Nintendo was founded in Kyoto to make these cards. The company still makes hanafuda decks.

Haori (羽織): A type of jacket worn over kimono. It reach to the thighs or hips, and there is a tie in the front to close the lapels. Decorative linings and family crests are also often found on haori.

Happi (法被 or 半被): A type of jacket or coat with straight sleeves and often a crest on the back. Usually they are indigo blue or brown. Today they are usually only worn at festivals. In the past they would have been worn by shop staff, family servants, and fire brigade members. They reach to the thighs or hips and are closed by a belt.

Honden (本殿): The inner or main hall of larger Shintō shrines. It is reserved for the kami and not open to the public. In front of the honden will be another building, the haiden, where people can worship.

Hondō (本堂): The main hall of a Buddhist temple. Some sects may call this structure by a different name.

Horigotatsu (掘り炬燵): A type of traditional table where you sit on a cushion on tatami but your legs fit into a recessed section of the floor. In the winter these can be heated.

Hyakudoishi (百度石): "One hundred times stone." Hyakudoishi are found at many temples and shrines, often with the kanji 百度石 carved on them. The idea is that you go from the stone to the temple or shrine hall, pray, and return 100 times, to equal 100 pilgrimages. Many people keep track of how often they do this by leaving a small object at the hyakudoishi or altar on each trip.

Inari (稲荷): In the Tokyo area, Inari is one of the most popular of the Shintō kami. Inari is associated with agriculture and business, and people often pray at Inari shrines for financial success. Inari shrines were so common in the Edo period that there was a saying, "As common as Inari shrines and dog turds."

Jizō (地蔵): A Bodhisattva who is depicted as a simple monk. He protects the spirits of children who have died and works to reduce the suffering of those sent to hell. In Shingon he is one of the thirteen major Buddhas and Bodhisattvas.

Jōdo Shinshū (浄土真宗) and Jōdoshū ((浄土宗): Two sects of Pure Land Buddhism founded by Tendai monks: Jodo Shu by Hōnen and Jōdo Shinshū by his disciple Shinran. Both sought to establish a way for ordinary people to become closer to Buddhahood and be reborn in the Pure Land. Pure Land Buddhism is perhaps the most common form of Buddhism in Japan.

Jōmon period / Jōmon jidai (縄文時代): The period of Japanese pre-history from around 14,000 to 300 BC. This was a stone age culture with mainly a hunting and gathering culture but some agricultural practices. The Jōmon people created some of the earliest pottery in the world, the most striking examples of which come from eastern Japan.

Kabayaki (蒲焼): A method of cooking fish where the fish is boned, split open, skewered, and grilled. It is basted with a sauce during the grilling. Eel kabayaki is a popular dish, often served on hot rice.

Kabuki (歌舞伎): A theatrical form that originated in the very early Edo period when a woman named Izumo no Okuni began performing in Kyoto with her troupe. Originally performed by both men and women, kabuki came to be an all-male theatrical form, which it remains today.

Kaiseki ryōri (会席料理): A multicourse Japanese meal. This is very much haute cuisine and not for ordinary meals. Kaiseki is commonly served in ryōtei and better ryokan. There is a related term that is also pronounced kaiseki but is written with different kanji (懐石). This refers to a multicourse Japanese meal that is served at a tea ceremony, and also a type of haute cuisine that is derived from the dishes served at tea ceremonies.

Kamakura period / Kamakura jidai (鎌倉時代): 1185–1333. A period when the samurai took political power in Japan, starting with Minamoto no Yoritomo. The government resided in Kamakura while the emperor stayed in Kyoto performing a ceremonial role. The city of Kamakura has many locations related to that history as well as many temples and shrines dating to the period.

Kami (神): The native Japanese deities worshipped in Shintō. The term is very nebulous and does not always equate to the Western concepts of gods.

Kaminari Okoshi (雷おこし): A sweet made of crisped rice, syrup and sugar. Some varieties have other ingredients mixed in such as peanuts, sesame seeds, or powdered green tea.

Kana (仮名): Japanese characters that represent syllables. There are two kinds of kana: hiragana is used for Japanese words and katakana for foreign words. For example, ta is written as た in hiragana and as タ in katakana. These days the Japanese also use the Roman alphabet in some cases.

Kanji (漢字): Chinese characters used in Japanese writing. Each kanji can have more than one pronunciation depending on the context. For example, 山 means mountain and can be pronounced yama or san.

Kannon (観音): A bodhisattva also known as Avalokiteśvara, Guan Yin, and Kwan Yin in other languages. Kannon is known for great compassion and is a major figure in Buddhist worship in Japan. Common depictions of Kannon mentioned in this book include:

- Batō Kannon "Horse-headed Kannon," which has a horse head on the headdress.
- Eleven Headed Kannon, which has a headdress that includes eleven heads.
- Kosodate Kannon, who people pray to if they want a child.
- Senju Kannon, "Kannon with a thousand arms."

Kantō region / Kantō chihō (関東地方): A region in eastern Japan that includes Tokyo as well as the prefectures of Chiba, Gunma, Ibaraki, Kanagawa, Saitama, and Tochigi. Much of this area is a plain; the rest consists of the hills and mountains surrounding the plain.

Kappa (河童): A mythical creature. Kappa dwell in the water and are said to drown people and horses. They are usually depicted with a beaked face, a turtle-like shell, and walking upright like a person.

Karēpan (カレーパン): A bread (pan) bun made by filling dough with karē (curry), coating it with bread crumbs, and then deep frying it.

Katsuobushi (鰹節): Skipjack tuna that has been smoked and dried. The result is a hard, almost wood-like slab. To use it in cooking it is shaved with an inverted plane. It is possible to buy bags of pre-shaved katsuobushi—this is often referred to as bonito flakes in English.

Kirin (麒麟): A mythical animal, originally from China, associated with wise rulers and peace. In Japan some images of kirin have wings. It is also the brand name for a famous beer.

Komainu (狛犬): Guardian statues found at the entrance to many Shintō shrines as well as some Buddhist temples and private residences. These are sometimes called lion-dogs in English.

Konnyaku (蒟蒻 or 菎蒻): A gelatinous paste made from the root of devil's tongue. It may be produced as small bricks or in the form of a noodle-like string. It is boiled before eating.

Kōshin (庚申): A folk belief with continental origins. Every sixty days on the traditional calendar there is a Kōshin day. The tradition has it that your bad actions would be reported to heaven on that night as you slept. Believers would gather and stay up all night to prevent this. In the Meiji period, the government attempted to suppress such beliefs, so it is rarely practiced these days.

Manga (漫画): Japanese comics. They can range from four-panel strips in newspapers or magazines to entire books and multivolume series. Manga are written for all ages, and a significant portion of the market is aimed at a female audience.

Masugata (桝形): In castle fortifications, a masugata is a square between two gates, usually with one gate at a right angle to the first. An attacking army that broke through the first gate into the masugata would be delayed and could be attacked from above.

Matoi (纏): A standard for an Edo-period fire brigade. These were elaborate, consisting of a staff topped by a three-dimensional shape and leather fringe unique to each brigade.

Mie (見得): A type of pose done during dramatic moments of kabuki performances by the lead actor. Usually mie are accompanied by the beating of wooden blocks and stylized head movements before the pose is held.

Meiji period / Meiji jidai (明治時代): The reign of Emperor Meiji, from 1868 to 1912. This period began with the overthrow of the shōgun's government and saw Japan transform itself from an isolated state to a global power and young empire.

Meireki Fire / Meireki no taika (明暦の大火): See page 15 in the the front.

Melon Pan (メロンパン): A sweet bun that gets its name from its shape—it does not contain melon. They can range from small to as large as your hand. They can be plain, flavored, or served with a filling such as ice cream.

Mikoshi (神輿): Often translated as palanquin, a mikoshi is used to ritually transport a kami borne on the shoulders. Such transport can take place when there is a relocation of a kami to a different shrine or, more commonly, when carried through the streets at festivals.

Mirin (味醂): Mirin is made by adding fermenting rice to shōchū. After forty to sixty days the result is a sweet liquid with about 14% alcohol that is used for cooking rather than drinking. Sometimes mirin is mistakenly called sweet cooking sake, which it is not. Stores commonly also sell low alcohol imitation mirin.

Miso (味噌): A seasoning made from fermenting a salted mixture of ground soybeans and barley or rice. It is used to make miso soup, as a condiment, and as an ingredient in many dishes. Before modern techniques made soy sauce affordable, most households used miso in cooking.

Mochi (餅): A cake made of pounded glutinous rice. Mochi can be eaten grilled, in soups, and as the outer wrapping for various sweet fillings. Mochi ice cream is a recent confection dating from Los Angeles in the early 1990s that is made by wrapping a ball of ice cream in mochi.

Monaka (最中): Crispy wafers in any of several shapes made of rice then stuffed with sweetened bean paste (an). A modern variant uses ice cream rather than an.

Nabe (鍋): A cooking pot or pan. These can be ceramic or metal. Foods cooked in nabe may have the term as a suffix in their name.

Nattō (納豆): Fermented soybeans. This food is often disliked by non-Japanese as it is stinky and has a slimy texture. The smell reminds me of some French cheeses and the flavor is mild. While eating it can be a little messy, with practice that problem can be dealt with. Nattō is popular in eastern Japan, which includes Tokyo; it is not so popular in western Japan.

Nigirizushi (握り寿司): A style of sushi that originated in Edo, consisting of a small bunch of rice with a topping added. The topping can be anything and sushi chefs keep coming up with new dishes.

Ningyōyaki (人形焼): A confection consisting of a pastry shell in the shape of some object, usually with a filling of sweet bean paste. Ningyō means "doll" and yaki refers to the use of a griddle mold for the cooking.

Niō (仁王), Niōmon (仁王門): Wrathful protectors of Buddhism. Statues of muscular Niō are often found at Buddhist temples. If they are mounted in a gate, usually in alcoves on either side, the gate itself may be called a Niōmon.

Noren (暖簾): A length of cloth hung over a doorway, usually with one or more vertical slits to make passage easier. They are rectangular and the dimensions vary depending on the particular use. Indoors, noren are sometimes hung between rooms. Shops and restaurants may hang them out front to indicate they are open for business.

Nori (海苔): A type of seaweed that is gathered, pressed into sheets, and used for making a variety of dishes.

Onigiri (お握り or 御握り): A rice ball. These typically have a filling, usually something with a strong flavor such as pickled ume, salmon, or other seafood. Onigiri often have a piece of nori wrapped around part of them. Some shops specialize in onigiri, and you can buy them in convenience stores.

Otaku (御宅 or お宅 or おたく or オタク): A term for those who are so into their hobbies that it has an effect on their lives. At times this is translated as nerd, geek, or fan. Often applied to hardcore fans of video games, anime, manga, or railways.

Oyakodon (親子丼): A simple dish of cooked chicken and egg on top of rice, served in a bowl. The term is a combination of the kanji for parent (oya), child (ko), and bowl (donburi).

Rakugo (落語): A traditional storytelling performing art. The performances are done in a sitting position with minimal props. In the Tokyo area these props would be a fan and a handcloth. The stories are often humorous, and ghost stories are a popular subject for the heat of the summer months.

Ryokan (旅館): A traditional Japanese inn. These usually are found in rural areas, such as hot spring towns, rather than cities. Often they provide excellent services with a price tag to match. However, there are budget ones if you take time to look for them.

Ryōtei (料亭): Very expensive high-class restaurants. Guests are served in private rooms, usually with traditional Japanese seating. The foods served are typically decided by the chef. Some will only accept new customers by referral.

Sashimi (刺身): Any raw sliced meat served as part of a meal.

Senryū (川柳): A form of poetry that shares the five-seven-five syllable structure with haiku. Unlike haiku, senryū are about humanity, often about human failings, and can tend to dark humor and cynicism at times.

Shabu Shabu (しゃぶしゃぶ): A hotpot dish where vegetables and meat, usually beef, are cooked in a hot pot. Each piece of meat or vegetable is stirred in a cooking pot until it is ready to eat. The name is an onomatopoeia for the sound of ingredients being stirred in the hot broth.

Shamisen (三味線): A three-stringed instrument with a long neck and hollow square body covered with animal skin. The shamisen was introduced to the rest of Japan from Okinawa in the 16th century. It is still used professionally by such traditional arts as kabuki and bunraku, and by geisha. It has also been used, in both acoustic and electric forms, in jazz, rock, and pop performances.

Shichifukujin (七福神): Known in English as the Seven Lucky Gods. They are seven deities from various traditions that in Japan came to be gathered in a group. They are Benzaiten (Benten), Bishamonten, Daikokuten, Fukurokuju, Hotei, Jurōjin, and Ebisu. There are several groupings of shrines and temples in Tokyo where people go from one to the other in a type of pilgrimage. This is commonly done during the first few days of the year.

Shichigosan (七五三): A literal translation of shichigosan is "Seven-Five-Three." Each November 15, girls who are three or seven years old and boys who are five are taken to a shrine. Usually the children are dressed in kimono.

Shin hanga (新版画): A movement of the Taishō and early Shōwa periods that revitalized ukiyo-e printmaking. Shin hanga was influenced by the Western art of the times such as Impressionism. The movement faded away under the military government, which rationed materials and decreed that the subjects of art needed to be approved. Shin hanga never recovered once the war ended.

Shingon Buddhism / Shingonshū (真言宗): An esoteric sect of Buddhism introduced from China in the 9th century by Kūkai. It is one of the last surviving esoteric mikkyō traditions of Buddhism. While similar to the Vajrayāna traditions of Tibet, Nepal, and Mongolia, the two have many significant differences.

Shintō (神道): The indigenous religion of Japan. Shrines (jinja) range in size from minuscule to entire complexes of buildings. A popular saying is that there are eight million gods, and the diversity of the kami in Shintō reflects this.

Shitamachi (下町): The low town of the commoners, the artisans, and the workers, as contrasted with the high city, yamanote (山の手), of the samurai, the administrators, and the rulers.

Shōchū (焼酎): A Japanese distilled alcoholic beverage that is typically 25% alcohol. Some brands can be as high as 45% alcohol. Shōchū can be made from a variety of ingredients, such as rice, sweet potatoes, crude sugar, or barley. As it can be made from such a variety of foods, it is often compared to vodka. Often it is diluted with water or used as a base for cocktails.

Shōgun (将軍): Originally a special title, the Sei-i Taishōgun, given to generals tasked with the suppression of peoples not under the control of the emperor's government. Starting in the Kamakura period the shōguns became military rulers of Japan. Shōguns held political and military power while the emperor continued to reign in Kyoto in a ceremonial role.

Shōwa emperor / Shōwa tennō (昭和天皇): The emperor during the Shōwa period. In the West he is commonly referred to as Hirohito. I follow the Japanese etiquette of referring to deceased emperors by the name of their reign. Japanese refer to the present emperor as Kinjō Heika, Kinjō Tennō, or Tōgin. The etiquette gets a little complex for us non-Japanese.

Shōwa period / Shōwa jidai (昭和時代): The longest reign of a Japanese emperor, lasting from 1926 to 1989. In its first half, the Shōwa period saw the rise of right-wing power during the Great Depression and the Fifteen Years War. This lasted from 1931 to the end of World War II. During the second half, after the war, Japan experienced the greatest period of democratization and eventually prosperity in its history. In this period the arts especially flourished after censorship was abolished.

Soba (蕎麦), Sobaya (蕎麦屋), Sobayu (蕎麦湯): Buckwheat noodles, a popular dish with both Japanese and tourists. A sobaya is a restaurant that specializes in soba dishes. There are several dishes made with soba. Warm soba is usually served in a soup, either plain or with any of several kinds of toppings such as tempura or meat. Cold noodles can be plain, like morisoba, or with a topping: Zarusoba, for example, is topped with shredded seaweed. Both are served with a dipping sauce and a small dish of wasabi and onion that you can add to the sauce if you wish. Better restaurants will bring a pot of sobayu, the water the soba was cooked in, after you finish the noodles. Pour the sobayu into the remaining dipping sauce and sip it.

Sukiyaki (鋤焼): A hot pot dish of meat, usually beef, cooked with other ingredients such as tōfu, vegetables, and konnyaku or shirataki noodles. Usually ingredients are dipped in raw egg before being eaten.

Sumidagawa (隅田川): The Sumida river, flowing through the shitamachi area of

Tokyo. The river cuts through so much of Tokyo that it is spanned by thirty-five bridges. The city wards that it flows next to as it heads to Tokyo Bay are Itabashi, Kita, Adachi, Arakawa, Sumida, Taitō, Chūō, and Kōtō. It has also been referred to as the Ōkawa, the Great River.

Taishō period (大正時代): The period in modern Japanese history from 1912 to 1926. This time was marked with a great deal of social change and the spread of voting rights. Jazz, cinema, and literature all flourished. It was also a time when the right-wing resistance to change started to expand.

Tanuki (狸): Often translated as "raccoon dog" or mistranslated as "raccoon" or "badger." Increasingly the Japanese word is just left as is by translators, as anime and manga have spread knowledge of the term outside Japan. In folklore tanuki have the power to shapeshift and are seen as mischievous tricksters.

Tatami (畳): Mats used as floor covering in Japanese traditional-style rooms. Some restaurants will either have tatami rooms or separate seating areas covered in tatami. One should never wear shoes or slippers when walking on tatami.

Tempura / Tenpura (天麩羅): Any of a variety of foods dipped in a light batter and deep fried. Edo-style tempura has no vegetables, only seafood.

Tendai Buddhism / Tendaishū (天台宗): A sect of Buddhism introduced from China by Saichō in the 9th century. By imperial order, Japanese Tendai absorbed many elements of mikkyō from Shingon in the early years of its history.

Tenugui (手拭い): Long lengths of cotton cloth usually measuring about 14 by 35 inches (35 by 90 centimeters). Although often translated as "hand towel," tenugui are more than towels. They can also be used as head coverings in several ways, as headbands, as a wrapping to help carry things, and more. It is common for them to be printed with attractive designs, so they often are hung as decorations, either framed or with kakejikubō, a type of mounting for hanging things like tenugui and wall scrolls.

Tokonoma (床の間):The tokonoma is an alcove built into some traditional Japanese rooms, where artistic pieces are displayed, commonly scrolls, flower arrangements, and pottery.

Tokugawa clan (徳川氏): The Tokugawa family held political power in Japan as shōguns during the Edo period. Starting with Tokugawa Ieyasu and ending with Tokugawa Yoshinobu, there were fifteen Tokugawa shōguns. The Tokugawa clan still exists today, headed by Tokugawa Tsunenari, the eighteenth head of the clan.

Tori no Ichi (酉の市): A festival held at some shrines and temples on the day of the rooster in November. There are usually two such days, but some years have three days. People commonly pray for good luck and prosperity for their business.

Torii (鳥居): A simple gate consisting of at least two uprights and a crosspiece, which is found at Shintō shrines and a few Buddhist temples. The materials can vary: usually they are wood, stone, or metal.

Tōto Norenkai (東都のれん会): An association of over fifty businesses intent on preserving their crafts. To join, a business needs to have been in operation in Tokyo for more than 100 years and at least three generations.

Tsukudani (佃煮): A food that originated among fishing families in Edo as a way to preserve seafood. Food is slowly simmered in a blend of mirin and soy sauce, the ratios of which would vary according to the season. While originally tsukudani involved seafood such as shellfish, in time it came to be applied to pretty much anything.

Udon (饂飩): Fat wheat noodles usually served in soup. They can also be served separately with a dipping sauce or even grilled.

Ukiyo-e (浮世絵): An art form from the Edo period. While originating in the Buddhist term ukiyo "world of sorrow," different kanji with the same pronunciation are used that mean "floating world." Ukiyo-e art can be prints, paintings, or even sculptures.

Ume (梅), umeshu (梅酒): Ume is usually translated as "plum," but it is actually an apricot. The trees have beautiful blossoms that bloom earlier than cherries. The green fruit is used to make umeshu, a tart infusion of fruit, crude crystallized sugar, and distilled alcohol. Umeshu is sometimes erroneously called plum wine and should not be confused with sweet plum drinks.

Wataire Hanten (綿入れ袢纏): A short winter coat for indoor wear. The body goes to the hips, the arms to the wrists, and there is a tie in the front to close the two sides. Wataire hanten are padded with cotton for warmth and similar in shape to haori. Not to be confused with an ordinary hanten (袢纏), which is a type of jacket similar to a happi that can be worn outdoors.

Yaguramon (櫓門): A second gate within castle walls, specifically the second gate of a masugata.

Yamabushi (山伏): A practitioner of Shugendō, a religious movement said to have originated in the 7th century. Yamabushi practices are a mixture of Shintō and esoteric Buddhism, with an emphasis on ascetic practices on sacred mountains.

Yayoi period / Yayoi jidai (弥生時代): The period of Japanese history from 300 BC to AD 300. This was the period when rice cultivation and ironworking spread in Japan.

Yōkai (妖怪): A general term for all sorts of supernatural critters that are not deities or Buddhas. Some may be actual animals with legends of supernatural powers such as fox and tanuki. Others are mythical, such as kappa.

Yose (寄席): A type of variety theater with acts similar to vaudeville in the West. Yose are mainly known as venues for rakugo, but shows may also include stand-up comedy, magicians, jugglers, paper cut artists, and more.

Yoshiwara (吉原): See pages 462 and 464 in the guide.

Yukata (浴衣): A type of light cotton kimono that is often worn in warm or hot weather.

Zen (禅): A school of Buddhism that places an emphasis on meditation. In Japan the three major sects are Sōtō, Rinzai, and Ōbaku Zen.

Zōri (草履): A type of sandal traditionally made of rice straw or wood with cloth straps. Today they are also made of leather, rubber, or synthetics. At times they are worn with tabi, a type of sock with a separation between the big toe and the other toes for the strap to fit through. The common beach wear flip-flop sandal is based on the zōri and originated in Kobe in the 1950s.

Index of Place Names

NOTES

NOTES

Other Titles of Interest From Stone Bridge Press

Amy's Guide to Best Behavior in Japan: Do It Right and Be Polite!
By Amy Chavez
ISBN 978-1-61172-043-3

The Inland Sea
By Donald Richie
ISBN 978-1-61172-024-2

Japan from Anime to Zen: Quick Takes on Culture, Art, History, Food . . . and More
By David Watts Barton
ISBN 978-1-61172-063-1

Exploring Kyoto, Revised Edition: On Foot in the Ancient Capital
By Judith Clancy
ISBN 978-1-61172-041-9

Tokyo Junkie: 60 Years of Bright Lights and Back Alleys . . . and Baseball
By Robert Whiting
ISBN 978-1-61172-067-9

Available at Bookstores Worldwide and Online